NEW MASTERS OF PHOTOSHOP

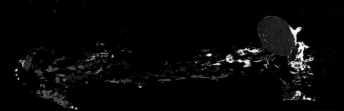

D1632911

Tim Bird
Michael Cina
Gavin Cromhout
Josh Fallon
Jens Magnus Karlsson
Derek Lea
Adrian Luna
Catherine McIntyre
Wojtek Madej
Jason Mohr
Eun-Ha Paek
Andrew Park
Paul Sinclair
Colin Smith
Yoshi Sodeoka
Peter Stanick
Johann Terrettaz
Norma V. Toraya
Michael Young

friendsof

DESIGNER TO DESIGNER™

NEW MASTERS

NEW MASTERS OF PHOTOSHOP

Trademark Acknowledgements

First printed August 2001

Published by friends of ED Ltd. 30 Lincoln Road, Olton, Birmingham. B27 6PA
Printed in USA
ISBN 1903450624

NEW MASTERS OF PHOTOSHOP

Credits

Authors
Tim Bird
Michael Cina
Gavin Cromhout
Josh Fallon
Jens Magnus Karlsson
Derek Lea
Adrian Luna
Wojtek Madej
Catherine McIntyre
Jason Mohr
Eun-Ha Paek
Andrew Park
Paul Sinclair
Colin Smith
Yoshi Sodeoka
Peter Stanick
Johann Terrettaz
Norma V. Toraya
Michael Young

Author Agent
Sophie Edwards

Project Administrator
Thomas Stiff

Copyright Research
David Spurgeon
Thomas Stiff

Team Leader
Joanna Farmer

CD Design
New Media Works
3rd Floor, Lupus House
11-13 Macklin Street
Covent Garden
London WC2B 5NH

Index
Simon Collins

Content Architect
Jon Hill

Editors
Julia Gilbert
Luke Harvey

Graphic Editors
Katy Freer
Deb Murray

Technical Reviewers
Kristian Besley
Garrett Carr
Kim 'Bimmer' Christensen
Rowan Dodds
John Flanagan
Denis E. Graham
Simon Gurney
Vicki Loader
William B. McIntyre
Glain Martin
Richard Pearman
Weston Skye
Jerome Turner
Andrew Zack

Proof Readers
Pauline Briggs
Luke Brown
Mel Jehs
Louise Kitchen
Alan McCann
Fionnuala Meacher
Alice Myers
Mel Orgee
Paul Samuels
Paul Thewlis

Creative Consultants
Catherine O'Flynn
Sunny Ralph
www.freshfroot.com

Contents

1   Tim Bird   **Samples** 1

2   Johann Terrettaz   **Diverse** 25

3   Jens Magnus Karlsson   **Light**...............................55

4   Jason Mohr & Yoshi Sodeoka   **Yellow** 93

5   Josh Fallon   **Metamorphose** 117

6   Paul Sinclair   **Personal Space** 141

7   Colin Smith   **Photorealism** 177

8   Catherine McIntyre   **Finders, Keepers**..............213

Contents

9   Peter Stanick   **Pop**..........................247

10   Gavin Cromhout   **Message**..........................271

11   Derek Lea   **Psychosurgery**..........................311

12   Eun-Ha Paek   **Daydream**..........................347

13   Michael Young   **Structure**..........................379

14   Norma V. Toraya   **Obsession**..........................401

15   Wojtek Madej & Andrew Park   **Effective Spaces**..........................437

16   Adrian Luna   **Reflective**..........................467

17   Michael Cina   **Edge**..........................497

Foreword

Photoshop is a drug. It is as ubiquitous in professional imaging as aspirin in the home. This book is meant to help you get your usage under control.

When Adobe raised the layers limit to 8,000 in Photoshop 6.0, there were artists formerly in full control of their habit who promptly overdosed. The Liquify tool has mashed the brains of many an otherwise sober and "Less is More" designer.

So there are two things that the 19 artists in this book share.
One: their art is highly influential.
Two: they have Photoshop firmly under control.

It may seem strange to state this here, but it's an important point: these 19 artists are not necessarily the planet's unequalled wizards in how to use every last feature of the giant landscape that spreads out when you start Photoshop.

But these artists are in control. Control is about judgment. Knowing when to do less, knowing when to leave something alone, is a far, far greater expression of Photoshop mastery than throwing every possible flavor and texture into the dish.

How to use this book
Use it as a birdfeeder – ideas need sustenance when food is scarce.
Use it as an accelerator – send techniques into high-energy collision.
Use it as a bone – bury it, dig it up again, chew on it.
Just don't use it as a manual. It won't teach you How To Use Photoshop.

It will however help you to place Photoshop in the context of your work.
It will, if it works the way it's meant to, help you exercise more self-control.
It will, we hope, release your innate sense of judgment from feature bondage.

Give it a couple of months and get in touch if you haven't gone cold turkey.

friends of ED
08.04.01

PS >   Different artists use different platforms. To avoid boring repetition throughout the text, we only supply the key combinations for the platform being used in context. The conversions are:

(PC) Right-click = (Mac) Ctrl-click
(PC) Ctrl-click = (Mac) Command-click

Tim Bird

Tim has known from a young age that he wanted to pursue a career in the creative field. He left school at 16 and went straight into a design studio as a junior. "Further education didn't appeal to me; I just wanted to get on and get some hands-on experience." It was a couple of years later that he started to use the Mac, and was soon hooked on Photoshop. "I wasn't fazed by its complexity, and in turn was given more interesting and challenging jobs. I went freelance in 1996 and have worked on a wide variety of projects." He now supplies photography to a leading photo library, where his Photoshop skills play a big part.

michael cina

michael cina is an artist and designer living in a small village outside of minneapolis. he creates stuff (mikecina.com) and things (trueistrue.com) out of his house in that village. companies like mtv or adobe may even call him to do some work. every now and then he leaves his village to speak at design conferences. often he will leave his house to buy cds or books (or both if he got paid). otherwise he rides his bike, fishes, chases his cat or girlfriend, takes pictures, makes fonts, paints, e-mails people, struggles over writing things like books and bios...

currently michael is working on his new company, weworkforthem.com, with michael young. WeWorkForThem is half art and half design studio.

Gavin Cromhout

Gavin Cromhout lives in Cape Town, South Africa. He studied art formally at the University of Cape Town, but owes most of his Photoshop skills to work avoidance behavior (not wanting to write his Masters thesis in psychology). He strongly believes that Photoshop is about as much fun as a person can have by themselves. You can drop him a line at gavin@lodestone.co.za, or catch up with him on his work web site: www.lodestone.co.za. If you're a Maitre Luthier, all the better – he can use all the help he can get for his hobby.

Gavin would like to thank Alison for all her help with this project.

Josh Fallon

Studio artist turned graphic designer Josh Fallon, 24, works out of Los Angeles, providing illustration and web design services. Notable work includes his personal project entitled *Inspired*, a tribute to the late graphic artist M.C. Escher. Josh has recently been featured by Adobe.com and Computer Arts Special magazine (#20), and he is currently working on additions to the *Inspired* series, as well as developing DesignLaunchpad.com, a web site where beginning graphic designers will be able to go to study the fundamentals of design. Fallon's work can be seen at www.fallondesign.com, and he can be reached by e-mail at josh@fallondesign.com.

About the Authors

Jens Magnus Karlsson

Jens Karlsson is a Swedish digital artist and designer. He studied information and advertising for four years, partly in the US, and later graduated from Hyperisland School of New Media Design. At Hyperisland, Jens worked as a freelance art director, along with his studies, doing print, animation, and online work for clients such as CBS, Sony, Volkswagen, and Digital Vision. From there he moved on to a position as Senior Designer at Kioken Incorporated. Jens is currently a freelance designer through Chapter3.net, and he is actively involved in enriching the online design culture with news, articles, and events, mainly as assistant creative director at threeoh.com.

Derek Lea

Derek Lea's work is a unique combination of original photography, traditional illustration, and digital art. His work has captured the attention of prestigious advertising and corporate clients in Canada, as well as a large number of editorial clients in Canada, the United States, the United Kingdom, Italy, and Japan.

Boasting a number of awards to his name, Derek resides in Toronto, Canada. He works out of a studio in his home where he lives with his wife Janet, and their three cats. To see more of his work, visit his web site: www.dereklea.com.

Adrian Luna

I have been searching for my edge for many years, and have endeavored upon many creative theories and methods that have become a base formula for my designs. By day I am a designer working with freelance clients on projects ranging from Flash animation engines to creative high-res imagery. By night I am a new media artist. I have five years' user interface experience with such clients as Adidas, Sempra Energy, Home Depot, Farmers Insurance, Beckton Dickinson, Duke University Medical Center, and William Morris Agency. I was recently the Creative Director for Digital Evolution (formerly US Interactive), but have just moved to freelance. This in turn opened the door to a lazy beach bum lifestyle and offers genuine thinking time. I love it!

Catherine McIntyre

Catherine McIntyre is a digital artist living and working in Scotland. She makes book and CD cover illustrations, greetings cards, and magazine editorial imagery. She also pursues her own personal work, a selection of which appears in a monograph, *Deliquescence*, published by Pohlmann Press in 2000. Her work has been published in magazines and books worldwide.

Her work can be seen on the World Wide Web at http://members.madasafish.com/~cmci, and www.intangible.org/Features/mcintyre/mcihome.html

Wojtek Madej

Wojtek Madej lives in Sulkowice, Poland, where he enjoys time with his wife Asia and son Jano. He also spends time driving to and from Krakow, listening to funky music and thinking about the Universe's great movements. He contemplates life and has four large rocks at the four corners of his house that block harmful energies. He likes to study details and will often surprise his friends with observations from the most bizarre sources. A connoisseur of funk, Wojtek can often be found walking in the fields smiling and singing songs from James Brown's *Funky People* album. As well as the *Days of Code* book with Andrew Park, Wojtek is currently building a new studio at the side of his house so that he can continue to work with his friends.

Jason Mohr

Jason Mohr is an artist and designer who trained at Pasadena's Art Center, College of Design, where he earned a Bachelor of Fine Arts degree in graphic and packaging design, with an emphasis on interactive media. After moving to New York and working briefly for Razorfish and as a freelance designer, he designed for Word.com. As Word's Senior Designer, Jason designed sites such as Pixeltime.com and Sissyfight.com, and helped earn Word recognition from organizations such as the New York Art Director's Club and Siggraph, and appearances in publications including I.D. Magazine and The New Yorker. He's currently working with Yoshi Sodeoka as C404, creating specialty digital media including web sites, web content, animation, videos, films, television graphics, magazines, books, exhibitions, interactive art pieces, games, digital audio, CD-ROMs, kiosk interfaces, and installations.

Eun-Ha Paek

Eun-Ha Paek specializes in storytelling for propaganda and happiness. Her personal work has been screened at numerous festivals and venues, including the Los Angeles Museum of Modern Art and the New York Expo. Professionally, she provides art direction and animation for clients like LEGO, The San Francisco Symphony, The Gap, and Wieden + Kennedy. She is one of the founding members of Milky Elephant, along with Karl Ackermann and Mumbleboy. Milky Elephant makes sweet design, fancy characters, funny games, and loads of motion.
www.milkyelephant.com
www.eun-ha.com

Andrew Park

Andrew Park lives in South London, and at 6 a.m. every morning he is woken by the noisiest dustmen in the world! One might think he would spring out of bed and pray to the Sun God of Bermondsey, whose radiance shines directly onto his head through the gap in his broken curtains? No, not quite... he often lies there trying to avoid the strip of light that manages to follow him around the bed for several hours. The rest of the day is spent trying to get the many different components in his computer to talk nicely with each other. Tea is consumed in vat-like quantities, and ideas flow at glacial pace. Andrew is currently working on an animation that is hurting his brain. He and Wojtek Madej are also producing a book for their medieval series of prints, *Days of Code*.

About the Authors

Paul Sinclair

Paul Sinclair was born just outside Edinburgh, Scotland in 1973. He qualified in General Art and Design at Worcester College of Technology in 1992, and went on to complete an HND in Electronic Graphics from the same college three years later. His work has appeared in Computer Arts (issues 47 and 59) and Graphic Design magazine, and is also featured on several web sites including www.whitelists.co.uk and www.wysi.org. His own web site, www.silverdemon.com, went online at the end of March this year.

Thanks to Mum and to Nadine for believing and letting it happen.

Colin Smith

Colin Smith is an award winning Graphic Designer who has caused a stir in the design community with his stunning photorealistic illustrations composed entirely in Photoshop. He is also founder of the popular *PhotoshopCAFE* web resource for Photoshop users and web designers. His images have been featured on the National Association Of Photoshop Professionals web site. He has won numerous design contests and awards, including the Guru Award at the 2001 Photoshop World Convention in LA. Colin's work has been recognized by Photoshop User, Mac Design, Dynamic Graphics, and WWW Internet Life magazines. Colin is listed in the International Who's Who of Professional Management, and is is an active member of the National Association Of Photoshop Professionals (NAPP). He also moderates the forum for the web portal Planet Photoshop.

Yoshi Sodeoka

Yoshi Sodeoka is best known as the founding art director of one of the Web's oldest and most influential e-zines, Word.com, launched in 1995. His inventive, playful, and groundbreaking designs for Word have won awards from I.D. Magazine and Print, among others. His interactive digital artwork has been featured on numerous CD-ROMs and web sites, and in exhibitions at the San Francisco MoMA, Design Museum, Germany, and Art & Design Museum, Brazil. He has also lectured widely on digital design, and has juried design awards for PDN magazine and the One Club. He holds a degree in computer graphics from Brooklyn's Pratt Institute and studied art in his native Japan from age five. He started his career as one of the first designers for Viacom's New Media department, where he worked on experimental interactive music projects for MTV. He is currently working with Jason as C404.

Peter Stanick

Peter Stanick was born in Pittsburgh on May 27, 1953. He received a BFA in painting from Carnegie Mellon University in 1975, and a MFA in painting from Indiana University of Pennsylvania in 1977. Since 1981, Stanick has had numerous solo exhibitions in New York, Chicago, Miami, London, Stockholm, and Osaka. He is included in the collections of the Metropolitan Museum of Art in New York, Carnegie Museum of Art in Pittsburgh, and the Museum of Art in Osaka. Stanick currently lives and works in Florida.

Johann Terrettaz

I started graphic design because I have always been attracted by images. After studying for years at the School of Decorative Arts in Geneva, and at the ERAG in Lausannes, I joined a small graphics studio in Geneva in 1990. I chose a small agency so that I could learn all aspects of design: the process of creation, the relationship with the client, and the different production demands. After nearly ten years, a colleague and I decided that we wanted more control over design direction and project choice. So I opened my studio (twice2) in Geneva on 01/01/2000, with the aim of creating exchanges with other designers. My clients are from a wide variety of fields, including sport and finance.

Norma V. Toraya

Norma V. Toraya, who goes by crankbunny, created Crankbunny.com. She works in NYC as a senior web designer. She lives in Queens, NY. Crankbunny is three years old, an evolving Internet project about the future and the human evolution of emotion and technology – together. Crankbunny projects are done in video and Flash formats.

Before moving to New York, she lived in Miami, Florida as web designer and video editor for a production company in South Beach. She graduated from Syracuse University, NY where she studied sculpture. In her spare time she continually creates for Crankbunny.com, buys toys and Japanese action figures, takes last-minute trips to see bands play, and eats a lot of deep-fried things.

Mike Young

Mike Young is an artist currently residing in Washington, DC, USA. Mike has created and maintained sites such as designgraphik.com and submethod.com, and is currently starting weworkforthem.com with Michael Cina of trueistrue.com. While working on these projects, Mike has also served as art director for two years at Vir2l Studios, where he directed and designed on projects such as vir2l.com, which won prestigious awards such as the New York Festivals New Media Competition, Cannes Cyber Lion: Gold, Clio Award, Art Directors Club, and also Invision Award. Not only has Mike worked on many personal and experimental web art-based projects, but also he has worked with clients such as MTV, Dc Shoes, Mercury Automobiles, Dj Dieselboy, Dj Dara, Dj Ak1200, and Walker Art Center.

chapter 1

chapter 2

chapter 3

chapter 4

chapter 5

chapter 6

chapter 7

chapter 8

chapter 9

chapter 10

chapter 11

chapter 12

chapter 13

chapter 14

chapter 15

chapter 16

outro

"Tim, can you make this computer explode?"

Tim Bird
www.timbird.co.uk

Samples

I think my fascination with unreal and surreal imagery began while reading books about ghosts, UFOs, and other strange happenings. I came across a story about a man who photographed his wife sitting in her car alone – but when the pictures came back, a faint image of the woman's mother, who had died several months before the picture had been taken, was clearly visible on the back seat. It doesn't matter that it might have been faked using the multiple exposure technique; I was fascinated, and I spent a long time studying it.

A similarly strange picture I saw was of a young girl sitting on some grass, clutching a few flowers – but when her father got the film developed, he was in for a shock. In the background, you could clearly see a man in a spacesuit – just standing there in broad daylight! Again, it doesn't matter how it was done; this was a picture that you really couldn't ignore. If the girl had been alone, it would have been a pretty ordinary photo for the family album, but the presence of this uninvited guest broke all the rules of what a normal picture should be, and turned it into an extraordinary one.

For me personally, Photoshop is all about breaking the rules and making extraordinary pictures that you can't take your eyes off – whether they're beautiful and clean, or dark and complex. As you'll see from some of my pictures in this chapter, my style changes a lot – this can depend on my mood, the kind of pictures I've been looking at on the Internet that day, or (if I'm working on a commercial project) what other people have had to say about an image. Whatever style I use, though, Photoshop always feels like it's been tailor-made to suit my needs.

I started working in London as a junior in a design studio in 1987. It was a time when there was talk of computers coming in to do all the work, but it wasn't until 1990 that I really got my hands on one and started experimenting with it, and tried to learn QuarkXpress. One day, I watched a colleague open a picture of a skyscraper in a program that I wasn't familiar with; the skyscraper had tinted windows, but some of the lower ones contained reflections of distant fluffy clouds. I wasn't sure what he was going to do with it, but I was pretty shocked to see him drag the cursor across one of the windows, and make the clouds disappear. I'd always been keen on photography as well as graphics, so I was amazed and intrigued at what I'd just seen.

I squinted my eyes and pulled my chair up to his desk.

"What did you just do with those clouds? How did you make them disappear?"
"I'm using the rubber stamp tool in Photoshop. I just wanted to get rid of them."

He could tell that I was keen, and showed me some of its other features. I'd just seen the line between graphics and photography blurred. This was my first encounter with Photoshop, and I was seriously impressed.

I had to get stuck in and experiment, and there was no shortage of material to use – inspiration was (and still is) everywhere. In 1990, the UK rave scene was in full swing: big parties with colorful visuals, colorful music, and colorful people. The club flyer was an important part of promoting these events, and the artists creating them quickly tapped into the creativity Photoshop could provide. Just as important, there were no prima donna art directors or creatively-challenged clients having their say, so a lot of cutting-edge and stimulating art was getting printed.

For once in my life, I think I was in the right place at the right time. I've been very lucky to work in one of the most creative cities in the world, at a time when sophisticated software and hardware was being placed in the hands of people other than rocket scientists or the government. I feel lucky in the same way that footballers and pop stars feel – I do something I love, and I get paid to do it!

Samples

The more I learn about Photoshop, the more I push myself to do better, and I experiment constantly. Many hours are spent trying out new things, and many pictures don't see the light of day – they just get backed up onto CD, never to be seen again. A lot of my early work involved experimentation with filters, and blending elements together using alpha channels, before layers were introduced in version three.

I think it's interesting that filters aren't used as often as they were a few years ago. There was a period of overuse due to artists experimenting with their newly discovered digital tools, but the novelty has worn off. People have moved on from creating pictures that are just a mishmash of instantly recognizable presets, and digital art is becoming more refined and natural. I strongly suspect that future developments in Photoshop will encourage this trend by providing ever more features for simulating nature with incredible realism.

My reasoning is based on what we already have. Photoshop is driven by some seriously powerful mathematics and algorithms that define how each individual pixel reacts to your commands. Whether it's the stroke of a brush or the application of a filter, the laws of physics have been broken down and turned into raw code that Photoshop can translate into pixels, in turn emulating an airbrush, a smudge, etc. It's not really groundbreaking; I just think that it's something we can expect to see more of in the future. There are many natural effects whose 'code' has yet to be properly cracked and digitized.

Something else that will surely become more common is the use of Photoshop by professional photographers. Despite its name, right now you're more likely to see Photoshop in a graphics studio than a photographer's studio. This is because many of today's photographers have dedicated their time to learning about the physical side of photography – lighting, composition, developing, etc – and spent their money on lenses and lighting. It's understandable that some are put off by the extra expense of a computer and the software, not to mention the time-consuming process of learning how to use it to its full potential. Despite this, however, photographers are gradually getting more involved in the digital process, which is a good thing.

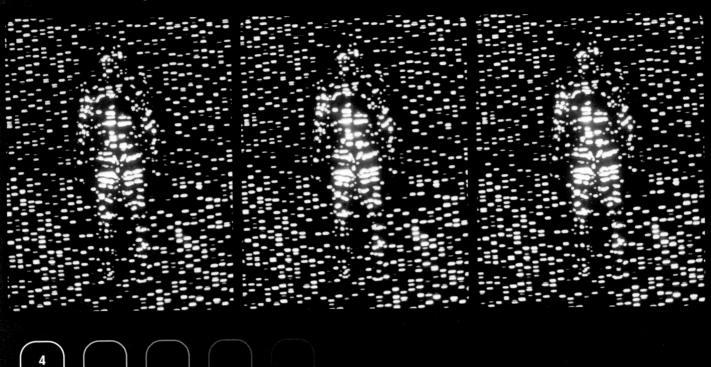

Over the past few years, I've moved in the opposite direction – that is, from the graphics industry into the photographic industry. This process started when I landed the job as retoucher for a major stock photography library. It was 100% Photoshop, retouching high quality, drum-scanned, medium-format photography. I had to be adaptable, because every day and every picture threw up something different.

"Tim, can you make this computer explode?"
"Tim, can you fill those empty seats in the stadium with some of the existing crowd?"

I loved this challenge. If I didn't know how to do something, I was usually given the time to work it out, thanks to the fact that photo libraries tend only to have a few deadlines a year. One of the main benefits of constant use over a long period is that I became fluent, and my work at the photo library took that fluency to another level. This is really important with Photoshop, as the technical issues become less of a drain on the brain, leaving you to think freely and creatively.

Inspiration comes easily to me: every single day, without fail, I see something that makes me want to create. A good example is The Aphex Twin's video for *Come To Daddy*, which contained an old TV sitting in a puddle after it had been unplugged and cast aside – yet despite this, it was emitting pictures that corresponded to the video. I found this to be a really powerful image, and it was definitely the motivation behind my Trellick TV shot. I used to live quite close to a huge tower block in West London called Trellick Tower, so I got my friend Kevin Muggleton to photograph it at a menacing angle. Then I stood in the same position, holding my old black-and-white portable (making sure that it was lit by the same surroundings, as opposed to shooting it in a studio). I dropped the cutout TV onto the Trellick picture, and took care to position and blur it so that it looked as natural as possible.

Sometimes I feel like a camcorder, scanning my surroundings looking for something interesting. A recent picture (*Man in Gas Mask*) came about from the purchase of a Russian gas mask that I picked up in a market. I like to explore markets for interesting things that can be photographed or placed under a scanner, and I thought it would make a good subject for a stock picture. Luckily, my friend Paul Hames (a great photographer) didn't mind modeling it on a very hot, sunny day! I also had a shot of a broken window, and combined the two. I was really happy with the result, despite the fact that it was scanned on a really low quality scanner.

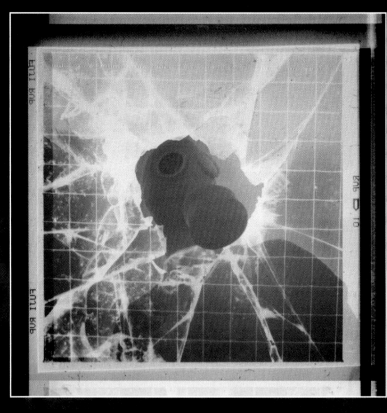

I'm always struck by great photography, and it was after seeing the work of Kevin Muggleton that my passion for it was rekindled. His black and white work is great, the subject matter is always varied, and his timing for capturing the right moment is spot on. Kevin has given me good advice as I have ventured into the world of medium-format photography. Another great black and white photographer is Rolfe Horn, whose work really has the "wow" factor – his site at www.f45.com is a must-see. I also love the night photography of Troy Paiva, so check out www.designshed.com, and bear in mind that none of his pictures have been retouched.

Other digital artists are a great inspiration, most notably people like Magic Torch (www.magictorch.com): their style is sleek, hi-tech, and beautifully crafted. These guys really use Photoshop well; the composition, the often-abstract subject matter, and the way they combine Photoshop with other software is excellent. Jason Brooks (www.folioart.co.uk) is another artist who creates jaw-dropping, slick illustrations – his work seems to be everywhere, and rightly so. He uses a combination of Photoshop and Illustrator, his work is refined and clean, his colors complement each other really well, and he uses light and dark variations of these colors to enhance this effect. Also, his subject matter is usually gorgeous women looking oh-so-cool. Very nice.

© Kevin Muggleton/CORBIS Stockmarket
www.corbisstockmarket.com

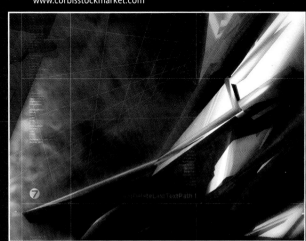

www.magictorch.com ©Magictorch 2001

Samples

Moving to (slightly) more conventional art, Salvador Dali has always been a great influence on me. People usually think of *The Persistence Of Memory* (commonly referred to as "the melting clocks") or *The Metamorphosis Of Narcissus* (the hand holding the egg with the emerging narcissus flower), but my favorite by far is *The Hallucinogenic Toreador*. This was started in 1968 and completed in 1970, and its dimensions are approximately twelve feet tall by nine feet wide. Dali himself described it himself as being "all of Dali in one painting". Its many elements are carefully and beautifully composed, the colors are vivid, and absolutely nothing has been left to the imagination. It's Dali who inspired me to take my time and not rush my work, and a good example of this is my camera illustration – although I confess that it took me rather less than two years!

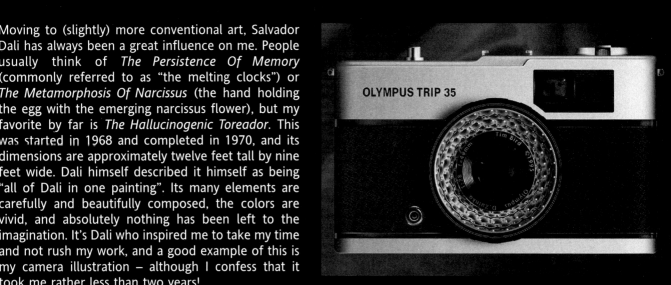

I've got huge respect for Dali and what he achieved; there aren't too many artists who take that long, go to so much trouble, and pay so much attention to detail. One that does is another whom I admire: Nick Cudworth creates art that has many similarities with Dali's. It's usually vivid and surreal, and a lot of time and care has clearly been taken to get the pictures looking just right. His gallery and web site are both well worth a visit, at www.cudworthartworks.co.uk.

Conversation between two chairs by Nick Cudworth
©Nick Cudworth www.cudworthartworks.co.uk

As I said at the beginning of this section, I like to vary my style whenever possible. I don't have a set formula; sometimes I can clearly see a picture in my head and work towards that, while at other times I might just open Photoshop and start playing around. Perhaps I'll just draw a squiggle, then duplicate that layer, rotate it through 180 degrees, and change the layer mode until something interesting comes up. I'll then continue this process, almost randomly adding things, taking them away, changing layer modes, and so on. Sometimes, I'll be pleasantly surprised at what evolves – I've created some really nice abstract pictures just by using this technique. If I've made a busy picture, I may flatten the layers, zoom right in, and look at the picture close up. Then, if I see a small section I like, I can select it with the Marquee tool, turn it into a layer, and enlarge it. If you ever need to use abstract backgrounds in your work, you should give this technique a try. Despite the process being digital, you can often come up with some very natural, organic-looking shapes.

Another technique I like to use is the 'rough and loose' look, with inspiration coming from Stanley Donwood, who did the artwork for Radiohead's *OK Computer* album, and Kyle Cooper's opening sequence for the film *Seven*. This is a great style to try if you want to create stuff, but have limited resources. Just have a look at your immediate surroundings; if you like the look of something, chuck it under the scanner until you have a handful of elements, fire up Photoshop, drag all your elements into one file, then let your creativity take over.

For the tutorial, I have created a fairly abstract picture that has used random photos and bitmapped clipart. It took me a fair amount of experimentation to get the elements how I wanted them, so I'm just going to show you the picture's final construction in terms of layer placement. If you work your way through, you'll see that this picture is actually quite simple to create – Photoshop isn't actually too hard to learn; there's just rather a lot of it! Feel free to try out different things with the elements that have been supplied, but please respect the copyright laws and don't use them for anything other than personal erudition.

Samples

It was a big thing when layers were introduced in Version 3 of Photoshop. I remember the feature being demonstrated at a trade show: the woman was showing how a parachutist could be selected and then moved around to different parts of the sky. In earlier versions, your placement of elements was permanent: once you deselected (apart from one undo), that was it. Now, things are very different. Adobe has made layers very powerful, and with a bit of experimenting they aren't too difficult to get to grips with. Layers lie at the core of all my work (and that of many other users too), and sometimes the Layers palette is the only one you'll use in the creation of an image.

This is one of those pictures in which I just threw stuff together until I came up with something that appealed to me. It doesn't really have a theme; it's art for art's sake. I got the elements for it from various sources – they're a combination of photos that I've taken while out and about, and low-resolution bitmapped illustrations taken from a cheap and cheerful clipart CD. To begin it, create a new file called Rough with a width of 1864 pixels, and a height of 1931 pixels. Set the Resolution to 300 pixels per inch, and the Mode to RGB color. (In case you were wondering, these measurements were taken from the file I used in order to experiment for this project; it was originally 2000 x 2000, but I did a bit of cropping.) Also, make sure that Transparent is selected in the Contents section.

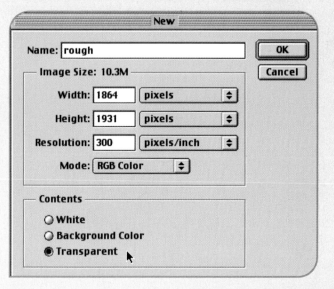

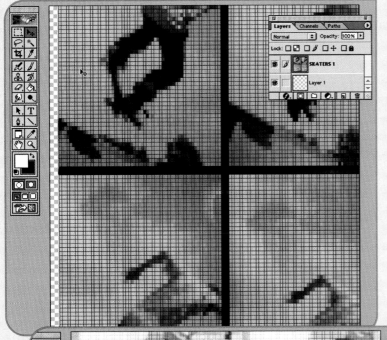

Now open the file called `skate1.jpg`, and drag the image straight into your Rough file with the Move tool. Name the resulting layer SKATERS 1, and drag it until it hangs slightly off the right edge of the canvas, and the trousers of the bottom left skater are just showing.

(I've actually already applied a filter to this image, but it's not one that ships with Photoshop as standard. If you're interested, it's called Plain Mosaic, and comes from a collection of filters called Toadies that can be downloaded from a number of sites on the Internet.)

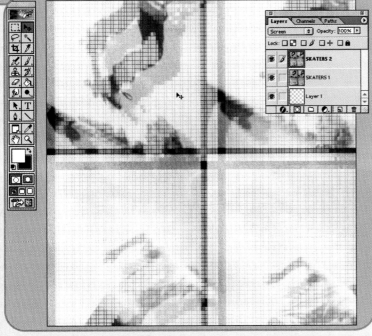

Repeat this process with the picture called `skate2.jpg`, and position it slightly above and to the left of the first image. Name the new layer SKATERS 2. We want to combine these two layers to create the foundation of the picture, so set the layer blending mode of SKATERS 2 to Screen in order to create this abstract effect.

Next, open `fuzz.tif`. I took this image from a de-tuned TV screen, and it seems to work well here in adding some noise to the picture. Drag and drop it into the file; if you hold the Shift key down as you do so, it will automatically be centered. Name the resulting layer TV FUZZ.

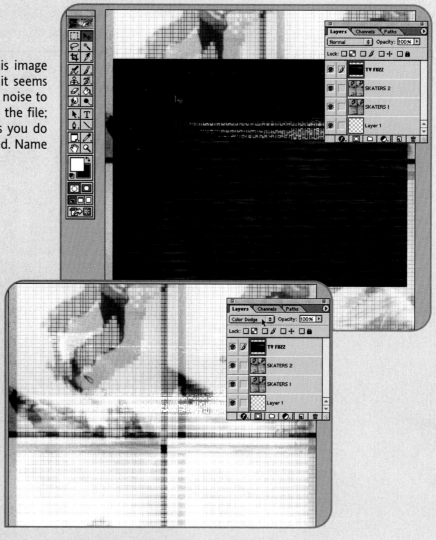

Finally for this stage, give the new layer a blending mode of Color Dodge.

As I said earlier, abstract backgrounds act as great foundations for many of the pictures I produce. They're easy to make (or find), and you don't have to spend lots of money on royalty-free CDs. A good source can be photos you've taken that might be blurred, washed out, or over-exposed. Everyday objects can look very different once they're placed under a scanner — what about the controller for your PlayStation? Your favorite item of clothing? Screwed up newspapers? Or that box of spare video and computer cables? Material is all around you.

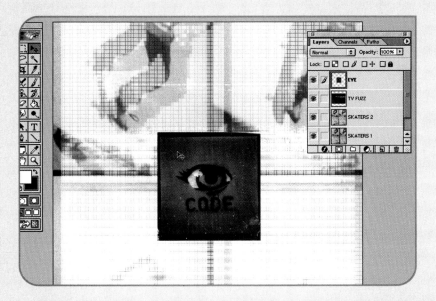

Now that we've sorted out the background, let's start adding the foreground elements. The next image that we're going to add is in the file `eye.tif`. I usually get my transparencies drum-scanned, but I put this one on my cheap and cheerful flatbed scanner and placed my light box on top of it, giving me a really rough scan that was completely covered in dust – perfect for this picture. Drag and drop the image and position it as opposite, naming the new layer EYE.

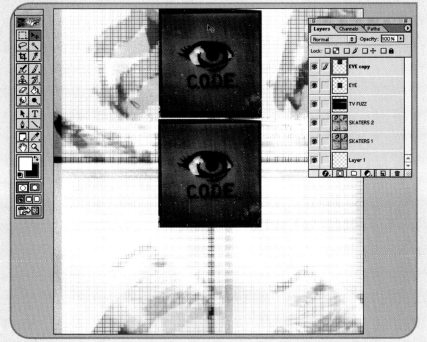

If a lot of your work uses photography, I strongly recommend that you use transparencies (positive) as opposed to prints or negatives. I've found that prints tend to show up imperfections and scratches, while negatives seem to come out grainy. The advantage of having the master sharp and in color is that you can always tone it down or make it black and white, but you can't turn a grainy black and white into a sharp, colorful picture.

We're now going to duplicate this layer by dragging the eye image upwards with the Move tool, while holding down the Alt/Option key. Photoshop will automatically create a new layer above the existing one, and assign it the same name followed by "copy".

Samples

Repeat this process, and position another eye at the bottom of the image.

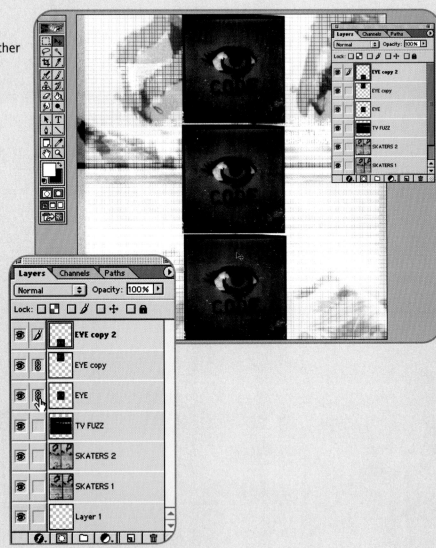

Having lots of separate layers can sometimes be useful – for example, you might want to color each layer individually, using adjustment layers. In this case, however, we want to apply a single layer blending mode, and reduce any unnecessary clutter in the Layers palette. The next step is therefore to combine all three EYE layers, a process that starts when you link them together by clicking in the boxes alongside.

One purpose of linking is to enable multiple layers to be moved around simultaneously, but in this case we want to combine them. If you go into the Layers palette menu and choose Merge Linked, your three EYE layers will become one, making the application layer effects much simpler. If it isn't already named, rename this merged layer as EYE.

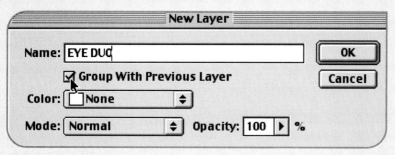

We're now going apply a sepia tone to the eyes, so go to Layer > New Adjustment Layer > Hue/Saturation, name the new layer EYE DUO, and check the Group With Previous Layer box. This will apply any effects we specify only to the contents of the EYE layer, and not to the rest of the picture.

In the Hue/Saturation dialog box, check Colorize to apply a wash of color to the whole layer (you can also check the Preview box to see your changes as they happen). Change the Hue value to 31 and the Saturation value to 14, and then press OK.

When you added the adjustment layer, Photoshop also added a layer mask, in case you wanted to apply the adjustment only to a specific area of the image. In this case, we don't need that facility – and as it increases the final file size, we'll remove it. Go to Layer > Remove Layer Mask > Discard.

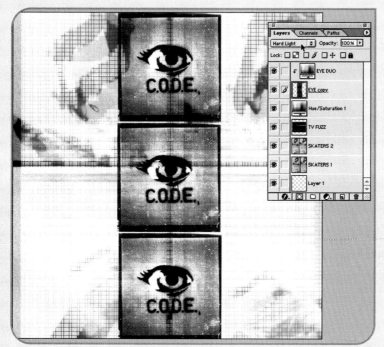

We now want to apply a global color to the layers *below* the EYE layer. The uppermost of these is TV FUZZ, so select it in the Layers palette, and go to Layer > New Adjustment Layer > Hue/Saturation. This time, make sure Group with Previous Layer is *not* checked. Check the Colorize box, and change the Hue value to 191 and the Saturation value to 8, and press OK. Again, you can remove the layer mask using the same method we employed in the previous step.

Now I want to blend the EYE layer into the layers below it, allowing some of the detail from the lower layers to show through. Selecting Hard Light as the layer blending mode gave me the effect I was after.

Samples

On the subject of blending modes, I tend to use Multiply if I have a picture that seems to have lost some detail due to overexposure – maybe something like a wispy sky. By simply duplicating the layer and applying the Multiply mode to the top layer, you'll be surprised at how much detail you can retrieve. The layers don't have to be identical, though – you can get some great creative effects by running through the various modes and experimenting. The different calculations used by each mode can throw up some really interesting stuff.

I have a great little Russian camera that gives noticeably darker edges to a picture, and draws you into the center of an image by doing so. I'm going to do something similar here. Go to Layer > New Adjustment Layer > Brightness/Contrast, and uncheck Group with Previous Layer. Change the Brightness value to -100 and the Contrast to -33, and move this adjustment layer up to the top of the Layers palette.

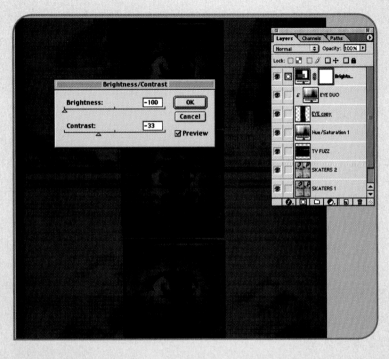

In this case, we *do* need the layer mask. In the Layers palette, click the square on the right of this adjustment layer. Then, select the Gradient tool and make sure your settings are the same as in the screenshot below (a radial gradient, foreground to background, with black as the former and white as the latter). Now click in the center of the picture, hold down the mouse and drag to one of the corners.

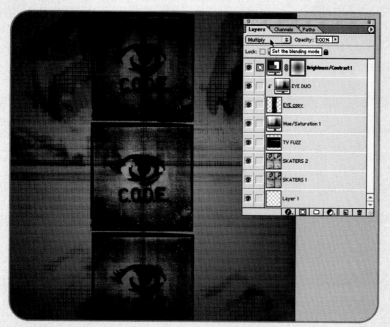

The more you work with layers, the more things you'll find to do with layer masks. As another example, you might have a color picture of a woman that you want to turn into a grayscale image, but retain the blue of her eyes. One way to do this would be to apply a Hue/Saturation adjustment layer and key in -100 in the Saturation box, leaving you with a grayscale image. To bring back the color of her eyes, you'd simply select a small brush, make sure that black is the foreground color and that the right-hand square on the adjustment layer is active, and then brush the blue back in. You're effectively painting 'holes' in the mask to show the color in the layer below.

In the layer mask thumbnail in the Layers palette, you can now see the radial graduation from black to white, showing that the center has had less brightness and contrast adjustment applied. Adjustment layers can also have layer blending modes assigned to them, and I strengthened the effect of this one by applying Multiply mode to it.

Next, open the file called deep.tif. This contains some text that spells out the title of a song, and like the other elements in this picture, I'm throwing it in simply because I felt that it fitted. I needed, though, to 'extract' the text from its background – and while there are a number of ways of making such specific selections, in this case it will be quick and easy to use Color Range. Go to Select > Color Range, set the Fuzziness to 0 (this is a tolerance level), and then click on the area you want to select (the black text).

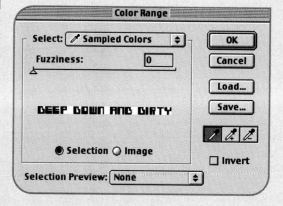

Samples

Press OK, and you should see the 'marching ants' around the edge of the text. Using the Move tool, drag and drop the text into the main picture, and name the resulting layer DEEP.

We're now going to turn the text on its side. Go to Edit > Free Transform, click outside the box, and then drag the box round until it has turned 90 degrees counterclockwise. (If you hold down the Shift key while doing this, your layer will be constrained to rotate in 15-degree increments.) Once rotated, you can move it into place using the Move tool, or nudge it by using the arrow keys. Once you're happy with the position, apply Overlay mode to the layer.

Open the file called barcode.tif, drag and drop its contents into the working file, naming the resulting layer BARCODE 1. You can get rid of the white background quickly and easily by applying the Multiply layer mode. Now drag it to the top left corner.

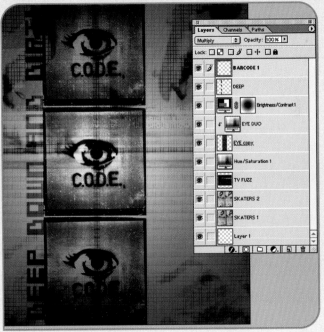

Repeat this process by copying the BARCODE 1 layer, rotating it, and placing it in the bottom left corner.

Open the file called site.tif, which contains a picture of a crane on a building site, and drag and drop it into the main file above the SKATERS 2 layer. Position it as shown below, and invert it (Image > Adjust > Invert). Then apply the Hard Light layer mode, and set the opacity to 90%.

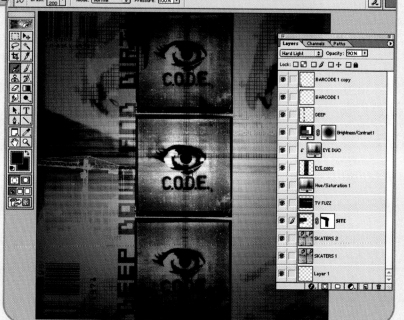

I don't want the hard edge to show at the top of this layer, so I'm going to remove it by using a layer mask that I added by clicking on the icon at the bottom of the Layers palette. Select the Airbrush tool and a 200-pixel brush, and create a similar shape to the one you can see in the screenshot opposite. (As you paint, the layer mask thumbnail will update to show you where your brush strokes have been made.)

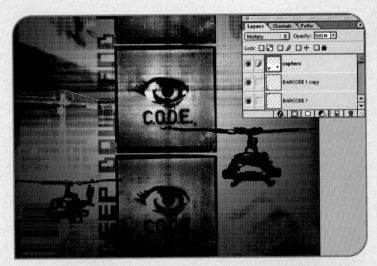

I found this helicopter picture (`copters.tif`) on a clip-art CD, and thought that it would also look good in this picture, with its bold lines and jagged edges. Drag and drop it into the composition, and position it as shown. Name the layer COPTERS, make sure that it's at the top of the Layers palette, and then apply the Multiply layer mode.

I love the strength of the black lines that are now a feature of the picture, so I'm going to add a black border as well. As with so many things in Photoshop, there are several ways of achieving this, but here I'm going to fill a layer with black, and delete a square in the middle. Add a new layer named BORDER, and then go to Edit > Fill, set the Contents to Black, and make sure that Preserve Transparency is not checked. Press OK.

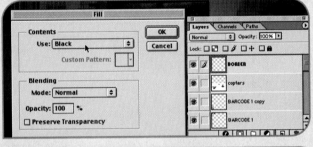

Your picture will now go completely black, so select the Rectangular Marquee tool, and use it to define the inside edge of the border. It will help if you reduce the opacity of the BORDER layer while you perform this step. When you're happy with the position, delete the selection.

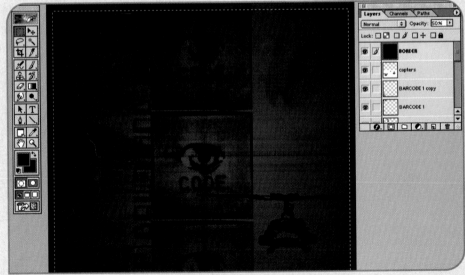

Your picture is nearly there, but I think it would be better if the skateboarders at the top were more visible, so once again we'll take advantage of a layer mask, this time on the SKATERS 1 layer. Select the Gradient tool (a linear gradient, on this occasion), place the mouse just above the top eye, and click and drag until you're lower than the skateboard. The skateboarders should now be clearer, and the Layers palette will update to show the area you have masked off.

Finish off by selecting the SKATERS 2 layer, going to Filter > Noise > Add Noise, keying in a setting of about 12, and selecting Uniform Distribution. This defines how the speckled pixels we're about to create are dispersed. Now check the Monochromatic box (if you don't do this, the noise will contain specks of color that can sometimes spoil the effect). This is the final step, and your picture should now be a close match for the one you saw at the start of the section.

I hope that you've enjoyed this tutorial, and that you've picked up a few new tricks along the way. If you like this look and feel, why not reuse these elements in a new image of your own? Maybe you could add some of your own elements too? Just experiment, and never be afraid to try new things. Good luck, and enjoy!

chapter 1

chapter 2

chapter 3

chapter 4

chapter 5

chapter 6

chapter 7

chapter 8

chapter 9

chapter 10

chapter 11

chapter 12

chapter 13

chapter 14

chapter 15

chapter 16

outro

"I can be as fascinated by a complex tree shape as I am by a simple pebble."

Johann Terrettaz
www.twice2.ch

Diverse

I find inspiration in everything around me – drawings, television, cinema, or just everyday life – and there's no single style, period, or fashion that's particularly compelling. I don't have any prejudices regarding the things that surround me: it's like a landscape, and I can be as fascinated by a complex tree shape as I am by a simple pebble. When I design, I feel exactly the same way, and that's why my interest in certain styles or designers can change according to my mood.

I live in one of the most populated areas of Geneva, where there is a multitude of different nationalities and cultures, and you can change from one continent to another just by crossing the road. I like being among different cultures and mentalities: it helps me to open my mind. Tradition, folklore and custom are a rich source of inspiration. I'm like a sponge, absorbing most of it for reuse later, when I need it.

I love the aesthetic of design, and of images in general. I like to understand the method, the vision, the thought process, and the realization of other designers – especially those from other countries whom I've met when collaborating on projects like k10k, Shift Rojo, Cubadust, etc. I like discussing their philosophy, and the way they see their work – it helps me to broaden my mind, and my horizons.

Very often, the most talented designers are simply the most enthusiastic: they are open-minded and curious about everything. I think that in this job, it's when you believe that you know, that you're not progressing anymore. Personally, I'm always surprised and amazed by the creations of other artists, but I find it quite difficult to put my finger on exactly why any particular person has influenced me. The best I can do is to list a few of the people and things that have made me think and work in a different way.

Diverse

To begin, there's Joe Duffy and Charles S Anderson of Duffy Design (www.duffy.com). The characteristic of their work is the profusion of graphical elements; they have a very current vision of the past. Their work is never boring, so no matter how much time I spend looking at it, I can always discover new details. Enthusiasm emanates from each and every one of their creations, and yet they've got a very sharp sense for color, and manage to keep the overall mix subtle. For me, their posters and logos symbolize how joyful design can be.

Margo Chase has always interested me, because she seems to hold strong opinions about the images she creates. Whereas other people would have done things in a simpler way, she imposes her complex and very detailed vision, and you're forced to admit that it couldn't have been done any better. She pays close attention to detail, color, and typography; and she's so far ahead in her thinking about these things that it acts as a motivator for the rest of us. Her designs evince a gothic mood, but always with a disconcerting coolness.

I have to mention Max Bill, a Swiss who had the same 'traditional' background as me (the old days, when you couldn't use a computer for everything). I'm fascinated by his technique and his design philosophy: everything is in the right place – pure, structured, and always in the service of the subject, without blurring the vision with an overload of useless elements. I like the dynamic and the clarity of his work, as well as his use of typography, which becomes a graphic element in its own right.

Typography is one of my passions: it helped me to understand that pictures and their subjects can be interpreted in thousands of different ways. I like the way that the structured shapes of letters contrast with fluid pictures. When computers started to be widely used, everybody had a go at typography and lithography with generally mediocre results. Work generated on the computer was soulless – too rigid and plain – until the arrival of designers like David Carson and Neville Brody, who tried new ways of bringing life back into designs, with their 'loose', and organic layouts. They showed me that the computer wasn't an obstacle to creation, but rather that it could be used to experiment, to discover new ways of working with pictures; that it could mean more freedom, and not more barriers.

© Design: Margo Chase

I've always been fascinated by H.R. Giger (who conceived, among other things, the sets and creatures for the movie Alien). His drawings are sometimes morbid, but he's got a style that's incredibly powerful – his images are almost overloaded with detail. And if we're talking about detail, I should also mention the illustrations of M.C. Escher. The first time I saw his work, I was amazed at these apparently old prints that were at the same time incredibly modern. There were geometric and organic forms overlapping one another, and incredible optical illusions – just complete mastery of the art of illustration. I believe that, unconsciously, a lot of designers have been inspired by Escher's work.

In another field, I'm often moved by the photography of Herb Ritts – his work shows extreme sensitivity. Processing black and white pictures in CMYK gives very interesting tones, bringing a dramatic or sensual touch to the photos. The way he frames his subjects is sometimes surprising, but it brings an incredible atmosphere. He also demonstrates that you can always do something different, even with subjects that have been used thousands of times before. Ritts can adapt his vision and search for a detail, an angle, or a pose that will show his subject in a whole new light. I'm never bored looking at his work, as I feel that I share his ideas about beauty.

And then there's Andy Warhol! I love his way of 'diverting' pictures – of transforming them from something rather plain into something interesting by combining them together, or by working on their colors. I like the idea that everything can be interesting; that a surprising combination can make a feeling, an emotion, or a memory spring into our minds.

Finally, a great big "thank you" goes to Kyle Cooper for making movie title sequences fashionable again. I used to enjoy it when every film began with an introduction that gave some clues about its mood and atmosphere – and the one for Seven, in particular, is a real masterpiece. Cooper's work is incredibly creative, and very well conceived. Every element supports every other: without sound, the sequence would lose some of its intensity; the typography supports the rhythm of the music; and the style of the pictures gives an indication to the audience of the subject matter.

Skoda Detail – 1J0615301D

Skoda Detail – 02C409053M

Skoda Detail – 6Y08372461NB

© Duffy 2001

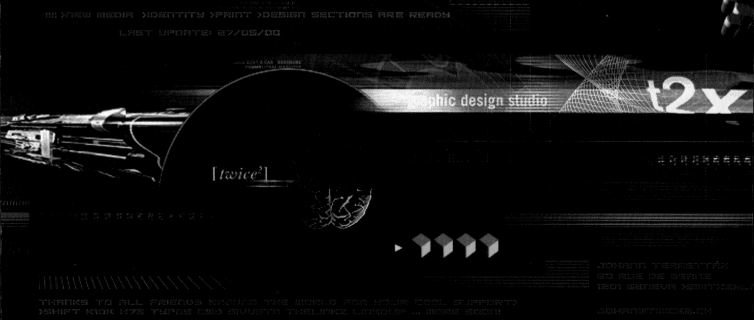

I started using Photoshop at the same time as I started to use a computer, and I grew with it. At the beginning, I thought we were already at the limit of what could be achieved using 'accessible' programs, as I came from a traditional design background of using Rotring equipment, compass, and drawing pens. As the years passed, the program evolved and became more complex, but that didn't cause me too many problems because my style and my expectations grew with it. I think that in the near future, Photoshop will become more intuitive, and I hope that one day it will incorporate more vector functions like the ones in Adobe Illustrator. I also hope that processor power will continue to increase apace, as one of the inconveniences of working with tools such as Photoshop and large, high-resolution images is that the processing time can be a bit long!

Photoshop has made it considerably easier for me to work without barriers to the realization of my ideas, and above all to avoid wasting precious time. Little more than ten years ago, it was a complicated procedure to put a shadow onto text or to change the colors of a photo, let alone to create images of the kind we produce now. You had to discuss the project with the photolithographer and the photocompositor, increasing the chances that the final project would not resemble the original idea at all. Also, one of the enormous opportunities that Photoshop gives us is the power to test, correct, and modify (or go back to a previous step) very quickly – and because of this, our work has become much more playful and instinctive than before.

The trouble with this, of course, is that sometimes clients don't see your work as being very complicated, and imagine that a job can therefore be done very quickly. At times like this, I remind myself of the time when Picasso was asked why one of his pieces was so expensive, when it only took him three hours to create. (Far be it from me to consider graphic designers as artists – I think we are more like craftsmen, but that reinforces the kind of perception that we have to face.) I truly believe that work created in a short space of time is often the fruit of many years of permeation, association, and personal research, vital to the realization of the end product.

My education will probably never end. Every day, I learn, see, read, and discover new things. I read lots of books about graphic design, especially the Graphis and Print series, which both demonstrate how imaginative graphic design can be. It also keeps me humble with regard to whom I consider to be real artists. Books are a huge inspirational resource for me, as you can jump from one style to another quickly, but still understand what makes a designer unique, and what techniques they employ. They also help me to refocus when I'm working on a project for a long period of time.

When it comes to professional projects, I've got two ways of working. Either I set up a carefully considered structure and stick to it, without any space for improvisation, or else I work in a more instinctive and organic way. It pretty much depends on my mood, the complexity of the project, or my current inspiration.

At the moment, for example, I'm working simultaneously on a collection of designs for surfboards and snowboards. For projects of this type I usually have a briefing with the client first, in which we define the broad direction of design. Above all, we discuss what they don't want, as it's often easier to start by getting to know what the client doesn't like – they usually have a stronger idea of that, than of what they do like. Next, I'll make myself aware of all the other brands in the market, and try to see the emerging trends (colors, themes, complexity/simplicity, and so on). I'll take notes to help me remember the big ideas, and I'll start to sketch out ideas of my own.

This particular project is quite demanding, because of the constraints of the medium. Surfboards and snowboards have very specific forms, and you can't forget that your design will spend a lot of its life in contact with water or snow! Restrictions like these can reduce the range of materials you can use, and thereby harm (or at least, affect) an otherwise perfectly good design.

Depending on whether the motif of my design is in a technical style or something more textural, I draw up models in Illustrator or Photoshop to present to the client, in order to show them my 'starting point'. Then the client will give me an idea of their vision according to my design, in order to refine the idea of what he really wants, and I'll redo a series of models based on our discussions, keeping as close as possible to the client's ideal.

A number of the logos I've produced for this project were inspired by the style of Tracy Sabin (http://tracy.sabin.com): direct and sensual, fusing illustration and typography in order to be as legible as possible, but still conveying personality.

I like my logos to have a sense of 'life', through the of use pictograms or illustrations like Tracy Sabin's, or Charles S Anderson's fonts. In turn, the brand or the product becomes more 'friendly' and 'lively'. Clearly, I can't suggest this kind of logo to every client – it's always necessary to adapt – but that can be just as stimulating.

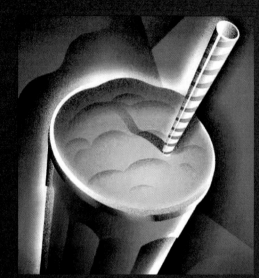

Design Firm: Mires Design, Art Director: Scott Mires
Client: Boyd's Coffee, Illustrator: Tracy Sabin

As a rule, I try to combine the influences I have discovered, as in this commission for a design magazine. In it, I believe that you can see the echoes of a number of the people who have inspired me.

My work is often characterized by a richness of elements, and you can see that the picture above is 'cut' in half by two styles and two processes. The left hand side is very refined – it's simplified to the maximum without degrading the image – while the right hand side is quite different, being along the lines of a 'cutaway' medical diagram. (I've always been fascinated by drawings like these – it's the combination of the fluid but complex work in the textures, and the rigor of the graphics and legends.) The image has been decomposed, and I've played with the colors and textures to get a complex result that doesn't allow you to see everything at first sight. I like the contrast of the simplistic (for the colors, as much as for the graphical aspect) and the complex; this is how I feel in the city, and about life in general.

Diverse

The image that we're going to look at in this tutorial was constructed for the Web, so it uses a fairly low resolution, and RGB. When I'm doing this kind of work, I tend to work on backgrounds in Photoshop, and then import them into Macromedia Flash. Once there, I add animations and little details. Using a low resolution is quite convenient, because it allows you to work on documents with a small file size, and to see how the final result will look while you're working. This is not generally the case when you work on a high-resolution document in CMYK, because what you see on the screen can be quite different from the printed document.

What I like about Photoshop is that you can achieve a result that often exceeds your expectations in terms of quality, color, structure, and detail. Also, there is almost no limit to the creativity it allows — whether in the construction of an image from scratch, or in aiding the creative process by means of the effects and techniques that it offers. I often try to give an image life and depth; with Photoshop, this can be done by refining, modifying, or adding effects that make the image more 'real'. I find that it's the ideal complement to programs such as Illustrator or FreeHand, which allow the creation of very precise elements or images that are generally too cold. When you mix or modify them in Photoshop, you can bring a little life to them that they were lacking.

In Photoshop, you can work on images in a completely intuitive way. It's quite likely that you could achieve an almost identical end result to mine by going through a process that's totally different from the one I'm going to use. I often compare it to a journey from one place to another: you could take several different paths and still reach your destination.

Images that are made with lots of layers have a kind of 'uncertain' side to them. I find this quite stimulating, because you can be carried away by the combinations available. A little experimentation can lead you to change your initial ideas about the level of color, or the arrangement of elements. It's a bit like a game that opens a door to the unknown: when an image evolves during its construction, the methods that you use can give you new ideas along the way, according to your inspiration. I find the unknown part exciting, and it can lead to places I never would have thought of otherwise.

It can be instructive, too, to play the game in the role of other graphic designers: to try and understand the route that they have taken to achieve a certain result. In the past, I've had to work on images that other designers have made, and I've always been interested to see that each of them have their own methods, some more complicated than others.

Because I work for a very varied clientele, I must adapt to their 'environment'. I don't have any fixed ideas at the start, nor do I use identical methods for each project. It all depends on the style (retro, corporate, avant-garde...), but I think that having to adapt to a different world and different constraints each time is an advantage, because it allows me to discover new techniques and ways of working. The mock-ups that I present to clients, though, are usually always created in Photoshop, rather than being sketched in pencil or pen. This allows me and the client to have a definitive vision of the project – there's no way that the direction I'm taking with the piece can be misinterpreted. This avoids any misunderstandings from the start, and allows me to foresee any problems that the final version of the project could pose.

In Photoshop, I try to use filter effects as little as possible, or to mix them in new ways, so that the image has a more human feel. For example, anyone is capable of using a pretty lens flare – and because it's so easy, a lot of people do! This tends to result in a lot of images that look the same: pre-built, and impersonal. I prefer to make my images look a little 'imprecise' through the use of less structured, more complex techniques, rather than effects that are ready-made.

This preference for 'living' images has paid off, because it has allowed me to persuade (or at least, arouse the curiosity of) clients about the choice available to them. I have some new clients who contacted me simply because of this style, and our collaboration is extraordinary because a real trust is established between us. The problem that can arise if your style is too 'cold' is that certain clients may not believe you really have a 'vision' of the order they have given you. When you try to have your own style, on the other hand, the client will see that you have been able to produce work that they could not have imagined themselves.

Before beginning an image in the style that I'm going to deconstruct here, I prepare as many graphical elements as I can in Illustrator: structures, outlines, text, logos, geometric shapes, etc. In the end, I may or may not use them in the construction of the image – it all depends whether they 'fit'. I only make use of what is the most coherent, to my taste, and to the benefit of the whole.

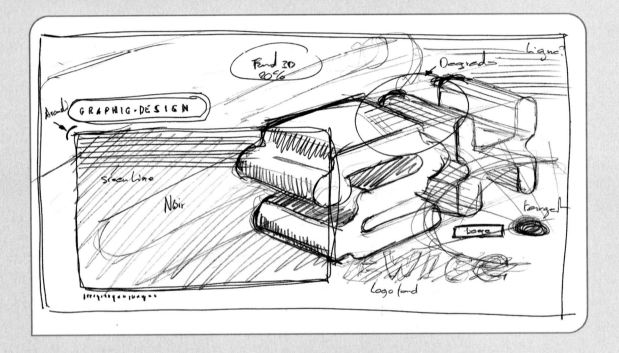

For the image that you can preview by taking a look at `basetwice2.psd` on the accompanying CD, I started from a sketch, in order to make myself aware of the placement of the main elements. (In other words, the format of the whole composition, the two black rectangles, and the three-dimensional "2X" element that overlaps them.) The other elements were placed in a more intuitive way as the project progressed – sometimes, the availability of graphical elements and the different sorts of blending modes between layers can completely change my original idea. As for my choice of colors, I generally start with quite a precise idea of the feel I want to have, so the elements I import from Illustrator tend to be in neutral colors (black, gray, or white), and I add the color in Photoshop.

To begin with, change Photoshop's background color to quite a deep green – I entered #669900 in the edit box at the bottom of the Color Picker dialog box. Then, create a new RGB document that's 794 x 397 pixels in size, at 72dpi.

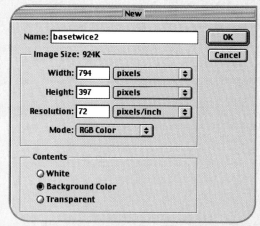

This image is going to comprise graphic elements that are imported from Illustrator and mixed together in Photoshop. Now, going from a vector program like Illustrator to a raster program like Photoshop invariably involves some approximations, which are reflected in the dialog box that you'll see when you try to open the `matosill.ai` file. For simplicity in this tutorial, I left all the settings at their defaults, but it's possible to (say) increase the dimensions of the representation that Photoshop creates in order to produce higher-resolution elements, should you require them.

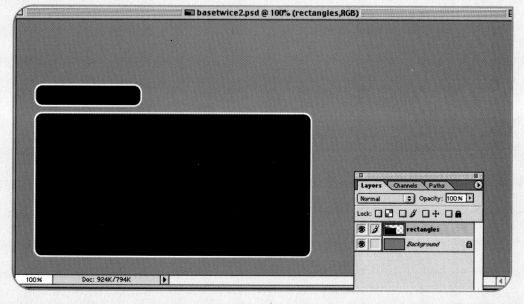

Once you've opened the file, select the rectangular elements using the Rectangular Marquee tool, and copy and paste them onto a new layer in your `basetwice2.psd` file. Don't forget to name each of the new layers that you create – when there are many of them, you'll be able to retrieve the one you want to work on quickly. We'll call this new layer rectangles.

Diverse

Next, we're going to bring in a 3D graphical element from the `matosill.ai` file. I created this element in Illustrator, with the KPT Vector Effects plug-in.

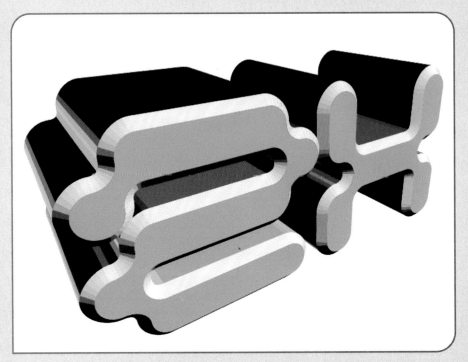

Import the element, and place it on a new layer named back 3D element. Then use Edit > Transform > Scale to make the element around twice its original size. Set the layer blending mode of this layer to Luminosity, at 35% opacity.

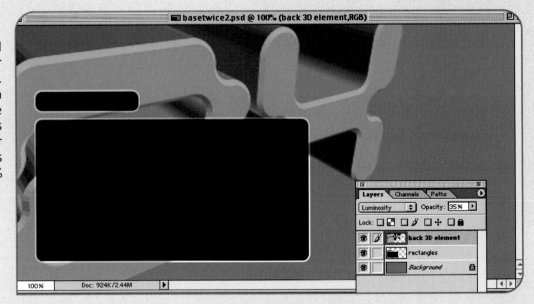

Next, Command-click on the rectangles layer in the Layers palette to make a selection of its contents, so that we can erase some areas of the 3D element that we don't want. Select the Eraser tool, and work on the back 3D element layer. First of all, erase everything that appears in the top rectangle, and then just the edges of the large rectangle with the eraser brush (use the soft, round shape at 45 pixels). You will then give an impression of depth to the black rectangles.

On the finished web site, the large rectangle is going to display information, so we're going to make it look more like a 'screen'. To get this effect, you can start by creating a new document that's just ten pixels by four pixels. Then, set the Pencil tool to a single black pixel, and color in the top line of the document. After that, Edit > Define Pattern, and save your new creation as a pattern called lines. If you like, you can close the tiny document – we won't need it again.

Now, create a new layer called lines, make a selection from the rectangles layer again, and use the Paint Bucket tool to fill the selection with your new pattern.

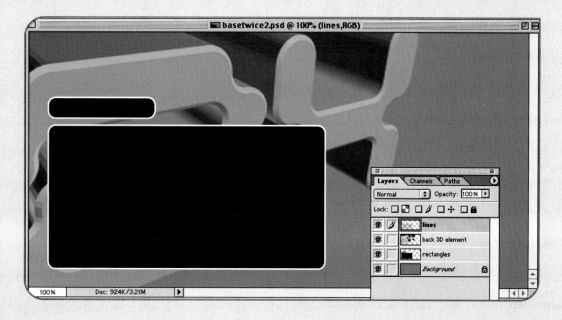

I didn't create these lines in Illustrator because I wanted them to be as perfect as possible, and the process of importing them could have compromised that. In the screenshot above, I've deleted the parts of the fill pattern that extended into the white lines by shrinking the selection a little (Select > Modify > Contract), taking the inverse of the selection, and then using the Eraser tool on the lines layer.

Diverse

Next, creating the two 'ruler' elements involves the same principle as the horizontal lines that we added earlier. I made a new 197 x 8 pixel document, used the Eyedropper to sample the lightest green in the composition, and produced the following with the help of a custom fill pattern.

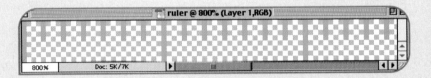

Now you can copy and paste this image into `basetwice2.psd` twice, creating layers called ruler and ruler 180. As its name suggests, the second of these should be rotated through 180 degrees (Edit > Transform > Rotate), and both should employ the Screen layer blending mode. Finally, maneuver the two layers so that the complete image looks something like this.

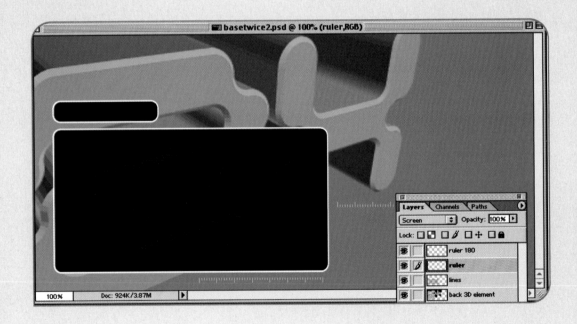

The next step is to bring in the "graphic design" text from the Illustrator file, and to name the new layer graphic text. After that, you can import another copy of the 3D element – without altering its size, this time – onto a new layer named front 3D element. Change the hue/saturation of this layer (Image > Adjust > Hue/Saturation) to the values shown here.

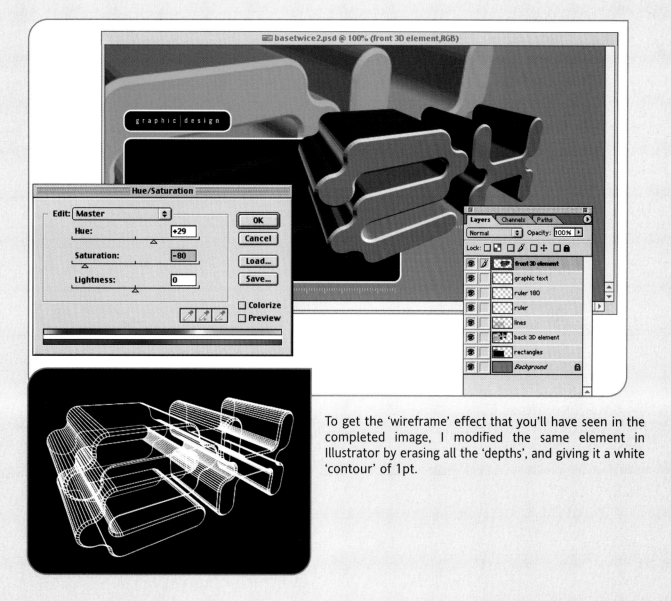

To get the 'wireframe' effect that you'll have seen in the completed image, I modified the same element in Illustrator by erasing all the 'depths', and giving it a white 'contour' of 1pt.

One way to bring this element into our composition from the `matosill.ai` file is to use the Magic Wand tool with a tolerance of around 200. If you click on a white area, you'll also pick up the gray anti-aliasing, but not the black background. Copy the selection you made and paste it into a new layer called skeleton 3D element. Switch the layer blending mode to Lighten, and position the new shape squarely over the existing one.

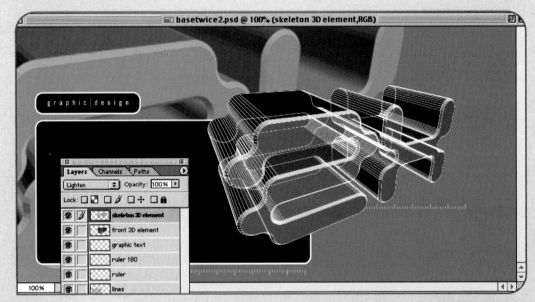

We'll change the color of the skeleton lines to complement the background green color, so use the Eyedropper tool to sample it, and then use the Hue/Saturation dialog box to redefine the color, giving it a slightly warmer look than the background. Make sure that you check the Colorize box as you do so.

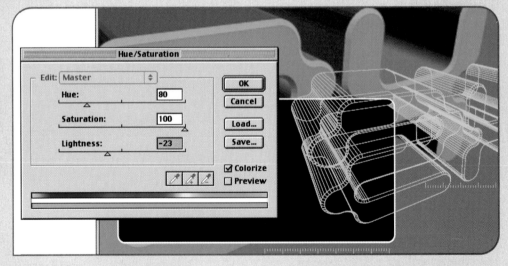

Next, Command-click on the front 3D element layer to select its contents, and save the selection (Select > Save Selection) as 2x. It's important to do this now, as we'll need it later when we modify this layer.

It's relatively simple to create the effect of a 3D object that's 'half-finished' – you just need to erase part of the 'solid' 3D element with the Eraser tool in Airbrush mode at 100 pixels. It can help to change the layer order and put the 'solid' drawing above the 'wireframe' one, and also to erase the part of the wireframe layer towards the left of the selection. There are no rules for creating the effect that you want – try erasing various amounts to achieve a result that you like. You can always go back if you make a mistake.

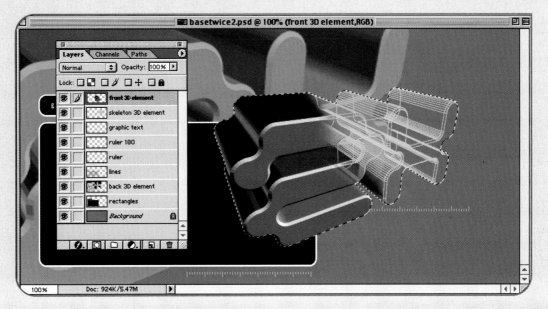

Many graphic designers have asked me about this effect – they thought it was created in 3D Max, or that it must be very complicated. That's what I like about Photoshop: you can experiment, look for effects with blending, and modify imported elements to achieve a more personalized result.

Diverse

Now that we have the basic elements of the image, we need to dress it up with a few more graphical elements to give it 'life'. Pick up the set of three small cylinders from the Illustrator document, paste them into a new layer called cylinders, and click on Colorize in the Hue/Saturation dialog box to give them a color that complements the background. Then, import the "twice2" logo, place it on a new layer called logo, and change the blending mode to Overlay at 100% opacity. Once again, this is to give the new element a color that fits with the rest of the composition.

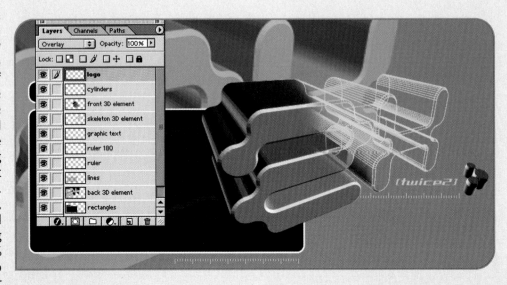

The elements we need to add now are the pixelated writing ("...wxyz"), and the lines that look a bit like crop circles. Getting the size and balance right here required a little experimentation, but in the end I chose Overlay mode at 40% opacity for the wxyz layer, while the crop circles layer was scaled to 75%, and set to Overlay mode at 70%. Since these elements were to be partially obscured by some of the others, their position in the layer stack was equally important.

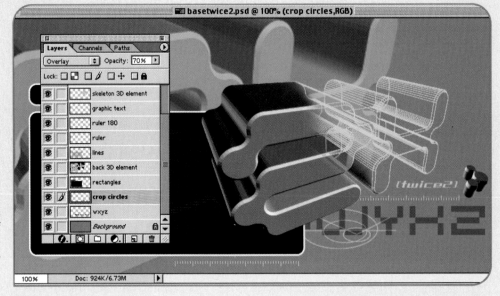

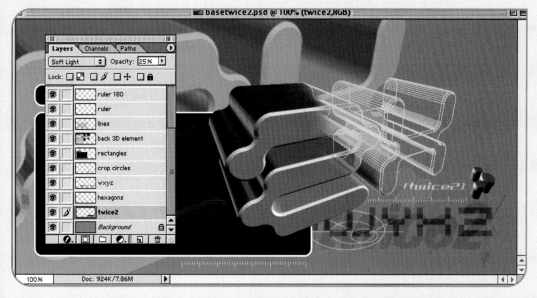

The next few steps are all about adding extra detail and interest to the right hand side of the image. Import the hexagons from Illustrator, and change the layer blending mode to Hard Light at 33% opacity. You can also bring in the "twice2" element and change the mode of *its* layer to Soft Light at 25% opacity.

Bring in the gray, square-shaped grille from `matosill.ai`, changing the blending mode of the new layer to Soft Light. Once that's done, delete part of it using the Eraser tool in Airbrush mode at 100 pixels. Then, go to Select > Load Selection to load the 2x selection that we saved earlier (you can choose it from the Channel drop-down), and completely erase the part of the grille that's inside the 3D element. Here's the result I got:

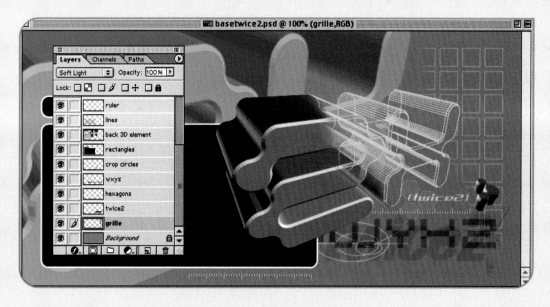

The 'target' design that we'll import next was created in Illustrator and modified with KPT Vector Effects. It also resides in a separate file: `target.ai`. Apart from that, though, the procedure is the same as ever; you can call the new layer target.

Some of the colors here are clearly rather out-of-place – but as usual, we can soon do something about that. First of all, invert the colors (Image > Adjust > Invert). Then, modify the hue and saturation of the target layer.

Finally, change the blending mode of the layer to Hard Light at 44% opacity, place the 'target' over the cylinders, and then erase part of the target with the Eraser tool in Airbrush mode at 15% pressure. If everything has gone to plan so far, here's what your composition should look like.

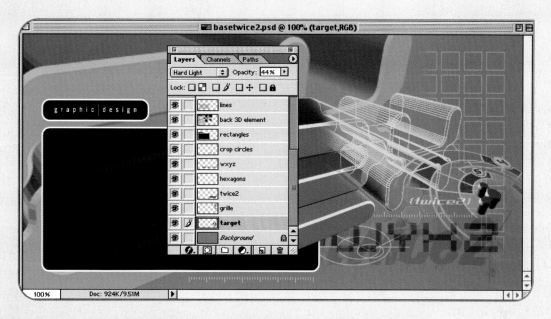

We're on the home stretch now. Import the radiation lines from Illustrator onto a new layer called radiation. They start out black, so you'll need to invert the layer before you attempt to center it on the cylinders. Once you have it in the right place, change the blending mode to Overlay at 70% opacity.

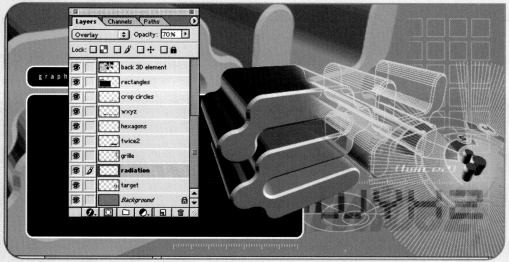

Then, simply erase the greater part of the pattern (the top-left semicircle) using the Eraser tool in Airbrush mode at 200 pixels.

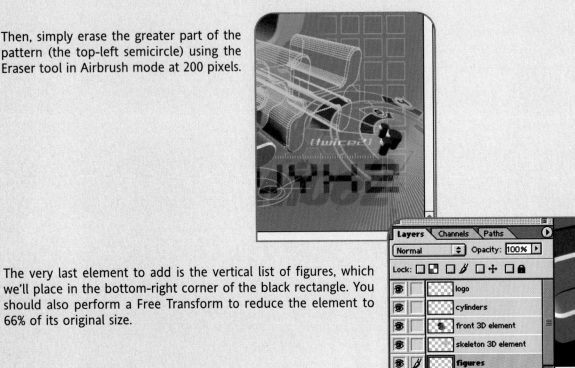

The very last element to add is the vertical list of figures, which we'll place in the bottom-right corner of the black rectangle. You should also perform a Free Transform to reduce the element to 66% of its original size.

We've now finished the imports, and can concentrate on the image itself to give it more depth and relief with shadows. For this, create a new layer that we'll use for all the shadows we add, and change the blending mode to Multiply. Name this layer shadows, and locate it just beneath the rectangles layer.

To create the shadows, we're going to load the 2x selection once again. Then, inverse the selection, so that you're only able to draw the shadows *outside* the 3D object. Next, use the Eyedropper tool to select a dark green color from the background, but not 100% black. Then choose the Paintbrush tool with quite a large, graduated brush, and start to create shadows underneath the main 3D element.

(In order to see the action of the paintbrush on your image better, it can help to go into the View menu and uncheck Show Extras. The selection will still be active, but it will become invisible.)

Continue the shadows under the three-dimensional "2", and feel free to change the shape of your paintbrush to create your own details. Eventually, your image will look something like this one.

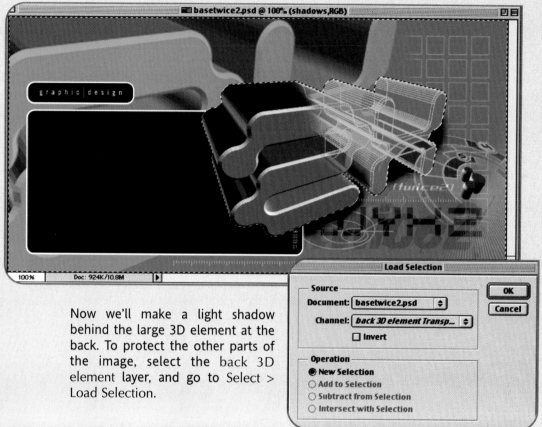

Now we'll make a light shadow behind the large 3D element at the back. To protect the other parts of the image, select the back 3D element layer, and go to Select > Load Selection.

Do the same with the rectangles layer, but this time choose the Add to Selection radio button.

Diverse

Finally, add our old 2x selection to the mix as well. Once you've done this, take the inverse of the selection (Select > Inverse) to draw outside the elements. At this stage, you can go back to the shadows layer, choose the Paintbrush tool and create some small shadows above and below the large 3D element.

In a similar way as previously described, recall the rectangles selection, take *its* inverse, and make a small shadow (still on the shadows layer) under the rectangles with the Paintbrush tool. To constrain them to a straight line, press the Shift key as you paint.

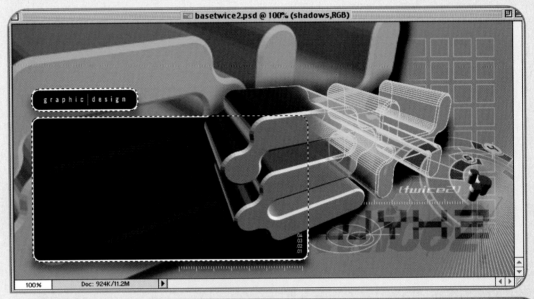

We're now going to make a small shadow to the left of the "2" in the large black rectangle. To do this, recall the 2x selection for a final time, inverse it, place it on back 3D element, and erase part of that layer.

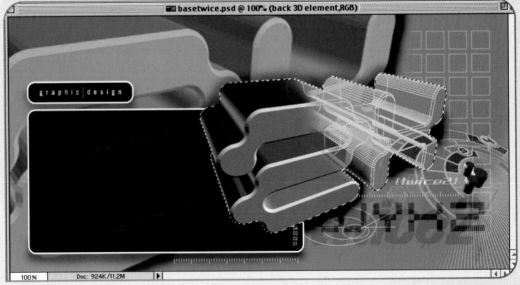

Last of all, for the shadow under the cylinders to the right of the image, we'll create a new paintbrush. To do this, click the arrow at the top right of the paintbrush selection palette and choose New Brush. Change the roundness to give an impression of perspective, and use it to put your shadow on the shadows layer.

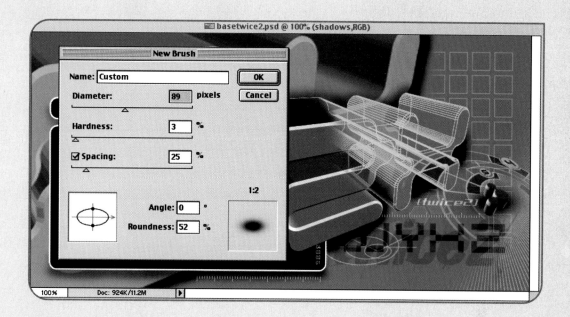

Now the image is almost finished, all that remains is to correct any little unaesthetic details. Once you're happy that everything is as it should be, finish off by going to the Layers palette and choosing Flatten Image from the drop-down menu. When you're working on complex images with many layers, always save a 'non-flattened' version too – this will be useful if you have any final modifications to make, or you need to remember the different effects that allowed you to reach your result. Good luck!

graphic | design

[twice2]

chapter 1

chapter 2

chapter 3

chapter 4

chapter 5

chapter 6

chapter 7

chapter 8

chapter 9

chapter 10

chapter 11

chapter 12

chapter 13

chapter 14

chapter 15

chapter 16

outro

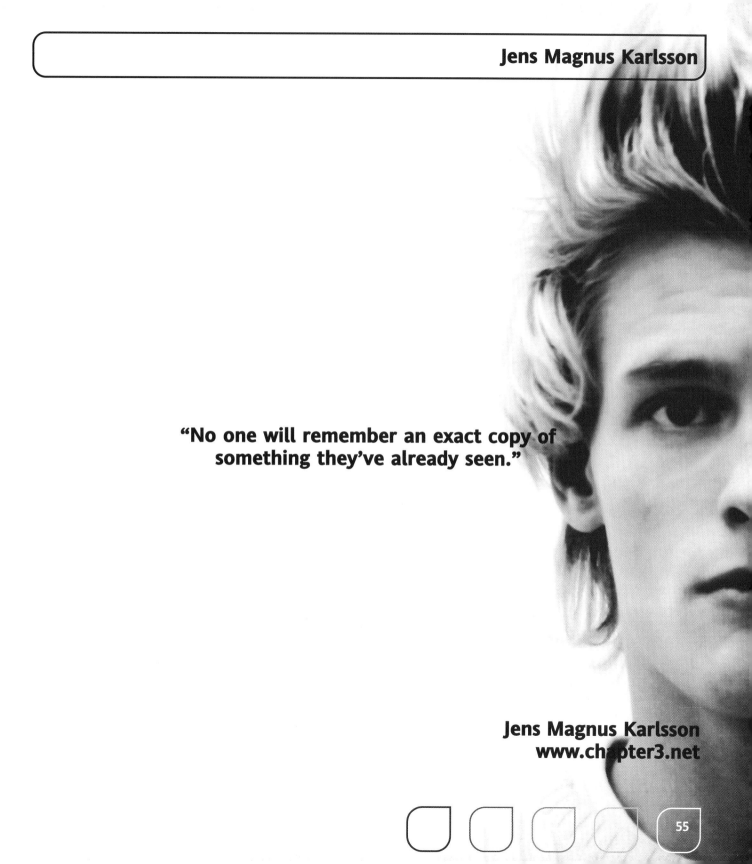

"No one will remember an exact copy of something they've already seen."

Jens Magnus Karlsson
www.chapter3.net

Light

MESSAGE BOARD
PROJECTS
NEWS LETTER
REQUIREMENTS
CONTACT

MESSAGE BOARD
April 24, 2001
I was one of the 4 nominees for Sweden's second largest advertising price Guldeken. The category was 'Rookie of the year' and here's the winner.

April 02, 2001
Oh my, the Teragroup site gotta be one of the most beautiful works ever online. Also make sure you didn't miss Danny Browns incredible bitsandpieces.

March 29, 2001
Untitled issue 02 is out and Lab79 got a new portfolio up.

March 17, 2001
My interview is up at Surfstation and there's a feature on chapter3 at Mediainspiration. Also check out my snowboard design for the Monson competition.

February 22, 2001
May 1st Reboot – A Reinvigoration of the Web. Curated by THREE.OH. Read more and sign up!

Hungry for inspiration? Like always, ThreeOh is the place to hang out and you know it.
/Jens

Take a photograph of your mom. It's likely that although (of course) you'll remember what your own mother looks like, you probably won't remember the photo itself. However, if the photographer had cropped the picture of her horizontally, right through her forehead, shot it up close with a fisheye lens, and added a second exposure to the frame with two male sex organs replacing her eyes, you would surely have experienced an emotional reaction looking at it. You'd remember it as, "That offensive picture where mom's face looks like a balloon with someone else's very personal belongings duplicated on it, by that stupid photographer we never should have hired for the family tree collection." People don't always have to be offended by your work – but if it's different, they'll find it far more interesting.

Early in my adolescence, I discovered a strong interest in light and photography that later made me apply for a three-year-long study of media communication (information and advertising), in the hope of becoming a professional photographer. At that time, I had no insight whatsoever into graphic design or digital media. My parents had always been interested in art, but I never comprehended their love for the realistic pieces that decorated the walls of the house where I grew up.

I studied form, film, multimedia, and photography – with emphasis on the last – but after two years I felt that I hadn't found an outlet for my creative visions. The limitation was rooted in the fact that everything I could create with the camera had to be based on a depiction of existing environments in the real world. In the final analysis, photography is about the light reflected from matter, a copy of something already present, and despite the thousands of possibilities offered by manual manipulation, from double exposures to experimenting with development processes, I always felt constrained.

I tried to focus on finding ways to look at things that untrained people would never think of. My goal was to shock my audience – to start a process in their minds, and to affect their personal interpretation of my work. I never got hooked on the use of a 50mm lens, which best reproduces the view of the human eye. Instead, I loved wide lenses, short focal lengths, motion blurs, and extreme close-ups from perspectives that you don't normally experience unless you make an effort to do so. Distorting the world – whether it's the one we all know, or the one inside of me – and making people think differently are things that I always try to achieve in my artwork, because no one will remember an exact copy of something they have already seen.

Jens Magnus Karlsson

© Web Agency – SEVEN srl
Inferentia DNM group company (Italy)
Art Director – Michele Gulielmin (Seven)

Despite this experimentation, I still felt frustrated by the limitations of traditional techniques, and so I started a search for other areas that would open up for a more artistic Jens. I began trying out the scanner that was available in the graphic design department, and subsequently acquired some hardware and software of my own. I was introduced to the Internet for the first time, and became familiar with the online design community while learning HTML and publishing my very first web presence. At the time, the online scene was led by a web site called Swanky, a forum and collective of web designers. I remember Miika Saksi's Finnish, dirty pixel style being born, and another designer who frequently caught my attention: Mirco Pasciolini (now at www.seven.it). His work was playful, contrast-rich, and like nothing I had seen before.

As a photographer, one always has to wait for an exhibition to take place (or arrange one yourself) in order for people to see the work you produce. The ability to present my photography online was revolutionizing. I could get feedback and input instantly, and even chat with people live. I was blown away by the digital medium, and felt very comfortable with the option to Ctrl+Z, Ctrl+C, and Ctrl+V – I didn't have to make a totally new paper copy if something went wrong.

On returning to Sweden after a spell as an intern at a small design studio in the US, I noticed that Photoshop 3.0 had arrived. Layers! I think this was the point at which I really got hooked on graphics. Layers allowed me to change my mind the next day, to reposition elements, and to distort certain elements further by using the different layer modes. I had found my favorite 24-hour hobby – Photoshopping – and planned on selling my work as art some day, even though it looked like crap at the time. On my course, I found another student who seemed to share the same passion: James Widegren of www.threeoh.com. We became great friends, and started collaborating on projects, pushing each other harder and harder. We even competed at who could sleep the least, just so we could get more time digging into the core of Photoshop, and pushing the envelope with our designs.

Light

These days, a couple of years and several experiences richer, I don't focus on image manipulation in particular, but on design as a whole. I've found a stronger love for communication that's targeted at a specific audience. The camera is always in my pocket wherever I go, though, and when time allows I still try to exhibit new graphical experiments at www.chapter3.net. For me, art is something I do when I feel like it – my body and soul tell me when it's time to let something out. When I feel that urge, I don't find much resistance in terms of creativity – I just paint, play, and experiment at a high tempo. I don't feel that I have to challenge my mind as much as when I'm developing a concept with a specific audience in mind.

My art and design go hand-in-hand: they help each other on the way to better results. I couldn't do one without the other, because sometimes you get so angry that you're only fulfilling others' needs, rather than what you need in order to feel that creative calm. It's a fact, though, that clients do turn to me because of the material exhibited on my site. For example, an LA-based company called Highly Graphic Technology, which manufactures graphical overlays and electro-luminescent light circuit systems, hired me to do their profile, their print catalog, a business presentation, and their web site (www.highlygraphic.com). Day to day, though, it's more common for me just to work with forms that suit the project at hand.

© www.highlygraphic.com

Jens Magnus Karlsson

What I do at Chapter Three is purely ornamental. Eye candy. It's infected with design bacteria, but it doesn't communicate a legible message – hence the name, Emotional Abstracts, which was influenced by my visitors' comments. Nevertheless, I hope my artwork elicits some sense of mystique. I've never worried about the people who don't find purpose in my work, but for those that do I hope it inspires them, setting their brains on fire when they try to delineate the subliminal intention. Art is subjective, and one should decide whether one appreciates a piece on an individual basis. Design has to be implemented with an audience in mind, and a clear purpose. It's about predetermined communication.

Light

I love astronomy, the enigma of the obscure, and imagining what might exist deep down in the sea where no man has set foot. I love the appearance of carefully illuminated things in darkness, or watching the sky behave at dawn – how the clouds morph into new shapes, letting a few light rays through here and there. Every aspect of lighting amazes me.

On my computer at home is an image library, which is very often where I find the bases for my graphical compositions. Not by using the actual pictures, but rather by looking at how things in the image have changed through the use of different camera techniques, and then exaggerating those in the final piece. I often try to observe my surroundings differently by rotating my head through 110 degrees, looking through a dirty window, or by stepping up on things or lying down on the ground. Try walking around for a day viewing the world through an 18mm wide-angle lens, and push the shutter when you find something interesting. Or put the camera in places you wouldn't normally put it, and experiment with foreground, focus, exposure, rotation, shutter speed, iris sizes, motion, etc. to find fresh compositions.

If you don't currently own a camera, I recommend that you get one as soon as you can, and start using it. You'll find it a great asset to your design/artwork, enabling you to re-establish those Kodak moments, and get inspired again. If you don't have a camera with you, try this: Put an object 20cm in front of you, and look at it with both eyes. Now, switch focus from the object to the horizon. Then try the same thing with only one eye. What you see when using two eyes is that the 20cm object is half transparent, duplicated, and not really out of focus. Using one eye, you should see that focal depth appears, in the sense that the object goes in and out of focus, just like looking through the viewfinder of an SLR camera.

Of course, I enjoy physical photo exhibitions, or just surfing around the Net, in both amateur and professional galleries. A definite must-visit is the web site of Floria Sigismondi (www.floriasigismondi.com), an artist who has greatly inspired me – her use of color and light is incredible. Other names whose work I'd like to study in more detail are Man Ray, because there are few photographers with such a feel for composition and 'catching moments', and Cindy Sherman, because her portraits are so moving.

Even though I generally prefer the science fiction genre, the films of the cinematographer and director Lars Von Trier are astonishing. If you're familiar with his work, you'll know that he's tired of cheesy Hollywood movies. In his films, which are produced according to the Dogme rules, he uses neither a tripod for the camera, nor artificial light sources, and the themes are often very intense. Watching these films is like taking a break from the mainstream of media influences, opening up a personal discussion about what is right, and what is wrong.

Photo by Floria Sigismondi,
© Floria Sigismondi/taken from Redemption published by
Die Gestalten Verlag, Berlin 1998

And then there's music. Hip hop, trip hop, soul, electronica, or jazz; whatever I'm listening to affects my thoughts and moods. Without my stereo system, my creativity would lack variety. All my senses are more or less controlled by music, and I see it as an enormous fountain of ideas. Albums by De La Soul, Mandalay, Crustation, Stacey Kent, and The Temprees generate more heat in my speakers than others, but two particular songs that have really built up inspiration are The Doors' *The End* and Dire Straits' *Brothers In Arms*.

Without music, I wouldn't fall asleep – I use it for relaxation as well. It's hard to cool down your brain after a long jamming session, but with the help of music I manage to stay away from counting sheep. That moment when I'm about to close my eyes is a treasured one. It's the best time for brainstorming, and for making notes on concepts and solutions that I would never think of during the day.

When I'm awake and looking for help (not usually in terms of concepts and solutions, but to stay up to date with software and techniques), magazines such as *EFX Art & Design*, *Computer Arts*, and *CAP&Design* come in handy. Also, Element K Journals' *Inside Photoshop* mailing list sends tips that you can subscribe to for free at www.elementkjournals.com/tips.

My involvement in the online design community has given me the opportunity to work and share ideas with talents that I would never have met if it wasn't for the Internet. I love the idea of sharing, so I try to spend any spare time I have posting news at threeoh.com, helping out with online events, or just participating in art groups. Currently, I'm also working on the fourth edition of Desktop Imperium (www.desktopimp.com), which should be online when this book is published. The web site has features such as user messaging (for direct feedback on artwork by other members), wallpaper challenges, asset libraries, interviews, and a forum for people to grow as designers and chat with their peers. The sole purpose of the project is to create relationships between designers that allow them to educate each other, and to exhibit the best desktop wallpaper around.

I love the process of creating wallpaper as a break from the work I do for my clients. It's a way to develop new techniques, and to play around in Photoshop without someone telling you what to do – and the promotional value of wallpaper shouldn't be underestimated. When I first developed Desktop Imperium in 1997, as a way of getting people to return to my portfolio, I never figured how successful the idea would become. Good wallpaper gets spread around quickly through e-mail, ICQ, newsgroups, etc., and I promise that you'll be happy with the appreciation that arrives in your inbox. It's a wonderful way of sharing art, and of getting your name known out there.

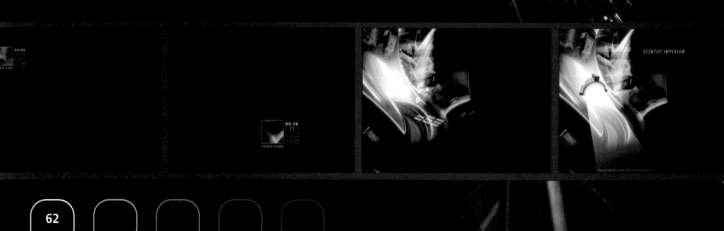

INTERSECTION500

The pages of the chapter that you're reading right now contain a collection of my surrealist environments. They represent my love for ambience out of our earthly nature. Each day, I get a few e-mail messages that ask about particular techniques for creating the light effects that appear frequently in these pieces, and what software I use. In fact, most of the tools I use for my creations come from Adobe. If we look at the process of creating the image on this page, for example, it went from my head, to Discreet's 3ds max, to Photoshop, to Illustrator for the line work, and finally back to Photoshop again.

Using 3ds max provides me with the ability to create things that can't be caught on camera. However, the final stage always takes place in Photoshop, where I compose and retouch my renders, producing a look that's quite different from making everything with a 3D package. Layering your objects manually, using the transform tools for perspective and so on, adds errors to the natural view of the composition – but they're positive errors. The 'camera' in 3D software imitates the real world, as though you're looking through a viewfinder, but I prefer it when things diverge from reality, or the imagined reality, into a deformed rendition of one's final idea.

Photoshop is definitely the only image-editing tool that I would use. Yes, there are programs that might be better for one particular task, but I see Photoshop as the most stable, powerful, and extensive tool that I can use for both Web and print – especially when working with the rest of Adobe's products, since they are all compatible. Being able to have 180 layers active and still feel comfortable with the performance is something I don't think any other program can offer me.

Part One

In the first part of my tutorial, I'll show you how to create the electric light waves that explode out of a meteoroid. You'll learn the process of using different layer modes, transform tools, and duplicated layers, in combination with external assets, to make the complete image. You should experiment with all the settings and values afterwards, of course, but try to complete the tutorial according to the book once, just to get the basics of everything. When using these techniques in your future work, bear in mind that the effect is not as successful when working with a bright background. A dark background adds contrast, and makes the light more prominent.

Let's start by opening the `base.psd` and `spiral.psd` files in Photoshop – you can find these on the accompanying CD, along with the other files you'll need to complete the tutorial. You can also find `complete.psd` on the CD, which shows what the end result should look like.

I created `base.psd`, which is the composition you will be enhancing with light effects, by assembling a few 3D Studio Max renders in Photoshop. `spiral.psd` is a really simple render made with a 3D package, and should really only be seen as an example of the kind of shape you can use when forming your 'light'. It could just as easily be a shape drawn in Illustrator or Photoshop, but what's important is that whatever shape you use, it should allow for tiling. It's also good to use a high-resolution file, since you might want to bend and distort the shape. The result of doing that with a low-resolution shape will look pixelated and poor.

In `spiral.psd`, choose Load Selection from the Select menu. Choose Alpha 1 as the Channel, and then press OK. This was saved as a selection when I created the file.

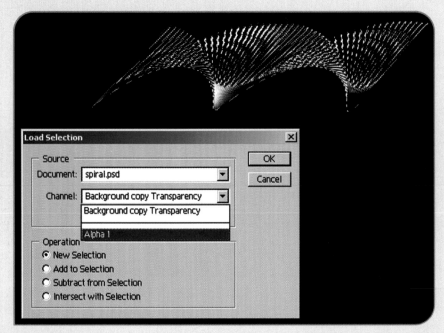

Now select the Rectangular Marquee tool, put the cursor over the selected spiral shape, and right-click on the selection. From the menu that appears, select Layer via Copy. Now use Free Transform (Edit > Free Transform) to scale the spiral down to about 40% of its original size, holding down the Shift key to scale it proportionally. Use the Info panel to monitor your scaling – or, alternatively, click the Link button and type 40% into the top bar for the Transform tool.

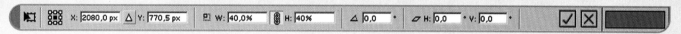

Next, we'll use the shape in Layer1, and duplicate it horizontally until we have six copies tiled in a row. Ctrl+click Layer1 in the Layers palette to select the layer's transparency. Keeping the Alt key pressed, duplicate the shape using the Move tool until you have something like this.

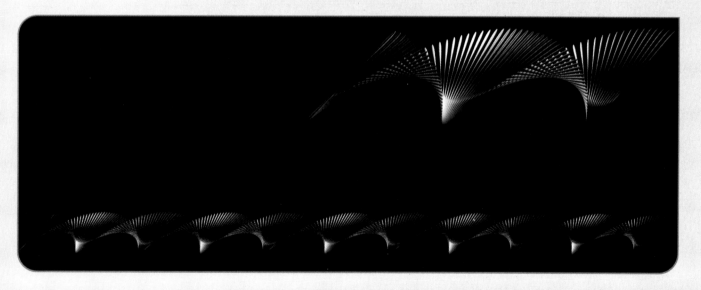

Don't worry if the tiling is not seamlessly perfect – it won't matter after all the work we're about to do to it!

You should now be ready to use the tiled spiral to create the light rays on top of the existing artwork in base.psd, but first we're going to make the color scheme of the latter more interesting. Create a new layer and name it RED. (This was originally red, as you'll see in the screenshots of the Layers palette. I later changed it to a much pinker color, but didn't change the Layer name!)

Fill the new layer with pink using the following RGB values: R: 238, G: 0, B: 242. Set the layer blending mode to Hue, with 72% opacity.

Then, create another new layer named BLUE, and fill it using these settings: R: 2, G: 0, B: 95. This time, set the layer blending mode to Overlay at 43%. Your image should now look like the one here.

When I'm working with colors, I frequently play around with adjustment layers. These are perfect, because they can be turned off at any time, and you can always change your mind if you're not satisfied with the look. This is much better than adjusting the colors in each layer separately, which you can't undo. For adjustment layers, I find Channel Mixer, Hue/Saturation, Levels, and Curves very useful – but when I was setting up this tutorial, I thought it would be more appropriate to use the alternative method of filling layers with solid colors. When you do so, the visual thumbnail in the Layers palette gives a better overview of how each layer's color affects the overall look of the image.

Drag and drop Layer1 from spiral.psd to base.psd, giving the layer the name blur 1.3. You'll understand why soon!

Let's create the first light ray, which will explode out from the opening in the meteoroid that points at the upper left corner of the image. Go to Edit > Transform > Scale (you may find it useful to zoom out a bit, to help see the edges of the boundary boxes). Now scale the horizontal width of the spiral to about 1/3, and then flip the spiral vertically (Edit > Transform > Flip Vertical).

Next, rotate it (Edit > Transform > Rotate) so that it lines up with the direction of the upper left opening.

What you want to do next is to add perspective to the spiral (Edit > Transform > Perspective). This transformation stretches out the image in the direction in which you are adding perspective, and therefore it's important that you complete all the steps before you hit Enter, which renders the transformation. Each time you hit Enter, the object you're transforming trashes the image data from the previous state, replacing it with the data for the new state. By using an object much larger than the canvas can hold, and by not rendering in between the different transformation stages, we can make full use of the original image data and keep the quality of the spiral.

Light

After adding perspective, you should also distort things a little by widening the spaces in between the upper corner nodes of the transformation box.

Finally, hit Enter to render the spiral in its new state, and don't worry on this occasion about the loss of quality that's inherent when you enlarge a bitmap graphic. We'll be adding a lot of blur to the image, so you won't notice that problem. I guess you could say that in this case, the rule doesn't fully apply.

How do we turn the 3D spiral into light? Well, first of all, the spiral has to be made a lot brighter, so let's adjust the Hue/Saturation (Image > Adjust > Hue/Saturation) to add 100 to the Lightness. Then, by using different values of Gaussian blur in multiple layers (all of these being copies of Blur 1.3), we'll bring the light to life.

To start this process, apply the Gaussian blur filter (Filter > Blur > Gaussian Blur), with a radius of 1.3 pixels, to the Blur 1.3 layer.

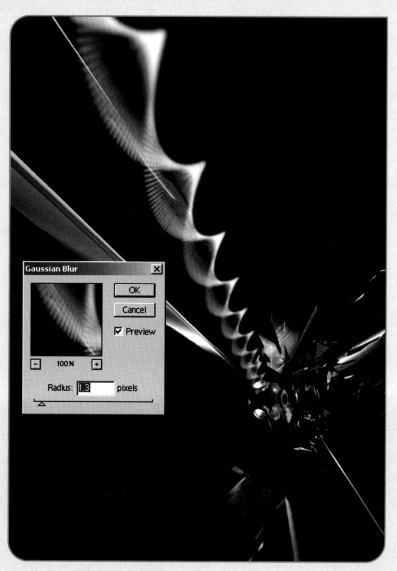

We want the part of the light ray that is heading out of the picture to be more blurred than the rest, to strengthen the feeling of depth. By doing this, we're imitating the focal depth you get by using a large iris when shooting a picture with a camera. Some of the work involving depth by other designers that I've seen often lacks this treatment; by putting everything in focus, you distract the eye of the viewer. When you're working with depth, always try to find a focal point in the image where the eye can rest.

The easiest way to blur the end of the spiral alone is by using the Blur tool, setting its strength to 50%, and brushing out the detail manually (preferably with a 200-pixel brush). Another option you could try is making a 546 x 200 pixel selection (monitor the size of your selection in the Info panel) at the top of the image, feathering the selection by 50 pixels, and applying a Gaussian blur with a 4-pixel radius.

Light

Next, make a copy of Blur 1.3, call it Blur 10.0, and add a Gaussian blur with a radius of 10 pixels to it. After that, make *another* copy of Blur 1.3, call it Blur 45, and add a Gaussian blur with a radius of 45 pixels to that. The whole thing should now look something like this.

To blend the 'light wave' more into the color scheme of the environment, we're going to colorize it. To do this, we'll use copies of existing layers. Duplicate Blur 10.0 and call the new layer Colorize 10.0; also duplicate Blur 45 and call the new layer Colorize 45.

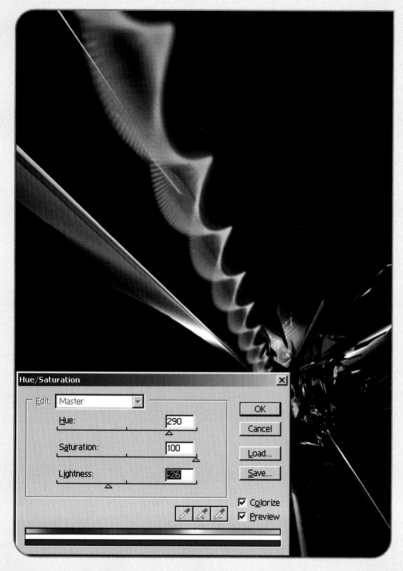

Select the Colorize 10.0 layer, go to Image > Adjust > Hue/Saturation, and check the Colorize box. Colorize it using the following settings: Hue: 290, Saturation: 100, Lightness: -26.

Notice how, when changing hue and saturation, you can't see any difference in the preview until you've changed the lightness to a negative value. Trying to do so would be the same as trying to turn the volume up on a stereo without pushing play on your CD player. If there are no values to start with, you can't modify them – and white doesn't hold any color values. (Well, this is almost true. On a monitor, white consists of red, green, and blue (RGB), but I think you know what I mean.)

Now select the Colorize 45 layer, go to Image > Adjust > Hue/Saturation again, and check the Colorize box. This time, use the following values: Hue: 240, Saturation: 90, Lightness: -45.

Light

The current look of the light wave is still not very pleasing, so let's make it more exciting by adding a glow to it. Do this by duplicating Blur 1.3, naming it Dodge, setting its blending mode to Color Dodge, and putting the layer at the top of the layer hierarchy. (For making changes to graphical environments, I most often use the Dodge and Burn tools, adding highlights to the backdrop where the light is intense, and darkening the areas where there is no light present. This is something you can experiment with later; I won't go into that technique here.)

Next, let's imitate the use of a slow shutter speed in photography. The light wave is moving, and if this were a real shot, we'd see traces of that motion. Duplicate Blur 1.3 once again, this time naming it Trace, and placing it directly below the Dodge layer. Now, since all the layers based on the original Blur 1.3 contain information outside the canvas that we don't need, we should remove them. This will enable easier control of the elements, and also save disk space. Do this by selecting everything inside the canvas area (Select > All), and cropping the selection (Image > Crop).

When you're working with potentially hundreds of layers, it's important to try to speed up your process as much as possible. When I took my first gig creating imagery of this kind, I didn't think of cropping out unnecessary image data. This caused me to end up with files whose sizes were more than 700Mb! Files that big require a lot of computer power, and take forever to open up and save in Photoshop. Due to this, sometimes I didn't worry about saving until I was done creating the whole image, after 30 hours, and you can imagine how devastating it can be if your system freezes after the 29th hour. Since I started cropping out the inessential layer data, I noticed that I could sometimes even halve the file size. Try keeping this in mind; it will save you so much time, and many sad moments.

For the 'motion' effect, we'll distort the Trace layer – particularly in the background, and in the area surrounding the light wave. Select the layer, go to Edit > Transform > Distort, and adjust the nodes (zooming out may help again) so that you get a similar result to this image. Then set the blending mode for the Trace layer to Overlay, with 43% opacity.

We only have one little thing to add before we're done with the first light wave: the meteorite opening needs to be covered with a more intense light. Add this by making a new layer named opening glow, and airbrush some white right at the opening and a little bit along the light wave. A 15-pixel airbrush and 100% pressure will do the job nicely. To achieve the glow effect, use similar layer modes and layer hierarchy as for the light wave (have a look at the Layers palette if you need a reminder). Brush the white around the opening onto a new layer, duplicate the layer, put it below the original, and then colorize the duplicate with a color that blends in nicely with the color of the light wave. Finally, add a 20-pixel Gaussian blur to the duplicate layer.

The first light ray is complete, and I think you can probably figure out how to add the other two (or as many as you want), using the techniques we just considered. All you have to do is link your light wave layers (except for Trace, which is using the Overlay mode), and then merge them. (In Photoshop 6, you can group them together as a set.) Now you can easily duplicate the light wave and the Trace layer separately – and using the different transform options, it's a quick job to resize and distort it to fit into the other two openings. No one will ever know that you're using the same layer repeatedly! Have in mind that resizing and distorting the light wave would *not* have been an option, though, if we'd started out with one of the other openings on the meteoroid. Remember: you can't enlarge a bitmap graphic without losing quality.

When light passes through an environment where gravity exists, you will most likely find particles in the atmosphere. Those particles reflect the light, and in this image we're going to do two things to add some atmospheric light to the scene. First of all, the whole scene needs some ambient light, which you can add by duplicating the BLUE layer, changing the layer mode to Screen, and setting the opacity to 25%. Name the layer ambient light, and put it at the top of the layer hierarchy.

In the next step, we'll use an actual photograph to add some sparks and fog around the meteoroid. This is a trick I've used many times, involving material from the 'lights in motion' category of my photo library. Open up the image called `light_in_motion.jpg` from the CD, and copy it into `base.psd`. Name the new layer light sparks, and place it just above the BLUE layer. Change the layer blending mode to Screen, and rotate and scale down the photo like this.

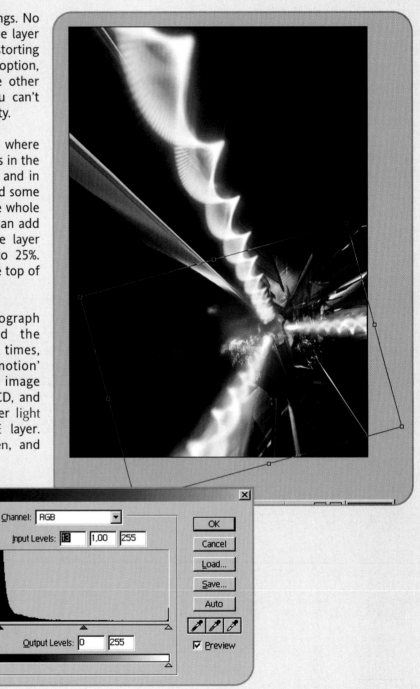

Now go to Image > Adjust > Levels to bring up the Levels dialog box. Change the first Input Levels field to 13, and press OK. This field adjusts the levels of the shadows in the image, while the following two fields adjust the mid-tones and the highlights levels.

That change should have removed any ugly edges that were visible, so now you can go to Image > Adjust > Hue/Saturation and colorize the layer in any color that you find looks good with the current scheme – I suggest purple or blue. You'll need to decrease the saturation of the photo before you press OK, so that it blends in smoothly.

When you use photography alongside objects that have been completely created inside the computer, you'll notice how prominent the grain appears in the areas where you've been using photos. The way to get rid of this, losing some detail in the image at the same time, is to apply either the Median or the Despeckle filter. We're going to use the former here, so go to Filter > Noise > Median, and specify a radius of one pixel.

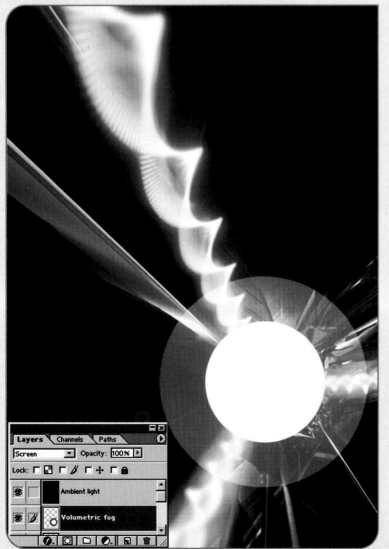

(When I'm in working in Photoshop, I quite often change my mind regarding colors somewhere along the way. This happened when setting up this tutorial as well, so let's make a little change. Fill the RED layer with this purple RGB color: R: 127, G: 81, B: 161.)

If you imagine the scene to be a 3D environment, the particle reflection would be most noticeable around the light source. The second thing we'll do to create the volumetric particle reflection light also involves using the Screen layer mode. Create a new layer named Volumetric fog, and place it just beneath the ambient light layer. Use the Elliptical Marquee tool and draw a circular selection originating at the center of the meteoroid, while holding down the Shift+Alt keys. Your selection should have a radius that's close to 300 pixels, which you can use the Info panel to monitor. Fill the selection using these RGB values: R: 121, G: 53, B: 226.

Now make a new circular selection on top of the purple circle, and fill it with white using a selection radius of 170 pixels. Set the layer blending mode to Screen.

Deselect everything, apply the Gaussian blur filter with a radius of 95 pixels, and reduce the layer opacity to 80%. That completes our graphic, and the image you see in front of you should look close to the one at the end of this chapter. Congratulations!

Part Two

In the second part of this tutorial, we'll create another kind of light – fluorescent lamps – and look at techniques for quickly turning a photographic image into a cool graphic. Our starting point will be a picture I shot at Arlanda airport in Stockholm; we'll add graphical elements to it, while retaining the existing composition and depth. To make the process of distorting shapes using Photoshop's transformation possibilities easier, we will work in *twice* the target output resolution, which in this case is the resolution of the airport shot. We'll need to be precise in using the perspective lines in the photo as a guide for how we should add depth to flat artwork.

You can start by opening the file Stockholm_airport.jpg from the accompanying CD. Now, to make the image layer-based, double click on the background layer in the Layers palette and click OK in the dialog box that appears. This enables editing of the layer.

The first thing we're going to do to it is rotate the picture 180 degrees, so go to Edit > Transform > Rotate 180. Next, we'll remove the 'daylight' look from the image, give it a different color tone, and make it darker. Go to Image > Adjust > Levels, and use these input levels: 50, 1.0, 255.

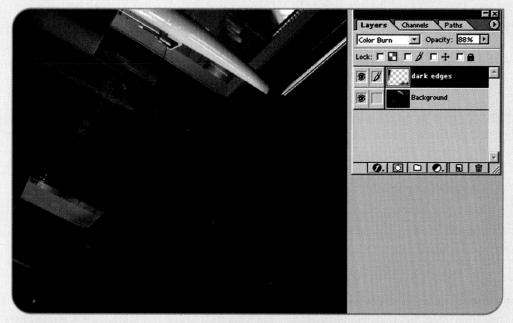

To take away some of the daylight reflections in the image, and make it look like the windows are the only light sources (for now, at least), we will darken the edges of the photo by using the Airbrush tool and the Color Burn layer mode. Create a new layer called dark edges, and use a 100-pixel, 100% pressure airbrush to brush some black around the top left and bottom right edges. Change the layer blending mode to Color Burn, and reduce the opacity to 88%.

Now we'll change the color scheme to green and yellow, which suits fluorescent light better. First, make a copy of the background layer, name it yellow, and hide it – we'll be using it soon enough. Select the original background layer, go to Image > Adjust > Hue/Saturation, and check the Colorize box. We'll colorize the layer with these values: Hue: 76, Saturation: 32.

Light

Now make the yellow layer visible, set its mode to Overlay, and give it 62% opacity. After that, change the saturation to -55.

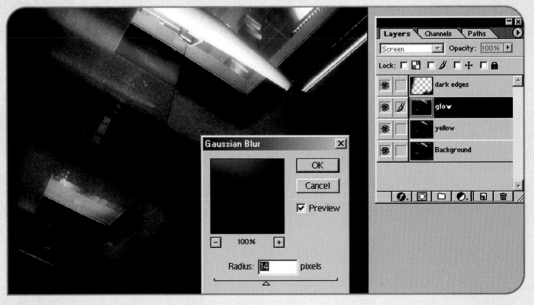

The windows in the picture have now started to look more like lamps, so let's add some glow and fog to heighten that impression. Duplicate the original background layer again, name it glow, place it above the yellow layer, and set the layer mode to Screen. Then, add a Gaussian blur with a radius of 14 pixels.

Since we're using Screen mode, only the light part of the blurred layer affects the background. What we want to do next is to add some of that blurry glow to the dark parts as well. Duplicate the glow layer, name it dark glow, and desaturate it (Image > Adjust > Desaturate). Then set the layer mode to Overlay at 47%.

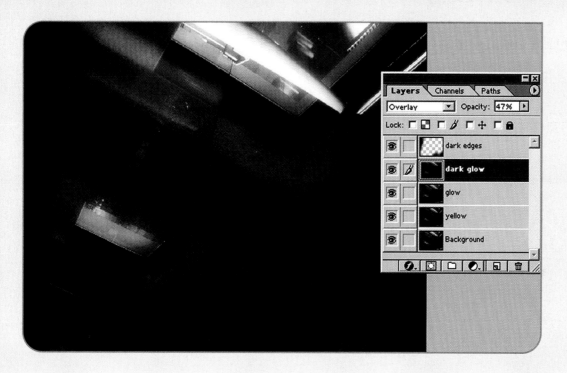

The changes to the photographic image are complete; now we can add some 2D graphics, and make them look 3D. Open up the sample file called 2d_grid_sample.psd from the CD, and then drag and drop the 2d layer on top of all the layers in our main picture.

It's no coincidence that I'm using a grid in this sample image. By using a grid when you're adding perspective, you can use the gridlines as guides to match with the perspective lines in the photo. When you try this technique with your own graphics, it's useful to have a grid in another layer that you can link with your graphics layer before you start transforming it.

Go to Edit > Transform > Rotate, and rotate the grid so that it looks like this.

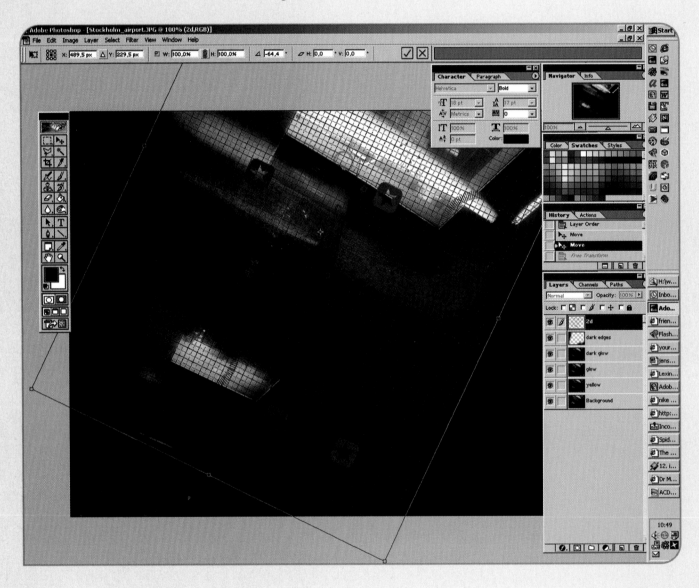

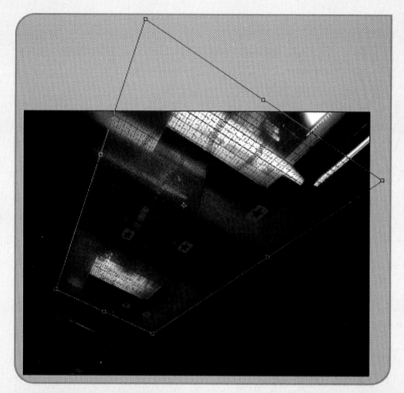

We're now going to distort the grid, so go to Edit > Transform > Distort, and adjust the corner nodes of the transform selection box like this.

Use the outlines of all the windows as references for how to add depth to the grid. When it looks good, hit Enter on your keyboard to render the selection.

Now, once again, drag and drop the grid from `2d_grid_sample.psd` into the main composition, and use the same techniques to slap the grid onto the ceiling in the back area of the environment. When you're done, you should merge your two 2d layers, and name the resulting layer grid. The grid should now look as though it's been mounted onto the ceiling of the photographic environment.

Light

If you look closely, you'll notice that the outline around the windows is not totally straight. This is because I was using a wide-angle lens when shooting the picture, but don't worry too much about that now, because we'll be adding elements of light on top of the grid to cover it up.

First, though, we're going to make use of an element in the picture in order to blend in the grid even more. Look at the right of the picture. What was originally a handrail now looks more like a metal pillar holding the ceiling up. We'll cut some parts out from the grid, to make it look like the pillar is passing through it.

Zoom in to about 400% around the area where the grid overlays the pipe, and use the Polygonal Lasso tool to draw a selection like this.

Make sure that you're using the grid layer, and then delete the selection before zooming back out to 100%.

Now the grid blends in with the background a bit too much, so let's make it a little more prominent. Duplicate the grid layer, name the new layer grid glow, drag it below the grid layer, and invert the color (Image > Adjust > Invert). Then add a Gaussian blur with a radius of 1 pixel to the layer. Offset the grid glow layer by 4 pixels up and to the left, using the arrow keys on your keyboard. Finally, set the layer mode to Overlay with 60% opacity.

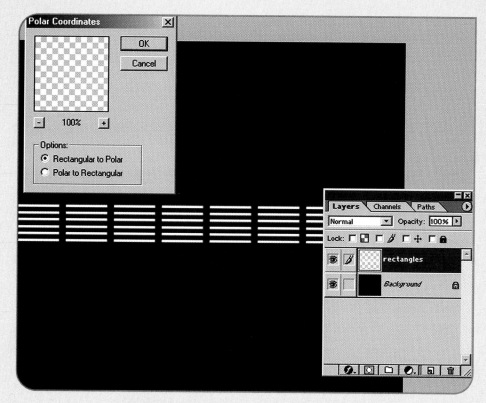

By using a simple photographic image and a few quick tricks, we've already created a pretty nice graphic in no time. To give you some more practice at creating light in Photoshop, though, we will now (as in Part One) look at a technique that uses a repeated simple shape to build up the light source.

Open the `rectangles.psd` file from the CD. Using the rectangles image, we'll create a wavy, snakelike, fluorescent light that we will then import to the airport photo and add into the ceiling of our environment. First of all, to add some wavy light rays and sparks, go to Filter > Distort > Polar Coordinates. Choose the Rectangular to Polar option, and then press OK.

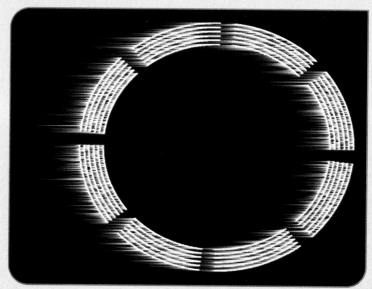

Now go back to the Filter menu and select Stylize > Wind, using these settings in the dialog box (Method: Wind, Direction: From the Right). After pressing OK, repeat the filter twice more.

Don't worry about the edges of the circle looking jagged – remember we're working at twice the resolution, so that when we scale everything down at the end, the anti-aliasing will look perfect. Apply the Polar Coordinates filter again, this time selecting the Polar to Rectangular option.

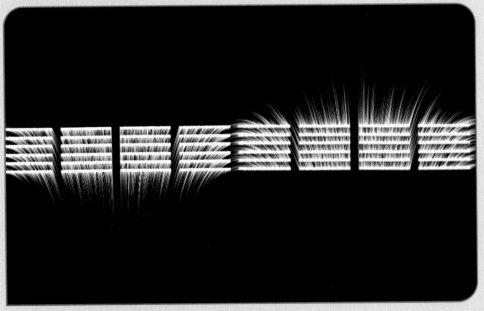

To make the shape more dynamic, we'll twist it a bit. From the Filter menu, select Distort > Wave, and use the parameters shown here. (Note that for the Wavelength values, you'll need to enter the Max value first, as the Min cannot exceed the Max.)

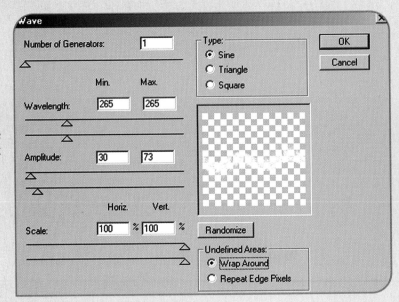

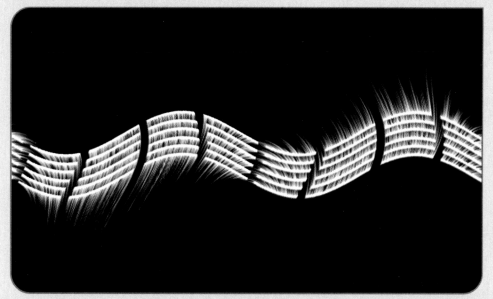

Add a Gaussian blur with a radius of 1 pixel to get rid of any jagged edges, then duplicate the layer, name the copy blur 11, and apply a Gaussian blur with a radius of 11 pixels to that. As in the first part of the tutorial, this blur adds a little light to the surrounding environment and atmosphere, around the light source where it's most intense.

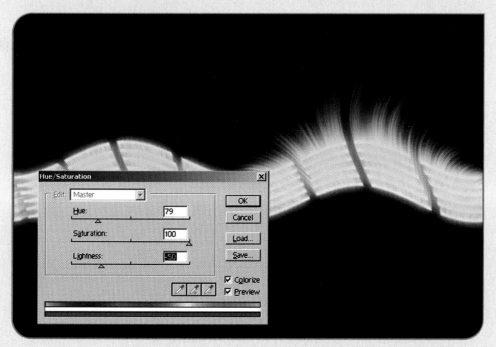

This time, duplicate the blur 11 layer, and name the copy green 26. Then go to Image > Adjust > Hue/Saturation, make sure that you check the Colorize box, and colorize it like this: Hue: 79, Saturation: 100, Lightness: -50.

Light

Add a Gaussian blur to green 26, using a 26-pixel radius, and then move it below rectangles in the Layers palette.

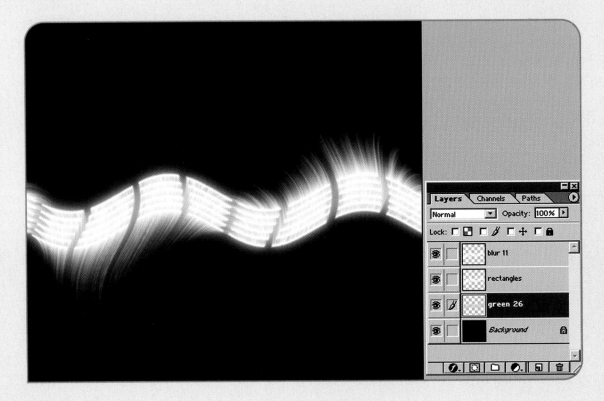

Next, we'll start the process of repeating the shape to create a long, snakelike light. Link the three light layers, merge them (Layer > Merge Linked), and then scale the light down to a fifth of its original size (Edit > Transform > Scale). Now duplicate the light using the Move tool while pressing the Alt key, so that you have a total of five lights tiled together horizontally, like this.

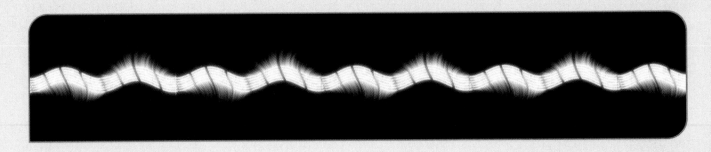

Link these five layers in the Layers palette, merge them, and name the resulting layer fluorescent. It's now ready for use in our photographic environment, so drag it in, place it at the top of the Layers palette, make a duplicate of the layer (fluorescent 2), and hide that for the moment. Using the same transform technique that we used earlier for the grid graphic, add fluorescent to the 'ceiling' in the picture, along the left edge of the grid. Then make fluorescent 2 visible, and transform the light in it in the same way, but this time along the right edge of the grid.

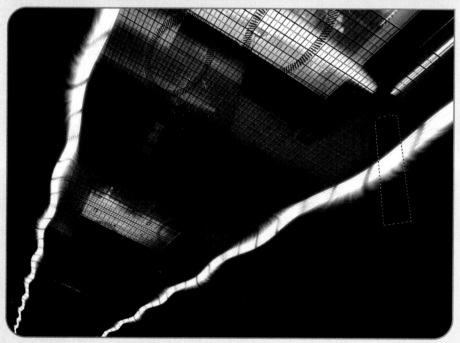

Remember how we cut a part of the grid out, so it looked like the metal pillar was running through it? Well, if fluorescent 2 is placed outside the edge of the grid that we cut, it means that if this were a light that was an actual part of the picture, it would go behind the pillar. Make a selection like the one in this screenshot, feather it by 2 pixels (Select > Feather), and delete the selection from the fluorescent 2 layer.

Light

If you look at the fluorescent lamps now, you'll see that something looks wrong at the back end of them. The hindmost parts are too sharp to blend in with the focal blur in the photography. This problem is solved very easily by using the Blur tool. Set the pressure to 40%, use a 100-pixel diameter, and simply brush the light so that it fits in with the blur in the environment. If you look at the depth in the photographic background layer, you'll notice that it has its focal point in the upper right corner. We're using the Blur tool to alter the blur of our added graphical elements, so that they get the same focal depth as the photograph.

Congratulate yourself once again! I hope you found these tutorials interesting, and that the techniques become useful in your future work. Find the areas of design where they can be applied, and use your intelligence to see where they are improper.

Remember too that these tutorials are only one way of achieving the effects they exhibit. Play around with different layer blending modes and opacities, and find something that suits you. If you're doing work for presentation online, keep in mind that the look of your light effect will vary a lot depending on people's monitor settings. Always be self-critical, and ask others for constructive feedback. Try to have a good eye for detail, and get a good night's sleep before you decide that your piece is complete.

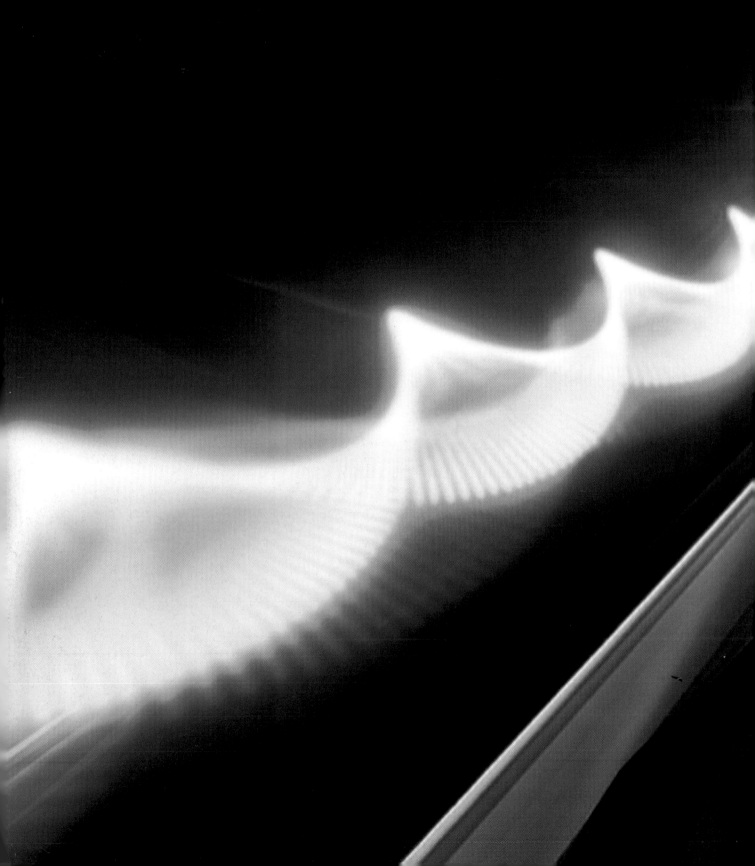

chapter 1

chapter 2

chapter 3

chapter 4

chapter 5

chapter 6

chapter 7

chapter 8

chapter 9

chapter 10

chapter 11

chapter 12

chapter 13

chapter 14

chapter 15

chapter 16

outro

"I grew up in "The Valley". The, like, San Fernando Valley in Southern California, for sure..."

Jason Mohr & Yoshi Sodeoka
www.c404.com

One of the best ways to learn a skill is to be forced to do it. Beginning in kindergarten, the private school I was attending 'encouraged' children to keep personal notebooks for every subject. In these, we illustrated lessons and copied notes and drawings from the blackboard. We were even told precisely how to draw; how to make 'correct', uniform-length, uniform-width, evenly spaced strokes with our Caran d'Ache colored pencils and oil pastels. We would actually get scolded for 'against-the-grain' contour shading, scrubbing, and outlining objects! Regardless, I loved it. I lost myself in my work; found myself creating work for classmates. In the third grade, I distinctly remember illustrating a blue Cadillac Fleetwood for a friend, using his toy die-cast metal car as a model. Cars, monsters, dragons, aliens, animals, BMX riders, and anything space-related were my most frequent creations, in the margins of math, Spanish, English, and history lessons.

For many years, my weekend morning ritual involved sifting through a huge denim bag full of colored plastic. Emotionally speaking, I was submerging myself in a world of infinite possibility. Technically speaking, I was having my first lessons in creating in three dimensions. Anything I could think of, I would build. In the process, without my awareness, I learned about space and form, and the interaction of forms and colors. Gradually, by studying and following the patterns in the LEGO idea books, I noticed that not only could the LEGO creators in Denmark design amazing-looking structures, but also they engineered them precisely to insure their structural integrity. Though proud of my own creations, I found that I couldn't play with them as roughly as I did with the official LEGO ones. This became my first inspiration for designing for other-than-aesthetic reasons.

The lessons about form and function continued with more hands-on experience while working during summer vacations with my father, a carpenter and general contractor. Observing a house, and participating in its stages of production – foundation, framing, plumbing, heating, wiring, insulation, dry walling, finish-carpentry, painting, and landscaping – drastically changed my perception of the house as the final product.

These experiences have undoubtedly affected my method and style of creation. I have applied three dimensions to a variety of interfaces, including this one for *Furniture*, an online gallery of paintings of 50s' interiors. The icons for the paintings were line tracings of their dominant forms, which gave the interface its blueprint-meets-wireframe style. Once clicked, paintings loaded within a simple three-dimensional room, sitting as if they themselves were solitary pieces of furniture.

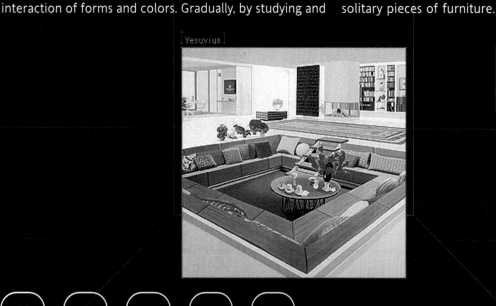

[Vesuvius]

At times, I let the process of creation contribute to the visual impact of the final work. Revealing, and even emphasizing particular techniques can add an additional layer of depth to a piece, or contribute to its emotion or essence. For a Word.com text feature, Be Prepared, I cropped images very crudely using Photoshop's rectangular selection, block eraser, and/or magic wand tools without anti-aliasing. I collaged these images just as crudely, combining different styles and using saturated, solid background colors to highlight their grit. Many of these images were animated, also in a crude and choppy manner, and the page was topped off with an annoying dose of a bugle-call-to-arms audio. This created a sense of uneasiness that complemented the twisted tale of boy scouting, and also parodied web design itself — at the way people frequently cram gratuitous graphics, animations, and audio into their sites simply for the sake of having them.

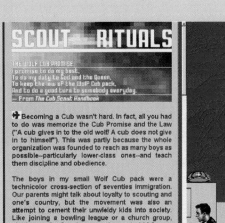

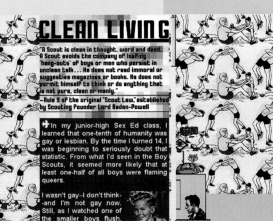

Yellow

There were many things that triggered my imagination as a child, but not even the fantastic, medieval powers of the role-playing game Dungeons & Dragons came close to the 'force' of Star Wars. That wasn't a movie; it was a drug. I was an eight-year-old sponge, just sucked it up. It went straight to my brain, and wove itself into my psyche. It had both short-term and long-term side effects, increasing my ability and courage to use and believe in my imagination.

The film itself was a venture into the unknown. It gave me a glimpse of what life could be like beyond our world. Like Luke Skywalker, I learned the importance of pursuing my dreams and fulfilling my destiny. Not a prescribed destiny, but one that always evolves and changes. At times you take control of it, at times you let go, but it's a destiny that you 'feel' to be right. Immediately after seeing the movie, I was granted the power to see things that weren't there. From my flashlight came a glowing saber of blue light, my lunchbox hovered from my cubbyhole to the desk, and the galaxy would stretch as I jumped to light speed on my bike. This ability was most rewarding during visits to parents' friends' houses, during long drives through the desert, and now while designing international investment companies' web sites.

I'm fortunate to have parents who have always supported and encouraged my decisions and creative endeavors. They took an active role in exposing me to many different sights, sounds, and tastes, and provided me with resources to accomplish whatever it was I wanted to create. They accompanied me to concerts, plays, films, and museums, and chauffeured me back and forth from still life, figure drawing, oil painting, ceramics, and sculpting classes. My first real art-as-a-career inspiration came unexpectedly in one of these classes. A painter and illustrator, Drew Struzan – a name I wasn't familiar with at the time – came to our class to speak about his work, with which I was thoroughly familiar. He was the creator of film posters for Star Wars, the Indiana Jones trilogy, Blade Runner, E.T., the Back to the Future trilogy... and thus, a god. Still receiving an allowance from my parents, it had never occurred to me that you could make money from art – "awesome" art – and even work for such "radical" clients.

Silhouette au Repos Against the UNESCO Headquarters in Paris
© Paul Almasy/CORBIS

Large Marble Sculpture by Henry Moore
© David Lees/CORBIS

Henry Moore Makes a Miniature
English sculptor Henry Moore making a miniature in his studio.
© Hulton-Deutsch Collection/CORBIS

At home, I was surrounded with many sources of inspiration. Most memorable were a few books, paintings and calendars that have undoubtedly influenced the way I think, observe, and create.

With Henry Moore, by Gemma Levine, was a beautiful, weighty, coffee-table book. Moore's sculptures revealed how the scale and texture of a piece could affect its emotional impact. When designing for the computer, though I don't have much of a chance to utilize the interaction of scale between a piece and the human body, I pay close attention to the scaling of objects and their relationship to one another. At its most basic level, scale has the power to infuse a sense of tranquility, stability, anxiety, and even humor into a piece.

Henry Moore also introduced me to the fact that a piece interacts with its surroundings, affecting its viewers' perception. This also applies to computer creations, where the environment – in this case hardware and software – dictates how a piece is perceived.

Following his ritual, I began my own collection of organic objects: bones, stones, shells, and branches. By studying them, drawing them, and combining them to form new objects, I began to learn to observe, appreciate, and draw creatively from forms, patterns, and textures in nature. I swooned over Moore's free-flowing developmental sketches for his sculptures, at how they captured not just the shape of the objects, but their emotion and spirit. Up until that point, my experience of drawing had been entirely technical, and my 'style' was very analytical and detail-oriented. I soon realized how frustrating it was to attempt to be so realistic, and how it can hinder new ideas from being expressed or discovered. Over the years, my sketches have attained a 'Moore-ish' likeness.

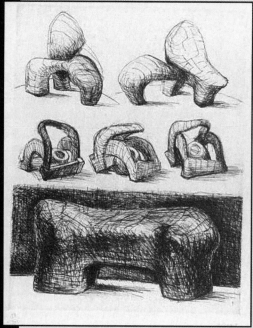

Preparatory Sketches for Sheep Piece and Other Bronze Sculptures by Henry Moore
© Geoffrey Clements/CORBIS

In a similar way, the magical illusions of M.C. Escher, and the graphically bold visual tricks created by Shigeo Fukuda, have inspired me to incorporate twists of reality into my own work. This is no easy task – there are times when I've focused all of my effort on pulling off a visual prank, and after having solved it, realized that the piece as a whole failed to fulfill the overall objective. It's an intriguing and enveloping challenge to create an illusion, and it often takes an outside opinion to bring things back into perspective. Is the trick gratifying enough for the viewer to solve, and is it complex and/or aesthetically pleasing enough for the viewer to want to solve it? Otherwise, as Yoshi (my favorite outside opinion) has pointed out on occasion, "...yeah, so what?"

All Japan: The Catalogue of Everything Japanese was an abundant source of wonder. I can't put my finger on exactly why this book was so interesting to me as a child, but my eyes gravitated to the brightly colored carp-kites, toys, and signage; opened to the bold iconic crests and pictographic calligraphy; and wandered about the beautiful woodblock prints, minimal interiors, and manicured gardens. Everything seemed exciting and different, yet at the same time, serene and fulfilling. I believe this again was due to expertise in the application of the properties and knowledge of nature, intense attention to detail, and a high regard for simplicity. These are a few of the traits that have attracted me to many works by contemporary Japanese artists, craftsmen, and designers.

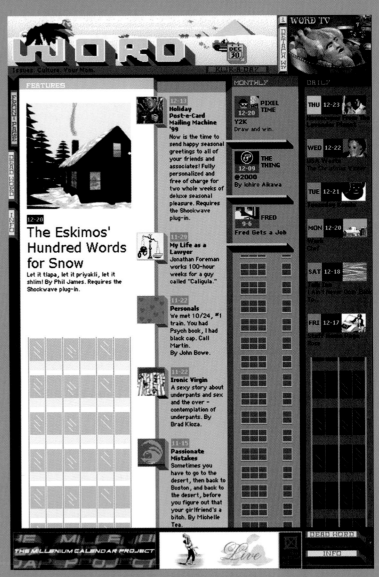

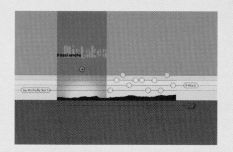 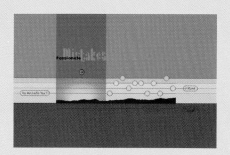 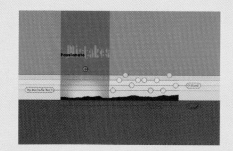

I grew up in "The Valley". The, like, San Fernando Valley in Southern California, for sure, amongst preppies, heschers, skaters, surfers, punks, cholos, cholas, and dweebs. I'm sure I emulated all of these groups at one point or another. Whatever you were, there was no avoiding the influence of the perpetually warm, dry climate, the burgundy smog that frequently blanketed the place, and the increasing number of 7-Eleven and Subway Sandwich chains that were taking root at every intersection.

Many people in The Valley, including myself, aspired to be not from "The Valley". We idolized the surfer culture, and wished it didn't take us at least an hour to get to Santa Monica beach, a full hour to Malibu, or an hour and a half to County Line, without traffic. So we dressed like surfers, bought lots of surf gear, and even, to an extent, adapted their laid-back, environmentally enhanced, spiritually connected mindset. Along with this image came so many visual influences: the checkered patterns and color combination of customized Vans lace-up or slip-on sneakers; post-psychedelic/speed culture airbrush art on boards, trucks, vans, album covers, and t-shirts; and the bold, brightly colored, tiki-meets-garage logos of surf brands that we advertised all over our bodies. Many of these elements captured a sense of speeding, free-floating, gliding, letting go, perfect enlightenment, ultimate fantasy – the fusion of the physical, spiritual, and natural worlds.

When we weren't sitting on the curb wishing we were at the beach, or buying all of this surf paraphernalia at the Northridge mall, we'd be at the arcade playing video games. I never tired of Tempest: it was lightning fast, with an array of beautiful, sharp, brightly colored webs of geometric, vector graphics protruding from a black void. Its dial was the most perfectly ergonomic controller, to be rotated ever so slightly for precise maneuvers, or spun frantically in a last attempt to destroy advancing enemies. Tron, on the other hand, was more than a game. It was a movie, and yet another colorful reality to submerge myself into. Just like in the movie, I could be transported inside the computer to race sleek, hairpin-turning light cycles, battle tanks in a glowing green maze, destroy an onslaught of replicating grid bugs, and attempt to penetrate a cone of deadly, rotating blocks to defeat the MCP. Everything in the Tron universe was glowing, and (much like Tempest) the arcade game utilized bright colors on black, sometimes grid-covered backgrounds. The game's graphics were very basic, but with the scenes I carried with me from the movie, and with the fluorescent blue lights emanating from within the joystick and from the console all around me, its little bits of color, blips, and drones took on monumental significance.

Yokoo Tadanori, a more recent influence, was a master of the complexity of simplicity. His theater and film posters of the mid-to-late 60s juxtaposed solid and gradated graphic shapes and colors, high contrast photographs, typography, and playfully stylized illustrations. The compositions are cosmic. At first, they might seem overly simplistic, but gradually they penetrate your subconscious, convincing you that they are as perfect and as right as nature itself. Once drawn in by color and composition, your eyes are arrested by his poetic use of scale and proportion. They will continue to explore every detail, every millimeter of the piece, until you discover each pop-culture symbol, nationalistic or religious icon, and finally the ironic and humorous way his world mirrors our own.

A piece of mine that closely mirrored the style of Yokoo's posters was Fifteen, for yet another www.word.com text feature. Bright clashing colors, collaged high contrast photos, and iconic symbols were all incorporated. The compositions were based on complex framesets that refreshed often one pane at a time, showing a gradual evolution that paralleled the loss of innocence of the story's main character.

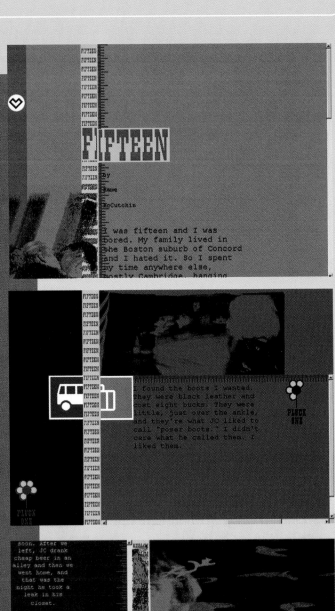

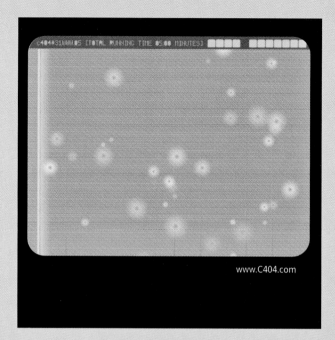

www.C404.com

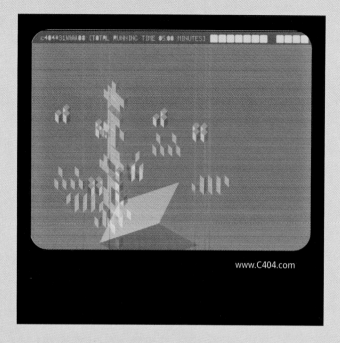

www.C404.com

I'm currently the Senior Designer at C404, a small digital design company started by Matthew McGregor-Mento, Melissa Dallal, Yoshi Sodeoka, and me. Within C404, we have set up a loose, creative atmosphere that was hard to find elsewhere. The four of us, and our two office mates Eric Rosevear (e13.com) and David Oppenheim (Day-Dream.com), bring so many different experiences, points of view, hobbies, tools, and toys to our office, that it's impossible not to be inspired.

In its short, nine-month history, C404 has produced a Superstitial, mock web site screenshots for a TV commercial, an online homepage builder, three-fourths of a 60-minute electronic noise audio-visual DVD, a touch-screen kiosk interface for a museum, prototypes for an original skateboard and chair, an album cover, a magazine column on digital culture, illustrated spreads for two design books, and a C404-curated online art gallery for a Japanese web site. In addition, we maintain C404.cc, which is a growing collection of sketches, animations and interactive pieces that C404 and its friends make on a regular (sometimes daily) basis.

Yoshi is C404's Art Director and my 'boss', in the best sense of the word. We've been working together since 1996 (nearly five years at Word; the remainder at C404), and in the process have perfected an efficient, collaborative work system that often occurs at a subliminal level. Over time, we have become aware of each other's strengths and shortcomings, and have learned how and when it is necessary to provide feedback, guidance and support. Often, we bounce projects back and forth as a way of pushing them beyond our original expectations or vision.

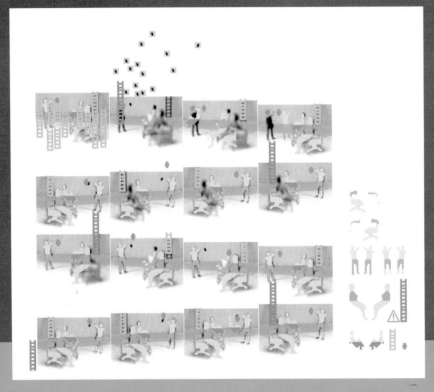

My individual creative process is conscious and subconscious, project- and time-dependent, and varies from being entirely spontaneous to super-systematic. Many of my ideas come from dreams or visions, observations, collaborations, or reactions to the inspiring photographs, books, drawings, raw materials, and music that I collect on a regular basis. For more involved projects, ideas come only after I've saturated myself with the subject matter.

If I don't have an idea before I begin sketching in my notebook, they usually come after a bit of brainstorming and doodling. I prefer to use a fine-tipped black pen, and the typical black-bound, 8" x 10" white-paged sketchbook. With these simple tools, I'm not required to make so many decisions, and ideas can just flow. When designing logos, three-dimensional objects, or illustrations, evolution might occur exclusively in the sketchbook. Trusty tracing paper and a drafting pencil make small refinements very

efficient. In these instances, the computer is reserved for the final touches, when I'll scan or re-render the image or logo for printing or web-based applications.

Sometimes, when under a time constraint, I'll skip the sketchbook and go straight to the computer – and that generally means going to Photoshop. Having used it for many years, performing functions with Photoshop has become intuitive. I no longer have to think about how to create, and can focus on what I create. Most of the projects I'm currently involved with at C404 are interface related. Using the sketchbook for such projects is a useful first step, but there are simply too many details and factors that can only be discovered and addressed on and by the computer. Similarly, even after developing an interface with Photoshop, if the final product is web-based, there are issues that will arise only when it hits your browser.

I'd like to think that I don't adhere to an underlying style when designing. If I'm working on a client project, I aim to apply the style that most thoroughly solves the design problem. Realistically though, I have found myself repeating certain looks, either due to convenience, a desire to explore another aspect of that look, or simply acknowledging that the look was once again appropriate for the subject or medium. For example, I've made repeated use of the now-trendy pixel-perfect style, which satisfied my craving for grid systems, lean web-compliant color palettes, and lo-fi video game and computer operating system aesthetics. For projects such as Sissyfight.com (an online, multiplayer game) and Pixeltime.com (an online drawing application), this style was a perfect match.

Some of my work, though, has surfaced as a protest against excessive pixel pushing. I get the urge to use traditional cut-and-paste tools in order to create something tactile that won't appear differently depending upon the platform, monitor settings, or browser. It is very refreshing, and often rewarding; some of my favorite projects have been conceived in this manner. I think this is due to the fact that I have less control over the medium, and beautiful 'accidents' can happen. If I'm ever having difficulty with a project while working on the computer, it's almost because I'm thinking too analytically — I'm too focused on a specific detail of the project. It's easy for me to get buried under many layers of detail and lose sight of the original concept, the essence of a piece. At these times, taking a step back, or even giving the project a rest for a short time, helps me gain a new perspective, or rediscover the original one.

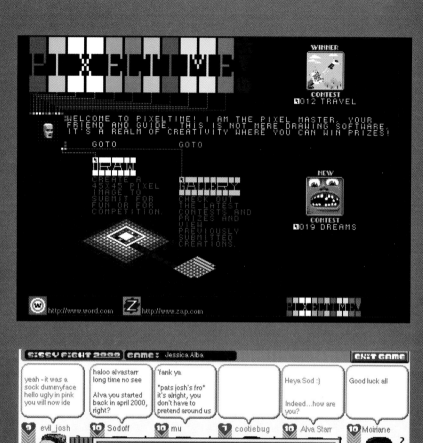

Yellow

The following project was a recent spontaneous creation. It began with scissors, glue, and the Value-Pak (a junk-mailer full of coupons), and was later introduced to a digital photo that I took in the restroom of our office building.

I love collage – old-school collage – where you can get dirty, or even slice your hand open. It produces physical as well as visual satisfaction. Except for the sheer pleasure of the process, I had no goal, concept, or expectation when I started creating. I snipped and collected bits and pieces of cheesy, gaudy, clip-art-laden coupons, responding primarily to the more abstract shapes, graphic borders, and bright colors. From a thick stack of coupons, not much made the cut.

Atop the next blank page in my sketchbook, I began shifting and arranging the pieces, responding to the cutouts' interactions with one another. My father used to wear the style of glasses I found on an optician's coupon, so for nostalgic reasons, they were salvaged. I played with the repetition of shapes, first grouping the circular glasses with the circular, upside-down wheels of the car outline on the Carmel Car Service logo. This transformed the wheels into eyes.

The dark navy and yellow colors of the seafaring rope and sand dollar border jived nicely with the car outline's yellow background, forming an almost symmetrical arch. Until the end, all the pieces were free of glue, which enabled me to try many variations of position and alignment. While free, I manicured them, either to fit with each other, or to suggest relationships with non-neighboring pieces better. The shorter right leg of the arch beckoned for support, and the red swallow volunteered to be the candidate for stability. Actually, the red swallow fluttered in from a Chinese takeaway coupon...

What looks like a destructive, tragic stabbing, is really the constructive achievement of visual symmetry. Actually, I wasn't turned off by the stabbing association, because it turned a cheesy graphic seafood-coupon border into a deadly weapon. On a symbolic level, it could represent humankind's abuse of the environment to attain control and order. Yeah, that's it!

Grouping the pointy elements, I placed the star within the border of the jagged, burst shape. This combination created another eye that mimicked those of the wheels-turned-eyes.

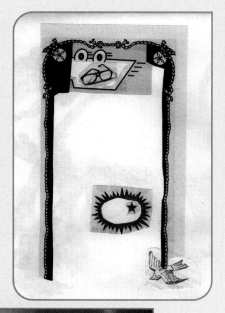

It took some time to find this new eye a home. In the end, its proximity to the swallow gives it the impression of being the bird's last exclamatory speech bubble. Simultaneously, the position of the star/pupil within the burst/eye suggests that the eye is coldly ignoring the swallow's perilous state.

That was the end of the collage session. I had fun, was happy with the piece, and had no future intentions for it. Then, Yoshi Sodeoka and I were asked to submit images for a publication being created by the German design collective, *Eikes Grafischer Hort*. We were given four spreads, eight square pages, to do with as we pleased. I decided to give this collage a life beyond my sketchbook.

I thought that on its own, the collage was a bit sparse. It needed some visual complexity – something to keep viewers engaged for long enough to grasp the 'humans vs. nature' symbolism. For our submission to the book, I had also begun taking digital photos of the insides of the restrooms in our office building. They were attractive subjects because of their bleak, sloppily painted, deteriorating mint-green walls; makeshift plumbing; ageing tiles; and life-sucking fluorescent lights. After examining all of the photos, three of which are pictured here, the third ranked as being most appealing. Its more subtle perspective would complement the flatness of the collage, as would its texture, linear elements, and open space.

Yellow

I scanned the collage, and decided that it required some heavy-duty clean up. On the spread following the collage in my sketchbook, I had already painted a watercolor, which was now visible through the page. Also, the colors were darker and muddier in the scan than in the original, probably because of the settings I'd used when scanning. Photoshop is ideal for these types of clean-up jobs. Its selection tools can be as precise as you want them to be.

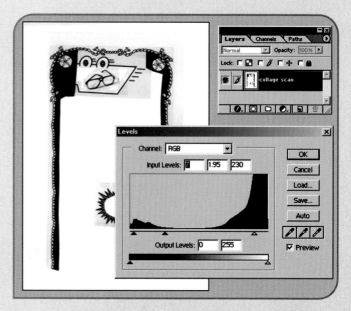

Open up `CollageOrigScan600dpi.psd` in Photoshop. To return the colors to their original glory, and to flush out the watercolor, open the Levels dialog (Image > Adjust > Levels). Slide the right highlight arrow a little to the left, to where the white level peaks on the chart (an input level of about 230). Moving too far to the left would blow out the colors, and lose the realism of their printed quality. Then, to compensate for the dark scan, slide the mid-tones arrow also to the left, to about 1.95. This returns the seafood arch to its original navy-ness, and cuts out some of the graphics printed on the back of the pieces. I also shifted the shadow arrow to the right just a tad, to about 7, to make sure I had a true black in there somewhere.

That done, I whipped out the trusty Sharpen filter (Filter > Sharpen > Sharpen), the solid, automatic settings of which I've really grown to rely on. It came through for me once again, giving to the collage the crispness I pay optometrists and contact lens manufacturers good money to see.

Now it was really time to dig in. I zoomed into the image, and hunted for spots and blemishes that survived the frying of the highlights. I only pursued those that were on the sketchbook page, ignoring those on the actual paper pieces of the collage. After verifying that the background color was set to white, I used the Rectangular Marquee tool to select larger patches of to-be-white space and deleted their impure contents. For cleaning tight spots near the pieces, I employed the Eraser tool, set to both Block and Paintbrush. When in Paintbrush mode, use different brushes depending on the intricacy of the erasure – and use the non-feathered, anti-aliased ones located on the top row of the Brush drop-down menu.

Next, as a pre-integration step for the bathroom image, I honed in on the best way to crop it. Open `BathroomPic_3_Orig.jpg`, select all of it, copy it, and then close the file. Now open a new Photoshop file (which conveniently sets the width

and height to match the image just copied), paste it in, and save it. With the Rectangular Marquee tool's style set to Constrained Aspect Ratio, width set to 1, and height set to 1, I played around, framing different square selections. You could simply use Image > Duplicate instead, but that doesn't give you the same feeling of traditional cut-and-paste that you get from my method.

I chose the final crop to incorporate the air vent, the vertical pipe, and the "GUESS" graffiti at the bottom right of the photo, and to allow for the most space to the left of the pipe to accommodate the collage. When making the final crop, I went much wider than I anticipated the final image would be. This gave me room to make fine adjustments once the images were integrated, and allowed for a required bleed (this is the overlap needed for printing, to ensure that the image fills the entire space intended).

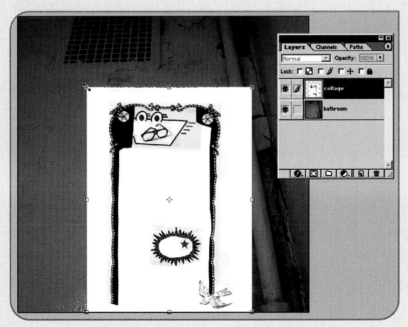

In order to loosen up the integration and exploration process, I copied the cropped bathroom, opened a new file, pasted the bathroom, and then shrank it down to 67% of its original size (Image > Image Size). Decreasing the size of the file makes it easier to cake on those layers, and cuts down on the time it takes filters to render. The drawback is that you eventually have to recreate the entire process in the final format with the larger images, but I think that it saves me time in the end.

Finally, it's time to unite the two images. Open the cleaned up collage file, copy it all, close it, and then paste it into the cropped, shrunken bathroom file. Name this new layer Collage. Since it's about eight times larger than the shrunken bathroom, you'll need to scale it down (Edit > Transform > Scale) to bring it down to a manageable size – it's much easier if you zoom out a long way before you hit the Transform button, as this will help you to see the bounding box. Remember to hold down Shift while you drag the corners in order to maintain the proportions.

Yellow

I wasn't exactly sure how I would eventually treat the collage, but I knew I wanted to eliminate its harsh, white background. Once it's pasted and scaled down, reduce its opacity to 40% while getting it into position. This makes the whole collage transparent, and much easier to place.

After a few more shrinking sessions, the collage nestled nicely, front and center. Its scale was determined roughly by applying a three-column grid to the background, where the width of the arch spanned the center column. I was paying attention to the way the cracked and missing paint on the bottom right side of the bathroom wall enveloped the burst and the supportive/stabbed swallow, and how those elements triangulated with the vertical pipe and vent.

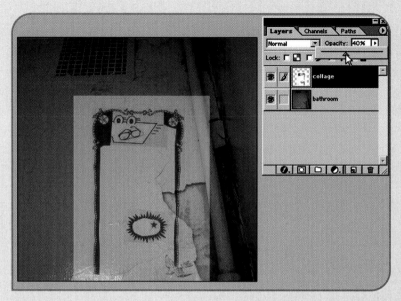

After contemplating the fate of the collage's white background, I decided (rather mercifully, I thought) against its total annihilation. I opted for a treatment that mimicked the decrepit condition of the wall behind it. In the event that I'd not be satisfied with this technique, I duplicated the Collage layer as a back up, and worked on the copy instead.

With the Magic Wand tool set to a Tolerance of 10, and with Contiguous unchecked in its Options panel, select the whitest of the white background, and then delete it. Deselecting Contiguous enabled the Magic Wand to select all the whites within a tolerance range of 10 that existed within the entire Collage copy layer, not just the ones that were adjacent and 'connected' to the white part selected.

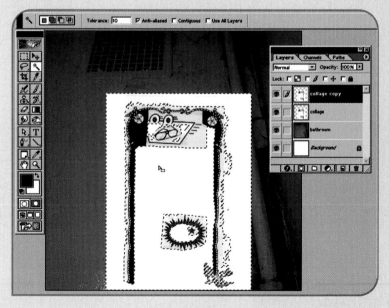

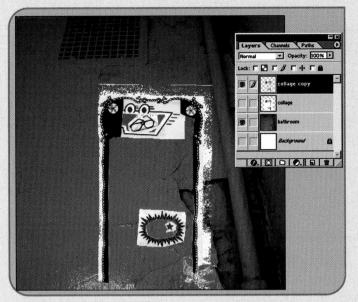

Make the original Collage layer invisible, and you'll see the effect when you delete the selection.

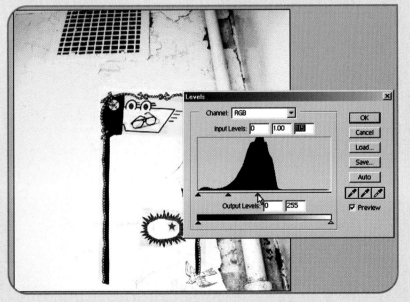

It was time now for the bathroom to make some compromises, but not until its layer was duplicated too, just in case. As much as I loved the dreary green of the wall, there was just too much contrast between it and the bright collage. Select the Bathroom layer, and choose Select > Deselect. Changing the levels (Image > Adjust > Levels) of the bathroom background, moving the highlights arrow left to about 115, was a good start in bringing the values of the layers together.

Yellow

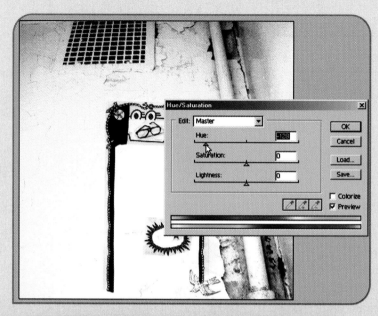

With the Hue/Saturation controls (Image > Adjust > Hue/Saturation), I cranked the Hue arrow left to about -128, until a slight magenta cast began to emanate from the wall and the pipe. This brought out the reds of the collage's burst/eye and swallow. With its new hue, the wall's beautiful dimples, cracks, and gaping holes could now be perceived more clearly as graphic shapes and textures.

Even after the Level and Hue alterations, the layers still felt too distant. I needed to flatten the background even further to disguise the difference in depth. While experimenting with the settings of the background (because it clearly wasn't going to be as simple as a shift here and a crank there), I'd started inserting solid fields of color into a new layer, above the Bathroom layer and below the Collage layer. Nothing was working, until I applied a yellow as saturated as the one in the collage. I took a sample of the brightest yellow using the Eyedropper tool, created a new layer, selected the entire layer (Ctrl+A), filled it with the selected foreground yellow (Alt+Delete), and set its blending mode in the Layers palette to Multiply. In fact, I tried various layer effects, but Multiply was most successful. It preserved the high saturation of the yellow without sacrificing the depth of the darker details in the wall, making the background seem more two-dimensional.

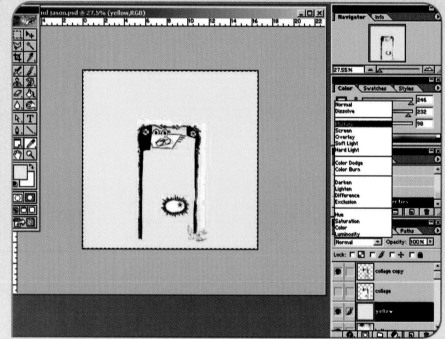

Mostly, this fused the layers together, but it also peeled them apart by highlighting the contrast between the collage's white, foamy border, and the bright yellow background. In addition, the overall composition was becoming uncomfortably vertical, and the shapes and textures of the wall began to detract from the focus on the eyes/glasses and burst/swallow clusters of the collage. After experimenting with deleting various horizontal patches of yellow, selected with the Rectangular Marquee tool, I finally reached a conclusion that solved both of these problems.

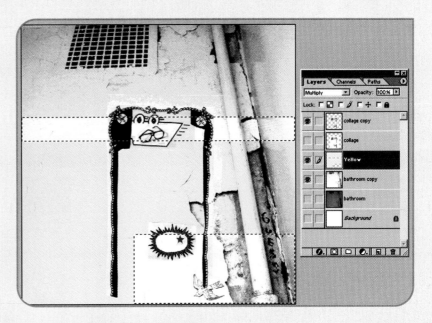

I based the top omission on its horizontal alignment with the white, upside-down car of the collage, and extended it across the entire width of the piece, to counteract the verticality of the legs of the arch and the corner pipe. It created a kind of three-row horizontal grid, separating the top third of the piece from its lower two thirds. I used the second omission not only to define part of the middle row of that grid, but also to frame and emphasize the burst and the swallow.

Since this was only a small composition, I then recreated the full-size piece, which took a fraction of the time. We submitted Photoshop and Illustrator files to Hort, both with grid lines indicating the bleed.

Conclusion

It's very refreshing to approach a piece with no initial objectives. At C404, we incorporate a generous amount of time for free expression and experimentation into our production schedules. The experience gained through this process is invaluable. It generates an abundance of enthusiasm, and allows for the discovery of ideas and techniques that undoubtedly contribute to other projects.

Photoshop helps me to visualize many vague thoughts and ideas, and also to fine tune more complete concepts. Its user-friendliness encourages the emergence of many different styles. The collage work for this piece, originally created by hand with scissors and glue, could have been replicated using Photoshop: layers allow for pieces to be shifted easily, and the selection tools facilitate a range of 'cutting', from the crudest to the most incredibly accurate. The types of 'accidents' or discoveries that can occur during these two processes, however, are quite different. Flattening a layer in Photoshop will not cause a small amount of glue to ooze from under the object's perimeter; nor would your paper cutouts miraculously shrink to fit your composition. Since I can never tell which of these processes will yield the best results, I often choose to use them both.

I'm looking forward to seeing this piece printed. It's very rewarding, after producing mainly digital work, to actually hold one of your own creations. It's there. It will always be this way. Its colors, layout, and fonts will never change. This permanence can sometimes be a source of anxiety – knowing that you can't make changes to the final piece can influence the way you design it, and even cause you to over-design it. The fact that we had only three spreads to design for Hort's publication may have also prodded me to ramp up their complexity. Fortunately, whichever the case, I was happy with the collage's evolution. I'm very satisfied with the many ways your eyes can navigate this piece, and that it's engaging while maintaining its simplicity. These are characteristics I respond to most in the work of others, and strive to achieve in my own.

After the analytical process of creating this tutorial, I discovered one detail that I wish I'd incorporated into the final piece we submitted for the book. In order to weave the yellow color more tightly into the three dimensions of the wall background, I would have liked to remove just one half of an ellipse from it where it covered the drainpipe. After magnifying the lower right-hand corner of the yellow layer with the Zoom tool, I would take the Lasso (with no feathering, and Anti-aliased checked in the Options bar) and use the Alt key to select small increments of straight lines in order to create a visually correct wedge selection. Delete!

Sometimes, this takes additional passes to get the curve smooth and realistic. Thankfully, there's always the History panel that can return your piece to a previous state if you'd like to have another go at it.

This would create the illusion that the yellow was painted along the wall, and around the base of the cylindrical pipe. I tried the same effect where the top stripe intersects the pipe, but it was too much, and interfered with the detailed cluster to the left. I even tried skewing the top stripe to follow the contour of the wall that juts out from the right corner, but that too seemed heavy-handed. Yes, the added perspective to the base of the pipe was just perfect, and as a bonus, harmonized with the round shapes of the letters "G", "U", "S", and "S" of the word "GUESS".

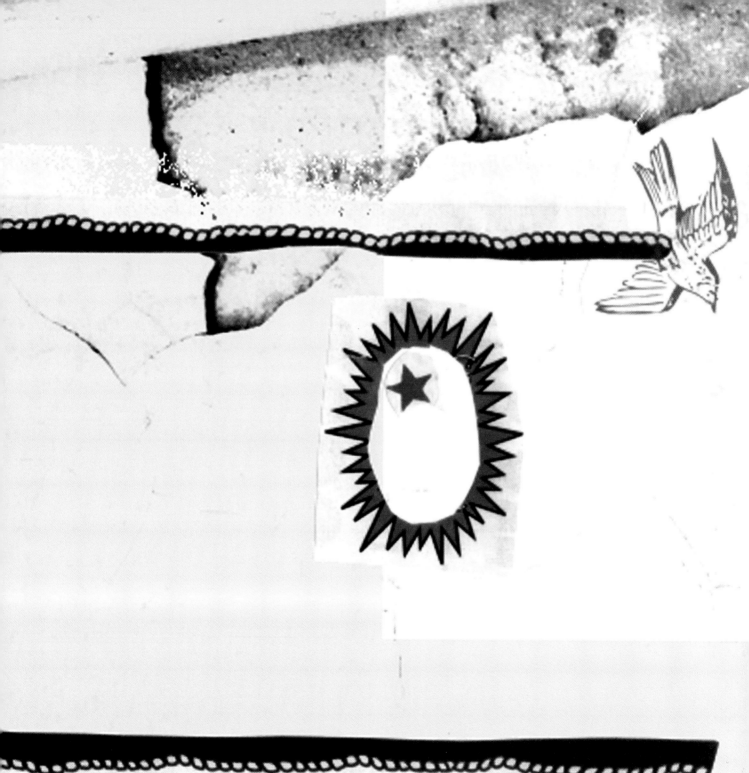

chapter   1

chapter   2

chapter   3

chapter   4

chapter   5

chapter   6

chapter   7

chapter   8

chapter   9

chapter 10

chapter 11

chapter 12

chapter 13

chapter 14

chapter 15

chapter 16

outro

"I see the work of great artists, and feel challenged to create images that in turn inspire others to create."

Josh Fallon
www.fallondesign.com

Metamorphose

I used to be a studio artist, pure and simple. Paint, brushes, charcoal, and pencils were all I knew. I'd dabbled in sculpture and ceramics as part of my course as a studio art undergraduate, but in the spring of 1999 my arsenal of artistic weapons was limited to the traditional tools. It wasn't until then that I began to take notice of graphic design, and my work was transformed.

The title of this chapter, Metamorphose, has a double meaning: it's representative of my transition from studio artist to graphic designer, and it's the title of a piece by the most influential artist on my design style, M.C. Escher. In the following pages, I hope to reveal what inspires my work and where I see it going in the future, and to explore Photoshop's developmental role in its evolution.

The paintings for my senior project were on large canvases that featured a background of pixelated images of hands. Now, anyone with a basic knowledge of Photoshop knows that the easy way to get this effect is to use the Mosaic filter. What did I do? I took the original line drawing of my hand that I was working with (on an 8.5" x 11" sheet of paper), and drew an intricate grid on it, numbering each row and lettering each column. On my 3' x 6' canvas, I drew another grid, with the same number of rows and columns. Next, on the paper, I developed a system to determine what color each block (or pixel) should be on the canvas grid. Depending on how close to the center of each individual block the lines of the drawing were, I numbered the blocks on the large canvas 1, 2, 3, or 4 – to represent the four shades of blue I was going to paint the pixels. This arduous process ended up looking great, but it was extremely inefficient. Imagine the time I could have saved myself had I learned Photoshop earlier!

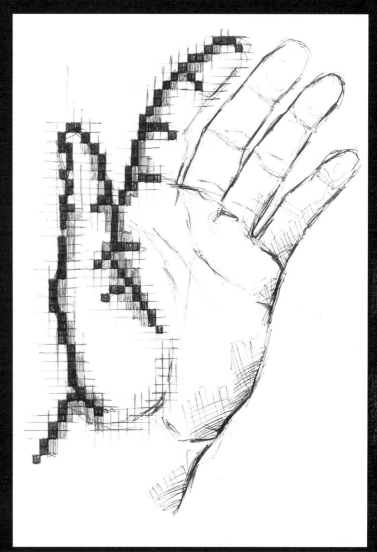

I would never have admitted it, but I was intimidated by computer software. Having limited computer experience, and no knowledge at all of graphics software, my natural reflex was to push away my curiosity, and tell myself that the computer was a crutch used by artists who couldn't hack it with traditional media. But some of the things I saw in the graphic design lab truly inspired me. Even worse, I knew that a lot of the work I saw there, I could never produce with paint or pencils alone. That, combined with the snowballing popularity of the Internet as a showcase of artistic talent, was too much for me to ignore.

That same semester, the final one of my college career, I could regularly be found in the school's computer lab (not the design lab, no way I would have been seen there) playing with Photoshop 4.0, pretending to be typing a paper. I went through what I assume is the standard "Damn, these filters are awesome!" phase, making sure all of my images had at least three lens flares, and a frosted glass distortion. I tested every filter, every text effect, and every tool in the palette. For the first year or so that I worked with Photoshop, I made a complete mockery of it – but I was learning quickly, coming to realize that Photoshop offered a host of features to complement my existing work in paint and pencil.

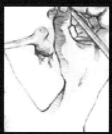

Metamorphose

The first thing I discovered was how beneficial Photoshop could be for generating quick compositions of projects that I intended eventually to paint on canvas. In particular, the ability to save all of these compositions in one layered file was extremely efficient. Before Photoshop, I would make quick sketches of new projects in my sketchbook using pen or pencil, but this method never moved beyond basic visual layout – I never experimented with color schemes, or alternative canvas layouts. I'd sketch until I was happy with the concept, then hit the canvas and see what happened. This works perfectly well for some artists, but I found that I would get midway through a project and be unhappy with the color selections, or discover a better way I could have arranged the visual elements.

With Photoshop, although my sketchbooks remained an integral part of the design process, I could scan in pen and pencil sketches, and use them as layout templates. Once I'd imported the imagery, I could use color balance, hue/saturation, and channel mixer adjustment layers to create different color schemes. The freedom of working in layers allowed me to compose various layout alternatives as well. What would take me ten or eleven pages in my sketchbook could be accomplished in a single Photoshop document! I soon found that I could get a far better feel for how a project would turn out before I opened even the first tube of paint.

Despite my experience in the graphic design lab, though, and regardless of the benefits mentioned above, I've never thought of Photoshop as a tool that would eventually replace my traditional means of creation. Rather, these days it's the place where all my efforts to create a composition come together to take their final form. I still begin nearly all projects that contain Photoshop elements (web layout, print design, digital illustration) with pencil and paper, because that's where I feel most comfortable.

Detail of Hands from Creation of Adam by Michelangelo Buonarroti
© World Films Enterprise/CORBIS

I've talked about how Photoshop has changed my creative process, but I haven't yet said much about what inspires me to create – the artists whose works I've admired, studied, and pondered throughout the developmental years of my career. It usually works like this: I see the work of great artists, and feel challenged to create images that in turn inspire others to create. It's almost ironic, though, that with all of the amazing, computer-generated art in contemporary graphic design, the majority of work from which I draw motivation is at least fifty years old.

My favorite period in art history is the High Renaissance – there's a quality to the work from this era that evokes a sense of mystery and wonder, none more so than that of Leonardo da Vinci and Michelangelo. These two master artists were considered by their peers to be driven by divine forces, undertaking massive projects that often took several years to complete. It is awe inspiring to comprehend the dedication of these artists, and their bodies of work exemplify unmatched artistic passion.

What I take from them more than anything else is the way they depicted the human form. They both went beyond strict physical accuracy when painting the human body, often sacrificing rational order to attain visual effectiveness. Their works are distinctive because they took artistic license not just to represent reality, but to shape it as they felt necessary in order to communicate emotion. Artists before them had placed an ideal on the true and accurate representation of nature, but the Renaissance masters focused on conveying mood by manipulating the composition. Hands, for example, feature in my work quite often – they can be so expressive – and there can be few more striking representations of them in art than in the Mona Lisa, or in the scene of man's creation on the ceiling of the Sistine Chapel. Through the study of the techniques of the Masters of the Renaissance I learned early on that composition is ultimately more important than visual accuracy – and I still keep that in mind in the work I do today.

Metamorphose

I think it's important to be well rounded as a graphic artist, and there's no standard higher than that set by da Vinci, whose method has had a great impact on the way I go about creating my work. The pages of his sketchbooks are testament to the fact that he was not only a great artist, but a great scientist, architect, and inventor as well. Rather as he did, I try to fill my sketchbooks with anything I can't quite visualize in my mind alone. Nearly all of my work is born there, often starting out as something insignificant that follows several different tangents before it becomes a fully-fledged project.

Leonardo's sketches lead me to another source of inspiration. There's something oddly intriguing about the line drawings that feature in old dictionaries. These anonymous pieces of visual stimulus appear in many of my paintings and drawings, and I like to reference them because of their dual symbolic and literal meanings. Taken out of the context of a dictionary, they become powerful elements – fragments that I routinely scan into Photoshop and manipulate as pieces to be integrated into my work.

The strongest influence on my work, however, is that of M.C. Escher, who began producing his work in the 1920s and continued through the early 60s. Most of his pieces were woodcuts and lithographs, art forms that he mastered through diligent study. A lot of Escher's work, and the visual paradoxes he explored, are begging to be attempted in Photoshop. The piece that particularly intrigued me at first was Bond of Union, an illustration of his head and his father's head, shaped by a single, spiraling rind of flesh. After experimenting briefly with masking, I knew it would be possible to recreate this effect. Soon, I began to study others of his pieces, marking in a book of his work the images I thought would bear similar investigation. That group of images still drives an ongoing project of mine, titled *Inspiration*.

The images that enthuse me most now are those that portray a dual reality – *Up and Down*, *Belvedere*, and *Waterfall* contain effects that I'm currently developing projects for. I hope to use Photoshop to fuse several different photographs to achieve a similar effect. The toughest part is finding architecture suitable for the project; most of the fun lies in using Photoshop's Clone Stamp tool to manipulate the digital photos to my liking.

What initially fascinated me about Escher's work was the degree to which he absolutely mastered his craft. Technically, his work is beautiful. What set him apart, however, and what drives me to try to master Photoshop, was the manner in which his skills became second nature, such that he was able to shift his focus to creating art that mocked reality, but at the same time followed strict guidelines of nature and/or mathematics. In an introduction to one of his collections, Escher wrote, "...there came a moment when it seemed as though scales fell from my eyes. I discovered that technical mastery was no longer my sole aim ... Ideas came into my mind quite unrelated to graphic art, notions which so fascinated me that I longed to communicate them to other people." For me, taking a concept for a project from my mind to a visual form is still the most enjoyable aspect of graphic design, whether it is for the Web, print, or multimedia.

M.C Escher's "Waterfall"

Metamorphose

So now let's jump forward to the 21st century. These days, there's no better place to look for inspiration than the Internet, where thousands of artists' portfolios reside, and where there are countless design forums in which to discover new artists. The ability to communicate designer-to-designer, discuss contemporary issues, and trade tips is invaluable. There's a sizable group of sites on the Web that I regularly visit for inspiration, as well as to see the latest work.

There's nothing I like to see more than a designer just turning it loose in Photoshop. I look at the work on Chapter3.net, Onyro.com, 2Advanced.com, and WebAgent007.com, and imagine Photoshop files with hundreds of layers – just a massive composition of blending modes, adjustment layers, and layer styles. Yet they manage to bring it all together to form visual expressions that are so beautiful. It's a style that many designers emulate, but few pull off so well. Work of this caliber inspires me to break loose from the rigid, exacting techniques that I often work on and freestyle a little in Photoshop. Just to take an emotion or concept and translate it into an abstract composition that you could stare at for hours.

Then there's the work on CemGul.com, cmart.design.ru, and Konstruktiv.net. These artists represent another style that I admire and am driven by: it's a darker vision of design that I relate to the work of the great Renaissance artists I spoke of earlier. The ability these designers have to evoke a mood of mystery, horror, or wonder is unquestionable. When I was younger, a lot of my pencil drawings involved dark themes, and I can foresee this style eventually working its way into future graphic design projects. If that does happen, I will definitely consult these sites first for inspiration.

At the other end of the spectrum is the corporate design firm, Attik.com. To browse the portfolio of the Attik is downright depressing – when I first drooled over their work, I wondered what I'd been doing wrong as a designer. What impresses me most, I think, is the way they manage to blend corporate and experimental design styles. It's great to see the boundaries of corporate design being challenged, and accepted – their clients include Microsoft, Nike, and Ford.

©www.onyro.com

WWW.CHAPTER3.NET ©2001 Jens Karlsson

© Cem Gul www.cemgul.com

©www.WebAgent007.com

I don't know any of these artists personally, but to me they consistently define the standard for design excellence. If you want to see some amazing work that Photoshop has obviously played a huge role in, take a look at any of these sites. Between them, they contain an amazing variety of styles, speaking to both ends of the array of artists that use Photoshop to complement their design work.

With that, let's move on to the tutorial, in which I'll demonstrate the 'rind' effect that I mentioned earlier in this chapter, as seen in *Bond of Union 2001* and *Spiral Hand*. My intention with these projects was to create contemporary translations of Escher's efforts in his piece *Bond of Union*, using a combination of original photography, pencil sketches, and Photoshop techniques.

Metamorphose

In this tutorial, we'll take a crack at putting together the same rind effect that I created in *Bond of Union 2001* and *Spiral Hand*. However, to keep this project under the 20-25 hours that it took to finish each of those two pieces, we'll be trying it on a simple, organic object: an orange. To follow along, you can either use the image provided on the CD, or choose one of your own - just make sure that it's a good, clean shot of a round object. With the knowledge you gain from this tutorial, you can move on to apply the technique to more complex objects if you so desire.

The first question to answer, though, is, "Why use Photoshop for these images?" I could just as easily have done them in pencil, or painted them - but I was drawn to the challenge of creating composites of digital photography with pencil and pen sketches, rather than using only one medium. I also wanted to test the flexibility of Photoshop - maybe after experimenting, I would discover that it would have been better to draw or paint it. At the time, I wasn't completely sure that my attempts would be successful, and my methods were really just instinctive. I realize now that there are several different ways I could have gone about it, but I'm not sure I would change too much if I had to do them over. Even though a lot of the steps can be tedious and frustrating, the great thing about masking in Photoshop is that the original image you're working with is always preserved. Should you have to make adjustments later on, such as erasing or drawing back in portions of a layer, masking ensures that you can always do it. I found this a necessity, as I'm sure you will, for there are many small corrections that will inevitably have to be made during the course of the tutorial, no matter how accurately the steps are followed.

To follow the tutorial *exactly* as I did it, there are a couple of things you're going to need in addition to the main image we're going to work on. You need to get hold of some tracing paper, your favorite drawing pencil, a fine-tipped ink pen, and access to a printer and scanner. If you don't have these materials handy right now, don't worry – you can still do the tutorial, as all the necessary source files are provided for you on the CD. Just skip ahead to the section where the rind sketch is imported into Photoshop, after you've loaded `orange.tif`.

Before we get started, it's probably a good idea to give you a general sense of what we're going to accomplish. No matter how your final image turns out, I hope to demonstrate how effective masking can be, and show you how to incorporate freehand sketch work into your compositions. If you're unfamiliar or uncomfortable with using masks in Photoshop, I hope you'll find that they're actually not too scary, once you've played around with them a bit.

Basically, what we're going to do is take an image of a simple object and make it look like you've taken the outer skin off it, as if you've carved a spiral rind using a potato peeler. First, we'll prepare the image in Photoshop, using a simple mask to isolate it on a clear background. Next, we'll draw a pencil sketch of the rind that will be then scanned into Photoshop, and used as a guide for masking the object to match the drawing. We will then perform any necessary touch up and adjustments using the same mask. We'll finish off by creating a simple background to make the final image pop a little more.

To start off, then, open up the image we're going to use in Photoshop. As stated, I'm going to use an orange, but you're free to substitute. The file `orange.tif` is a 5-inch by 5-inch image at 300dpi resolution, so if you're working at a different image size or resolution, you might experience slightly different results with some of the pixel-specific effects and tools (such as selection feathering and brush sizes). Double-click the locked layer called Background to make it an active layer, and title it orange. Then, add a new layer (by selecting New Layer from the Layers palette menu), name it white background, and drag it below the orange layer. Fill this layer with white, so we're not working against a transparent background when we mask the orange.

Metamorphose

Using the Mask button in the Layers palette, add a mask to the orange layer. This is important, because we'll be using this mask throughout the tutorial to carve out the rind. (If you're new to masking, keep in mind that a mask does nothing to alter the layers below it – think of it as a separate layer that you can add to and subtract from, to show or hide portions of a lower layer. Painting or filling with black on a mask hides that area of the layer below it, while white will make it visible again.)

Then, using the Pen tool or the Lasso tool – whichever you're more comfortable with – create a selection around the edge of the orange, and feather it 0.5 pixels to soften the edges just a little. Now choose the *inverse* of the selection, and make sure that the mask is active in the Layers palette (click on it; it's the preview box linked to the orange layer). Fill this selection with black to mask the area outside the orange, and we should now have the orange isolated against a white background. Deselect the selection, and we have our orange, ready for carving. Go ahead and save this project as `orange.psd`.

Now we're at the point where we have to summon up some drawing skills to sketch the outline of the rind. The first thing we need to do, though, is print out the orange that we just masked, so that we can trace it – make sure that you print it at 100% scale! Then, tape it to a drawing surface, and tape a sheet of tracing paper over the printout.

I originally considered executing this step from within Photoshop too, but personally I draw much quicker and more accurately on paper. Previous attempts at sketching in Photoshop have proved unsuccessful – my drawings have looked too choppy, even when using a Wacom pen and tablet. What it comes down to for me is the direct, natural feeling of pencil on paper, and being able to see the tip of my pencil and the drawing it's producing at the same time.

This is by far the most time-consuming step of the project, and the most crucial. You definitely need an eraser close at hand, and you mustn't get discouraged if it takes a few attempts to get the right look for the rind sketch. The best tactic is probably to draw the 'front' of the rind first – on a small object like an orange, we only need to draw four bands. Try to visualize the rind as one continual strand, starting at the top of the object, and wrapping around to the bottom. Once you're happy with the front, move on to the back, where the bands should all bend in the opposite direction. When you draw these, actually draw *through* the front rinds, to ensure the back curves look accurate. In this example, what you end up with should be horizontally symmetrical. (Of course, this only holds true for symmetrical objects – sketches for a hand or a head, for example, will not end up symmetrical.)

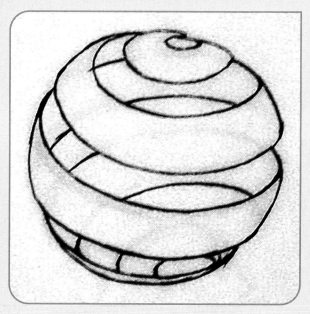

Our pencil sketch now complete, tape another sheet of tracing paper on top of the first. (It can help to put a piece of white paper between the original print and the first sheet of tracing paper, so that all you see is the pencil sketch.) Now take your fine-tipped ink pen, and with an even stroke, trace the front of the rind. Then, trace the back of rind, but *don't* draw through the front rind this time. This ink drawing is what we'll end up using as a masking guide for the orange in Photoshop.

Take the tracing paper with the inked rind on it, and place it in your scanner with a clean sheet of white paper behind it. Scan it into Photoshop at 100% scale, 300dpi – we want it to be exactly the same size as the orange in the Photoshop file.

Metamorphose

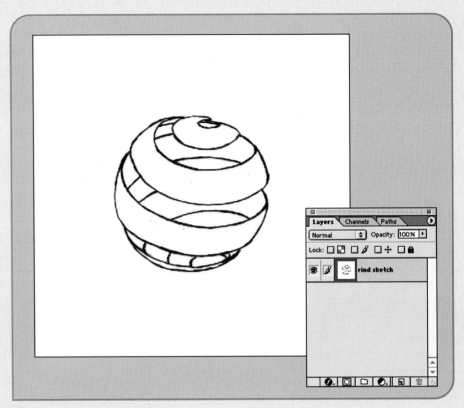

The scanned image is probably going to need some levels adjustment to get rid of any unwanted smudges, and to brighten the white area. Open up the levels (Image > Adjust > Levels), and pull both the white and dark points in, until the white area is clean and the rind drawing is dark enough, but not too bold. Use the Layer Properties menu in the Layers palette menu, or double-click the layer if the image is already flattened, to name the layer rind sketch. (If you don't want to draw the sketch yourself, you can use rindsketch.tif from the CD.)

With the orange.psd file open in the background, we can drag the rind sketch layer onto it. If it doesn't do so automatically, make sure that it ends up as the top layer. Then, by setting the layer blending mode of rind sketch to Multiply, you can 'knock out' the white background of the sketch, leaving only the lines of the sketch visible. Now, use the Move tool to align the rind sketch layer with the orange, lining it up as closely as possible. Use the arrow keys to nudge it into perfect position.

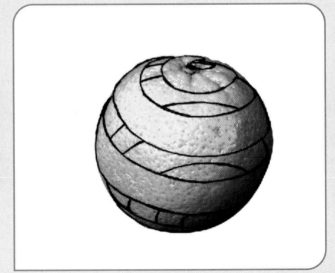

After trying the rind effect several times, that last step is the one that I'm most happy with. Layer blending modes can be incredibly effective and efficient. In my early attempts, I used the Magic Wand to select the pencil sketch and move it over to the main composition, but it just never looked right, with either too much white on the edges of the drawing, or too much black trimmed off. Using the Multiply blending mode achieves the perfect effect, with a single click. I definitely suggest experimenting with layer blending modes whenever possible – you'd be surprised how easily they can solve problems you wouldn't otherwise have been able to fix.

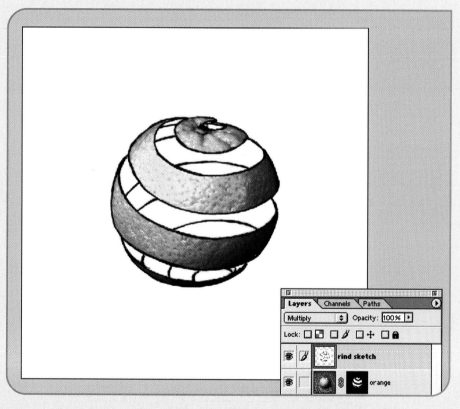

Next, we're going to mask the front of the rind on the orange layer, using the rind sketch layer as a guide for creating our selection. Using the Lasso or Pen tool again, create a selection that includes all of the front areas of the rind, tracing this area from the rind sketch layer. When the selection is complete, feather the selection by 0.5 pixels to soften the edges. Next, take the inverse of the selection, because we're going to want to mask the area surrounding the front rind. Make sure the orange mask is active, and fill the selection with black. This will mask everything on the layer, *except* the front rind of the orange.

Now that we have the front of the rind, we need to create the back of the rind. We've got to create this section from scratch, since we're depicting the *inside* of the object, which obviously couldn't be seen in the original image. Before we start, deselect the previous selection and change the white background layer to a dark gray – this will help us to see the back rinds better when we fill them in, since they'll be white against a gray background. Create a new layer just above the background layer, and name it back rind.

Metamorphose

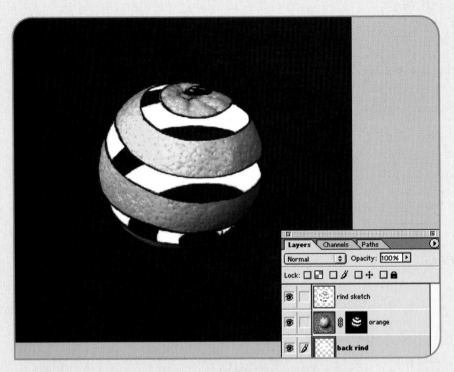

Using the rind sketch layer as a guide again, draw a selection that includes all of the *back* area of the rind, and feather it 0.5 pixels. Don't worry about the sections of the back rind that are covered by the front rind – as long as these areas are reasonably accurate, they will be fine. Since the front rind hides them, and we're only estimating their curvature anyway, they don't necessarily have to follow the path of the rind edges perfectly. On the back rind layer, fill this selection with white. If you hide the orange layer, you can see that I've taken several shortcuts to create the selection for the back rind layer.

We're now at a point where you can see the final composition coming together, but a few key elements are still lacking. If you look at the rind itself, it has no depth – right now, it's paper-thin. We can add some depth by giving it a white edge – but before we do that, we need to double-click on the back rind layer to give it a layer style; Color Overlay is the one we need. Leave the blend mode at Normal, and choose a red color. We'll turn this off later, but for now we want to be able to distinguish between the back rind, and the rind edge we're currently working with. Red is a bold enough color to create a definite distinction from the white edge we're going to draw. Also, you can hide the rind sketch layer – we're done with that now.

Now you can create a new layer above back rind, and name it rind edge. We'll start drawing the edge of the front of the rind first. Select the Airbrush tool, and create a new brush that's 20 pixels in diameter, 90% hardness, and 1% spacing – we want to use a brush that has just a little bit of softness to it, with a consistent stroke. The brush size might seem large, but since the edge we're drawing first will appear *below* the layer that the front rind is on, only the top edge of the brush stroke will actually show through. I find this makes it easier to control – you don't have to worry about the bottom edge of the brush showing, although we do have to stop short of the right and left edges of the front rind, to prevent drawing past it.

To draw in the left and right curves of the front rind edges, and the edges of the back rind, we need to switch to a 13-pixel brush, leaving the other settings unaltered. We need this smaller brush now because the back rind edges *aren't* covered by another layer. Especially with an organic object like an orange, drawing the edge in by hand gives it a more natural look, as any imperfections will actually end up benefiting the final image. Use the sharp edges of the front and back rind as guides – and when you're drawing the edges, try to make the ones that border the front rind a little bit thicker than those on the back rind, to add proper perspective.

Take some time to get the rind edges to look right – they're a vital feature that's important in the final image. If you're having trouble getting an effective rind edge, try experimenting with a layer mask on the rind edge layer. That way, you can afford to be less than perfect when you first draw it in, and go back afterwards with the mask, removing from or adding to the edge as necessary.

Metamorphose

The image is now almost complete, but the back rind still needs some work. If you go back to the back rind layer and disable the red overlay, you can see that it looks too flat, and the white rind edge blends right into it, which isn't what we want. Create another new layer above back rind, and name it back rind shading. Then, hold down Option/Alt and move your cursor between these two layers until you see the Clipping Group symbol, and click to group them.

This is a great feature; one that I frequently use to ensure that I'm 'painting within the lines'. Now, any shading we do on back rind shading will only appear on the back rind layer, as the latter is now a clipping mask for the former. It's the same concept as that of a layer mask, except that instead of creating a mask from scratch, we're using the boundaries of a chosen layer to define a masked area.

Select the Airbrush tool, and create a new brush that's 300 pixels in diameter with 0% hardness and 1% spacing. Again, 300 pixels might seem large, but the reason I've chosen it is so that we can get a lot of softness on the edge of the brush, which is important in achieving a smooth, well-blended shadow. Set the Pressure to 20% with black paint, and gently airbrush-in shading on the outer edges of the back rind, working on the back rind shading layer. Get it to a point where it is almost *too* dark – we're going to add an adjustment layer to it, to give it an orange tint. Doing so should help to create some unity between the front and back rinds.

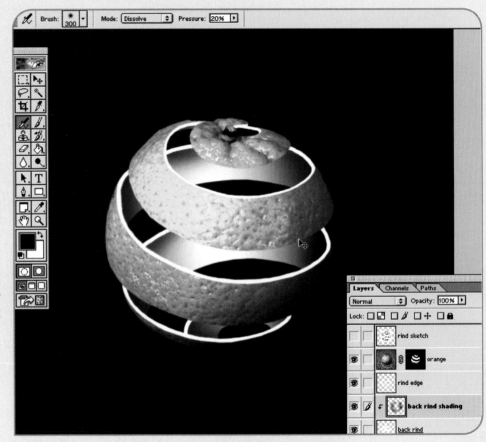

While still on the back rind shading layer, click on the Adjustment Layer button in the Layers palette, and select Color Balance. Adjust the top slider – Cyan and Red – to add 50 towards red, and adjust the bottom slider – Yellow and Blue – to subtract 50 towards the yellow side. Create a Clipping Group as previously explained, using the adjustment layer and the back rind shading layer, as again we only want the adjustment to affect this layer. This still looks too bold, though, so to tone it down we can set the blending mode of this adjustment layer to Screen. Screen is a good mode to use here, because it both lightens the shadow's tone, and maintains the color balance adjustment. As usual, I achieved this through trial and error – I still find blending modes very unpredictable, and I usually test a bunch of them before settling on one.

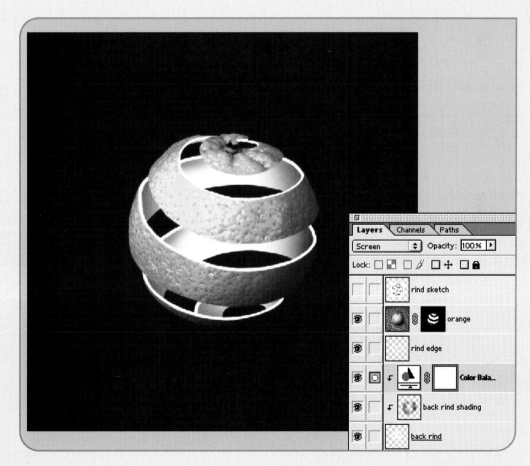

Metamorphose

Congratulations! We're now at a point where we have the completed image on a dark gray background, with complete flexibility to add any other background if we want. On this occasion, I'm going to make it a little more interesting by adding a blue color tint using a color balance adjustment layer, and a radial gradient overlay using the Gradient Overlay layer style at 60% opacity, set to soft light blending mode. Feel free to create your own background, though!

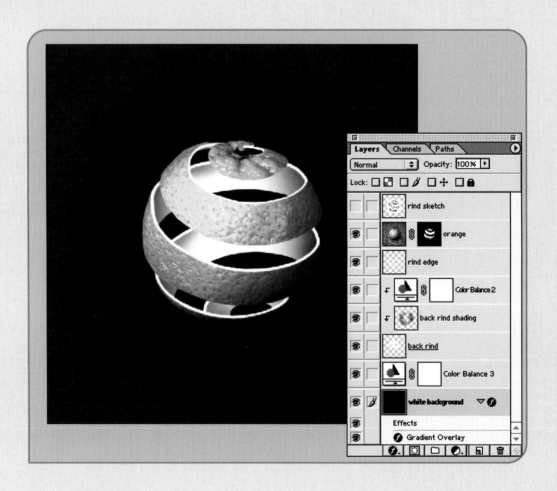

Frankly, I'm now unsure as to whether I should put these projects to rest, or explore them some more. The idea I keep coming back to is composing an entire human body, shaped by a single rind. This would be an extensive project, and I wonder if it would end up being too complex to form an interesting image. I'd also be curious to see someone attempt the effect using 3D rendering software. My fear is that it would end up looking unnatural and contrived, but some of the things I've seen composed in 3D make me think twice. I've even had someone ask me what plug-in I used to achieve the effect.

The point is, with all the different ways it might be possible to do it, I think the idea will continue to intrigue me until I take it to another level, and move beyond what I've currently done with it. For that reason, I encourage you to experiment with it as well, and to try applying it in ways that seem unconventional. You might just stumble onto something that provides you with inspiration for a whole series of projects.

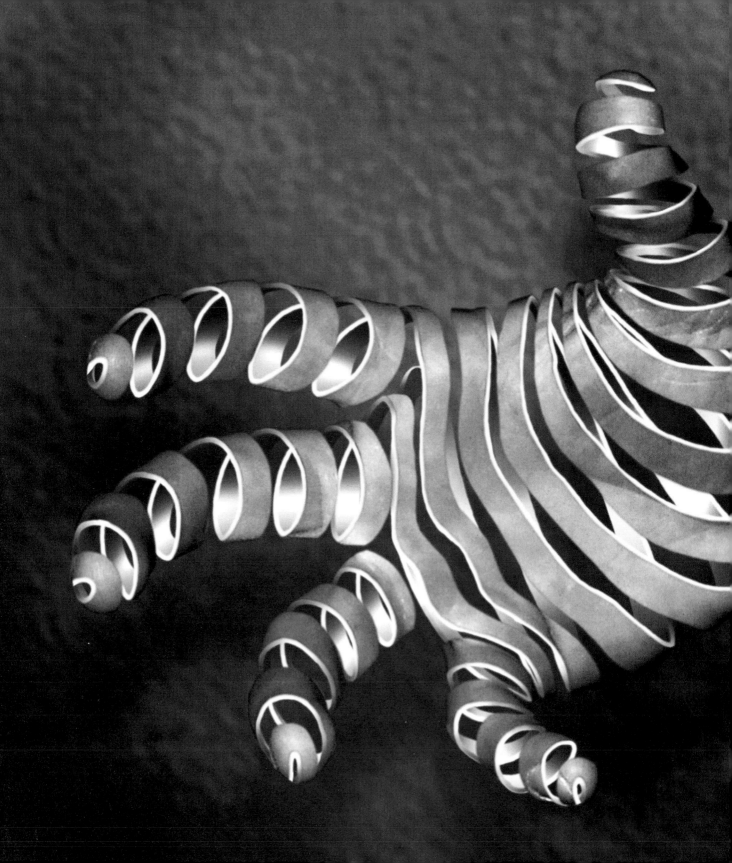

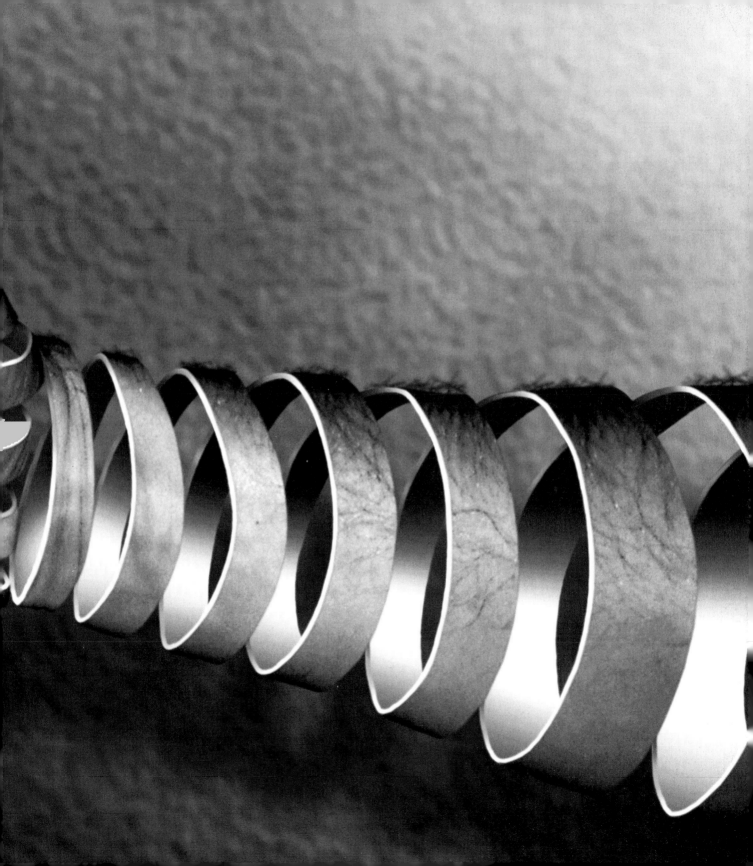

chapter 1

chapter 2

chapter 3

chapter 4

chapter 5

chapter 6

chapter 7

chapter 8

chapter 9

chapter 10

chapter 11

chapter 12

chapter 13

chapter 14

chapter 15

chapter 16

outro

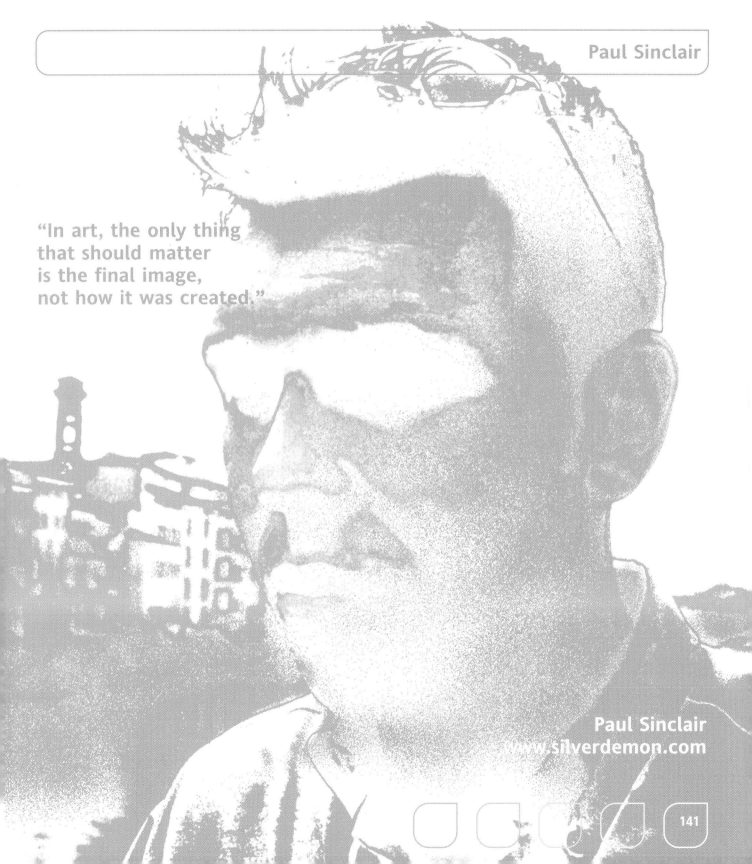

"In art, the only thing
that should matter
is the final image,
not how it was created."

Paul Sinclair
www.silverdemon.com

141

Personal Space

I remember as a small child of about 9 or 10 years old, sitting and drawing a neighbor's car and being asked by that neighbor what I'd like to be when I grew up. I replied, "An artist". Even at that age, I had an idea of what an artist was: it was someone who painted in a smock and a beret, and hung nice oil paintings in a gallery. My time since then has been filled with experimentation – not only with different media and materials, but also with ideas and influences, ranging from classical artists like Michelangelo, to contemporary artists like Dave McKean.

After years of using pencil, pen, gouache, and watercolor for illustration work, I discovered Photoshop, which has become my main tool in the creation of images. Whatever the style of the work, Photoshop offers a huge range of options that were previously impossible using natural media. Things like layers and history options enable me to defy the normal laws that govern traditional, non-digital works. There is no fixed timeline in place, scale doesn't come into it, and color can be manipulated at any point. It's the sheer freedom and control that it gives me that makes it such an invaluable part of my toolkit. The killer punch is that Photoshop places no constraints on its users, and because of this I've been able to develop my style according to what I *want* to produce, rather than what I *can* produce.

When I was young, I spent all of my spare time at home drawing or painting. At first, I'd just copy anything that took my fancy – usually from comic books, and almost always involving fantastic depictions of the human form. In particular, I remember being struck by Bernie Wrightson's cover for Meatloaf's *Dead Ringer*, with its white figures in sharp contrast against the dark night surrounding them. That kick-started something in my head that I pursued through the work of Boris Vallejo and Simon Bisley. Never before had I seen black and white artwork as clean and dramatic as that in Bisley's *ABC Warriors*, and the full-color *Slaine – Horned God* graphic novel nearly blew me away. It was this that directly inspired me to produce *Daemons*, ten years later. I was harking back to the days when all I'd paint were fantasy scenarios: muscles and swords, that sort of thing.

Unique Forms of Continuity in Space by Umberto Boccioni
© Burstein Collection/CORBIS

I've always been fascinated by the human anatomy, and this is something that has featured from time to time in my work – sometimes as a full figure, sometimes just as a suggestion of a skeletal form. The intricacies in the anatomy are fascinating, and almost limitless. Vertebrae, for example, are particularly interesting: the abstract qualities they have as a shape, and the way they fit together so neatly to form yet another shape. When I look at things in this way, it gets my mind firing off on all sorts of tangents, wanting to photograph, to model in a 3D package, to start sketching... anything at all, as long as I can record my response to the stimulus. I guess this is what it really boils down to: a desire to create and record an emotion; a snapshot of feeling.

Though it was the work of fantasy artists that first grabbed my attention, they're not my sole source of influence – there are classical pieces that can do it too. Boccioni's *Unique Forms of Continuity in Space* sculpture is a piece that stands out in my mind, because it's a rare example of a solid shape that seems to possess the qualities normally found in a liquid, almost like drawn-out mercury. The way that these ideas contrast in your head is one of the reasons why I remember the piece so clearly. It's not a case of looking at something and getting everything off it first time; rather, you spend time studying, and your perception of the sculpture can start to change. The way it appears to be heavy one minute, yet an instant later can seem incredibly light, is just fabulous.

Michelangelo's *Head of a Centaur* is striking, with its clean, solid, yet raw-looking pen and ink hatching. I love the classical profile, with its character clearly on show. I think that anyone interested in the human figure has at some point been overawed by the works of Michelangelo and his apprentices. There is always such a feeling of power and emotion in his works, as there is in so many of the works of the Renaissance. From the Baroque, Caravaggio's *Supper at Emmaus* in London's National Gallery just has the most fantastic lighting. It really draws you in, just as a play at the theatre makes you focus right up onto the stage by the use of light and space. And from the Art Nouveau movement, the first time that I saw Gustav Klimt's *Medicine* and *The Kiss*, they were revelations. His use of color, and the way he merges shapes into one another so that they almost unite, creates a magical atmosphere – although it's never an easy one to enjoy. You're never sure whether to feel happy or worried about what's going on.

There are elements in all of these pieces that I aspire to in my work, whether it is the precise and strong drawing of Michelangelo, the beautiful lighting and contrast displayed by Caravaggio, or the ethereal qualities shown in Klimt's work. Boccioni's sculpture and Klimt's *Kiss* were the first pieces of abstract art that I'd really been attracted to, and they opened my eyes to more abstract work in general – 2D and 3D – making me realize that art doesn't have to be instantly recognizable for it to work. I enjoy pieces that can be enjoyed on many levels, and that is what I aim to do with my personal works. Primarily, they need to satisfy my creative desires (after all that's why we create art, is it not?), but I also want them to be of interest to other people – for them to have a reaction to the works, the way I react to Caravaggio's. I'm not about to compare myself with him, but it's the passion that certain pieces arouse, the gut feeling inside when you see something so awesome that you just want to rip it off the wall and take it home. This is what I would like to achieve.

The Supper at Emmaus by Caravaggio
© National Gallery Collection; By kind permission of the Trustees of the National Gallery, London/CORBIS

Something that really gave my imagination a kick and made my perceptions stretch was the discovery of Clive Barker's books. I'd always liked the films *Hellraiser* and *Candyman*, but nothing prepared me for reading *The Great and Secret Show*. It really was a mental wake-up call, a completely refreshing twist on horror. He knows how to write in a way that makes you question the fabric of life itself, and that takes some skill. He is someone with a very individual way of looking at the world we live in, a true visionary, and someone whose work I would love to emulate in my own style. It was his sheer darkness that inspired me to produce *Death's Doorway*. An abstract piece with no specific visual objects, it leaves everything to the imagination.

The biggest change in my work occurred when I started a diploma in electronic graphics, and was introduced to the world of Photoshop and Illustrator. This was chiefly (at first) because I could work more efficiently just by having the ability to try out several variations of an idea in quick succession. It was also the first time I'd used a scanner properly, and the idea of scanning in sketches and then altering them in Photoshop was almost miraculous. This was the beginning of my use of the computer in the creation of my work, and the true beginning of the development of the style I have today.

On the same course that I was introduced to Photoshop, I discovered the artwork of Dave McKean, first of all on comics and graphic novels, and then on record covers – all the things that had first moved me to create images. He used photographs, scanned objects, drawings, and text to great effect, and managed always to produce something that looked dark or sinister. His illustrations in *Batman – Arkham Asylum*, for example, brought the book to life – he gave it an almost oppressive feeling of despair that drags you in deeply.

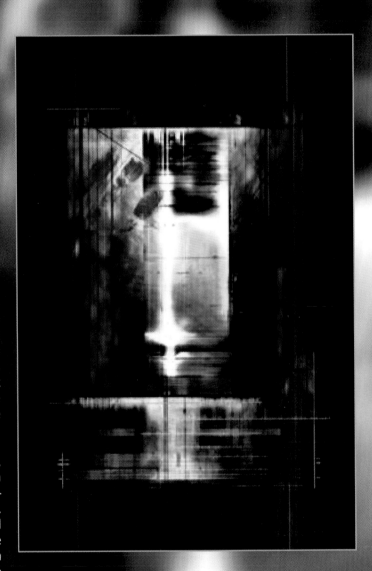

Something else that I came across at this time was David Carson's *Raygun* magazine, and later *BlahBlahBlah*. Using layers of text – over images, and over other text – was the opposite of everything we'd been taught to do. There was such freedom, almost to the point where it was secondary actually to read the content, the primary issue being the look and feel given off. It was all very contemporary, and made me think about boundaries – what could be pushed, and what couldn't. The very nature of art is experimentation: sometimes it works, and sometimes it doesn't. It's just a matter of thinking about something, trying it out, and then seeing if it does work in practice.

You might scan in a photograph, blur it by 10 pixels, and discover that it's not what you want. But blur it by 30 pixels, and it's just what you need. Making progress through trial and error is the way I like to work; if I find myself wandering down the road to ruin, I can use Photoshop's history feature to turn back. The personal pieces of work I've done tend to keep developing until they're finished – because there's no deadline involved, you just work at the piece until the moment arises when you think, "That's it". In some cases it's been 40 minutes, in others it's been days, and that's the beauty of the way the program works with you.

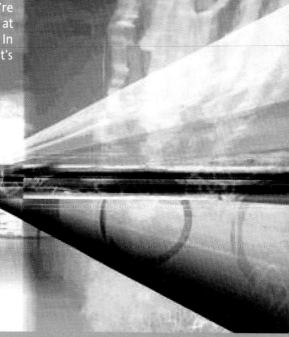

Personal Space

The book *Typography Now: The Next Wave* is a collection of commercial works by people like Vaughan Oliver, Why Not Associates, and Neville Brody. It showed me what people were actually buying and what designers were making money out of, and I became more and more interested in producing work that merged illustration, photography, and design to produce what amounted to art. I was becoming more and more engrossed in the image manipulation that Photoshop offered, and I realized that it was something I wanted to pursue further. To me, it was only natural that I should experiment as much as possible with both the software and the content, to create a fusion that I was happy with, something that excited me artistically. It's through years of creating personal pieces that I've developed my current style of illustration, having had few commercial opportunities to use Photoshop in the way that I would if given carte-blanche on a brief.

When you have to do brochure and corporate identity work to pay the bills, you really need a release, and these days photography is an increasingly important part of what I do. It gives me the complete freedom and control that I don't usually get when working with clients. I'll walk or drive around looking at things and framing them up for future shots, noticing the way the light catches a building at a certain time of day, or the way the morning mist clings to the fields. I'm currently taking a lot of industrial and urban shots, as part of an ongoing project. I'm looking into structure, organization, decay, and destruction, using photographs taken in the towns and cities I visit. Once I've amassed enough, I shall begin work on the final images, perhaps collating them in book form. The idea of commentary in pictures is an important one in my work; I believe that people respond better to visual stimuli.

I'm also keen on promoting digital art as a legitimate art form, and I'd love to see more large showings at major galleries of digital artists and illustrators. I believe that if the people 'in the know' act favorably toward digital art, then the general public will accept it too. It shouldn't be portrayed as something special, and attention should be focused on the final work, rather than the technology that produced it. I don't want people thinking that what I do is lessened by the fact that a computer is involved before it's finished. Hopefully, this book will help in displaying digital art as art; and in showing the creative process, make people realize what's involved, and accept that you still have to have talent to produce work of high standard.

Personal Space is a new piece that's typical of the work I've been doing lately. It features some urban photography, in the form of a bridge and a multistory car park. It has a sketched character overlaying a self-portrait, color treatments as used in a lot of editorial work just at the moment, and some clean type. The image essentially arose from the photographs, and the way that they fitted (or were made to fit) together. I usually find that having something to say, or having a message to get across with my work, gives me the focus I need, and with this one it was a bit of a mixture. There's the idea of the space in the background being personal to me because I created it; or there's the way that the self-portrait has been covered and boxed in, almost imprisoning it – perhaps that's the personal space? Then again, maybe it's a subconscious agoraphobic thing? This is exactly what I aim to create with my work: ambiguity and interest; some food for thought.

Personal Space

What I'm looking for here is a piece with good contrast, good lighting, and strong elements within it that give the viewer lots of things to see and think about when they examine it a little more closely. The theme of the piece is one of space, both physical and psychological – hence the title, *Personal Space*. Using a combination of photography and illustration within Photoshop, we're going to create something with good depth that works on many levels.

I'll start by going through my collection of photographs and sketches, looking for suitable images or ideas that I can use for the brief. If I can't find exactly what I'm looking for among my photos, then it's probably time to check out some stock images, or something from an alternative source (like someone else's pile of photos). Luckily, as I had no specific brief to work to for this piece, it was a case of going through all of my photographs until a few jumped out at me. I chose three that I'd taken of a multistory car park near to where I live, because of their interesting forms and their very strong lines.

As well as these, I found a photograph taken in Totnes (Devon, UK) of some steps leading up away from the road, a scanned illustration I'd created previously, a scanned self portrait, and a couple of excerpts from a Chambers 20th Century English Dictionary (dated 1921) referring to the two words of the title.

ŏn ; *then*. **Perspective**

stage: character: an individual, sometimes used slightingly: a living soul: a human being: the outward appearance, &c.: bodily form: one of the three hypostases or individualities in the triune God: (*gram.*) a distinction in form, according as the subject of the verb is the person speaking, spoken to, or spoken of.—*adj.* **Per′sonable**, having a well-formed body or person: of good appearance.—*n.* **Per′sonäge**, a person: character represented: an individual of eminence: external appearance.—*adj.* **Per′sonal**, belonging to a person: having the nature or quality of a person: peculiar to a person or to his private concerns: pertaining to the external appearance: done in person: relating to one's own self: applied offensively to one's character: (*gram.*) denoting the person.—*n.* **Personalisā′tion**, personification.—*v.t.* **Per′sonalise**, to make personal.—*ns.* **Per′sonalism**, the character of being personal; **Per′sonalist**, one who writes personal notes; **Per′sonal′ity**, that which distinguishes a person from a thing, or one person from another: individuality: [de]rogatory remark or reflection directly applied to [a per]son—esp. in *pl.* **Personal′ities**.—*adv.* **Per′son**[ally], in a personal or direct manner: in person: [indiv]idually.—*n.* **Per′sonalty** (*law*), all the property [whic]h, when a man dies, goes to his executor or [admin]istrator, as dist[inct] [whic]h goes to his he[ir] [na]me the likeness [co]unterfeit: to fei[gn] [c]orollary of the s[

Sowle, sown, *n.* (*Spens.*)
Sowse, sows, *v.* and *n.* (*Spens.*). Same as *Souse*, to strike.
Sowth, sowth, *v.i.* and *v.t.* (*Scot.*) to whistle softly, to whistle over a tune.
Soy, soi, *n.* a thick and piquant sauce made from the seeds of the soy bean or pea, a native of China, Japan, and the Moluccas.—Also **Soo′ja**. [Jap. *si-yax*, Chin. *shi-yu*.]
Soyle, soil, *n.* (*Spens.*) prey.
Sozzle, soz′l, *v.t.* to make wet or muddy.—*n.* disorder.—*adj.* **Sozz′ly**, sloppy.
Spa, spä, or spaw, *n.* a place where there is a mineral spring of water. [From *Spa* in Belgium.]
Space, spās, *n.* extension as distinct from material substances: room: largeness: distance between objects: interval between lines or words in books: quantity of time: distance between two points of time: opportunity, leisure: a short time: interval.—*v.t.* to make or arrange intervals between.—*ns.* **Spā′cer**, one who, or that which, spaces: an instrument by which to reverse a telegraphic current, esp. in a marine cable, for increasing the speed of transmission: a space-bar; **Space′-writ′er**, in journalism, one paid for his articles according to the space they occupy when printed; **Spā′cing**, the act of dividing into spaces, placing at suitable intervals, as in printing, &c.: the space thus made: spaces collectively.—*adj.* **Spā′cious**, having large space: large in extent roomy: wide.—*adv.* **Spā′ciously**.—*n.* **Spā′cious-ness**. [Fr. *espace*—L. *spatium*; Gr. *spān*.]
Spacial = *Spatial* (q.v.).
Spadassin, spad′a-sin, *n.* a swordsman, a bravo. [Fr.—It. *spadaccino*—*spada*, a sword.]
Spade, spād, *n.* a broad blade of iron with a handle used for digging: a playing-card of one of the [

Personal Space

During this tutorial, we'll see how these disparate elements can be used to lead the viewer into the piece, deliberately unsettle them, or just catch them unawares at a later date. Essentially, they break down into three basic groups. Firstly, there are the structural photographs – they set the scene. Secondly, there is the portrait section – there for the personal element. Finally, there are the blocks of color, and the text – these bring it all together and finish the piece.

The first stage, then, is to set up a blank canvas to work on. For personal pieces, I tend to use A4, 300dpi, and RGB, with a transparent background. The reason I use RGB is quite simply because not all of Photoshop's filters will work in CMYK. If the piece needs to be set to CMYK afterwards, it's straightforward to change the mode in Photoshop. I use a transparent background instead of white because it lets me see exactly where the different layers are. If I need to apply a white background to a piece at any point, I can drop in a new layer at the back with a white fill, no problem.

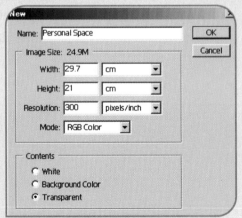

Next, we need to open `Bridge_1.jpg`, and transfer that image onto our blank canvas. To do that you can either select, copy, and paste; or use the Move tool. Which of these you choose is really personal preference, but if you're working with the image at full screen, as I tend to, then copying and pasting can be easier. Name the new layer that this process creates Bridge.

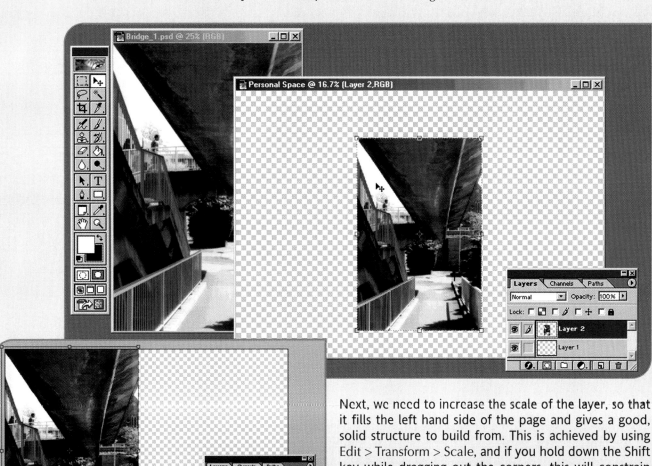

Next, we need to increase the scale of the layer, so that it fills the left hand side of the page and gives a good, solid structure to build from. This is achieved by using Edit > Transform > Scale, and if you hold down the Shift key while dragging out the corners, this will constrain the proportions for you. I've taken the layer so that it just goes off all three edges, because I don't want any gaps down the left side, which could spoil the effect.

Personal Space

The next thing to do with this layer is to remove the pedestrian who's just walked into the shot. This is where the Clone tool comes in very handy. I've used a 45-pixel brush with 100% opacity to clone from the tree behind the guy. This area is going to be fairly well bleached out later on, so it's not vitally important to do a perfect job, as long as it looks acceptable from a distance.

Once we've finished cloning, we need to bring in the next image. Open `Car Park_1.jpg`, and move (or copy and paste) the image into *Personal Space*. Before you do anything else, name the layer Car Park_1. When you're overlaying images, it helps if you drop the opacity down a bit on the top layer, so I've dropped Car Park_1 down to 70%, making it easier to line it up. I've also used Edit > Transform > Scale to scale it down to a size I'm happy with.

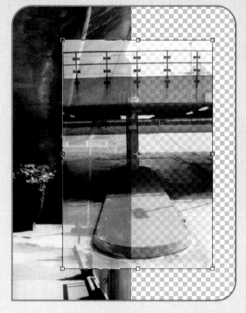

The aim here is to create the illusion of a real 3D space that doesn't actually work if you look at it for too long. With this new layer in place, a bit of removal work is necessary, which will be dealt with using layer masks. Go to Layer > Add Layer Mask > Reveal All, and once the mask is in place you can proceed to remove unwanted sections of the Car Park_1 layer by airbrushing black over them.

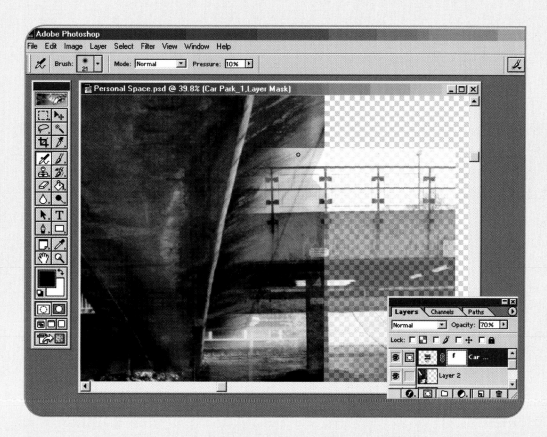

The main area to be removed is the section that overlaps the underside of the bridge. I tend to use a fairly large brush for large areas (100-200 pixels) at about 10% pressure, while for smaller areas I'll use brushes as small as 20 pixels and as low as 5% pressure. With the lower pressure, you can build up a nice smooth effect using several strokes. It's also a good idea to zoom in close when you're working on something detailed, or you're working up to an edge. Once you've removed enough, put the opacity of the layer back up to 100%, and remove any last bits that you may have missed.

Personal Space

The next section is going to extend the railings of the first section across the image to the right, disturbing the natural perspective and therefore adding a bit more interest to the piece. Open and drag Car Park_2.jpg onto our image, and name the layer Car Park_2.

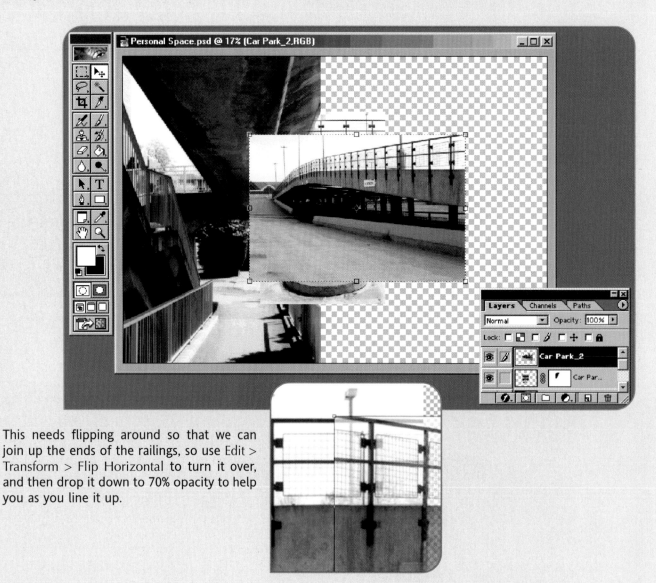

This needs flipping around so that we can join up the ends of the railings, so use Edit > Transform > Flip Horizontal to turn it over, and then drop it down to 70% opacity to help you as you line it up.

Then, using the Scale facility as before, you need to scale the Car Park_2 layer to match the layer below it. I've used one of the main railing supports as a reference point to match the layers up. This enables very easy layer masking to remove the excess railing material, because all I have to do to blend them is remove everything to the left of, and up to the mid-point of, the support itself. Using a 20-pixel brush at between 5% and 10% pressure, a fairly seamless effect can be achieved on this section.

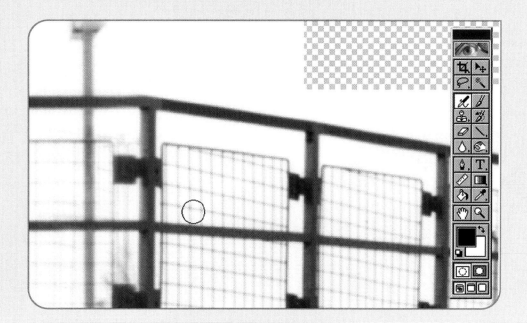

You can use the layer mask to soften up the edges of the new photo down the left side and along the bottom if you wish, but that area will be mostly obscured later anyway, so it doesn't really matter.

The next stage is really going to throw a visual spanner in the works, because we're going to insert a set of stone steps into the underside of the bridge. This will have the effect of adding more dimensions and levels, giving the viewer a suggestion of more behind the scenes, and adding to the whole idea of space.

Personal Space

Open and move `Steps_1.jpg` onto the image, and rename the layer Steps_1. This image will need scaling and positioning as the others did: I've located it so that the top of the steps is right near the top of the page. Should they notice the steps, the viewer is led up and away, straight through the top of the image.

Next, once again, is the layer mask process, to remove the hard edges of the photo. I've used a variety of brush sizes and pressures on this layer, from 100 pixels and 20% pressure on the large areas, down to a 20 pixels brush at 5% pressure around the railings. The trick this time is to take the left hand side back to the shadows with a 45-pixel brush, and the right hand side back to the drain pipe with a smaller brush (20 pixels), so that there's no obvious cut off point between the layers. The lower pavement doesn't cause any real problems because of the coloring; it's just a simple case of blending it out.

Once that's been fully blended, it's time to merge all visible layers (Layer > Merge Visible). The reason for doing this at this time is because I want to work with the layers combined, and I don't have any plans to alter the separate layers further into the piece. It also introduces a bit of finality into what has to be one of the most flexible working environments known to man!

Now we can take stock of what we've created so far, and get a feel for where it's going. It has a good solid structural feel, but the lighting is a bit flat, so we need to do something about that. Drag the merged layer down onto the New Layer icon at the bottom of the layer palette to create a duplicate layer, rename this layer Structures, and set the layer blending mode to Hard Light. Configuring things this way will intensify the contrast between the two layers, while keeping a nice color balance.

Personal Space

You can keep duplicating Hard Light layers to intensify the effect, and in this instance I've done it twice (duplicating once more, in other words) to give a nice weight to the piece. I think it's quite dramatic.

It's a good idea to experiment with layer blending modes, just to see what they do separately and in combination. I tend to use Hard Light the most, although Overlay gives a similar feel. I also use Color Dodge and Color Burn, which act pretty much like the tools of the same names, but affect the whole layer instead of small sections. There's always something to learn in Photoshop, no matter how long and how often you use it.

Once you've reached a level of contrast you're happy with, merge the layers again, and rename the merged layer Structures. Now bring in the file Text.jpg and rename its layer text. You'll notice that it's upside down, but this is not a mistake: I want to *suggest* written marks, not necessarily have them readable (that's not dissimilar to my handwriting anyway!), and I figure that placing it upside down will give me that. Drag this layer below the Structures layer.

Duplicate the text layer by dragging it down onto the New Layer icon. Then, drag the text copy layer so that it's *above* the Structures layer, and invert it (Image > Adjust > Invert). Set this new layer's blending mode to Color Dodge.

Next, with the text copy layer selected, click in the box next to the eye on the text layer to link the two together. Move them over to the right of the picture, so that the writing only just creeps onto the bridge section.

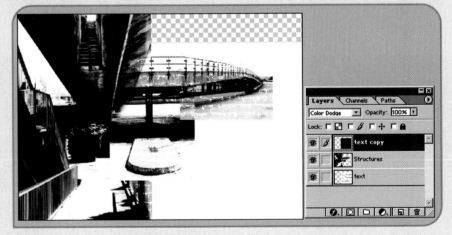

It's time for a bit of type. This will form part of the title of the piece, and give the viewer a kick-start into understanding what's going on in the image. Using the Eyedropper tool, select a dark color in the image, so that the text will be a good match. Now select the Type tool, and select a sans serif typeface (Arial, Helvetica, Gill sans, or Verdana will all work well). Set it at 50 point bold, and type the word "space" onto the image in lower case letters, placing it so that the "s" is half on top of a dark area.

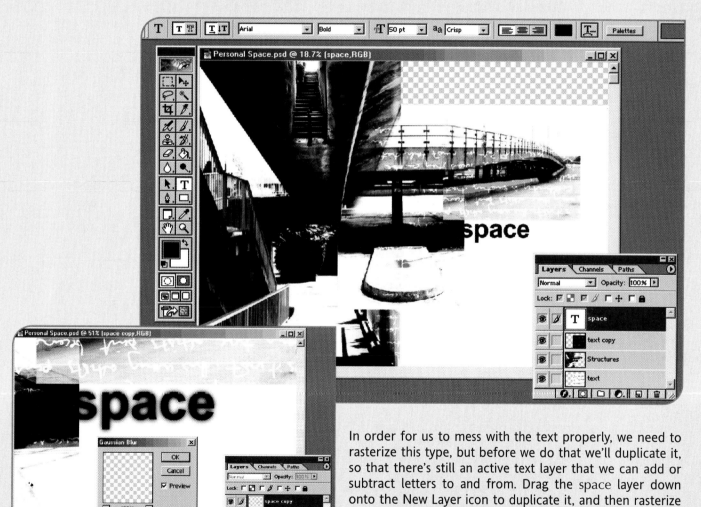

In order for us to mess with the text properly, we need to rasterize this type, but before we do that we'll duplicate it, so that there's still an active text layer that we can add or subtract letters to and from. Drag the space layer down onto the New Layer icon to duplicate it, and then rasterize the type on this new layer (Layer > Type > Rasterize). We're going to use a Gaussian blur filter on the text, so go to Filter > Blur > Gaussian Blur and set the radius to 10 pixels.

Personal Space

This will have the effect of giving the text a fuzzy edge, but as usual we can make it more interesting by experimenting with layer blending modes. Set the mode for this layer to Color Burn, and move it below the text copy layer. This should create a spidery halo around the type, because of the way the layer is interacting with the handwritten text layer.

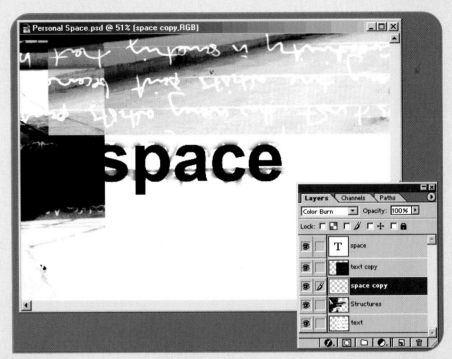

The next step is to add a human element to the piece by way of a scanned self-portrait, so bring in Portrait.jpg. This image has a level of distortion (due to the scanning process), and also has fairly flat coloring – but neither of these is going to cause major problems. Place the image to the bottom right area of the composition, and make sure its layer is above the others. Rename this layer Portrait, and set the layer blending mode to Hard Light.

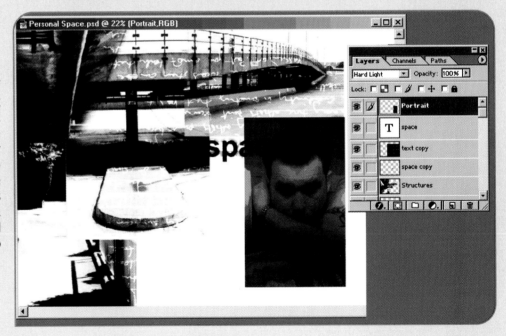

Duplicate the Portrait layer, and set the mode of the resulting layer to Color Burn. You'll notice that this darkens the portrait considerably, but dropping the opacity down to 30% should give just the right balance. We now need to merge the two portrait layers, again setting the resulting layer to Hard Light.

What we have now is a strong, high-contrast portrait that will act as a good base for the next stage. First, though, I'd like to change the coloring from red to blue-gray. Go to Layer > New Adjustment Layer > Hue/Saturation and check the Group With Previous Layer box (otherwise you'll alter the whole image).

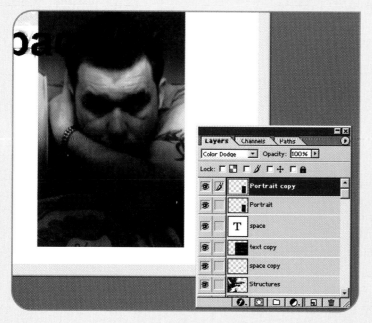

After you've clicked OK, open the Hue/Saturation dialog. Check the Colorize box, and move the Hue slider to 200 (this gives us the blue), the Saturation slider to 50 (this affects the color saturation and brightness), and leave the Lightness slider at 0. It's always a good idea to experiment with things like this as much as you can, because there are almost unending variations achievable with these sliders.

Now merge down the layer, duplicate it, and set the blending mode of the copy layer to Color Dodge (this just increases the light areas a fraction, giving them a lift).

Personal Space

The next stage is to create a mask and a bit of a frame for the portrait, and also to introduce some less tangible elements to the image, to contrast with the stark structures we've already introduced. This will also add to the idea of the image's theme. The viewer may consider that the title refers to the fact that I created this space, or that I'm hiding behind something while surrounded by this surreally structured world, or maybe that I'm claustrophobic or even agoraphobic. This is the beauty of this type of work: different minds will see different things.

Open up and bring in Mad_Pic.jpg, and name its layer Mad_Pic. I created this in Photoshop from a biro sketch, scanned in and painted up using the Brush tool at 30 pixels and 20% opacity. I also checked the Wet Edge box, which gives a more 'natural media' or 'non digital' look. The inspiration behind this was to create a deliberately distorted character, loosely based on me. I say "loosely" because we both have tattoos and short dark hair, but that's pretty much where the likeness ends!

Place the Mad_Pic layer over the self-portrait, set the layer blending mode to Hard Light, and drop its opacity down to 40%. To get the 'mask' effect to work well, though, the eyes (and preferably the nose too) need to be lined up on both images. This will require a bit of scaling, a bit of rotating, and just a little bit of repositioning. When using any of the options under the Edit > Transform menu, you can change from Rotate to Distort or Scale (for example) without having to apply the transformation, which saves a bit of time and hassle when working with something like this.

Once we've lined the layers up, they need linking so that they can be positioned and scaled together. With the Mad_Pic layer selected, click on the box next to the eye icon for *both* of the portrait layers on the Layers palette, and scale them up a bit and move them slightly higher in the image. Then, apply a layer mask to the Mad_Pic layer, so that we can remove some of the Mad_Pic illustration (particularly underneath the face), and achieve a better balance between the two images.

Once you've done this, I think it's time to remove the top and bottom from Portrait and Portrait copy, with the rectangular Marquee tool. If you drag out a selection, you can use that selection on any layer just by clicking in the Layers palette when the selection is active, so saving you from drawing it again and again. You can also move the selection with the Marquee tool, again saving time. So drag out a selection, and hit Delete.

Personal Space

At the moment, the portrait layers are a bit dark and overpowering, so if we drop the opacity on the Portrait layer down to about 66% (experiment with the percentages), it causes the 'mask' effect of the Mad_Pic layer to show more clearly. Finally, to tie this section in with the rest of the image, move the text copy layer to the top of the Layers palette, and then use a layer mask and a large brush (I used a 200-pixel brush at 5%) gradually to remove the contrast of the text over the face. I found that I had to go over the area several times, removing it and then bringing it back, to get just the right balance between the white text on the top and the black text underneath.

What we're going to do next is to bring in the "Personal" of the title, but before we can do that, we need somewhere to put it! Create a new layer named Orange Quadrangle (this will make sense, eventually!), and set the layer blending mode to (surprise) Hard Light. Then, using the polygonal Lasso tool, draw out what is effectively a distorted rectangle.

Now select the Paint Bucket tool, and while you're holding down the Alt key, move the cursor over to a suitable color. I used a selection from the Mad_Pic frame, just below the Space type. When you've found a color that you like, you can click the cursor on it (this will have changed to an Eyedropper tool when you pressed Alt), and then go over to your selection. Removing your finger from the Alt key, click the cursor (now returned to the usual Paint Bucket) in the selected area. It should fill with a nice red-orange. This may take a bit of trial and error because of the way the layers affect the colors, but if you select what looks like a light pink in the Foreground Color box, it should turn out fine. You can now deselect the area.

Personal Space

With that done, it's time for the type. Select the Type tool, and choose the same typeface as before, but set it to 40 point plain, instead of 50 point bold. For the color, I'm going to use a light blue-gray sampled from the car park in the background, using the same technique as I used for Space. The only other thing to remember here is to set the type layer to Hard Light.

At this stage, I want to bring in some dictionary scans to frame the portrait area further, and to add to the title. Open up `Personal_Scan.jpg` and, using the Lasso tool, select the definition of "personal". I chose not to include the actual word in my selection, because I didn't want to make things *too* obvious.

Copy and paste this selection into the main document, and place it to the top left of the portrait area, setting the layer blending mode to Hard Light.

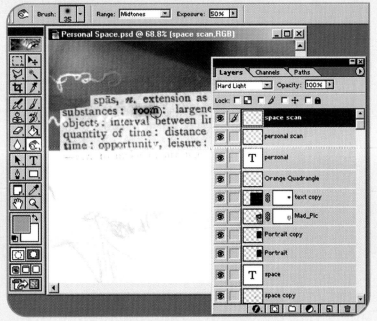

Open up `Space_Scan.jpg`, do the same to that one, and place it to the bottom right of the portrait area. Then, using the Burn tool with the Range set to Midtones at 50% exposure, and a brush size of 35 pixels, gradually stroke over a few select words on the two scanned dictionary layers. This is just to accentuate them slightly, and add a bit more interest and depth.

Personal Space

All that's needed now are the elements that bring the piece together, to add to the depth and interest of the final image, and draw the viewer's eye across to the portrait area more effectively. To tie in the colors, I'm going to use layer copies of Mad_Pic, distorted and placed across the image from the left.

The first step in this process is to duplicate the Mad_Pic layer and drag it over to the left-hand side of the image.

Then, use the distort facility (Edit > Transform > Distort) to bring the top right and bottom right corners towards the imaginary horizontal centerline. This will produce a shape similar to, though more exaggerated than, our Orange Quadrangle from earlier on.

Move this layer (Mad_Pic copy) over to the left a bit (so that it goes beyond the left line of the bridge) and down a fraction (so that the right end is overlaying the orange quadrangle). When this is in place, we need to duplicate it and then rotate it through 180 degrees (Edit > Transform > Rotate 180°) so that we can line them up nicely.

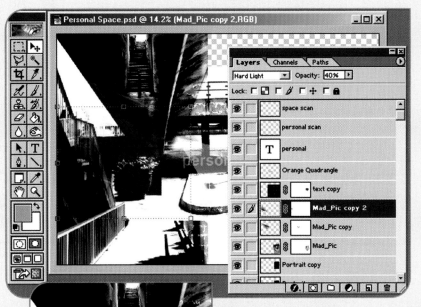

Drag the newest layer (Mad_Pic copy2) over to the left and down a bit, so that you leave a small gap between it and the previous one.

Duplicate Mad_Pic copy again, and move it down towards the bottom left of the image, leaving the same gap as before. Also duplicate Mad_Pic copy 2, and drag that right into the bottom left corner to complete the left section.

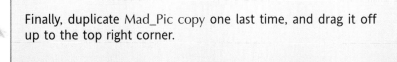

Finally, duplicate Mad_Pic copy one last time, and drag it off up to the top right corner.

Now that all the main elements are in place, I want to put a few horizontal lines straight across the middle of the image. Create a new layer named Lines and set it to Hard Light mode. Set the Line tool to a weight of 2 pixels, and holding down Shift to constrain the angle, drag a line across the middle of the page horizontally. Repeat this procedure another four times, so that you then have five lines in total (the spacing is up to you, but I like to keep the lines fairly tight). If you don't like the positioning, you can always move the layer up or down. Now move the Lines layer to just below the Portrait copy layer in the Layers palette, to integrate the lines into the image more effectively.

Right then. Here's one of those eleventh hour changes of mind that Photoshop lets you get away with! I don't think the type looks right. I think it's a bit too big and imposing, so I'm going to remove it, because I can! Off go the layers involved (Personal, Space, and Space copy), and in their place I will have a single, clean layer of type. Select the Type tool, and using the same typeface as before, type "*[personal]* **space**" in 20 point white text, as shown below.

And so here we have the finished article. With this image, I wanted to retain a clean photographic feel, albeit very abstracted, and I currently like the look that using the Hard Light layers gives to an image. I'm going through a phase at the moment where I don't want to distort things too much, and like to keep things filter-free if I can. This type of photographic treatment is currently quite popular in editorial pieces, especially in fashion/lifestyle/music magazines. It's a vibrant and edgy style that could find application almost anywhere, although it wouldn't be suitable for all magazines. Could you imagine *People's Friend* with this on the front?

It may have meandered a bit, but we got there in the end! Experimentation really is a key part of the process, and can't be over-stressed. With a program like Photoshop, you have to take chances, and (for as long as time permits) you have to have no fear for what might happen. Of course, there's almost always *something* in an image that I'd like to change, but you also have to know when to stop, when the balance is right, when to take advice from others who can view the piece objectively where you might not. The beauty of art, particularly digital art, is that it's constantly evolving. You should be able to extract something from everything you see, even if it's a mental note *not* to try it, because it clearly doesn't work for you!

For any number of reasons, the finished article can quite often be different from your original plans. You might go off on a tangent; you may find that changing the position and scale of certain elements improves things; or your idea may just suck when it gets on the screen. Anything can happen.

With this particular image, I found that changes were needed to get back the balance that had been lost through multiple points of focus, and off-putting use of type. The important thing is that you're able to rectify the problems when they do arise, even if it means accepting that you were actually a little lost during the creative process. In art, the only thing that should matter is the final image, not how it was created. That is for those of us that know, to create, and for those that don't, to wonder at.

[personal] space

belonging to a person : having the nature
or quality of a person : peculiar to a person or to his
private concerns : pertaining to the external appearance : done in person : relating to one's own self :
applied offensively to one's character : (*gram.*)
denoting the person.—*n.*

spās, *n.* extension as distinct from material
substances : room : largeness : distance between
objects : interval between lines or words in books :
quantity of time : distance between two points of
time : opportunity, leisure : a short time : interval.
—*v.t.* to make or arrange intervals between.—*ns.*

chapter 1

chapter 2

chapter 3

chapter 4

chapter 5

chapter 6

chapter 7

chapter 8

chapter 9

chapter 10

chapter 11

chapter 12

chapter 13

chapter 14

chapter 15

chapter 16

outro

"Photoshop is a tool... you can either use it, or abuse it."

Colin Smith
www.photoshopcafe.com

Photorealism

Oases in Thar Desert
An oasis lies in the Thar Desert, also called Great Indian Desert, in Rajasthan, India. This oasis provides desert villagers with water.
© Brian Vikander/CORBIS

Crawling on hands and feet, my lips swollen with thirst. The gritty sand feels like needles to my worn flesh. I pull my arms in agony; my body slowly slides forward a few inches. The desert sun is like a furnace to my burned head. I feel like I'm made of brick, not a drop of moisture in my body. Each breath is a gasp of pain as the dry, hot, rough air scrapes its way down my parched throat. Slowly, I slide to the top of another dune. My mind screams, "This is the last one, I cannot go on, but I don't want to die here!" Inspiration? What is it?

It's reaching the pinnacle of the sand dune in the desert and seeing a lush oasis spread before you, the waters sparkling in the sunlight with highlights dancing across the surface in the cool breeze, the sound of birds singing their songs from the treetops. Inspiration is the fuel for all creativity.

At times, we're each of us searching for our oasis of inspiration. Thanks to technology, the largest oasis of all is right at our fingertips: the World Wide Web.

Colin Smith

The Web is a fascinating place. I remember what it looked like in 1994, when a static image was considered hi-tech, and Microsoft was still to recognize its potential. At first, I wanted to ignore it, thinking it would go away – it seemed like such a fad at the time. It soon became apparent, though, that the WWW was here to stay, and so I – like other designers – reluctantly learned HTML, and complained about all the design limitations. Since then, the Web has evolved into an exciting, thriving medium. I was amazed that just three months after launching my own web site at www.photoshopcafe.com, I'd had visitors from 70 nations! We're now designing for a truly international audience.

tips, tricks, articles and shortcuts

PhotoshopCafe.com
THE FREE RESOURCE FOR PHOTOSHOP USERS
sponsors wanted - e-mail us today

PHOTOSHOPCAFE

home

tutorials

tips

actions

links

books

forum

e-mail

gallery

Bookmark this site. We are growing and just getting better!
Our content is constantly being updated.

Welcome to PhotoshopCafe

NEWS! I won the GURU Award for Illustration at the 2001 Photoshop World Convention

100% Photoshop

Check out my Camera, this image was created entirely in Photoshop. No scans, photos, 3rd Party plugins, 3d programs were used! See more stuff in the gallery

My buddy, Al Ward from Action-FX has interviewed me on his site. See it HERE!

Join our new mailing list!
Get cool Photoshop tips, tricks and announcements

Photorealism

The Web has had a tremendous effect on my design: it has enabled me to grow much faster as a designer by placing so much variety at my fingertips. I remember when I first saw sites by Anders Qvicker and Byron Rempel (a.k.a. Neofrog) and felt that I'd been taken to a whole new level – they raised the bar in my mind.

In turn, it's amazing just how much the Web has influenced traditional design. At the moment, for example, print and television are making heavy use of scan lines, grids, and interface shapes. Patterns and multi-layered images are everywhere. I think these elements are a great way to enhance a design. What people need to realize, though, is that these tricks don't constitute a 'design' in themselves – they're embellishments. Photoshop's layer effects and other one-click tricks can tempt us to try to impress people at the expense of the original message. If we put the latter first – if we build the basic shape, and then use the enhancements – we'll produce images that stand out from the crowd.

Most people know me for my realistic images of cameras, cell phones, and so forth – and it's some of the techniques that I use in creating such images that I'll be demonstrating later on. However, I do things like that mostly for fun – they come from experimentation, or just a desire to see how far I can push Photoshop. The side of my work that keeps me busy from day to day is graphic design. Whether designing a magazine cover, a web site, or an advertisement, I have a different challenge. I need to impact the emotions and spark a reaction in the viewer that's more than just curiosity over how the image was created.

In a perfect world, we'd always be in a perfect environment. I can't think of anything better than to be by the Waitahanui River in New Zealand. There's a big pool where the river sweeps around a bend, then suddenly fans out into a crystal clear sheet of water. The overhanging trees cause a trickling sound as the branches bounce on the breeze and skim the surface, and there's an old wooden arch bridge that completes this scene of tranquility. It's the most peaceful place I've ever seen. Unfortunately, of course, we can't be there all the time. In the real world, the sound of trickling water is replaced with the noise of a busy office. The ringing of telephones and the clatter of keyboards replace the singing of birds; the smell of coffee replaces the scent of the summer jasmine, and the only breeze around comes from the air conditioning!

The difference between a hobby artist and a production artist is that as hobbyists, we have the luxury of being creative only when the mood takes us – when we're in that perfect environment and we feel inspired. Working in a busy office with deadlines and pressure can easily eat away at one's creativity, but as production artists we have to figure out how to jump-start it. For example, I really like to look through magazines and books until I feel the desire to create swell up inside me. There's something about great work: when I see something that's really clever, it inspires me to do something clever. When I see something detailed and intricate, I want to go and build an image that's detailed too.

What is it about looking at other people's work that causes inspiration? It's always an education to see how other people tackle a design problem – how they combine color and form to come up with a solution. It's good to look at an image and ask yourself some questions: "Why do I like this?", "What does it say?", "How would I say the same thing in a different way?", "What does the combination of color tell me?", "The mood: is it serious, humorous, dark, or light?" Asking these kinds of questions helps me to come up with my own ideas.

Photorealism

Take, for example, this handbill for *Cherry Moon*. I picked it up in Brussels, and it totally inspired my new web page design. What grabbed me about it was the feel: it says hi-tech and hip. The colors – blue and orange – are opposites on the color wheel; cool and warm at the same time. The thumbnails are a classic 'broken rule': traditionally, if a face was too orange, the pressman would freak! The out-of-focus blurs imply movement and activity, while the simple square fonts give a feel like a song list on an album. It's perfect for a dance club.

If you point your browser toward my web page, or take a look at my business card, you might be able to see how I've taken inspiration from the handbill and created something new. I've adapted certain elements, and then given them a different message. I used the cogs to imply the software and the artist working together. I took the motion and applied it to the type and the buttons. I made an original production of my own as a result of seeing and being inspired by someone else's work. And, especially when I'm working rather than playing, that's the kind of thing I do all the time.

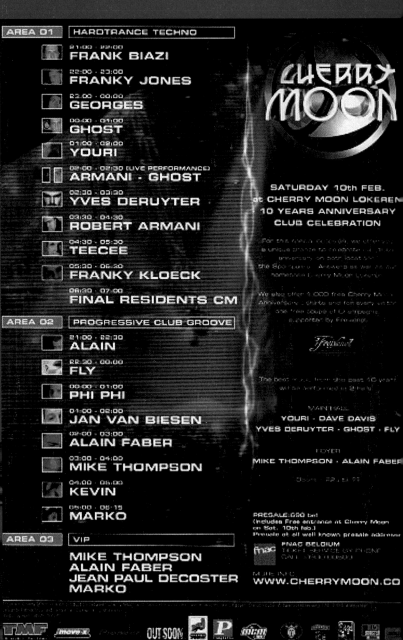

Like music, images have the almost magical ability to translate us through time and distance. Listen to a song you haven't heard in years, and there you are: all the memories come flooding back as if it were yesterday. Look at your photo album. A lot of the time, I can still remember what I was feeling when I took certain pictures. Sometimes, I think of famous photographs like the victory at Iwo Jima, or the man standing in front of the tank at Tiananmen Square. These are powerful images that jump-start the imagination, affect the emotions, and don't even need captions.

For about five years, from the time when I began as the designer for a monthly magazine called Voice, I had the privilege to be mentored by a very experienced artist and designer, Dr Jerry Jensen. By then, he'd been a designer for over 50 years, and produced many great pieces. He told me stories about how people would call him and beg to sit and watch him work. They just wanted to see how he did it. I recall him saying, while pointing to his head, "It's pointless watching me work; everything is going on in here, where they can't see it."

Dr Jensen taught me an important lesson. Back then I would put something into a design just because I thought it looked cool. He would ask me, "What does it say? How does the picture strengthen the message?" He taught me the importance of an image portraying a message – a picture should do more than just look good. I learned the art of functionality without sacrificing the 'coolness factor' – the hook in an image that catches the eye and causes the observer to say, "Wow!" More importantly, I learned the art of keeping the 'coolness factor' without sacrificing the message. For an example of this effect in action, I really love the old wartime propaganda posters. Everyone knows James Montgomery Flagg's "I want you" poster featuring Uncle Sam, but another of my favorites is the British one that warns, "Don't forget that walls have ears! Careless talk costs lives". They have a strong hook that serves to reinforce the message they convey.

Inspiration doesn't only come from still images, though. I remember when *Star Wars* was first released. The attention to detail, and the mood it created, were revelations. After watching the movie, people felt like they'd actually visited a faraway land and participated in an adventure. That's exactly what art should do. It can affect your imagination in such a way as to transport you to a different world.

More recently, *The Matrix* was another milestone. I just loved what they did with movement, as it seems did others. Many producers have since copied the effect of massive speed that's suddenly suspended in time to a lazy meander. If sudden stillness can be striking in a moving image, though, so too is the impression of movement in a still one. Just look at the way hair appears to blow in the wind here: the way it flows, waves, and the ends whip around is so dramatic. Watching the way water flows down a river, or wheat blowing in the wind, or waves breaking against the shore, are all sources of inspiration for me. Each explosion of surf is unique; each pattern in the wheat as the wind pushes golden waves of grain is a true original.

I simply don't recall the first time I drew a picture, or picked up a crayon – although the pencil was usually my weapon of choice. As a child, I would look at things from different angles, and be fascinated at the way light and shadows interact with objects. I think these are the most important considerations when creating believable images: light and shadow give dimension, positioning, and scale. That's probably why, as an artist, realistic works have always fascinated me. While I certainly appreciate the work of the Impressionists – the movement, color, and mood – it's been the likes of John Constable (*The Cornfield*, for example) that have made me look and say, "How do they do that?"

When I was young, I loved to build models and dioramas. I remember spending months on a little World War II desert scene. I built the huts out of matchsticks, and even went as far as making little maps for the walls. Each figure was painstakingly painted, right down to the color of the eyes. When I built the vehicles, I constructed them just as if I were building the real thing. I prepared the body and the chassis; I built the engine, piece by piece, painting each part; and then finally I pulled all the parts together and 'planted' the engine, as if it was a real vehicle.

I still transfer this method to my images today. I have to be patient and construct each part as if it were an image in its own right, but always keep the end result in mind. If anyone were to see my uncompleted work, they'd wonder where I was going with it. Then all of a sudden comes assembly time, and the image comes together as the separate parts unite into the whole. I have a directory of images on my hard drive that looks like a junkyard of bits and pieces. I approach many design projects like I'm building something in the real world.

Photorealism

It's truly amazing what you can come up with, just messing about. Some of my best Photoshop techniques have come out of 'playtime', and it's healthy for an artist to do that from time to time. Just start with a blank canvas and throw stuff at it, not trying to create anything in particular. This was born of a digital playtime, when I just started running filters and stuff to see how they would interact. The trick, though, is not to overdo it, especially if you plan on doing radical manipulation of an image. Less is more, particularly when it comes to filters and digital images. If you go nuts and apply everything full force, you'll just end up with big dark blob that says, "Too much"

Most of the things I do, I could do four or five different ways. The trick is to use the right technique for the result you're looking for – and to do that, you need to be thinking several steps ahead. For example, on the drawing of my watch, while I was making the parts for the face, I had to envision how they would fit into the overall illustration, and what they would look like when applied in a circumference around the face. That's why I added the chrome shading after I wrapped them in a circle, otherwise the light source would have looked wrong.

Microscopic

Colin Smith

My first real attempt at creating a realistic environment entirely in Photoshop was Alien Station. Looking at it now, there is a lot I would do differently, but I gave a lot of attention to the lighting and reflections. My best known piece, 100% Photoshop, I had wanted to do for a long time, but I didn't want to attempt it until my skills were at a level where I could make it convincingly real. I presented myself with the challenge of drawing my camera entirely in Photoshop, without the use of any third party plug-ins or scans – just Photoshop straight out of the box – and making it as realistic as possible. In the event, it won me a Guru Award at the Photoshop World Convention in L.A., and I've received a flood of e-mails asking how I did it. In the following tutorial, I'm going to share some of those techniques with you.

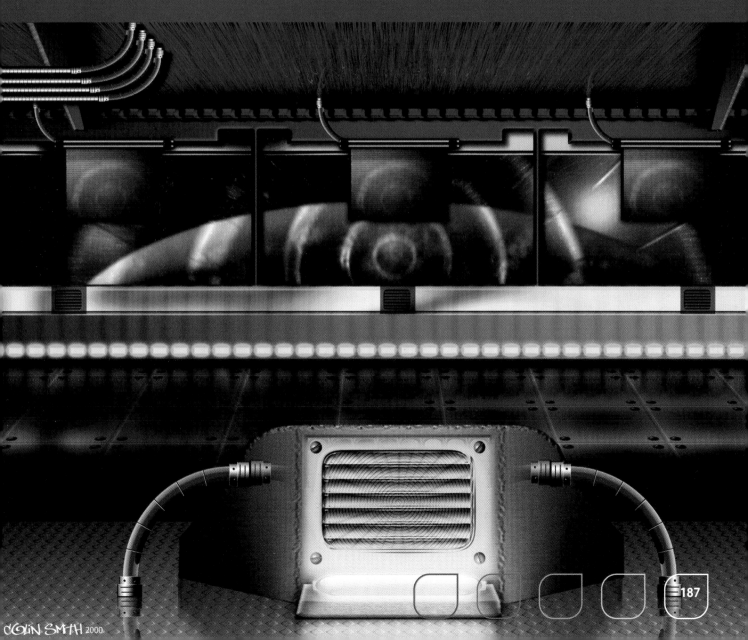

COLIN SMITH 2000

187

Photorealism

In this tutorial, I'm going to teach you some of the techniques that I use to create my photorealistic images. Because space is limited, my philosophy is going to be like the age-old saying: "Give a man a fish, and you feed him for a meal; teach him to fish, and you feed him for a lifetime". My goal is not so much to teach you how to complete an image; rather I want to show you the techniques that you can use to create your own images. Even more than that, hopefully I can help you to think about what's happening, and come up with some techniques of your own.

Art has a lot to do with illusion. It's not really what you do; it's what the viewer sees that's important. A prime example of this is process printing. Pretty much everything printed in the four-color process is fooling the viewer. That isn't *really* a picture of a person in full color. It's actually just a bunch of dots in a variety of different sizes and patterns, in cyan, yellow, magenta, and black. How you perceive those dots is down to the way your mind works. In a similar kind of way, a lot of the techniques that I use in Photoshop are designed to simulate realism, and to fool the viewer into seeing three dimensions where only two exist. A prime example of this is the camera lens that we'll be examining in the first part of this tutorial.

The Camera Lens

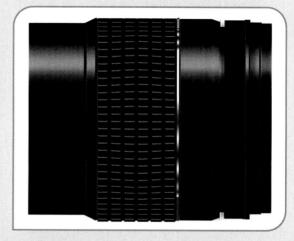

It would take several chapters for me to show you every technique involved in this project, so I've decided to concentrate on the main elements: the lens, and the body. My goal is to provide you with enough insight into my working procedure that you can take this tutorial and apply it to your own working style, and create a whole host of new images.

In this part of the tutorial then, we're going to explore the techniques necessary for reproducing a lifelike, cylindrical object: the lens of my Canon Rebel 2000 camera. As you'll soon see, the most important methods in play here involve the creation and use of gradients, with just a little pattern manipulation thrown in for good measure.

Let's start with the barrel of the lens. The challenge here was that the metal is most certainly *not* smooth and shiny – I had to create a 'dull' shine. In the real world, all objects reflect light. The smoother an object is, the more light it reflects. I try to deal with this in my images by defining 'levels' of reflectivity for different materials. The first level, for example, is when there's minor reflection, and only soft highlights are given off – you might see this with rubber, or rough stone. At the second level, there will be a bright white highlight, and perhaps the implication of some other colors – this is the kind of effect you get from plastics, or aluminum. At the third level, which I call 'full reflectivity', there will be identifiable images reflected – such as you'd see in a mirror, glass, water, or polished chrome. If we want to produce realistic artwork, we have to keep things like this in mind at all times.

The barrel falls between the first two levels, and the important point here is that the surface isn't shiny enough to produce a pure white highlight, so we're going to use two shades of gray to create the illusion of a matt surface. With that decided, let's see how to go about doing it. You can begin by creating a new document that's at least 1200 pixels wide by 800 high, in RGB mode, with a transparent background.

To create the correct highlights for the surface of the barrel, we'll have to make a new, customized gradient. Press G to select the Gradient tool (if this selects the Paint Bucket tool, press Shift+G). The gradient options will now appear in the toolbar:

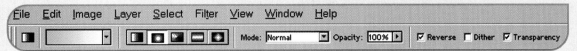

Click your mouse in the middle of the Gradient window to open the Gradient Editor. We're going to add some gray and black color stops to the gradient (remember, white would be too harsh for the plastic barrel), and then move the color stops to get the matt effect we're after.

So, click anywhere just below the gradient to add a color stop, and then click on Color at the bottom-left of the dialog to change it to a dark gray. Then add three more stops – two black, and one gray – but make the latter a lighter gray than the previous one. Position the two gray color stops between the black ones.

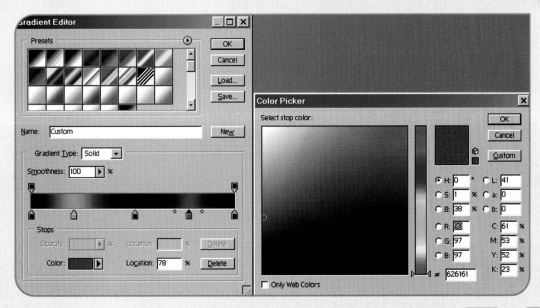

Photorealism

(To remove a color stop, just click on it, and drag it off the gradient – it will be deleted. To duplicate a color stop, hold down the Alt key, and drag to a new location. This is a *big* timesaver when you're creating complex gradients.)

When you click on a color stop, diamonds appear on either side. These are the color midpoints, which you can slide in or out to adjust the 'spread' of the color. You can see where I placed them in the screenshot, but in general you'll need to experiment to get the effect you want. Once you're happy with it, name this new gradient camera lens, and click New and OK. We now have our gradient for the lens stored in the Gradient library and ready for use. That means we can begin to create the lens barrel.

On your new document, draw a rectangle with the Marquee tool. Make it 1200 pixels by 800 high; this will be the basis of our lens. Select the Gradient tool and choose the Linear and Reverse settings, as shown in the screenshot below. Also, make sure that the new gradient we created is active!

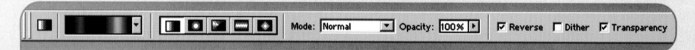

Now we're going to apply our custom gradient to the rectangle, to create a matt effect. The direction of the gradient is determined by a line that you draw inside a selected object, so click and drag the Gradient tool from the bottom to the top of the rectangle. If you hold down the Shift key as you do so, this will ensure that the gradient is perfectly vertical. Release the mouse button, and the rectangle should look more like a cylinder. (You may have to try this operation a few times, with different starting and ending points, before you get exactly the effect you want.)

So. It's looking pretty good so far – that 'dull shine' I was talking about is working – but it's still lacking something: a little texture. To give the lens that extra bit of realism, we'll add a small amount of noise. It's touches like these that make the difference between average images, and great images!

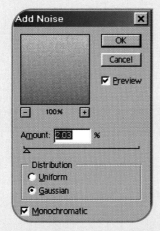

Go to Filters > Noise > Add Noise, and add just a small amount – don't overdo it. As soon as you see a slight change in the preview, that's enough.

The next stage is to 'break' the rectangle into three pieces, to produce the different sections of the lens. Duplicate the rectangle layer twice, by selecting the layer and clicking Ctrl+J. Then, resize each rectangle using the Free Transform tool (Ctrl+T), and use the scale feature by dragging on the resize handles (the eight little squares around the box). Do this to all three sections, until the image resembles the picture here.

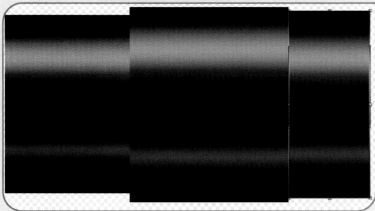

What about the beveled sections of the lens? Well, once again, duplicate a layer with one of the sections on it, and use the Free Transform tool to size the section until it's the height of the barrel's central piece, but very thin. Right-click in this selection, and a pop-up menu will open; choose Perspective from it. Now, click on the top-left handle, and drag downwards until the corner lines up with the narrower section of the barrel. Finally, press Enter to apply the transformation. The intended result can be seen below as two sections, joined by an angled piece. Note that the blends match perfectly – that's a little trick that happens as a result of *duplicating* the sections, rather than creating new ones.

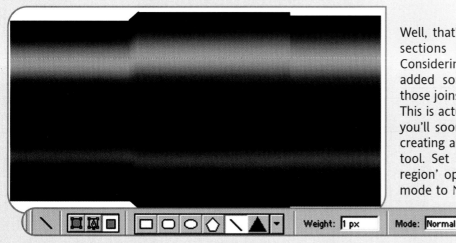

Well, that's not bad, but the 'joins' between the sections don't look very realistic, do they? Considering the final image, you can see that I've added some 'three-dimensional' grooves along those joins, and we're going to look at those next. This is actually a remarkably simple procedure, as you'll soon see. You can start the ball rolling by creating another new layer and selecting the Line tool. Set up the line as shown, with the 'filled region' option selected. You should also set the mode to Normal, and the weight to 1 pixel.

Press the D key to set the default foreground and background colors (black and white). Then, holding down the Shift key, click at the top of the barrel and drag down until the line meets the bottom. To add the little 3D touch, duplicate the line layer, and make this new line white by pressing Ctrl+I. On doing this, the color of the black line is inverted – in other words, it turns white.

Press the right cursor key twice to nudge the white line over a little, and change the Layer Blending Mode to Overlay. You now have a pretty good groove to separate the sections. The Overlay mode changes the way that white reacts with black, and causes a softer and more realistic blend between the line and the gradient. I encourage you to experiment a lot with the layer blending modes – they're one of the keys to getting great images.

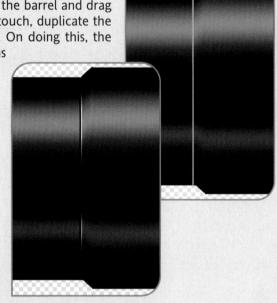

Believe it or not, using the different techniques that we've learned so far, you already know almost enough to create the completed lens I showed you at the start of the tutorial. The part you're probably wondering about, though, is the rubber grip that adds so much texture and detail to the image – but as you'll see, the solution is actually quite simple. I could have made it more complex, but why? As I said before, it's the illusion we are after.

The trick to the grip is Photoshop's patterns feature, which I use a lot – patterns are a really good way of saving time when you're using repeating elements. Not only that, but they also bring a cleaner sense of uniformity. Often, you could use Photoshop's alignment and distribution tools to do the same thing, but it would take a lot longer, and add so many extra layers. And on a personal note, another great thing about patterns is that they help me to avoid doing math – I used to get kicked out of math class when I was in school for doodling, but I guess it paid off in the end!

To kick things off, make a new document that's 25 pixels high by 35 wide. Again, choose RGB mode, and make the background transparent. Press the D key to reset the default foreground and background colors, and then Alt+Backspace to fill the rectangle with black.

The 'pimples' on the grip need to have equal spacing between them, so press Ctrl+T to enter Free Transform mode. Then, hold down the Alt and Shift keys (causing the transformation to happen from the center, and the proportions to remain the same), and drag from any of the corners toward the center, just a little bit. (For more freedom of movement, it helps to turn off the Snap feature.) The 'gap' you create here will be exactly half the space between the shapes.

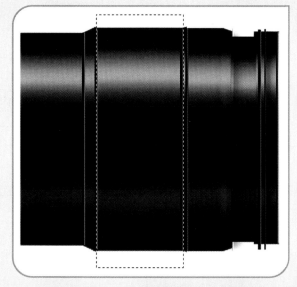

Next, press Ctrl+A to select the entire document, and then choose Edit > Define Pattern to save this pattern ready for use. Now let's get a grip on things! The image of the lens you can see to the left is a picture I prepared earlier, but it should be fairly clear to see how it's developed from the things you've already seen. (If you want to, you can extract it from the data in `lens.psd` on the CD.) On this document, create a new layer, and use the Rectangular Marquee tool to draw a rectangle around the area we want the grip to fill. Make it a little taller than we might at first seem to need; the reason for this will be obvious soon.

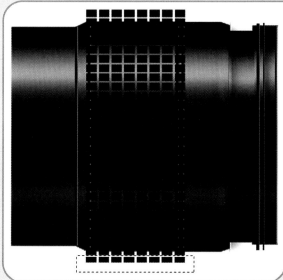

Open the Fill dialog box, set it for a Pattern fill, select our new pattern, and press OK. If there are any stray areas that contain portions of the pattern, trim them off by making a selection around them, and pressing Delete. Don't worry about perfect sizing; we can fix that later.

Photorealism

We now want to add some 'feel' to the pimples, and the quickest and easiest way is to add a Layer style. At the bottom of the Layers palette, click on the little f, and select Bevel and Emboss. For this effect, the important part is that we should use the Chisel Hard setting, which will give us a nice, sharp edge. Adjust the bevel size to your taste, and also add a drop shadow, for which the default settings should work fine.

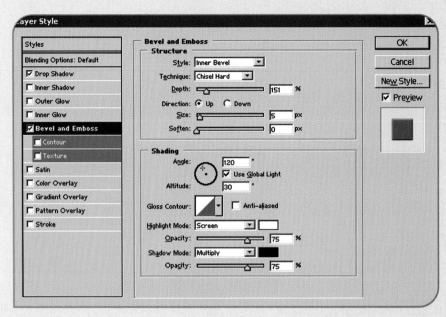

It's starting to take shape now, but what about that 'wraparound' look? This is so simple, it's almost cheating. Observe a real world object that wraps around a cylinder: what's the outstanding feature? As it gets nearer the edges, it looks narrower. In Photoshop, there are at least two ways of achieving this illusion, and I'll show you both of them here. The first one is quicker and works better on this image, but it doesn't work on asymmetrical objects. The second is more complicated, but it *will* work if you're ever dealing with images that don't have a perfectly rounded or symmetrical cross section.

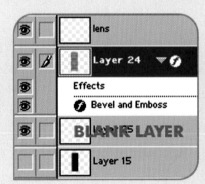

Whichever way we decide to proceed, the first thing we need to do is apply the Layer styles so that the beveling will be scaled too, to produce a more realistic result. In other words, we want to make the Layer styles a part of the image itself, rather than simply being 'attached' to it. The easy way to do this is to create a new layer, and move it directly under our 'grip' layer.

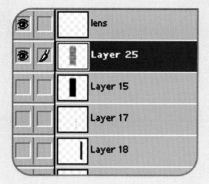

Click on the grip layer in the Layers palette, and press Ctrl+E to merge it with the layer directly beneath it. Now we can distort the image with the Layer style.

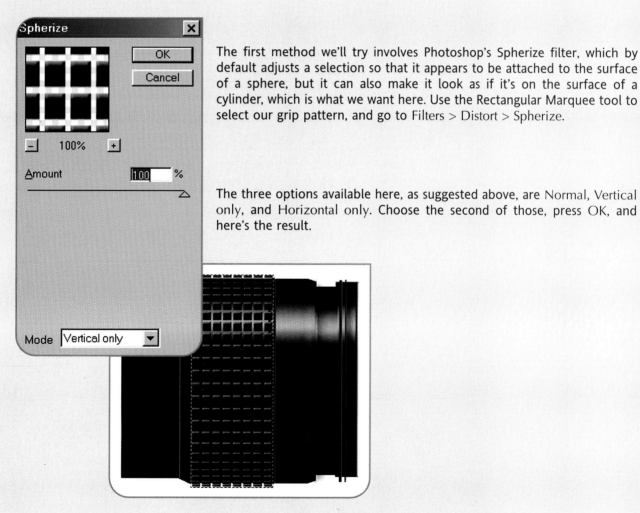

The first method we'll try involves Photoshop's Spherize filter, which by default adjusts a selection so that it appears to be attached to the surface of a sphere, but it can also make it look as if it's on the surface of a cylinder, which is what we want here. Use the Rectangular Marquee tool to select our grip pattern, and go to Filters > Distort > Spherize.

The three options available here, as suggested above, are Normal, Vertical only, and Horizontal only. Choose the second of those, press OK, and here's the result.

The second method is more 'hands-on' and takes longer, but it does give you the ability to 'wrap' around asymmetrical surfaces. Start by drawing a selection around just the top third of the pattern, being careful not to cut through any squares. Using a Free Transform, pull the top center handle down just a little. Then, draw another selection around the top half of the area you just adjusted, Free Transform again, and pull it down another fraction.

Follow the same procedure with the bottom third of the image, and you should come out with something that looks like this. Don't worry that the pattern probably isn't well aligned with the rest of the lens; we'll attend to that in a moment.

No matter which way you've gone about things so far, go into Free Transform mode (again), this time with the entire layer. Now you can position and resize your grip to fit the lens exactly, making sure that the pimples extend just beyond the edges.

For the finishing touches, we need to make a background for the grip, so create a new layer containing a solid, black rectangle, and drag it behind the pattern layer. Finally, select the pattern layer again, choose Filter > Distort > Pinch, and execute it with a setting of -5. The result of the pinch filter is like someone pulling on a piece of string attached to the center, giving a fatter, more rounded appearance to the image.

To complete our work on the lens, we just need to add the chrome ring that runs around it. As usual, the process begins with the creation of another new layer, which this time should contain a thin rectangle. Once again, select the Gradient tool, this time choosing the preset called Copper. Holding down the Shift key, drag from the top to the bottom.

The color variation in this gradient is nice, but we need to remove the copper color, so press Ctrl+U and desaturate the image – this will take out the color without affecting the grayscale. Now, to get the chrome effect, go to Image > Adjust > Curves and make a curve similar to the one in the next screenshot. Press OK.

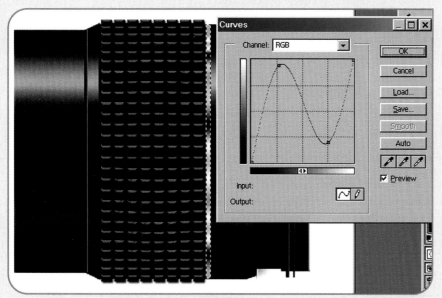

Now, holding down the Alt key, go to the Curves dialog again. By doing this, you retain the previous settings, and they get applied for a second time. Press OK, and presto: chrome. Curves are the most advanced tonal control available in Photoshop; by default, the tonal distribution of an image is shown by a smooth line, running from the bottom left to the top right. By making radical adjustments to the curve, we create much higher contrasts than are natural. These create color 'spikes' that give the illusion of chrome. By making the effect less defined, we could simulate aluminum, or other types of metal. Experiment, and remember that the shinier the surface you're after, the more radical the curve you'll need.

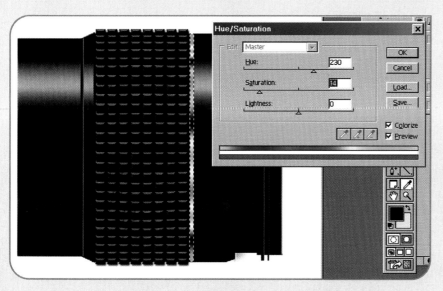

The last thing we need is just a touch of color, so press Ctrl+U again to open up the Hue/Saturation box. Click on Colorize to make the ring monochrome, and then slide the Hue slider until the image turns blue, and the Saturation slider to the left until just a hint of blue remains.

You can use this technique to add a chrome effect to anything at all, from shapes to text. The Hue/Saturation box is an incredibly useful tool, great for adding color, and for enhancing and changing the color of images, and it's worth just a little more explanation here before we go on.

Hue affects the actual color of an image, while saturation affects the *amount* of color – more saturation means more color. If you find yourself working with older pictures, the color often fades, but just pushing the saturation up some can make it look brand new again. Don't use too much, though, or your images will begin to appear artificial. When I was first learning Photoshop, I upped the saturation of some pictures of famous personalities for a convention ad in a magazine. I was horrified when the magazine came back from the printers and it looked like the men were wearing makeup and lipstick! I laugh about it now, but I didn't then – I'm just glad none of them saw the ad!

As for the other options available, lightness does exactly what it says it does, although I tend not to touch it here – levels (Image > Adjust > Levels) are better for adjusting brightness and darkness. Colorize, on the other hand, you've already seen in action, and I make no apology for using it a lot in my images. It's great for metal effects and on photos, or simply for colorizing a grayscale image.

The Camera Body

Now we have the lens, but what about the body of the camera? Once again, I can't hope to guide you through the whole thing, step-by-step, but I will show you the technique for the creation of one of its parts. After that, if you want to continue the image for yourself, it's just a matter of adapting the technique for the rest of the body.

In general, I like to compose my images in four stages. First, I create the rough shape; at this early stage, I'm only concerned with the proportions and positioning. Next, I add the detail, carving out the right shapes, adding dimension and surface texture, etc. Then, on the third pass, I add all the fine detail – little things like screws, fittings, contours on knobs, that kind of thing. Finally, I add the 'atmosphere' – shadowing, highlights, reflections, and any other touches necessary for total realism.

Putting aside for a moment the fact that we've already constructed the lens, let's look at the first stage. I put all the different parts on separate layers, and colored them different shades of gray for ease of identification. (The color is not at all important; I'm not building much more than a template at this stage.) Take your time with this; everything else will be built from it, so make sure that you have a strong foundation.

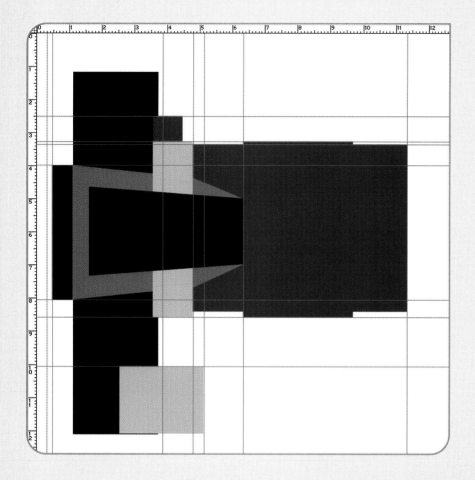

Essentially, this was just done by drawing boxes and using the Polygon Lasso tool, although there are a few neat tricks that you can use to make things easier. Whenever you want to constrain a shape to a circle or a square, or to rotate and draw in 45-degree increments, hold down the Shift key. Also, if you press Space while making a selection, you'll be able to move all of it – this is very useful for lining up circles or lines. Finally, if you hold down the Alt key, you'll be drawing from the center of the selection.

(Of course, it would also be possible to draw a basic shape like this in a vector program like Illustrator, FreeHand, or CorelDraw, and then import it to Photoshop. If you ever do this, though, remember to export each layer separately, so that you can manipulate them individually. It's amazing what you can do to a vector illustration in Photoshop!)

Photorealism

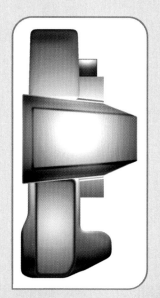

In the remainder of this chapter, I'm going to show you how I turned the block drawing you saw previously into the shiny, curvy thing you can see here. If you were ever scared by the thought of using Photoshop's Channels feature, this is your chance to learn how to master it!

The three things we're going to do are: get the shape right and make the rounded corners and curves; produce the 3D look using channels; and make the whole thing look as though it's made of aluminum. To start that process off, open the image `camera1.psd` from the accompanying CD, and hide all the layers except for 1 and 6.

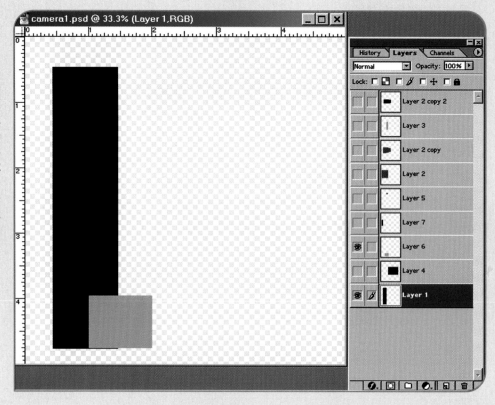

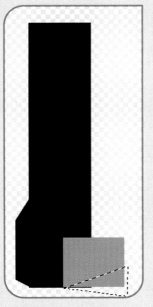

Since these two shapes are going to be joined up to make the main body of the camera, we're going to combine the two layers together. With Layer 1 active, click the box directly to the left of Layer 6, and a little 'chain' icon should appear to indicate that the layers are linked. Click on the Layers palette's menu, and select Merge Linked. The two layers have now been joined in holy matrimony and become one. Don't worry about the colors!

With the Polygon Lasso tool selected (this tool is great for drawing many-sided shapes with straight lines), draw in the little pieces that will be added to the shape. (Just click and click again in a different place; a straight line will join the two points you clicked. When you go back to the point of origin, a little circle will appear indicating that you are at the beginning.) Use Alt+Backspace to fill with any color; I used black here.

You can also use the Polygon Lasso tool to remove unwanted parts by making a selection around them and pressing Delete or Backspace.

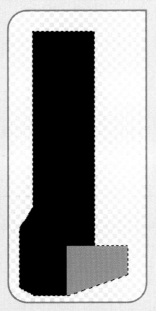

Is everything going well so far? Well, this is where we'll make it all look nice, with rounded corners. Click on the Layer 1 thumbnail while holding down the Ctrl key. This will load the whole layer as a selection.

Photorealism

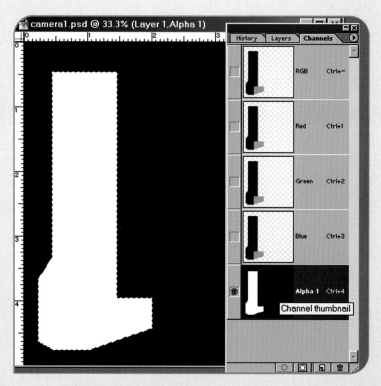

Open the Channels palette, and click on the Create new channel icon at the bottom (it's the third from the left; the page with the upturned corner). You've created an alpha channel, and you can click on it to activate it.

Channels are where all the color information is stored. Since this image is in RGB mode, there's a separate channel for each color. Mix the colors together, and you get your nice colored images.

Alpha channels, however, don't print; they're just places where we can store information to do cool things and get special effects – such as the one we're about to generate. Turn off the selection by pressing Ctrl+D, and then go to Filters > Blur > Gaussian Blur. You'll really need to eyeball this one, but adjust the radius of the blur until the edges look nice and soft. It may help to squint at the screen (seriously!). You should have something like this:

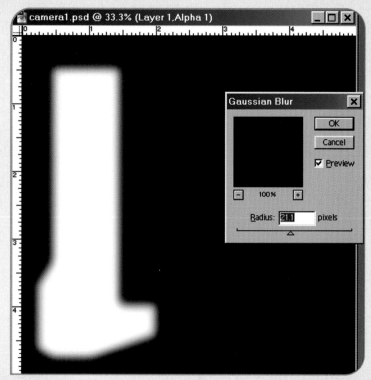

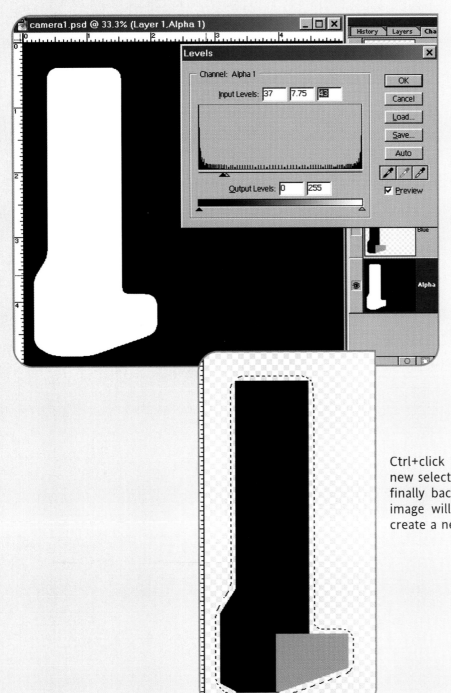

We now have our shape all soft and messed up – but how does that help us? It's time for another trick: open the Levels box with Ctrl+L, and pull the left slider to the right, just a little. Then, slide the middle one all the way into it, and do the same with the right one. Notice how clean the edges are now, and that our corners are neatly rounded. Just right!

Ctrl+click in the channel thumbnail to load our new selection, then click on the RGB channel, and finally back on the Layers palette, and the main image will be visible again. Without deselecting, create a new layer.

203

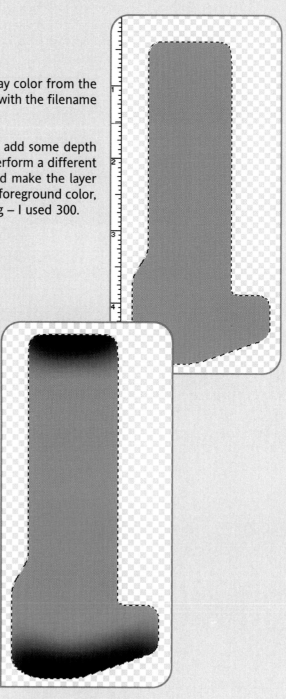

Finally, to make the finished shape, select a nice mid-gray color from the Color picker and fill the selection with it. Save it to disk with the filename `shape.psd`.

Now we're ready for stage two, in which we're going to add some depth to the image. For this, we can use channels again, and perform a different trick. If it isn't already, open that file you just made, and make the layer containing our curvy shape active. Selecting black as the foreground color, activate the Airbrush tool and give it a large, soft setting – I used 300.

Lightly spray some shadows at the top and bottom of the shape. We need a little more curvature in these places, and as you'll soon see, the shadows you draw now will determine how they look. While you're airbrushing, keep in mind that the grayscale will affect the 'depth' of the image: the whiter it is, the higher it will be. Think of 50% gray as being level – anything darker will be depressed, and anything brighter will be protruding. When you're done, press Ctrl+C to copy the selection to the clipboard.

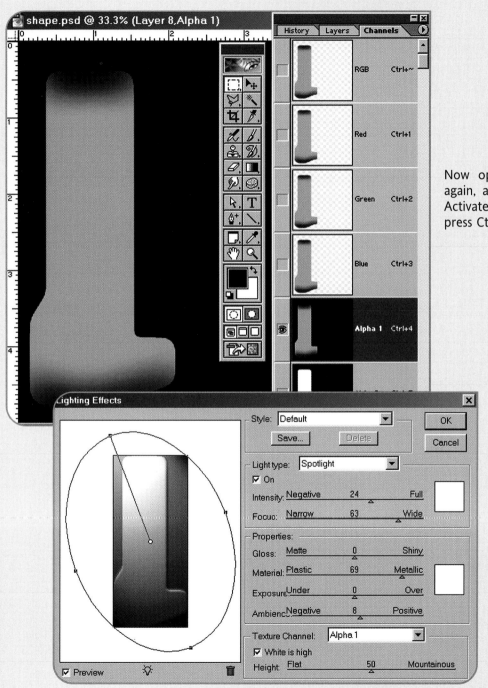

Now open the Channels palette once again, and create another new channel. Activate the channel by clicking on it, and press Ctrl+V to paste our image into it.

We're going to create a texture map, so deselect, and choose Filters > Blur > Gaussian Blur again, this time giving it a setting of about 5. As before, click on the RGB channel, and then back to the last layer we were working on. Ctrl+click on the thumbnail to activate the selection, and then go to Filters > Render > Lighting Effects, entering the settings shown here.

(The Texture Channel you use here will be called Alpha 2, if you used Alpha 1 to create the shape earlier on in the tutorial.)

Notice how the changes you make in this dialog affect the texture of the image? Press OK, and your shape will take on a 3D appearance.

At this stage, we could be satisfied with the image, but I think we need to clean it up a bit more. If you look closely, the gradient contains some abrupt changes in tone, but we can smooth those out with a two-step fix. First, go to Filters > Noise > Add Noise, and use a setting of just 1 pixel. Second, add a Gaussian Blur with a 1.2 pixel radius. See how nice and soft the gradients are now?

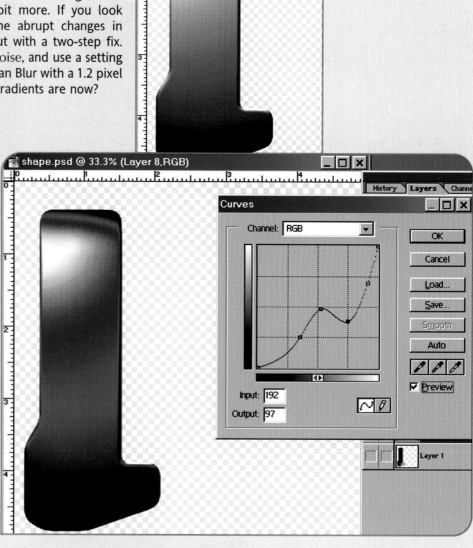

We have a pretty good shape, but it still needs a bit of sprucing up to make it look more like real metal. Let's go to stage three of my list of things to do. You'll no doubt remember how we did the chrome before, but since aluminum is not as reflective as that, we'll need to be more subtle. Go to Image > Adjust > Curves, and give it a setting something like this:

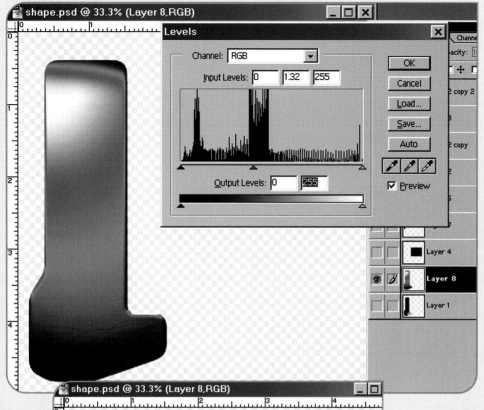

Press Shift+Ctrl+U to desaturate the layer, effectively removing the pink color cast. Then open the Levels box, and slide the midtones over just a little, to get a better looking metal. There... much more like it!

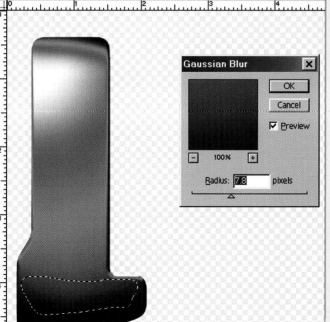

We really are almost done now! We just have a little blemish left over from the lighting effects – because only 256 levels of gray are used, the transitions can be a bit rough at times. So, with the Lasso tool, make a selection around the affected area. Then, go to Select > Feather, and give it a setting of 10. The feather will create a soft transition, so we don't create a whole new problem.

Now to remove the wrinkle, with yet another Gaussian blur. This time, just tweak the radius until the wrinkle is gone. Don't you wish that cosmetic surgery were this easy? Click OK, and just like magic...

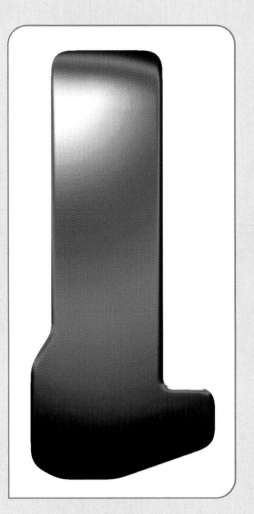

At long last, we have our finished section. I think this one is actually cleaner than the one I used on my original image!

Congratulations! You've just learned how to create realistic shapes with a three-dimensional feel. You can apply this new technique to all kinds of images and text, and watch your images come alive like never before.

If you wish, you can repeat these steps for all the different sections of the camera. Alternatively, you can take the techniques away and work on an even greater image of your own. When you've finished your image, the last thing you'll want to do is to add a soft drop-shadow using the Layer styles – these do a lot to add further realism to your images.

Don't be overwhelmed by the complexity of a subject. Like a lot of my work, this image is just constructed out of a lot of small parts that I put together later on. By breaking the task down, it becomes a much less frightening proposition.

The last thing I want to say is this: experiment, experiment, experiment. And when you stumble on something new, share it with the world. Isn't that what art is all about? Why create something if you don't share it with others?

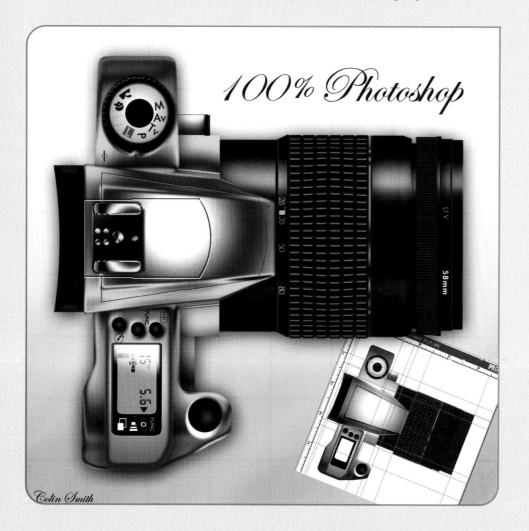

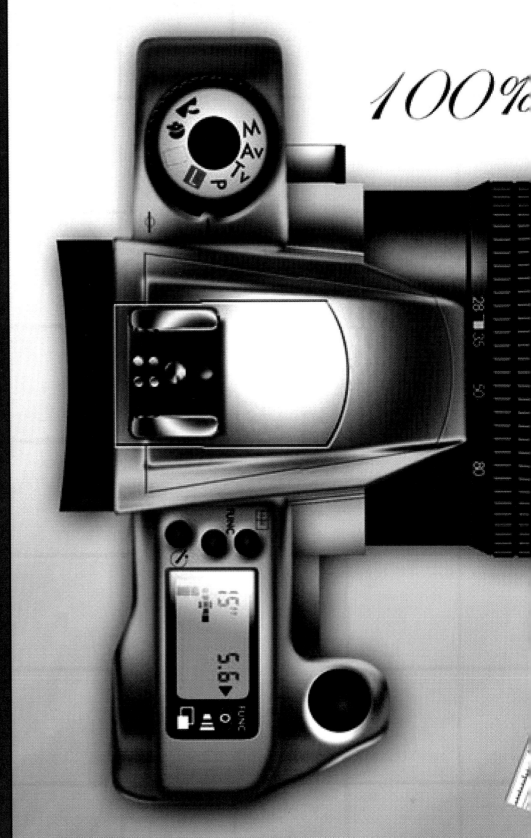

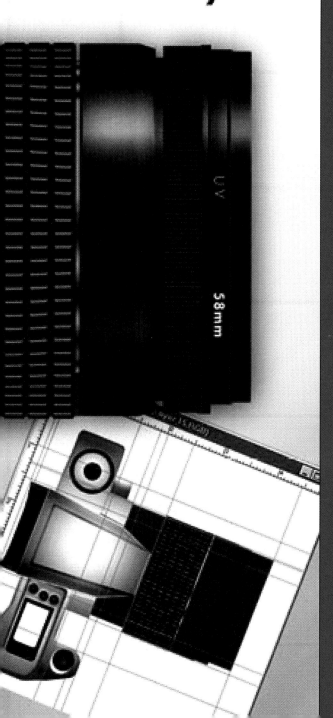

chapter 1

chapter 2

chapter 3

chapter 4

chapter 5

chapter 6

chapter 7

chapter 8

chapter 9

chapter 10

chapter 11

chapter 12

chapter 13

chapter 14

chapter 15

chapter 16

outro

"The most important part of any artistic effort
is what you communicate."

Catherine McIntyre
members.madasafish.com/~cmci/

213

Finders, Keepers

Originally a total technophobe, I was fortunate enough to be forced into computer graphic design out of the necessity to pay the mortgage. Using a completely digital working environment soon taught me what it was – and just as importantly, what it wasn't – possible to create with the medium. To someone with a natural propensity for collage – for organizing elements within an image, for selection, and for setting up gestalts from unrelated, recycled parts – Photoshop is a godsend. My initial belief that nothing emotional could happen without physical creation was completely overturned.

In particular, the layering techniques available in Photoshop were a revelation. My attempts at collage had always been restricted by the scale and color of the objects and photographs I found, and by the physical problems of attachment – some elements simply couldn't be included because they were three-dimensional, too large, or too precious. Translucency, too, was not a variable. In Photoshop, though, there are no such restrictions. Images can be compiled from widely differing sources, and fine-tuned with complete freedom and subtlety into a coherent whole.

The fact that the images I was creating were ideas trying to become visible suited perfectly a medium that allows you to operate somewhere between the two – that is, between pure thought and the physical result. In Photoshop, pictures in progress are always in flux, evanescent and growing simultaneously, allowing an unusual amount of decision-making both forwards and backwards in time. It is an instinctive process that allows technical problems to recede in importance, and the real business of communication to happen.

Like all art students, my first influence was the life studio, which provides an understanding of form, light, dimension, and composition. A fascination with anatomy, the mechanics and expressiveness of the body, and measurement began here. A Masters degree in photography continued the exploration of the nude, in ways both more and less literal than that of the drawing class; the 'reality' of photography could be countered with the 'surreality' of mixed media, collage and montage techniques. With these, the images became more complete than life drawings, which are simply explanations of what you see; they started to express very personal philosophies, obsessions, and emotions.

Since then, there have been many other influences upon my work, most of them visual or literary. The first one I can remember was that of an extraordinary book, *Transfigurations*. In 1986, Veruschka (Vera Lehndorff) and Holger Trülzsch collaborated on a series of photographs of the nude, painted and almost sculpted. This amazed, and still amazes, me with its approach to the body, to beauty, to human interaction with the world. In the most powerful images, Veruschka, an ex-model, painted herself and was painted by Trülzsch to blend almost imperceptibly with the background – a wall, a forest, a cave. Startlingly beautiful, the results are also frightening or amusing, horrific or tranquil, joyous or morbid, according to the background or pose chosen, and the relationship of the figure to its environment. The astonishing variety of responses engendered by these pictures is part of their power. A picture of Veruschka covered with mosses, almost engulfed in a forest floor, is simply beautiful, peaceful, yet terrifying in its frank admission of mortality.

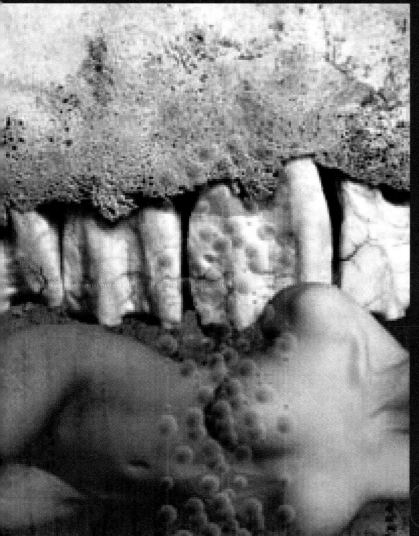

Depictions and explanations of the natural world also filter into my work continually, and I owe a great debt to *Gray's Anatomy* for an early fascination with the mechanics of the human body. What better way of explaining that one wants to address the internal, private, emotional aspects of a person, than by showing that person's physicality, both nude and stripped even further down, to the muscle and bone? What better visual analogy for feelings than the heart, for intellect than the brain, for structure than the skeleton?

Alongside this descriptive approach to human anatomy, an interest in animal osteology, taxonomy, and differentiation developed. The most beautiful books I've ever seen on this subject are both by Steven Jay Gould and Rosamond Wolff Purcell. In *Finders, Keepers* and *Illuminations*, this collaboration produced gorgeous collections of photographs of animals, preserved, fossilized, or stuffed. These animals are no longer related to their natural environment, but have become part of collections; they are arranged, organized and categorized. They are no longer what they once were, but have been assimilated by human minds and become another, captured, presence – sad, extraordinarily beautiful, and moving. Again, there are conflicting reactions to these images.

Finders, Keepers

In my own imagery, I try to remain grounded in some kind of reality – usually an emotional one, which is emphasized by using the 'reality' of photography as its basis. Reductive thinking, the empirical approach, would like to explain existence as an accident of atoms and amino acids, hormones, and DNA; but this has never explained what it is that we really are, just – up to a point – how it works. The part of us that leaves when we die, the emotions we feel, the really important stuff, is not to be confined to a series of chemicals and their reactions. This is shown so exactly by those relics of Gould and Purcell's: to me, they express man's desire always to pin down and document what is unknowable; and how in doing so, so much of importance is lost. On a map, the towns in Iran may be named, but you have no idea how the sand smells, or how a date tastes. When collecting butterflies, you can name them, and store them away in drawers, but those insects on pins are not the same as a butterfly in a field, and much less. This is an age-old problem for the artist who's trying to do the same thing: to translate real emotion – life – onto paper; to preserve the fleeting and precious.

That so much of life can be explained empirically does not, for me, reduce the mystery, but increases it – so much is known, yet so much more is still not known, and resists all attempts to be explained in this manner. Other, more intuitive, less clinical ways are needed. The parts that are not to be pinned down become more real by their contrast with the 'concrete', their very elusiveness emphasizing their existence. They cast a shadow, plainly showing that there is more to know, and it is these shadows that an artist strives to make pictures about.

There are purely artistic pieces that inspire me, too. Albert Watson has wonderful technique. His perfectly exposed, beautifully modeled, crisp and descriptive photography can be broken up and enlivened by a cyanotype exposure, or by a ragged edge to a liquid light print. His totemic images of fetishes, made in Marrakech, are extraordinary. In *Maroc* – my favorite of his books – I love his constant attack on the standard format, his lack of preciousness about the presentation of the images. Whatever it takes to show best the image's essence, he will do. There are some marvelous pages from sketchbooks, loose-edged and weathered, that have so much experience and life in them.

Javier Vallhonrat is another photographer whose work I find beautiful and moving. In *Animal-Vegetal*, he published a series of studio-based, unmanipulated shots of nudes with plant and animal material. The cover shot is of a model curled into a lovely pose reminiscent of a shell, with a string of mushrooms placed down her back; they so beautifully echo the spine beneath the skin, and eloquently allude to the interrelatedness of all living things.

Dave McKean is probably the most often cited influence on Photoshop users, and I'm no exception in admiring his surreal and evocative imagery. His subdued use of color – often duotone, or sepia – heightens the drama and tonal power of his pictures. Unsettling, funny, technically immaculate, full of atmosphere – it's no wonder his work is in such great demand with record companies, advertising agencies and book publishers all over the world. Many of his images appear to have been created using traditional cut-and-paste methods of collage, using photographs torn and montaged – although this may only be an illusion! His very personal vision chimes perfectly with the post-modern sensibility; he experiments with perception and plays with preconception.

There are other ways for a creative mind to express itself, beside the visual. I find the closest form to image-making is poetry; here, too, people try to condense and capture the most elusive of thoughts and feelings, and convey them to someone else in a small space (of time, rather than paper or screen). While working on my postgraduate degree, I made a series of illustrated books that had poems as their subject – in particular, the love poetry of women. While researching these – a joyous task – I discovered the work of Nina Cassian, a Romanian poet of great power whose poetry flings images at you with a concentrated energy. She gives me the same awestruck rush of mental images that the wonderful Sylvia Plath does – torrents of rich, twisting allusions that play with associations and alternative meanings. She's doing exactly what a Photoshop artist does – manipulating the audience's existing stock of ideas to create something wholly new.

The most important part of any artistic effort is what you communicate. The subject of an image is not necessarily just 'the things that are in it'. By association with each other, these elements can become symbolic of things above and beyond themselves. For example, the nude appears a lot in my work, and does not simply represent a naked human being. I see it as a natural symbol of the laying bare of innermost feelings: it can radiate hope or fear, strength or vulnerability; it can symbolize humanity's deepest essence, or that of the natural world; it can be idealized, realistic, impersonal, abstracted. There are endless ways of representing the nude, and they all carry with them resonances inevitably associated with the depiction of ourselves at our most unprotected.

Another recurring theme in my work is the difficulty of communication itself. This difficulty is one that artists face every day, and not only in their working lives. Any conversation is a microcosm of the dissembling, misunderstanding, and pretence of everyday transactions. The space between implication and inference, into which so much of importance seems to disappear; the gap between the projected and the true self; the misapprehensions inevitable when thoughts are translated, more or less efficiently, or not at all, into words – all of these can be translated into the visual.

The effects of ageing, on both organic and inorganic subjects, are also an important theme in the textural elements of my work. The beautiful effects of weathering and distressing on often unprepossessing substrates is at once destructive and creative; this paradox is mirrored in the ageing of the individual. The laws of physics act equally upon nature and the manufactured; some pictures show nature asserting itself and reducing man's efforts to their original elements, while others have nature under threat from encroaching industrialization.

The physical content of an image can express the less literal, emotional level of the work. Handwriting – an injection of the personal – or typeset text is an obvious way

of making thoughts visible. One can also use the figure, which can be an icon for honesty, openness and the inner soul. Dolls are another interesting symbol; I particularly like old porcelain doll heads, for their psychological overtones. Seen as transition objects in child psychology (objects on which to confer our love of someone, to ease the pain of losing them), they can be powerful images.

The theme of 'threat to nature' (and of course, to humanity) – pinned down and hemmed in, isolated and ultimately threatened by its surroundings – is an example of how ambiguity of message can make images more complex and thought-provoking. The environment can be the oppressor as well as the oppressed – particularly when it's an urban environment. Many of my images deal with the human form being trapped by an alien and unforgiving world. Peeling paint can be seen as either a lovely texture, or a candidate for redecoration, depending on its context; bolts can mean imprisonment or security. This confusion of perception is something for an artist to play with.

The wonderful thing about visual metaphors and symbols is that each viewer will interpret them differently, in a way that means something to them personally. Modern artists are not constrained by symbolism in the way that, for example, Renaissance artists were. St Jerome, for example, always had to have his lion, and St Catherine her wheel, in order that illiterate viewers might understand the narrative. Now, imagery tends to be in the service of the individual, rather than a religious or political body, and one has total freedom of expression and therefore content. Symbols can be more or less ambiguous; a chain around a neck will be pretty unequivocal, while an enclosed figure might suggest either security or entrapment, depending on the emotional outlook of the viewer. Personal interpretation of an image makes that image directly relevant to the viewer's experience, and therefore, hopefully, more powerful.

So the pieces work, I hope, on two levels. I believe that art should be interesting visually, as well as for its concept. The aesthetic level of the work is, for me, about finding correlations, echoes, and new resonances between disparate forms and surfaces, often between natural and manufactured objects in decay. Texture, color and pattern can all be brought into play here. I also think that the concept itself should be decipherable, and available to the viewer without the help of other knowledge – of the artist's history, for example, or anything else. The determinedly abstruse nature of much modern art seems to me to deny the very purpose of it. I believe pictures should inspire emotion, encourage exploration of the content – literally and psychically – and make inner landscapes visible.

The image in the tutorial that follows is part of an ongoing personal project that has been developing through a variety of media, along several themes, for many years.

Finders, Keepers

Photoshop is an admirable program for the retouching and manipulation of images. You can take a single image and perfect it, edit it subtly, or change it completely. However, there can be far more to it than that. When making a particular type of image – a montage – you combine many photographs and scans, and Photoshop is the perfect medium for this. Using layers, all of the traditional collage techniques are there, and much more besides.

Complex, multi-layered imagery is now so much a part of our lives that we hardly notice it. Quick-fire advertising, music videos, even simple reflections in layers of glass, all give our visual environment depth and multiplicity. How Braque and Picasso would have loved such intense and constant visual stimulus! When they began to make montages in the early twentieth century, they acknowledged the beginnings of this growing complexity of environment – and they were saying something completely new about what was worth making pictures about, too. The idea of using found objects, ephemera, even litter, to make something of interest and value was revolutionary. 'Real life' could be physically incorporated into a picture in a way only found before in the use of precious materials in painting. Gold leaf and lapis lazuli were used in Renaissance religious art not only for their color, but also to signify the wealth of the patron or donor, and literally to enrich the church. That less precious objects and substances might be worth the artist's attention was a thoroughly modern idea. Their worth was in their color, texture, content, and in their actuality – their being the 'real thing', and evidence of real lives.

All of the essential elements of collage were established before Photoshop came along. The fundamental idea of making relationships between previously unrelated items, and the resultant creation of a new gestalt – the idea of the whole being greater than the sum of the parts – was not new. The inclusion of 'real' objects, textures, or phenomena had been done. But collage was never really seen as a primary means of artistic expression; its limitations were felt to be too great. Where Photoshop revolutionized the medium was in its flexibility. The problems of the past – of attachment of fragile items, issues of permanence, scale, opacity – were instantly resolved when Photoshop 3 arrived, and with it, layers. As a means of artistic expression, collage now has all the capabilities of any other technique, and more than most.

The principle is the same. You still put things together on an image plane, and make new associations between things; the traditional skills of composition, tonal awareness, drawing, perspective, and so on are still vital. Now, though, you can do exactly what you want with the constituent parts of your image. You can make them any size in relation to each other, and see exactly how they relate as you're doing it. You can make something translucent, so that you don't lose the layers beneath it. You can change your mind about the color, contrast, or indeed any other attribute of any element at any time. You can remove things, and then put them back again. An image can take many unexpected turns – and you can keep all of them. And when you've finished, you can have as many versions, at as many different sizes, and on as many different substrates, as you like.

Applying Layers

There are three main methods that I use to blend together the parts of a Photoshop image. In order for a layer to be affected by those beneath it, you can reduce its opacity, change its layer mode, or apply a layer mask and remove parts of it. You can also use an adjustment layer or group layers together to blend the image, but I don't use these techniques much in my collages.

Using the Layers palette, it's possible to alter the opacity of any layer, except the background. If you want to change the opacity of your background, duplicate it, and fill the original background with white. That last step is important, because if you don't have a white background for the layers to work against, you may get unpredictable results when you come to flatten the image for printing.

Different blending modes affect different qualities of the layer they are applied to. For example, if you have a grayscale element that you want to take on the color of the layers below it, change its mode to Luminescence. Its hue will become that of the total of the layers below it, while its tonal range will stay the same. If you have a layer that's too flat, duplicate it and use Overlay – this will brighten the image in a way that's more controllable than simply changing its contrast.

The third main way of blending layers that I use is the layer mask. When you add a mask with no selection currently in place, you have two options: Reveal All or Hide All (if you already have a selection, there are two further options: Reveal Selection or Hide Selection). If you're likely to keep most of the layer visible, or you need to see which parts of the image to remove, go for Reveal All; if you only want a small area and you can easily find where to paint it in, use Hide All.

The layer mask works on a scale from black to white. By painting in black, you will remove the layer from view; by painting white, you will show it again. By working on the mask using the airbrush tool in various sizes and pressures, you can achieve a precise selection of the layer. The hidden information is not lost until you remove it and apply the mask; you can keep replacing it at any time until then. Using all these methods of affecting the contents of a layer together can give you complete control over each element's contribution to the final image.

A New Image

The collage in the following tutorial was inspired by an old photograph that I found in a junk shop. The woman has a lovely face – sensitive, intense, and intelligent – and she interested me. There was no clue as to her identity; the only wording was the name of the photographic studio, and its location – Edinburgh, Scotland. The image was obviously an old one, but otherwise I simply had to imagine who this woman was, and how she might have lived her life.

Throughout the long and venerable history of portraiture, the artist has always given the viewer clues as to the identity of the sitter – their status, interests, profession, and so on. These visual allusions strengthen the impression one already has of the subject's personality from their simple physicality – their expression, apparent age, etc. I wanted to give an impression of this woman and her time and place, so I included Scottish architecture (reflected in the broken window is a street scene from the Scottish town of Montrose), a map of Scotland in the background, and some portraits: a baby, a young man, and a group.

Of course, the story is all surmise, but a woman of that age and at that time must have been either living with her family, or married. Also, she was not poor – photography was not cheap then, and she is well dressed. More than that is impossible to know, so a background had to be provided. Some photographs I had taken of a notice board on the street, which had many old photographs and letters pinned to it, contained portraits of a similar vintage; some of these people became her family.

The triptych format I used was historically more common in religious works. It was a protective device, whereby a particularly precious or delicate painting might have the protection of its folding doors against the elements. It also implies privacy, since the doors might only be opened to a restricted audience. I decided that this secretive lady deserved a little shelter, but the format is a useful compositional device, too. By framing elements together, it categorizes them, and creates stronger connections. The left panel became her future, and the right her past – the one unknowable, the other defined by her relationships.

File Preparation

Having decided upon a subject for a picture, I collect all the necessary elements. I always keep photographs and scans as separate files on backup CDs for future use (and find it useful to keep a catalogue of exactly where to find each file – it can be difficult to locate a particular file in a growing bank of CDs).

A digital camera is a godsend for this type of work. The images are downloaded directly onto the computer, and suffer no loss of quality from being scanned. With no dust or scratches to touch out, a lot of tedious work is avoided. The files, which usually come from the camera at 72dpi, I change to 400dpi, as this is the resolution I tend to work at. Commercial magazine and book printers generally use 300dpi; so working at 400dpi allows a file to be scaled up a little with no loss of detail.

However the image gets into the computer, I do as much work as possible on the elements before beginning a piece; this leaves you free to think about more important things when you're making a picture. If the image is of a freestanding object, I use either the magic wand tool or paths to remove its background, and save it as a Photoshop file.

Creating Our File

Let's set up our file, `new.psd`, as 12.22 x 17.28cm, at 400dpi. That might sound arbitrary, but I can explain. 12.22cm is the width of a CD cover, and you never know when you might make an image that someone wants to crop square for their CD. Making it 17.28cm high then gives it proportions that will fit most paperbacks. Note that we'll be working with a lot of layers, so the file will become quite large – if your machine begins to struggle, try reducing the resolution of the image.

Another point to note is the file's mode: RGB, as opposed to CMYK, or any of the other possible formats. All of Photoshop's tools and filters work in RGB mode; when you work in CMYK, it has to keep converting between RGB and CMYK whenever any calculations are made, slowing your work considerably. Photoshop also runs faster in RGB mode because the file size is smaller than with CMYK – you're only working in three channels, not four.

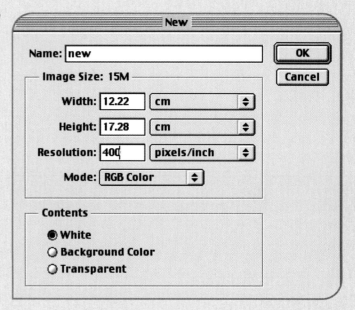

If you intend to use the completed image on the Web, you'll never need to touch this setting again. If the image is to go to commercial print, however, you *will* need to convert it to CMYK mode once flattened – but for the reasons above, it's always best to hold off the conversion until the image is finished. Be aware that the conversion may cause color shifts, as the two formats' color ranges are slightly different; it's sensible to examine a CMYK preview to avoid unpleasant surprises.

Finally, when setting up a file, I always start with a solid – usually white – background, rather than a transparent one. That way, you always see what the final result will look like once it's been flattened.

Tutorial

The first stage is to make a background to float the portrait of the woman against, so open the file `map.jpg`, select all, and copy-and-paste it into the `new.psd` document. The image needs to be enlarged slightly to fill the space (Edit > Transform > Scale); as it is a background the resultant increased softness is not a problem, I feel.

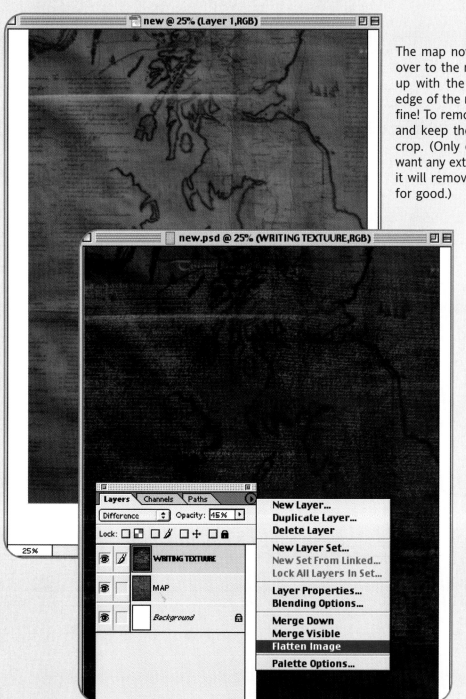

The map now bleeds off to the sides; I moved it over to the right, so that the left-hand edge lines up with the left of the picture, losing the right edge of the map. If you prefer it to the left, that's fine! To remove the unnecessary parts of the layer and keep the file size down, select all again, and crop. (Only do this if you're sure that you don't want any extra information in *any* of the layers, as it will remove everything outside the image edge for good.)

Now, add the `writing texture.jpg` file above the map layer in the same way; I left this layer centered. This is a good time to experiment with layer blending modes, and I eventually went for Difference mode at 45% opacity, allowing both layers to influence the result. I then flattened the image (which crops the second layer), as I'm confident that I won't need to change either layer's attributes again. I did this purely to reduce the file size, so that my clunky old machine wouldn't complain! If you have plenty of memory, and feel that you might want to mess with these layers later, don't flatten them.

Next, add the `portrait.jpg` file, and label its layer portrait:

The text at the bottom is a bit distracting – the information it provides can be imparted in the title later – so let's remove it using the Clone Stamp tool.

When you're cloning, keep choosing new places to sample from, as a repeating pattern would be obvious even in a subtle texture like this. Use a small brush for this detail, at 100% opacity to start with – you can always use a lower opacity to blend later if you need to. Also, you should always perform this task at a high magnification, checking the overall impression periodically with View > New View.

If file size is no object, and you want to check against the original, you can even work into a new layer. Select your original point to clone from in the first layer, and paint into a second. You could set the mode to Lighten or Darken, dependent on instance, if you like – although this tends to leave you with a discernable edge between cloned and original pixels. When you like the results, merge down so that any mode applied later to the layer will alter both equally.

new.psd @ 25% (Layer 1,RGB)

25%   Doc: 13.1M/33.5M

The Frames

Next, turn off the layer containing the portrait for the moment, place the first of the triptych frames into the file (copy and paste the contents of `reflections.jpg`), and label it reflections.

Assign this new layer Luminosity mode, which allows the tonal values of the layer to remain, while changing its apparent hues to those of the layers beneath it. This temporarily removes the distraction of the colors; you can see better how the tones relate to the background, and therefore how the composition is coming along.

Finders, Keepers

There was only the one frame, so we must manufacture the other two in order to complete the triptych. First, duplicate the frame layer, and flip it horizontally. It needs to be narrowed slightly to fit to one side of the existing, central frame – but don't just use Transform, as this would change the proportions, making the sides of the frame too shallow, and the top too deep. Rather, duplicate the flipped frame layer; add a layer mask to both layers, and remove the right hand side of one, and the left of the other. Now move the two together until they merge as a narrower frame. Once you're happy with the fit, merging these two layers will remove the layer masks. (It will also return the new layer's mode to Normal; remember to change it back to Luminosity.)

At this stage, I also took out the glass and board from inside the outer narrower frames; I selected the area to remove using paths, and removed it in a layer mask.

Duplicate this second frame layer, and move it to the other side of the central frame, then flip it horizontally. I also rotated the outer frames a fraction to change their alignment with the original. Finally, make small changes to all the frames with the Clone Stamp tool, so that they all look slightly different. If you now merge all three frame layers together, and copy and paste them into a new layer you can remove all but the original colored frame with the reflections (you'll need this for later color adjustments). This simplifies your work, and means that all future effects applied to one layer will apply across all the frames and their constituent parts. Label the merged layers frames – this layer now contains the three frames that make up your triptych.

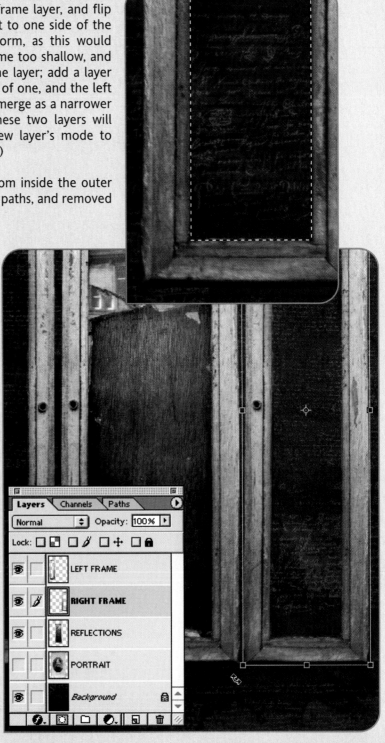

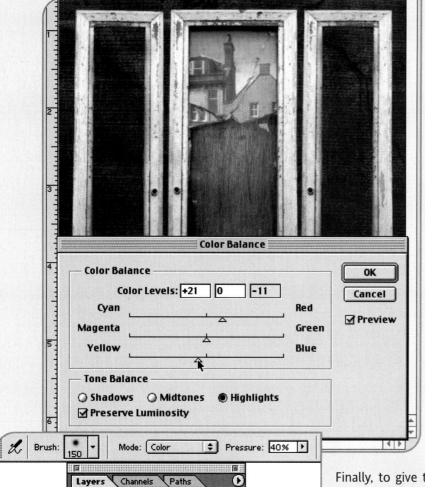

Leave the layer mode at Normal this time, as we'll now address the color of the frames. It would be better if they were warmer, to link them with the orange tones in the background, and with the hidden portrait. I don't want to lose the colors in the reflections and board, as these could be useful later, so select only the frames, remembering to feather your selection a little. Then, cut and paste into a new layer, label it frames, and desaturate (Image > Adjust > Desaturate). Adjust the image's Color Balance to give the frames a sepia hue (my settings were Shadows 20, 0, -9; Midtones 11, 0, -15; Highlights 21, 0, -11).

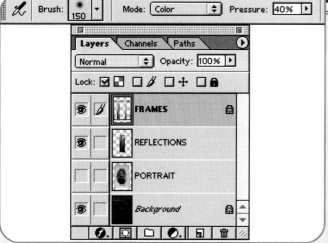

Finally, to give the color some variation, use the Airbrush tool set at Color mode (in the Tool Options bar) and a fairly low pressure. This will paint the hue of whichever color you've chosen in the upper paint swatch in the toolbar onto the image, leaving the tonal range unaltered. I used a fairly large brush (around 150) to avoid a 'striping' effect – and remember to check the Lock transparent pixels box at the top of the Layers palette for this layer, so that you don't paint into empty areas. The frames are now finished.

Adjusting The Portrait

Next, turn the portrait layer back on, and the reflections layer off. Assign the portrait
layer Soft Light mode, and leave the opacity at 100%.

Add a layer mask, and soften off the corners of the photograph. Then, turn the
reflections layer back on, and move it below the portrait layer.

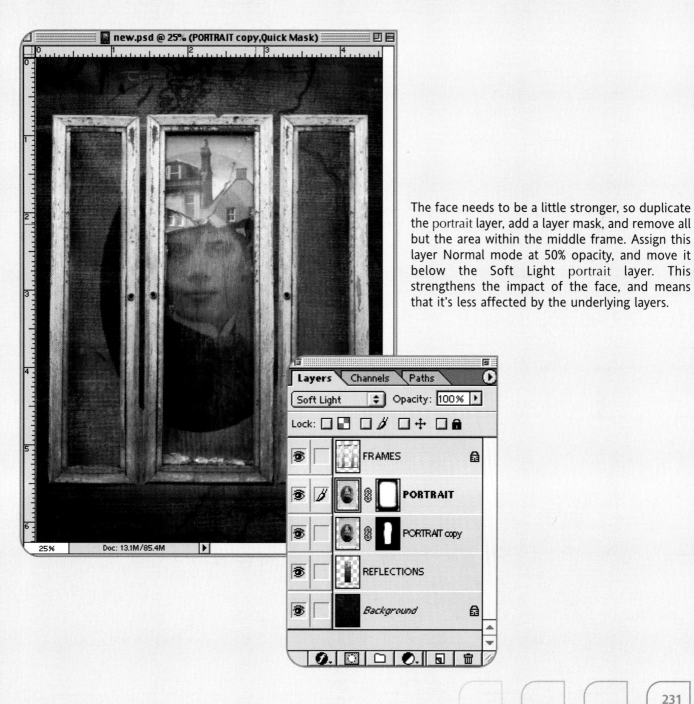

The face needs to be a little stronger, so duplicate the portrait layer, add a layer mask, and remove all but the area within the middle frame. Assign this layer Normal mode at 50% opacity, and move it below the Soft Light portrait layer. This strengthens the impact of the face, and means that it's less affected by the underlying layers.

To bring back the reflections a little, duplicate the reflections layer, and move it on top of the portrait layer. Assign it Multiply mode at 50% opacity; this adds the layer's contents to those below it and so darkens them. By reducing the opacity you 'knock it back' a little, so that the effect (and the reflection) doesn't become too strong.

To eradicate the slightly ruddy hue, go to Hue/Saturation (Image > Adjust...), and take the saturation of the red down by -40.

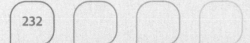

A Collage Within a Collage

It's time now to turn our attention to the contents of the other two frames. As detailed earlier, the one on the right is to contain signifiers of her relationships, and I've prepared two files (`pinboard 1.jpg` and `pinboard 2.jpg`) that contain ready-made assemblages of images and textures.

We're going to make a collage of these within the right-hand frame. Where the content is inappropriate – either anachronistic, as in modern advertisements for shops, or simply unattractive – we'll replace the area with another old photograph. I had the images `baby.jpg` and `man.jpg` on file already as possible candidates for inclusion in a picture, and so retrieved them from my CD collection.

The techniques involved here are ones you've already practised earlier in this tutorial. By opening each source file in turn, and copying parts that you like into the new image behind the frame layer; by sizing using Transform as before, and using layer masks to edit the visible parts, you will arrive at a collage within a collage. It will be different from mine, I'm sure; experiment with the composition in this area, remembering that the balance of this part of the image will affect the balance of the whole – both in content, and aesthetically. I made the young man quite dominant at the bottom of the frame, as I felt that her personal relationships would have been of great significance in her life.

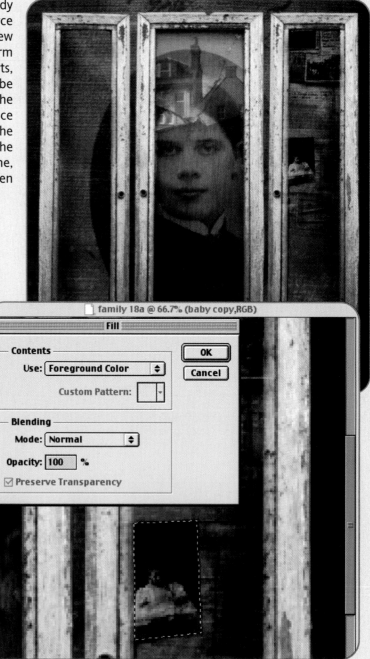

While you're working on this part, remember that you're making a simulacrum of a 'real' collage, and that each piece of paper overlapping another will create a shadow. You should keep these shadows realistic by noticing where the existing shadows fall in the pinboard shots, and make your new ones fall the same way. Also remember that the frame itself will shade the edges of the area; I made this shadow by gently removing these parts of the collage, and letting the background show through.

There are numerous shortcuts for making drop shadows, especially in later versions of Photoshop. I always make my own, though, as I feel it gives more control, and I can vary my technique to get unique results. To duplicate my method, make a copy of the area in which to cast the shadow, and paste it into a new layer. Then, check the Lock transparent pixels box in the Layers palette, choose a color from a shadowed area of the original image using the Eyedropper tool, and fill the layer with the color.

Then, unlock the transparent pixels, and apply a Gaussian Blur to the layer. Remember that the 'closer' you are to the object casting the shadow, the sharper the shadow should be, and vary your blur accordingly. Next, change the layer mode to Multiply, and its opacity to around 50%. Doing this with a darkened layer is a close equivalent to a real shadow and a good way of creating a realistic effect. If there is a large area of unnecessary pixels behind the object, you can remove them using a layer mask. Apply it immediately, as you won't need this information again.

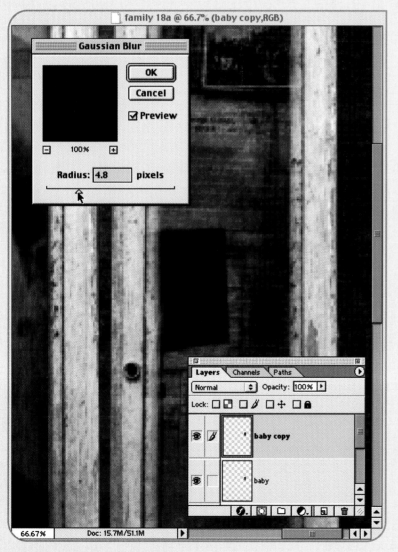

Shadows are not consistent across a texture, so use a layer mask to fade off corners and any areas where the background comes closer to the object casting the shadow. If the background slopes away rapidly from the object, you can distort the shadow to fit, either in Transform or, if a curving effect is required, using the Smudge tool.

Remember also that if you have information you don't want – some of the words in these shots, for example, are not appropriate to the atmosphere we're trying to create – cloning them out will often have a better result than removing them in a layer mask. You will then retain the illusion of a continuous plane, rather than developing holes through to the background.

Finders, Keepers

To blend this area of collage in with the rest of the image, I merged its layers together and applied Luminosity mode at 75%; this blends the hues with those of the background and warms them. Then, as this inevitably makes it recede, I duplicated the whole layer to 'lift' it again, and applied Hard Light at 50%, heightening both contrast and color. This way, the background still affects the whole area, but the collage still has enough depth and strength to weigh properly within the overall composition.

It is now obvious that, because Luminosity mode has been applied to the lower of the two collage layers, the edge of the portrait in the background is too prominent. By selecting an area within the outside edge of the frame, and working on the portrait layer, you can clone the layer across to blend this edge.

To complete the right-hand side, the man.jpg file should be added at the bottom of the frame. As this image has higher contrast and is darker than the others, it needs to be handled carefully or it will be too strong. I chose Normal mode at 40% opacity for the first layer, and then duplicated it at 70% for a Hard Light layer – this second gives it more substance, without allowing it to dominate.

The left-hand edge of the portrait is also too hard; I dealt with this differently, by fading it out using the layer mask. If you use quite a large paintbrush here (mine was 300 pixels, at around 60% opacity), you will achieve a softer result.

Now that we're dealing with the left-hand frame, copy and paste the `broken mirror.jpg` file behind the frame. You can have some fun here with cloning and painting; leaving the layer in Normal mode, try adding some bands of 'light' across it, using a paintbrush at a low opacity (remembering to check the Lock transparent pixels box in the Layers palette, so you don't paint outside its edge). I also thought the top edge profile was too rounded, so I cloned upwards to a sharply curving selection made in Paths. Then, soften the edges under the frame in a mask.

Tuning the Composition

After attending to all that detail, it's a good idea to take an overall look at how the composition is coming along.

At this stage, as a result of all our manipulations, the image is quite soft. The areas of most importance – the face, and the reflections – need to be boosted a little, and the tonal contrasts raised.

To do this, I selected the inside of the middle frame, and in the Soft Light portrait layer increased the contrast slightly and reduced the brightness (Image > Adjust > Brightness/Contrast; my settings were Brightness -30, Contrast +5). You could also make this adjustment in Curves (Image > Adjust > Curves).

It's now obvious that the frames themselves need drop shadows. Make a selection of the frames, add a new layer, fill the selection with a nice deep brown, deselect, move the layer downward a little (the light is nominally overhead, so no sideways nudge is necessary), and blur until it looks good. I felt that these shadows needed to be stronger than the more usual 50% opacity, and have set them at 85% – but play around with them until they fit your image. Remember to fade them off in a layer mask where they would be paler (where the frames lift a little from the background at the sides).

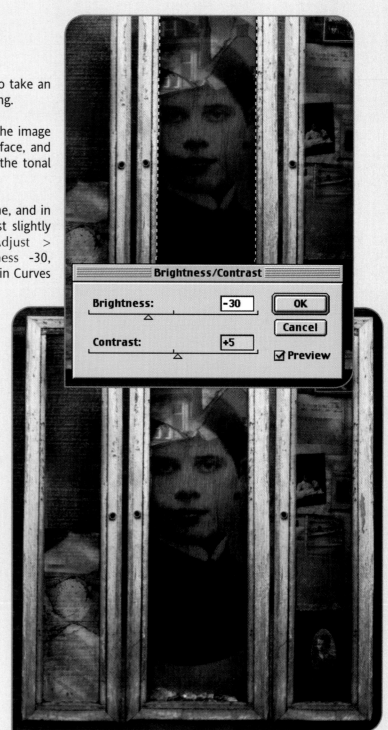

For me, the blues in the reflections appear too strong. (You may well disagree – I tend to use very subdued color, but if you prefer brighter hues, you could strengthen them instead.) Choosing the Multiply mode layer containing the reflections and board, I went into the Hue/Saturation palette and reduced the saturation of the blue alone (my setting was -65). This also affects the blue in the broken glass at the bottom of the frame, helping to blend it with the rest of the image.

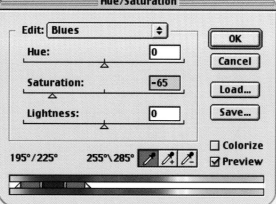

To lift the reflections a little more, I selected only the glass using paths (feathering the selection a touch will help to keep everything blending nicely – and do save paths until you're sure you won't need them again), and increased the contrast by 20 or so. This helps to separate it from the face below, and to enliven the tones across the image. Generally speaking, areas of greater contrast will be more important, so this sharper contrast will help to focus attention on the important areas of the composition.

The bottom-left mirror still jumps out a bit, but changing its mode from Normal to Hard Light (giving the background more influence) and moving the opacity down to around 80% helps it to fit better. I then increased the contrast a little to make the cracks more legible.

It still doesn't look like glass, though, so I duplicated the layer and changed its mode to Screen; this lightens the whole area, and by using this at a low opacity and removing areas in a layer mask, you can achieve a more translucent effect.

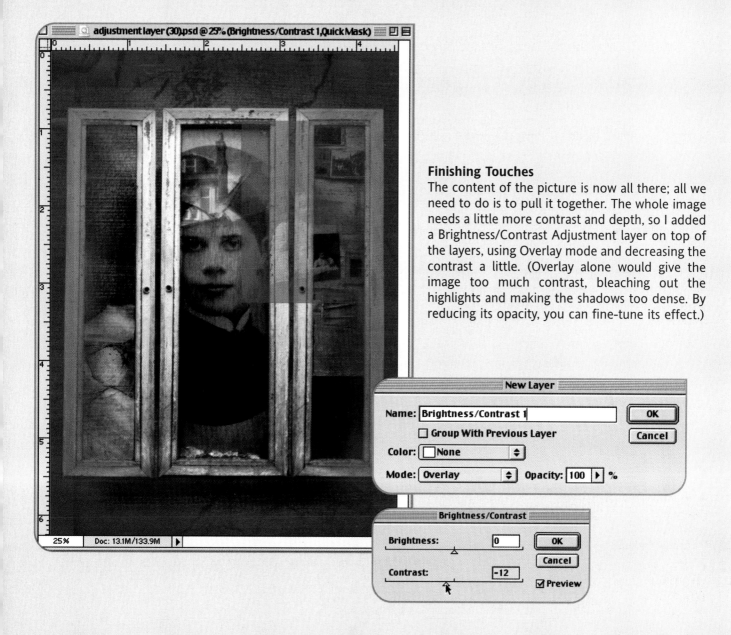

adjustment layer (30).psd @ 25% (Brightness/Contrast 1, Quick Mask)

New Layer

Name: Brightness/Contrast 1

☐ Group With Previous Layer

Color: ☐ None

Mode: Overlay   Opacity: 100 ▶ %

OK

Cancel

Brightness/Contrast

Brightness: 0

Contrast: -12

OK

Cancel

☑ Preview

25%   Doc: 13.1M/133.9M

Finishing Touches
The content of the picture is now all there; all we need to do is to pull it together. The whole image needs a little more contrast and depth, so I added a Brightness/Contrast Adjustment layer on top of the layers, using Overlay mode and decreasing the contrast a little. (Overlay alone would give the image too much contrast, bleaching out the highlights and making the shadows too dense. By reducing its opacity, you can fine-tune its effect.)

Finders, Keepers

The Overlay mode has brought out the reddish hue of the portrait, and I'll now reduce this a little to give a more subtle sepia color. Find the Normal mode reflections layer, and reduce its opacity. Also, using the selection made earlier with paths, I copied and pasted the glass area alone into another layer, and lightened the tones for a little more 'lift'. As you'll see, tiny changes made here and there at this late stage will make all the difference to the overall balance of the picture. We're not worrying about the content now, but the aesthetics: the composition, the bare bones of which were formed by the content, is subtly affected by the relative hues and tones across the image. Color psychology is a fascinating subject; it's apparent that different hues and collections of colors have an effect on a viewer's understanding of an image, so take advantage of this. Think about your message, and use color as another means of getting it across.

A final check over your flattened image at a high magnification will enable you to clone out any tiny imperfections you decide you don't want – I evened out the woman's skin tone where some paint flecks had marked it.

And that's it! I didn't have a particular idea of how this image would look when I started out; I just had a central subject, some other images that went with it, and an idea of what I wanted to say about it. Be flexible when you're working with this medium – it can be surprising when you experiment, and many happy accidents are worth keeping. The interactions between layers are often unpredictable, for example, so run through several alternative modes, as your original choice may not be the best.

Even the most basic things about an image – the placement of the main subject, its overall color, anything – can be changed at any stage in this way of working, so initial plans and sketches are less necessary than with traditional picture-making techniques. It's always a good idea, of course, to have a sketch-pad as well as your camera with you, as you'll keep your observational skills and drawing up to scratch too!

chapter   1

chapter   2

chapter   3

chapter   4

chapter   5

chapter   6

chapter   7

chapter   8

chapter   9

chapter 10

chapter 11

chapter 12

chapter 13

chapter 14

chapter 15

chapter 16

outro

"Creative people always question accepted principles."

Pop

When I was in college, I was intrigued by the work of the pop artists of the sixties. I found the approach used by Warhol, Wesselman and Lichtenstein appealing, but even more interesting to me was the choice of subject matter. The elevation of everyday images, objects, and situations caused me to look at everything differently. I related to their mechanical method, which was reassuring because it was the one that I used in my own paintings, probably a result of an emphasis on producing images that were informative rather than expressive. Although I found this imagery and approach to be very exciting, it didn't have any direct influence on my work until I saw an exhibition at Whitney Museum in New York in 1978.

Art About Art was an exhibition where the subject matter of each piece was art. The work showed me that while it was important to attract a viewer with strong images, there had to be a concept in any given piece too. On many occasions, the concept or thinking process was even more important than the imagery. Jasper Johns did a small piece, *Target*, which was fifty percent complete; the owner could finish the painting with the paint provided, and even sign their name next to Johns'. Robert Rauschenberg erased a drawing by de Kooning, signed it, and titled it *Erased de Kooning Drawing*. Andy Warhol's *Do It Yourself* was a replica of a partially completed 'paint-by-numbers' seascape. These pieces demonstrated to me that although they're often not as obvious, the conceptual qualities of pop art are as important as the visual imagery.

Estate by Robert Rauschenberg
© Philadelphia Museum of Art/CORBIS

Still Life # 25 by Tom Wesselman
© Burstein Collection/CORBIS

FIGHT GRIDLOCK, 1982

BEAT SURRENDER, 1982

My focus became even clearer during a 1981 trip to New York. The constant barrage of visual images directed at people in this urban environment seemed almost beyond stimulation. Billboards, signs and graffiti all had a message, but I couldn't help but wonder if the message was even perceived. Did the meaning become invisible because of the saturation? (Sort of like seeing something every day, but not really noticing it.)

This question of perception became the basis for my paintings that were shown at the Mendelson Gallery in Pittsburgh in 1983. *Fight Gridlock* (1982) and *Beat Surrender* (1982) represent the kind of visual overload that I saw in New York. My initial theory was that meaning would become less apparent as the quantity of images increased; the search for meaning would give way to an understanding of concept. I was wrong.

I found that the search for meaning or a message in art is relentless, even when one may not be present. I remember a woman insisting that I was making a statement about American society. When I told her I wasn't, she basically called me a liar.

This was also my first exposure to art critics. I understood the job of the critic, but their complex analysis of my paintings seemed almost comical to me. I could see how artists could be influenced by the reaction of others. From what I read about my work, I could easily have thought that I was doing things I wasn't even aware of.

I thought that maybe I should give people the meaning they were searching for – or maybe that I should make it seem like I was. In the next group of paintings, I made a conscious effort to make it appear as though there was some sort of message or meaning. This would be a much more complex test of perception, since I was putting together a format with the intent to mislead.

Pop

These new paintings were shown at Carnegie Museum of Art in 1984. John Caldwell, curator at the Museum, had seen my work at the Mendelson, and invited me to show. When I read John's statement in the exhibition catalog, I knew that he understood what I was doing.

"Looking at one of Peter Stanick's paintings is a little like moving very rapidly down an urban street. There is a kind of overload of images – traffic signs, billboards, pennants, direction signals, and pedestrians hurrying past. It is a stressful experience that causes the viewer to try with some anxiety to decipher the multiple images, and somehow decide upon an appropriate response. In *All Mod Cons* (1984) there are rock artists, whose messages cannot be understood, a self portrait, and soldiers combined with a connected line apparently taken from a chart of a constellation – clearly they add up to a message, but one that cannot quite be understood."

Just like the artists in *Art About Art*, the concept in my work became more important to me than the imagery. I was concerned that the imagery was overwhelming the concept, so in 1987 I began a series of paintings in which the figurative images became more like icons, almost symbolic in nature. I thought that the perceptual concept would become more obvious if the imagery was less intense, in a painting like *Hibiya Line Grey* (1987). These new paintings were shown in 1988, at the Frank Bustamante Gallery in New York.

ALL MOD CONS, 1984

HIBIYA LINE GREY, 1987

Pop art certainly had an impact on the way my work developed, but the major influence had become the work itself. Each painting had become the source of inspiration for the next. I was proud to have developed a cycle of images that was not influenced by outside sources. My goal was to produce paintings that were totally personal, images that reflected my interests. 'To be influenced' was something I avoided; to me it was a negative.

In 1990, I began to reintroduce stronger figurative images into my paintings. I found that the symbolic images were too subtle – it was much more enjoyable to deal with images that (in my mind) had an impact. Unlike the barrage of images that I directed at the viewer in the early Eighties, I was much more selective in my choice of images, which caused the paintings to become less complex. The paintings not only had a concept; they began to have content too. I started to use text as an additional element, and the paintings became humorous commentaries. Twelve years had passed since I first saw Art About Art and I was now using art as a subject in my work. I used a Jasper Johns flag in *It's Just a Flag* (1995), and made a comment about artists in *He's Not a Bum* (1995).

These new paintings, which had text and images, were shown at Carling Dalenson in Stockholm in 1996. This would be a new test in perception: a foreign audience that might have a completely different analysis, especially since the text was in English. As it turns out, Stockholm is a very Americanized city and although there were some subtle differences with regard to language, there was no unusual reaction.

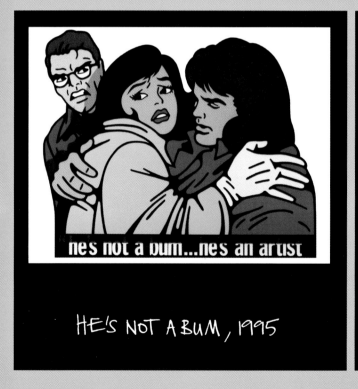

HE'S NOT A BUM, 1995

IT'S JUST A FLAG, 1995

Everything changed in 1996, when I started to use the Internet to present my paintings. The inevitable result – working with digital images – had a direct and immediate impact on my thinking. The Internet not only became part of the creative process, it would become the controlling factor.

My initial use of Photoshop was very simple: it was a tool to prepare images of my paintings for presentation on the Internet. It became apparent, though, that I needed to make the presentation as visually strong as the paintings. Photoshop defined the presentation, and the presentation started to influence the imagery. Everything started to revolve around how images were processed through Photoshop.

After a 1997 exhibition at Davies and Tooth in London, I came to the realization that my interest in producing digital images was equal to if not greater than doing the paintings themselves. I had been using Photoshop as a tool, but it was now time to take advantage of the digital skills that I had developed. I wanted to go beyond simply altering or enhancing images – I wanted somehow to create digital images that truly took advantage of existing technology. This technology was used in films, television, and music, but it seemed absent in the art world.

The decision presented quite a challenge. I knew that the art world was reluctant to accept digital work, and the computer world would be very demanding with regard to innovation. Ironically, my exhibition at Davies and Tooth was extremely successful. The easiest thing to do would have been to continue with my paintings as usual. Still, after seeing the influence of the Internet, I knew that I had to make a full commitment to producing digital images. To me, it was obvious that the digital world, via the Internet, was the future.

BATHROOM, 2001

RELAX, 2000

MARLBORO, 2000

The process that I first used in 1996 was reversed: a series of images would be constructed within Photoshop and viewed via a web browser. The completed images would first exist on the Internet. I found myself more involved with a system than with individual images – a system within which I had to create images that were not only Internet-based, but eventually had also to appear on canvas. Each image on the Internet had a corresponding file that would be used to transfer it to canvas using a large format plotter.

I couldn't help but notice that more and more web sites were using Flash, a vector-based program, and I wondered if I'd made a mistake by devoting so much time and effort to Photoshop, which was arguably less appropriate to the medium. Rather than choosing one format, I tried to use both, and after many frustrating months of trial and error, I finally devised a process. I would construct images within Photoshop, import those images into Flash for use on the Internet, and then export them back into Photoshop so that they could be finalized for canvas. These paintings were first shown on my web site (www.stanick.com) in October 2000.

TUBE, 2001

YAHOO, 2001

DANCE CRAZE, 2001

The method that I used to produce images had changed, but more importantly the graphic elements, interfaces, and visual imagery of the digital world had become a source of inspiration. Even with this change, though, the basic structure and content of paintings like *Relax* (2000) and *Marlboro* (2000) is very similar to the paintings I was doing in the Eighties.

In 2001, I was commissioned to do a series of paintings for Contact Music. I came to the realization that music had been an influence in my early work, but somewhere along the way it had stopped being a factor. In my most recent paintings, I have included references to music once again – not so much as an influence, but more as a kind of statement about the past, as in *Dance Craze* (2001) and *Yahoo* (2001). These references, and probably the influence of the iconic digital world, have caused me to take a renewed interest in symbols, as in *Tube* (2001).

The selection of images for use in a painting has always been the basis for my work. It's an ongoing process, in which I might be described as an 'image collector'. Within my collection, though, are images that have never been used in a painting – not because of a lack of appeal, but because I didn't think that I could give them the proper treatment. Photoshop has given me the opportunity to pursue those images that only a few years ago would not have been possible. The tool I needed in order to use those images was just not something that I used. While imagery and concepts are so very important to me, I learned that the ability to execute controls the entire process.

Pop

Creative people always question accepted principles, often finding ways to do things that are said to be not possible – or at least to try. Telling a creative person that there's no magic formula for, say, converting images perfectly from one size to another, will invariably prompt an attempt to prove that idea wrong. I suppose that thinking like this is what makes artists different, but at the same time it shows a possible conflict between creative and technical processes. I would much rather talk about the concept rather the technical aspects, but I now realize that the technical aspects are something that cannot be avoided.

When I made the commitment to producing digital images, I knew that I didn't want to alter existing images using Photoshop. In my opinion, that was a misuse of technology. A common practice among artists is to take an existing painting, reproduce it digitally, and then produce an edition. To me, this was using the computer as a color copier. I wanted to go further. I wanted to do something that took advantage of what I saw as a unique opportunity, but I didn't have a clear idea of what that was, what it would involve, or even if it would be possible. I could certainly deal with images and ideas – that's what I did every day in my painting. This was something different; there was the possibility that I could formulate something that I might not actually be able to execute on canvas.

My initial thought was that I could set up a system that included the interactive nature of the Internet, and the static images that would be used for final paintings. As I began to compose the paintings, I found that using the computer to manipulate images could be an endless process: one idea always leads to another. It always seemed like I could improve something, even when I had an image that I believed to be finalized. I could be dealing with hundreds of images for one painting on a daily basis, and not finalize it until I thought it was perfect. This showed me that working in the digital world would require discipline to define an end point to the process.

When you're dealing with digital images, image resolution is probably the most important issue to consider – as dpi increases, so too does file size. Images on the Internet are 72dpi, an ideal resolution for the monitor to display a clear picture. Images that appear in a magazine, on the other hand, are normally 300dpi; the higher resolution is needed because the printing process requires far more clarity. However, while 300dpi will provide clarity in any printing process, it is not mandatory, because today's printers emulate higher resolutions. Quite simply, they make an image that is 150dpi look like one that is 300dpi. While my printer is large, in that it prints on a roll of canvas 60" wide, it works on the same principle as any modern inkjet printer.

Painters like to do big paintings: it's very enjoyable to work on bigger and bigger pieces. I guess it sort of relates to the 'bigger is better' idea. Even though today's technology has made image creation easier, there is no magic formula for converting a small digital image into a much larger one. To create a small, Internet-based image in Photoshop is one thing, but how to convert that to the huge file necessary for a painting? I knew that, theoretically, it would be better to start with the large image and reduce it for the Internet, but working with large images was such a slow, tedious task that was more technical than creative. I didn't want to spend my days processing images; I wanted to work with small images and not have to worry about things like resolution and dpi.

Just like paintings, large images on the Internet have more impact than smaller ones. I like the idea of filling the entire screen with an image; in fact, the entire structure of my work is based on the 4:3 ratio of a standard TV or computer screen. When I was producing paintings by more traditional means, converting them to 1024 x 768 pixel images for presentation on the Internet produced files that were over 300 kilobytes in size. Over a 28.8kbps connection, that image would take about 90 seconds to download. Even if I could compress the JPEG to 150 or even 100 kilobytes, it would still take at least 40 seconds to download.

As a consequence of all the above, I want to produce an image that has a file size of 50 kilobytes or less, has perfect clarity, and fills the entire screen at 1024 X 768. At the same time, I want to be able to use that same image to produce a 72" x 54" painting. I want to use Photoshop because I enjoy working with pixels – but I also want to use Flash because I can use animation as a means to present the final work on my web site. For this tutorial, I want to show you that what I want is possible.

The picture I chose to use as a foundation for *Nova* came from a long-term interest in Japanese graphics that include lettering. Somehow, these graphics related to what I was doing in my paintings. Here was a language that I could not understand, so I was forced to go beyond the apparent message, and appreciate the beauty of each character at a visual level.

Now, as I've described, the two basic factors that determine the structure of my paintings are shape and size. Since the images are constructed for viewing via a monitor, the same ratio of 4:3 is used. The largest roll of canvas that can be accepted by my printer dictates size, so considering both factors, the maximum size painting is 72" x 54".

I began the project by scanning a photograph of some signs in Osaka, Japan. The file so generated (`japan.jpg`) is 400 x 400 pixels at 72dpi, and it's 118 kilobytes in size. As a result, the image it contains is clear on the monitor, but quality would suffer if it were enlarged.

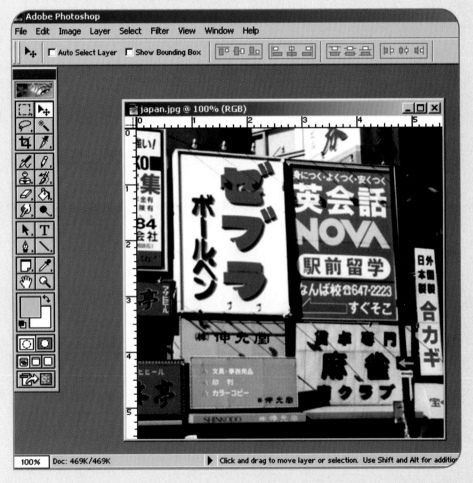

Looking at it like that, the problem isn't immediately apparent, but see what happens when we take a close-up of the "N" in "NOVA": the pixels are clearly visible.

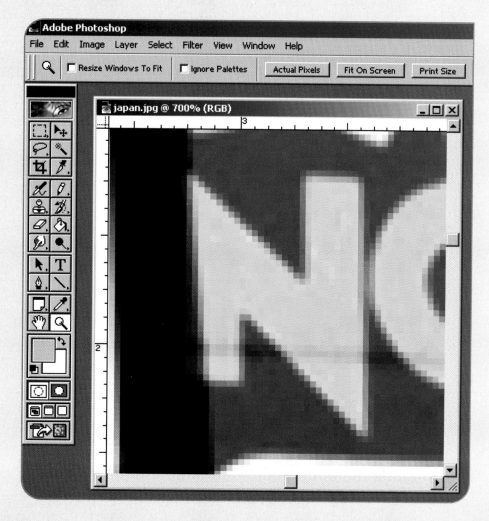

Pop

The first thing we're going to do is import the `japan.jpg` image into Flash – which, significantly for our purposes here, is a vector-based program. After opening Flash, select Modify > Movie and change the size to 400 x 400 pixels, corresponding to the image. Then, choose File > Import, and import `japan.jpg`.

The image *appears* to be the same, but zoom in on the "N" again, and you'll see that the pixels are far less obvious. Because Flash is vector-based, JPEGs are altered in this manner so that they can be more easily incorporated into the vector format. The outlines of shapes within the image are defined by vectors, so you still see a smooth outline when you zoom in.

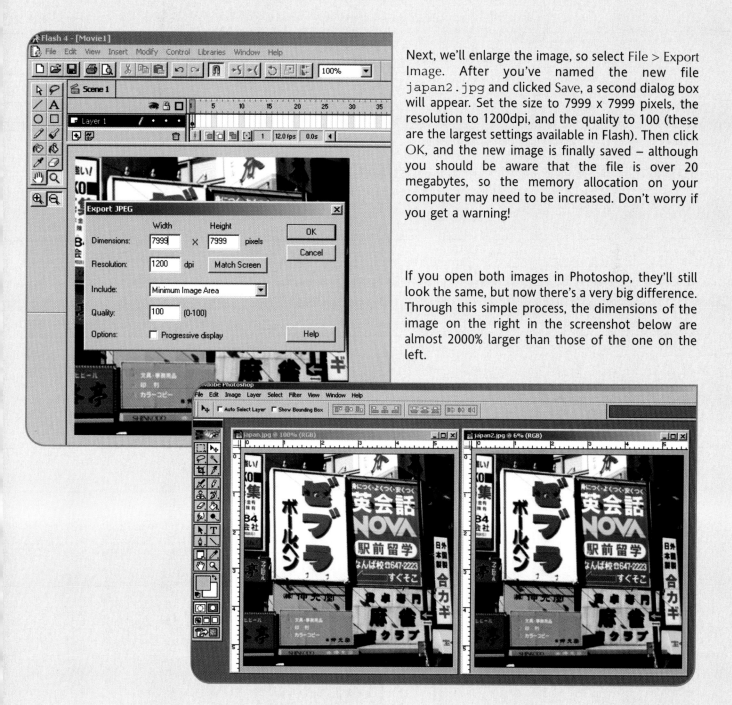

Next, we'll enlarge the image, so select File > Export Image. After you've named the new file `japan2.jpg` and clicked Save, a second dialog box will appear. Set the size to 7999 x 7999 pixels, the resolution to 1200dpi, and the quality to 100 (these are the largest settings available in Flash). Then click OK, and the new image is finally saved – although you should be aware that the file is over 20 megabytes, so the memory allocation on your computer may need to be increased. Don't worry if you get a warning!

If you open both images in Photoshop, they'll still look the same, but now there's a very big difference. Through this simple process, the dimensions of the image on the right in the screenshot below are almost 2000% larger than those of the one on the left.

Pop

The differences become very obvious when we compare close-ups of those "N"s again. We can clearly see the pixels in the original image on the left (shown at 400%), but they're far less obvious in our new enlarged image on the right (shown at 25%).

As I said, there's no magic formula for enlarging images, and the new one does require some work with regard to contrast and sharpness. Leaving that for now, though, my next step is to prepare this image (the first of three) for its final placement in the painting.

The final size of the painting is going to be 72" x 54", which means a JPEG that's 10800 x 8100 pixels at 150dpi. While it might not seem that 150 dpi would be good enough in an image that is 6 feet wide, keep in mind the advanced nature of today's printers that I mentioned earlier. The first step, then, is to increase the size of the image (Image > Image Size) to 8100 X 8100. After that, select Canvas Size, and set the final dimensions to 72 by 54", with the Japanese image on the left.

At this point you have an image that originated within Photoshop, was transferred to and enlarged in Flash, and then was returned to Photoshop. The second image is a very simple group of three line drawings that I drew and enlarged in Flash (I thought the linear images would be better suited to Flash's vectors), and then transferred to Photoshop using the exact steps that I described earlier. That image is then pasted on the right side.

Pop

At this point, I have two separate elements that consist of four distinct images. This particular composition might work, but normally I like to have at least three elements in a painting. As I looked at the image in Photoshop, I noticed the scroll bar, and took a screenshot of the screen. I decided to keep this in its pixelated state, since it would contrast nicely with the smooth image of the Japanese signs. The next thing I had to do was to calculate how big it should be on the painting.

In the screenshot, the scroll bar is 17 pixels wide. To make it fit with my image, though, it needs to be rather bigger! The actual size of the image of the scrollbar on the canvas should be 340 pixels wide by 54" high. To enlarge the screenshot in Photoshop so that it retains its graphical appearance, select Image Size and set Resample Image to Nearest Neighbor. Now, when enlargement occurs, no anti-aliasing takes place.

Finally, the image of the scroll bar can be pasted onto the left side of the painting – at which point the painting is complete, and ready to be transferred to canvas. After saving the file, I simply print directly from Photoshop to my printer, It takes about 30 minutes to complete the image on canvas, which is then stretched on heavy-duty stretcher strips. Here's the completed painting.

264

Once I'd completed the painting, I wanted to use the image on my web site. As you know, the image used to produce it was 10800 x 8100 pixels, but even after making a reduction to 1024 x 768, the image size was still 477 kilobytes. This could take about three minutes for the average user to download, and I didn't want them to have to wait that long.

My next port of call was the File > Save for web command in Photoshop. This command optimizes images so that files are as small as possible for use on the Internet, and it has numerous options. You can get the basic idea by clicking the 4-Up button at the top of the image – this will show the original image and three states of optimization. My 477-kilobyte image was presented with three options (high 158k, medium 85k, and low 49k – all JPEGs), but while the quality was fine at the medium level, the 85k file would still take about 30 seconds to download. That wasn't good enough for me, so the file needed to be smaller.

The approach I chose was to optimize the image in sections. Going back to my completed picture, I cut out the image of the Japanese signs (768 x 768 pixels), pasted it into a new document, and used File > Save for web again. Now I was down to 42 kilobytes, with good image quality, and an estimated download time of around 15 seconds. I was more than satisfied with that result, and after saving the new 42k image, I was ready to reconstruct the image of the painting using Flash.

First, I made sure that the movie size was set to 400 x 300 pixels, and then imported the optimized image of the Japanese signs. (Since that image is 768 x 768 pixels, I simply reduced it to fit into the frame by using Modify > Transform). Next, since the second part of the image (monkey, alien, and man) was created in Flash in the first place, I was able simply to add the vector image to the right side. The image of the scrollbar was a JPEG, but because it was made of simple shapes, I redrew it within Flash.

After saving the file, I used the Publish command, making sure that the Percent option was chosen in the HTML tab (Publish Settings > HTML > Dimensions) – this was done so that when the file is opened in a browser, it uses 100% of the available space. Since I've designed this image to be 1024 x 768 pixels, it will look great on screens of that size. If the screen is smaller, the image will be reduced with no loss of quality.

By using Photoshop to create and optimize, and Flash to present, I was able to take the same source material and produce a very large and a very small image that would be used for very distinct purposes.

Conclusion

As a painter, the past and the future are defined to me in terms of years. Working with digital images has changed that definition to days, and in some cases hours. This is an indication to me not only that the digital world has influenced my thinking, but that the entire process is open to change within a very short period of time. To me, this ongoing process requires an emphasis on logical thinking, and a willingness to evaluate everything at any given point. While this may be contrary to the expressive nature of art, or the art world in general, it may be an indication of my future. Technology has not only enabled me to define the content of my work, it has given me the freedom to define the environment on a daily basis if need be.

As I look at past paintings that I have done, I see images and ideas that I really didn't explore to the fullest extent. They remind me of other things that I was attracted to and didn't pursue at all. It's not so much that I chose something better, but I didn't feel that I made them work within the paintings that I was doing at the time. With Photoshop, I now have a tool to pursue and explore those images and ideas that, in my mind, were not possible before. While Photoshop is a program with almost unlimited image capabilities, the most important factor for me has been the realization that any concept may be possible, even those that I previously discarded.

This process is very much like surfing the Web, in that something always leads to something else. If someone had told me five years ago that I would be discussing things like 'file optimization' or 'image conversion', it would not have seemed possible. These kinds of things are not part of the world of the painter. Just as the digital world has affected everyone else, it has changed the way that I work. I let it influence me – I wanted it to, because I was a part of it – and there was no turning back.

For me, it seemed like a natural progression. I have always had a clear idea of what a painting would look like, even before I applied a drop of paint; to me the act of painting was more an execution of an idea. If I were an artist who enjoyed the act of painting, and allowed that to dictate content, then maybe working with digital images would not be right for me. I can easily see how Andy Warhol would be using Photoshop, but it probably would not work for Jackson Pollock. While it may seem that the type of image is the important factor, I believe the thinking process dictates an artist's involvement.

As I became more involved with digital images, I tried to envision the response to them in the future. I knew that the art world would be reluctant to embrace digital images, which is sort of ironic when you think that art is based on the concept of 'the shock of the new'. However, while making something simple or minimal is generally accepted as a creative act in the art world, the computer world has yet to pursue this concept. It's sort of understandable when you consider the dizzying array of options available, but the fact remains that simplification is a creative process that (right now, at least) is contrary to the complex nature of the digital world. Perhaps the almost unlimited capabilities of Photoshop do not promote simplicity? Certainly there are web sites and digital work that are minimal, but are they held in the same regard as complex and elaborate displays of every effect and filter possible?

Would my new paintings be too digital for the art world, and too simple for the computer world? I used to think that it was too early to tell, but I'm starting to believe that what I'm doing doesn't fit into either category. There seems to be another world that is taking shape. Difficult to define or describe, this new world is a product or a part of the Internet. I think it exists, I see signs of it, and I even like to think I'm part of it, but I can't explain. It's obvious that the most visually exciting work today is being produced by web designers, but is it art? Probably not, since art is defined as being non-functional – art that does have function becomes a craft. It's another of the ironies that's thrown up when art meets technology.

I've always had a clear focus as to what I wanted to do in my paintings; nothing could change my thinking or affect my confidence that only I knew what was best. I can honestly say that I've always made the right decisions – the only times I may have gone in the wrong direction is when I've let others influence me. My interest in digital images seems to be a logical progression from my past work, and I can't imagine doing anything differently. Due to the ever-increasing options before me, the future may not be clear. I know that I'll always be interested in working with images, but will the form change? I've always been a painter, but perhaps the end result won't be a painting? Whatever, I've never been so enthused about my work as I am today. When I consider the changes that have occurred in just the past five years, I realize that anything is possible.

chapter 1

chapter 2

chapter 3

chapter 4

chapter 5

chapter 6

chapter 7

chapter 8

chapter 9

chapter 10

chapter 11

chapter 12

chapter 13

chapter 14

chapter 15

"Imagine a monkey with a blowtorch in a shed full of paint... "

Gavin Cromhout
www.lodestone.co.za

My grandfather was a landscape photographer, and he introduced me to the magic of seeing an image form out of nothing on a blank sheet of paper. I think that I became the designer I am as a result of carrying his heavy camera bag around for him. He'd spend so long composing a photograph that the two of us would become a part of the scene; we felt like we belonged there. This comes through in his work, too: when you look at his photographs, you also feel you belong there. Of course, I was just grateful for the rest – I didn't realize until much later that this was an important part of the creative process! Now it's something that I hope comes through in my design too.

Being in my grandfather's darkroom and watching him use his projector fascinated me. He would often color his photographs by hand, and I saw how he altered and manipulated real images with different glass filters. At first, photography had seemed like truth to me – a mirror held up to reality. But in that darkroom, I realized that photography could also be art.

Years later, I studied art formally at university, but what History of Art taught me chiefly was that you could get at least an hour's good sleep out of a double lecture! If you're not creating the art, and you're not involved with it, I find that it's mostly lost to you. That's what I like about the Web: it's accessible and engaging. Interactive, you might say.

© Photograph by Ray Ryan

Photoshop is not just its drawing tools, its editing tools, or its selection tools. The strength of Photoshop lies in the combination of all three, and you can only discover it through experimentation – or, to use a less grand term, through playing. Experimenting with brush styles under various conditions, and differences in layer styles and opacities, is an unstructured but infinitely open way to learn.

Often, even if I think I already know what layer tool to use, I'll go through all the options, just to see. And most likely, I'll discover an effect that I can either use right there and then, or remember for later. I see Photoshop as more than just a 'development application', but a roomful of paints, brushes and canvases. It's an entirely new medium, and as such it needs to be explored in order for its character and potential to be realized. Photoshop can be a design adventure, not just a design tool.

In Photoshop, design elements can often come from what traditional artists would call mistakes. Selecting the wrong brush, or using the wrong layer style, can take you to a place further down the line in the design than your original intention. At first I thought I was just getting lucky, but now I think it's a matter of being open to different suggestions, and allowing yourself to grow with the design. It's another way of exploring the possibilities that Photoshop allows.

Message

Most of my experience in Photoshop doesn't come from the projects I've completed, but from my own exercises. I'd say to myself, "How badly can I mess this picture up?" or, "How weird can I make this man look?" After a while, I started to ask other questions, like, "How can I make this picture look aged?" and, "How can I create a mood of sadness?" Eventually, I asked myself, "How can I make this picture speak?" In this chapter, I'm going talk a lot about "the message". You may even get a little tired of it, but I think it's an essential consideration when you're designing professionally for functional web sites. These web sites are tools for communication, so the message they convey is paramount.

Artistic Influences

I did pay enough attention in History of Art to learn a bit about the Russian Avant-Garde. Neo-primitivists and cubo-futurists had the power to keep me awake, and some of their ideas have had a lasting influence on the way I think about design.

The artists of the Russian Avant-Garde belong to the early twentieth century – their contemporaries were Kandinsky, Duchamp, Braque, and Picasso. Their predecessors had seen art as a form of escape, a glorification and beautification of nature and culture, but as Russian society went through social and political revolution, a cultural revolution followed. The Russian Avant-Garde worked to bring about the death of easel art – to challenge and throw out the old ideas about the 'appropriate' and 'correct' ways of making art, and what the subject matter of art should be. They went from looking at the traditional to looking at the modern, in which reality was bound up with urbanization and industrialization.

Like the French cubists, they broke up the dimensional plane, creating a flat canvas in a rejection of the illusion of three dimensions. They were not trying to escape from their reality; rather, they sought to present their social situation honestly by abstracting it – by showing elements but not the whole; by breaking up planes; by including text. This was pretty weird stuff at the time, and it's stuff that works really well on the Web today. By its very nature, the Web also breaks traditional art paradigms.

Some of the Russian Avant-Garde's ideas on the creation of art and their sources of inspiration speak strongly as a good starting point for design on the Web. This goes not only to their methods, but also to their point of view on the way art should be created.

Nude Descending a Staircase (No. 2)
Marcel Duchamp, 1912
© Burstein Collection/CORBIS

The Panel No. 1 Vladimir Tatlin, 1916
© Archivo Iconografico, S.A./CORBIS

Message

> *"It is not necessary to copy nature and life, but it is necessary to observe and study them unceasingly."*

Alexander Shevchenko

> *"In the literal sense of the word, there is no such thing as a copy: no artist is able to produce two completely identical works. Painting is a visual art and, as such, can choose its object of imitation freely – that is, nature, or another work already in existence."*

From the manifesto of the neo-primitivists

A lot of people try to go it alone, but I think it's important to look at other people's design. It's not a matter of copying, because no two designs are ever alike, but it's important to see why things work, and to remind yourself constantly of this.

> *"An object is the sum of real units, a sum that has a utilitarian purpose."*

Ivan Puni

That last idea is quite similar to an area of psychology called Gestalt theory, which broadly suggests that the whole is greater than the sum of its parts. It's also central to my concept of design. In order to achieve this "sum of real units", you must build your final composition out of real, relevant, and complementary information – the elements in it should be directly related to the subject matter. If you're creating a web site for an opera house, for example, use pictures of that opera house, not just stock images. Some people will advocate adding bits and pieces that aren't relevant, but this is both distracting and detracting. It's fine to add neutral elements to act as part of the overall design, but they probably won't add to your theme.

For your opera house web site, for example, it would be fine to diversify your design with images that are not necessarily operatic: pictures of the surrounding city and its culture, perhaps. These can flesh out the core idea by showing some background and giving perspective. Including an unrelated image, on the other hand, such as a thunderstorm or a TV test pattern (and you do see these kinds of images on a lot of sites), doesn't speak to your viewers in any constructive way. Even if you want to use images like these as metaphors, such allusions are generally lost on the Web.

If you include elements that are cohesive, the finished product carries another level of information that might not be immediately apparent, but which contributes towards a richer overall design. Because you're using real images, you generate a design that is specific in its imagery, and therefore specific in its message.

> *"The most valuable and the most productive work is that which is guided by impression."*

Alexander Shevchenko

This final idea of Shevchenko's applies perfectly to the fast-forward world of the Web. When designing for this medium, the most valuable thing you can do is first to form the right impression in your mind, and then to recreate it in the viewer's mind.

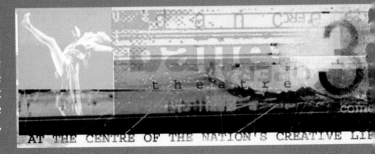

Process

Olga Rozanova, another Russian artist of the time, had some ideas on how to go about creating art in a way that makes sense. I think they're still very relevant. The process has three parts: the intuitive principle, the individual transformation of the visible, and abstract creation. I've chosen to interpret them in a way that works for me, and for the Web.

The intuitive principle

To me, the intuitive principle is all about presenting information that is not the design as such, but which nevertheless adds to its voice. And when I say "intuitive", I'm talking about something that's intuitive for both the designer and the viewer.

The intuitive elements of a design include combining things like color theory with form, to create a specific message. Have you noticed how the choice of palette can fuel the message of a design? Sometimes, this can be very obvious: if you're designing a web site for an insurance firm, for example, you probably won't use bright, garish colors, because you want to communicate an atmosphere of authority, reliability, solidity. (Although these days, all kinds of companies seem to want to get funky. The reason design is moving away from presenting this kind of message is that companies don't want to be seen as 'typical'. A result of competition, perhaps?)

The positioning of text, line work, and images can be far more subtle, but just as intuitive. If you imagine that you were designing a web site for architects, you might use clean, thin, exact line work to emphasize the message you want to convey: "This is a company you can rely on for style, sophistication, and professionalism."

The individual transformation of the visible

Individual transformation of the visible involves taking the raw material you need to work from, and adding your own interpretation and flavor to it – but never losing sight of the message. This is closely tied to the intuitive principle: it's how you link the main voice of the design to the message, bringing them together in an original way.

For the architectural web site, your raw material could be pictures of the firm's projects: maybe some buildings and blueprints. Incorporating the company logo is usually a good idea, too! The line work and color (which you might want to keep in tune with the logo) that you use to complement these pictures can then bring through the main voice of the design, which should be aesthetic, functional and precise.

Message

Abstract creation

During abstract creation, you develop design that is totally your own to bring the theme to life. This can mean manipulating the raw material by sinking it into the design so that it becomes fully a part of it. It can also involve putting in your own design touches, with further line work and new drawings.

From the raw material to the final design, an unbroken message should appear. Your design shouldn't be such that you've taken the original needs of the client and, through your creative process, totally obscured the message. Professional web design shouldn't be ego driven – the design is not about you, it's about the message you're trying to convey for your client. They will (usually) know their message better than you do, and the reality may be that you've forgotten that message in your design!

On the Web, people are bombarded with much that makes no sense at all, and the way they rapidly consume the medium means that there is confusion and smudging of style in their eyes. It's not enough just to create a piece of work that's individual in design; it must also be singular in meaning. This is where real strength in design lies. To be able to take your creative impetus and drive it into focused coherence is a true survival skill for the Web.

Artistic imperatives

What I seek to achieve in my work can be summarized in three key ideas expressed by Shevchenko and the other neo-primitivists: texture, structure, and style.

Texture

"We demand a good texture of our works – that is, the visual impression from a picture that is created by its surface, its painting (by brushstroke, density of paint, color, character of the painted layer); in a word, by everything that we see on the surface of the picture and that is related to its execution."

The computer designer does not have the luxury of paint. We do not have the freedom of a real canvas. But we do have some powerful tools, and texture is not out of our reach. Instead of using flat color, I often break up the surface by scratching out part of it, or putting low opacity text over it, for example. So if two elements are far apart and there is a flat area of color in between, I will try to break that area up by adding texture. Similarly, there are methods of creating a surface and a surface depth, some examples of which I'll demonstrate in the tutorial section that follows.

Structure

"We demand good structure – that is, a manner of execution that imparts a good density to the paint and to its disposition."

What is good structure? This can be difficult to define, and it's not always achieved consciously. It's about all the elements of a design working together. The surface is clearly delineated to enhance meaning. Focus points are highlighted. There is a marriage between the aesthetic and the functional. A good structure can impart a strong message, and a strong message will help deliver the intentions of your client to their clients. In the tutorial section, we'll see some concrete examples of how this works.

Style

"We demand good style of a work of art – that is, a style that expresses itself in a composition of lines, masses, and colors."

There are a number of elements in any work that you construct: color, line, form, content, and intent. These elements need to work together. It's possible to construct a work where all of these elements are well executed, but still don't deliver a cohesive message – and sometimes, this can be the client's fault. If you think of your final design as a puzzle, the client will often demand that you reshape one of the pieces. Suddenly, nothing fits together anymore. When this happens, it's really important that you don't just bang in the change, but try to rethink the design to encompass it. If you want to see how this can work in a real project, read on.

© Photograph by Ray Ryan

Message

My initial brief for this project, after meeting with the client, was: "We want something new, something dynamic for our web site. We want a look that will appeal to all our patrons." The client was a regional theater – *Artscape* – that hosts ballet, opera, stage productions, and other performing arts. This was a pretty open-ended brief, and I needed to know more about them – not just how they perceived themselves, but how they were perceived by their patrons. For that matter, who *were* their patrons?

The theater's own research showed patrons falling into two distinct categories: young, hip types (25-35), and your more conservative, older, traditional patrons of the arts (50-ancient). Considering their likely tastes, these were two very different groups, so my first challenge was to find a style that would marry them together – funky, but still austere.

I immediately made the decision to break up the design plane. Instead of trying to find something that was a compromise between these two very different styles, I wanted to try to represent both equally, and hopefully in a complementary fashion. At this point, I went and had a look at some design books – some traditional, some modern. I wanted to get an idea of what would appeal to each group, and then use elements of both in my look and feel.

First Scamps

The first images I looked at were ones that dealt with breaking up the visual plane. This was something that I wanted to get into my head before applying design styles from either group. I drew two initial scamps, the first of which was just a quick scribble of the way I first saw the idea represented graphically. Written underneath (I'll type it here, rather than make you suffer my handwriting) were my first ideas of how I wanted the image to speak:

1. Fine linework background, representing craftsmanship – analogous to the skill and precision of the arts.

2. A book (tattered, with an old-style picture on top) lying on top of the image. I'm not quite sure what I was getting at here, except that I know I wanted to present the concept of literature. In any event, I decided that I wasn't quite keeping to the theme, and changed this almost immediately to a torn-off ticket stub.

3. A line of dancers – mostly blurred, but with one of them in focus. I was trying to emphasize the idea that Artscape brings the arts into focus – perhaps a bit too literally. But from this evolved the idea that watching a performance at Artscape – a ballet, for instance – brought things out. Feelings and emotions that are normally hidden are brought to the fore and made vivid and real. This was closer to the route I wanted to go, and we'll see how this idea evolves later on.

The second scamp is a more detailed working of the same concept. In it, I was looking for *positioning*: how the elements I was thinking of would line up. Because I'm working with two fairly different styles, the way they work together is very important. I was looking for where to place focal points: where to center the gravity of the design, and which areas will draw your eyes to them.

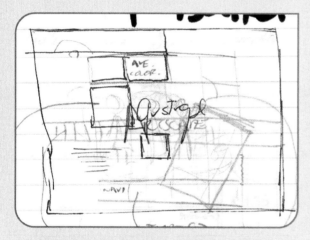

I also wanted to establish the relative proportions of the elements. It's a useful thing just to scribble the elements onto a page; it gives you a tangible idea of how things fit together, or jar into each other, or get in each other's way and run out of space. It forms a map in your mind that will be useful later, when you come to manipulating the raw material. I also added a thin 'strip' of a dancer in slightly changing poses, to be placed above the line of dancers – looking a bit like a film reel. I guess I wanted this here because the whole idea of slow motion photography – of seeing things that were right under your nose the whole time, but you missed – fascinates me. I wanted to get that kind of idea across: If you come to a show, you're going to be seeing something that otherwise you'd have missed.

Raw Material and Inspiration

I eventually chose to base the concept on a print design for a clothing manufacturer that I felt would be a useful starting point. The design plane is broken up into areas of strong photos, and flat color. I wasn't particularly looking for a design to do this, but I found that this image, more than most I looked at, represented both of the 'food groups' that I was trying to cater for. With the clean linework, you have a conservative aesthetic appeal, while the break-up gives it something fresh. I also like this design because it's not afraid of open space.

First Draft

I like to choose colors before I do anything else. In this particular case, the client had recently created a corporate look-and-feel that was based primarily on their logo, and three basic colors: an olive-khaki-to-blue-green, an ochre yellow, and a mauve-to-violet color. These colors were my initial departure point.

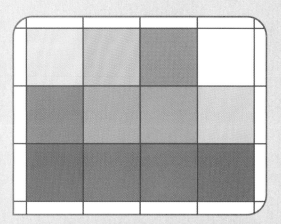

The other colors in my palette were chosen to go with these 'standards'. I decided not to include the mauve in my image, and to tone down the blue-green color. This left the ochre, which I built a fair bit of the palette around. These colors act as a guideline, and offer a point of reference when you're manipulating your raw material into the design. For the first draft, I worked primarily on the image of the dancers.

My first task was to blur the background dancers, but to leave the principal dancer in focus. I chose this particular picture for its striking presence. There is good flow from the pose of the dancer to the background dancers; it's the way the principal dancer brackets them, I think. Also, there is good use of light – the principal well lit, the other dancers far less so – which lends itself perfectly to blurring.

My initial plan was simply to leave the principal dancer in focus and blur everything else, but when I tried this technique it looked artificial. It's often that way with design: the way you picture something is very different from the way it comes out. Faced with this obstacle, I chose to differentiate the focused and blurred areas by segmenting the image.

Keeping one part of an image in focus and blurring the rest is particularly easy to achieve in Photoshop. For example, you could select the area you want to keep in focus (the lead dancer) using the Marquee tool, take the inverse of the selection (Select > Inverse), and apply a Gaussian blur filter (Filter > Blur > Gaussian Blur). All things considered, though, that's not a particularly aesthetic effect. I decided to break up my 'in focus' block a little further.

Instead of working with one layer and leaving a part of it in focus while blurring the rest, I used two identical layers of the same image, as I'll demonstrate. Open the file 1.dancers.psd, and copy the dancer 1 layer by simply dragging it to the new layer icon at the bottom of the Layers palette. Name the copied layer dancer 2, and then apply a Gaussian blur to the dancer 1 layer, with a radius of 12 pixels.

Message

Now, on the dancer 2 layer, use the Rectangular Marquee tool to make a selection of the head and upper body of the ballerina.

Next, apply a layer mask that will leave the selected part of the dancer in focus, and let the blurred layer below show through everywhere else (Layer > Add Layer Mask > Reveal Selection).

Why do this instead? Well, using a layer mask means that I can move the 'in focus' area around later if I choose. I can make any area I want in focus, and I'm not limited to my initial rectangle. This is very useful if you often change your mind while designing, as I do. Designs evolve, and it's vital to your sanity not to have to redo initial work because you've made it too static.

So. I've got my 'in focus' rectangle, as dictated by my layer mask. I found this contrast too stark, however, so I added a Hue/Saturation adjustment layer to dancer 2 (Layer > New Adjustment Layer > Hue/Saturation). Make sure Group With Previous Layer is checked, and in the Hue/Saturation dialog, check Colorize and change the Hue value to 45 and the Saturation value to 25.

I could have added just one adjustment layer to the whole project, but I chose to add one to each of the dancer layers. This means I can change the effect of the adjustment layer on either of the layers at a later date, which is worthwhile if you want to alter your color schemes subtly.

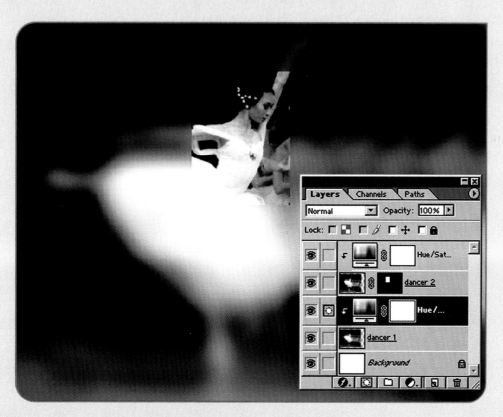

I still wasn't quite happy with this – the design was way too severe. In response, I filled the background layer (Edit > Fill) with a khaki color from our color scheme (RGB: 231, 215, 163), and used a mask on dancer 1 to blend the area surrounding the principal dancer into the background layer.

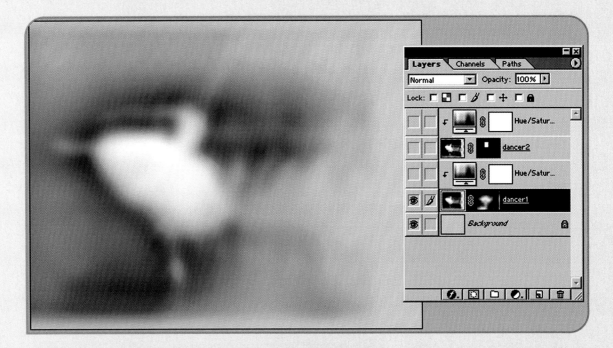

At this stage, my plan to contrast the focused and blurred areas hadn't quite been carried off the way I wanted it, so I decided to add a third dancer layer. Copy the dancer 2 layer, complete with mask, and name the copy dancer 3. Then change the blending mode of the dancer 2 layer to Screen, to contrast the blurred and in-focus areas once again. On the dancer 3 mask, we're going to erase the dark background around the dancer's head, letting the blurred layers below show through. Use a black paintbrush at 20% opacity to draw on the mask, which has the effect of erasing areas using a kind of spray-painting technique.

In the end, what we have is three layers: the topmost (dancer 3) is completely in focus, constrained to the size of a chosen rectangle (using a mask), but following the form of the principal dancer (we removed more from the mask by adding black paint). The layer below that (dancer 2), also constrained to the rectangle, is less in focus, having been blended to the dancer 1 layer – a very blurry and insubstantial layer – using the Screen blending mode. To each layer, I have applied an adjustment layer that removes a lot of the color. The effect of all of this is to contrast the in-focus and blurred areas, but in a less obvious and more interesting way (see `3.final dancer.psd`).

Also, the refinement of the contrast between the in-focus dancer and the blurred background has increased the surface depth of the work. It's not just totally flat, and that added volume draws the viewer in.

Now it's time to break up the image plane! I used some guides to help divide up the image, and brought in another, smaller, black and white photograph (`smalldancers.psd`).

I then added a Hue/Saturation adjustment layer to tone down the part of the block to the right of the picture.

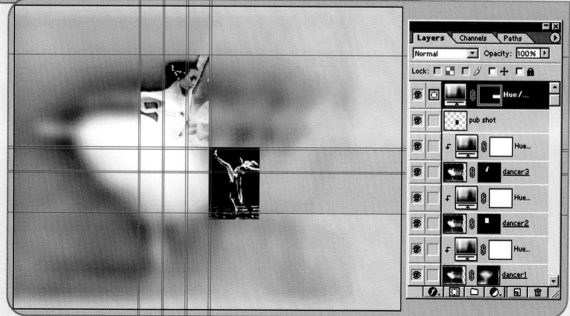

Message

Over the photo and adjustment layer, I placed a layer named color over with a block of yellow (RGB: 255, 204, 0) that I set to Screen. This area will be the base for the collage of text we'll be adding later.

I then added an eggshell-colored border to separate the sections of the plane, and to create a block of color at the bottom right of the image.

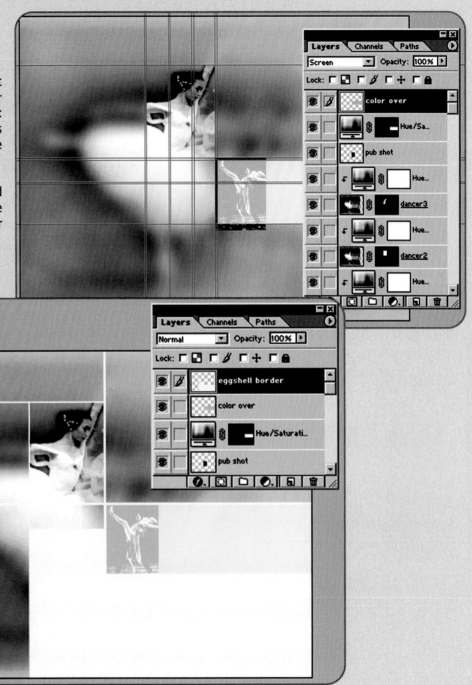

Referring back to the original inspirational image, you can see the beginnings of a similar technique: the combination of flat and complex color. The image (`4.fragmented dancer.psd`) is starting to look spliced together, which is part of the effect I'm going for.

Working Draft

Having got this far, and having broken up the image in more or less the way I wanted to, I now needed to add some more creative elements to complete the design. There were a number of considerations at this point.

Firstly, I found the use of flat color to be a little bland. I therefore planned to add some texture to those areas to break up the space a little. Secondly, I wanted to bring out a more funky, raw feel to some parts of the image. So far, the design was fairly conservative, and I wanted to change that. I also wanted to add more than just ballet to the design, as the clients should be able to demonstrate their entire creative offering. I therefore needed a generic and vibrant area as the focal point of the work, to bring this multifaceted face of the company to the fore.

I started by scanning in a handwritten list (`listofwords.psd`) of all the areas the theatre was involved in.

By writing them in black and inverting the scan that I had placed on a new layer (Image > Adjust > Invert), and then modifying the blending mode to Screen, the writing takes the appearance of being written onto the image surface in white. At first, this was how I intended to represent the different areas of the theater, but upon completion of this task I found that the result was not as visually interesting as I'd hoped for.

The image needed more. I left the handwritten part in, but dropped the opacity of the layer way down to 16%, so that it appears like an impression on a notepad after the page that was actually written on has been torn out. I also left it in because it added just a little bit of balance to an area of the image that was otherwise too starkly delineated by the plane lines. As you'll see later, I added some more design in that area to break up that delineation even more, but for the time being the writing was enough.

Although the top-right section of the image is broken up to some degree by the blurred remains of the dancers and the handwritten list, I wanted to increase this. I scanned in the messed up sides of an old photocopy – a perfect place to find some really interesting shapes and textures! Bring the scanned image (scanned_in.psd) onto a new layer called breakup, place this layer under the color over layer and apply Multiply mode.

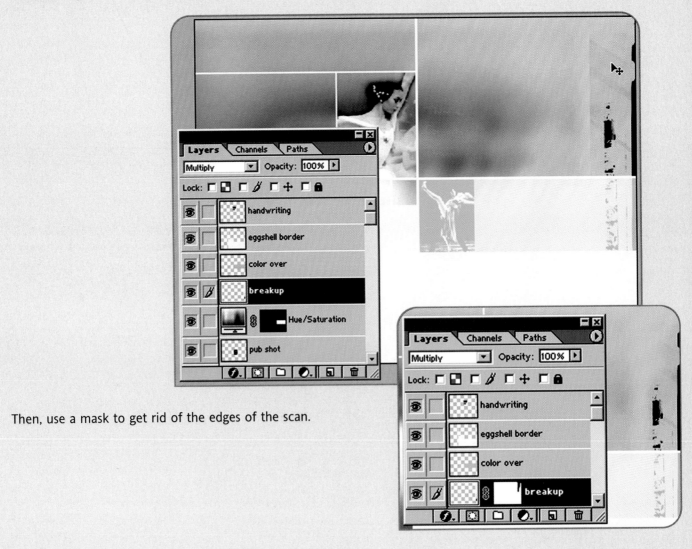

Then, use a mask to get rid of the edges of the scan.

The right hand collage of text is a complex piece to look at in its final form, but there are distinct elements, and it was constructed in a particular order that we will now look at.

Firstly, I wanted to retry representing all the facets of the theatre using text. Instead of using the handwriting technique that I wasn't happy with, I decided to go for a far more abstract approach. I started with a blank rectangle and then added one word at a time, breaking it up, inverting it, or flipping it on its side as it suited me. I used various fonts and layer blending modes to achieve this effect. (See `5.Adding information.psd`)

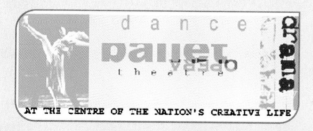

What I was saying with this was that people view the different arts differently. Each has its own unique style, and I wanted this individual character to come across in the design. Underneath this, I added the theatre's byline: AT THE CENTRE OF THE NATION'S CREATIVE LIFE.

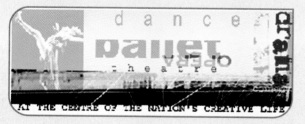

I now wanted to add elements that would cause the text to break up further. To the text, I added four bits of texture, the first of which was a scanned-in corner of an old photograph (`morebreakup.psd`), all scratched up (ready to serve!), which I added to the bottom of the rectangular area. I named the layer photobreakup, inverted it (Image > Adjust > Invert), and applied Multiply mode.

Message

On top of this, I added a textured block of yellow color (breakup.psd), on a new layer called yellowover, also with a blending mode of Multiply. I wanted to saturate the lower half of the rectangle with color, partly so that the word comedy (which I'd done in white) was more visible, and partly so that the photobreakup layer could be toned down (I felt it was a little too dominant).

The third bit of texture is a few blown up lines from a fax form. (You'll be amazed where you can find texture!) I added this above the photograph texture on a new layer called photocopy. Again, I used Multiply mode here.

The fourth piece of texture was a scratchy photograph of an old film number countdown sequence (`film3.psd`). I added it above the eggshell border layer, and used a mask to get rid of the edges of the photograph. I must admit that this last insertion was a little off the theme, and I did think about that at the time. However, I was going for the 'art across all mediums' approach, so I took a little artistic license myself!

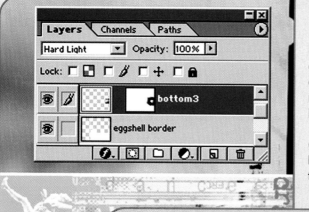

I had to break this image up into two layers, as I couldn't get a blending mode that showed enough of the image: Overlay caused it to be too light, and Multiply too dark, but only in certain areas. So I cut the scan in half, with the upper half represented through Luminosity blending mode, and the lower half through Hard Light.

(An alternative technique here could have been to mess with the levels of the image, through Image > Adjust > Levels. Pity I didn't think of that at the time!)

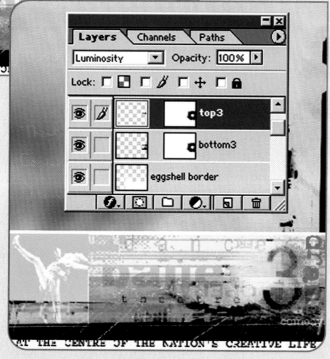

You'll have noticed that I used Multiply mode on a lot of the layers. The reason for this is that using Multiply allows for intersections between layers to be visible – you can see through the top layer to the layer underneath. Also, unlike Overlay or Screen, you don't lose a lot of the substance of the layer. Another reason why I used this particular blending mode was that I didn't want the upper layers to dominate those underneath them. Putting everything on one layer would solve this, of course, but then I would have lost the flexibility to change things later.

Message

The result, I think, is a very gritty look and feel. The reason I went for this is that the theater is currently in a process of transformation, of reinventing itself. Part of this process is the deconstruction of the idea that theater is inaccessible to youth – they don't want to be seen as a staid, boring old place. I've tried to bring across a feel of street culture, with an 'alleyway torn-down poster' combined with a 'digital information-flow'. Certainly it's a strange mix of ideas, but I was anxious to move the design into a funkier highland.

The last thing to do in this phase was to add the Artscape logo. Once I'd done this, I immediately noticed that it stood out too much, so I decided to break that up too.

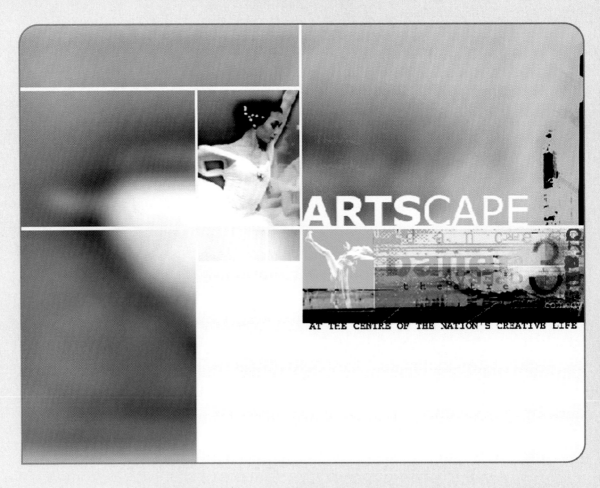

I applied a mask, chose a very grainy brush style (Spatter 58 pixels), and set the color to black and the opacity to about 15%. I could then scratch away at the mask to fit the logo into the style of the entire work better.

At this point, I sent the work off to the client for comments. While they liked the progress, they were concerned with the way the 'Artscape' text was so badly broken up. I guess I was messing with their corporate identity too much, so I went back and toned it down (see 6. Filling out and texturising.psd).

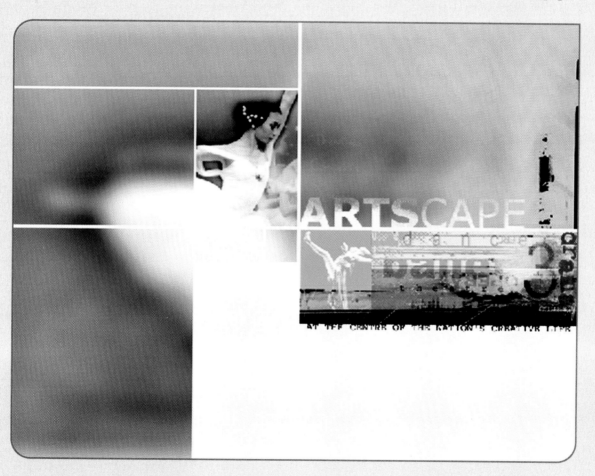

Final Draft

There are a number of elements still to be added. First, this was going to be the home page, so some elements for navigation would be required. Second, the one negative comment that I received from the client was that the design was very ballet-centric. I had to admit that was true, despite the fact that I'd been trying to avoid this all along! There was a reason, though: I planned for the site to be extremely customizable, to the extent that a viewer would be able to choose a different skin/theme when they came to the site. This, therefore, was the ballet theme. While a lot of the elements would stay the same across themes (it's always a bad idea to change how navigation works, for example), I planned to replace the dancers with (say) opera singers – a similar look, but a different feel. This idea was well met with by the client.

Unfortunately I had to abandon one of my earliest ideas – to have a sequence of the dancer in slightly changing poses, like a filmstrip – as I just couldn't get hold of any satisfactory raw material. I still liked the idea though, so I decided to try and represent it in a slightly different way, with the raw material available to me. I got the idea from glancing across at my Channels palette; have you ever noticed how you get this miniature version of your entire picture at three or four different intensities?

To me, this seemed like a good compromise. I hadn't wanted to have all the squares in the plane break-up the same size, so I'd included three small squares, right under the principal dancer rectangle. Currently the rest of the image overpowered them, so I decided to place differently modified versions of the principal dancer into each. For the third square, I took the original dancer layer, cropped it into a square and made it a lot smaller (Edit > Transform > Scale). I named the layer icondancer3 and then used the Exclusion blending mode on it.

I liked the way this amplified the principal dancer, so I made a copy of the layer, and dragged it into the first little square. I named this layer icondancer1 and applied a Luminosity blending mode; this removed the color, but was no less contrasting – a good counterpoint to the one on the right. I then copied *this* layer, dragged it onto the second square and named it icondancer2. I inverted it (Image > Adjust > Invert), left the mode at Luminosity, and dropped the opacity way down to 24%.

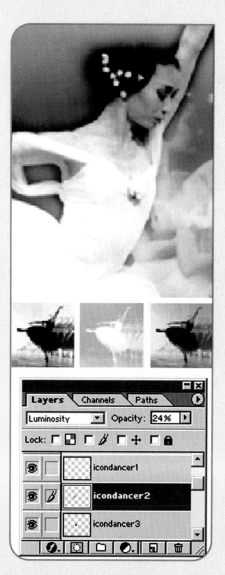

As a result of this work, I had changed my message from, "You will see things right under your nose," to, "You will see things from a different perspective." Actually, I think this design element turned out better than the animated strip of dancers would have.

Message

Now for the navigation. I've gone for something very simple at this point: just some text to click on. The reason for this is that the page will serve as a kind of 'portal' to major parts of the site, where the rest of the navigation will be situated – so there's no need to worry about that now. One thing that had been bothering me for a while, though, was the inequality of different sections of the work: some sections were sticking together, and others weren't. This was spreading the focus of the work too much, which is something I wanted to remedy by segmenting it further. I therefore selected the bottom left section, and applied an adjustment layer to lighten it up.

I then added a mask to this layer, and placed a gray strip over the all-white mask, to line up with the three small dancer squares.

Using gray meant that the adjustment layer wasn't as effective in the location of the strip, creating a darker band in this position. Doing this gave a greater horizontal flow to the work, which I felt was breaking down a bit too much. It also created a stronger division of the piece into halves, once again giving a better flow. Although I wanted to fragment the image a lot, this was isolating areas of it unnaturally, and spoiling the overall impact.

I then further emphasized the horizontal flow I'd created by changing the color of the adjustment layer where I'd applied the gray strip mask to it, making this part a complementary blue.

This area of the image was naturally lending itself to be used for navigation, so this is where I added the necessary elements, keeping them simple and fairly neutral. Remember, I was planning on adding different design themes, so the navigation would have to match all of them.

The flow of the work was *still* bothering me, so I added some new design where the handwritten text had been. For this, I used a scanned-in piece of torn, ring-bound paper (`ringunbound.psd`) with a Luminosity blending mode at around 30% opacity.

I then blended this into the rest of the image with some substantial masking.

With this completed, all that remained was to crop off the bottom of the image, something I only ever do right at the end of a project – just in case I need to use the space, and wind up constricting myself. Finally, I added the Artscape logo in the top left, and broke it up (just a little) to match the Artscape text.

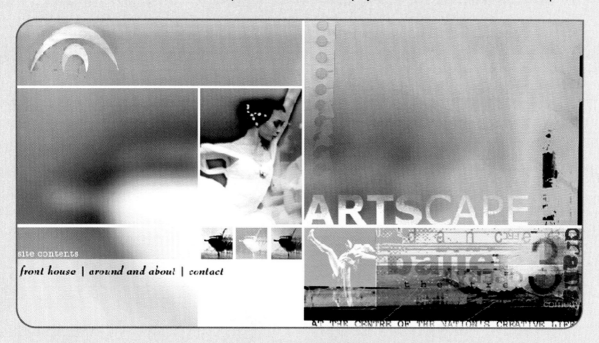

There were just two things remaining that troubled me. Firstly, the eggshell-colored boundary lines were a little too stark and artificial. To remedy this, I applied a mask to this layer, and then (using a black, low opacity, highly grained paintbrush) scratched out certain areas of the layer slightly. This blended these divisions into the work better.

Secondly, I still didn't feel that some of the sections were sufficiently fragmented from their neighbors. (Actually, some of this was probably caused by me mucking up the boundary lines – nothing like solving one problem and creating another!) But I did also notice that it's a bit artificial to have a boundary line slicing through two parts of an image that are identical in treatment. I didn't want the section boundaries to make the image look like I'd cut it up; rather, I wanted the feeling that I'd stuck different images together to form the same subject matter.

I decided to solve this problem by applying layers with blocks of color to neighboring sections at the very top of the Layers palette. I dropped their opacities right down, just allowing enough to make them visibly different from each other. I applied a red block to the section immediately to the left of the principal dancer, using Overlay mode at 8% opacity.

I used a green block for the large top right section, again using Overlay mode, but this time with a higher opacity of 16%.

For the top left section, I used a yellow color block at 18% opacity, this time with Soft Light mode.

In this way, I've slightly tinted some of the sections.

Finally, just to be difficult, I added in a vertical strip of break-up to the extreme left of the picture, to make it a little more textured. This was another piece of scanned, messy photocopy to which I applied Multiply mode and then dropped to low layer opacity: 8%. Here, then, is the final image (see 8. `final.psd`):

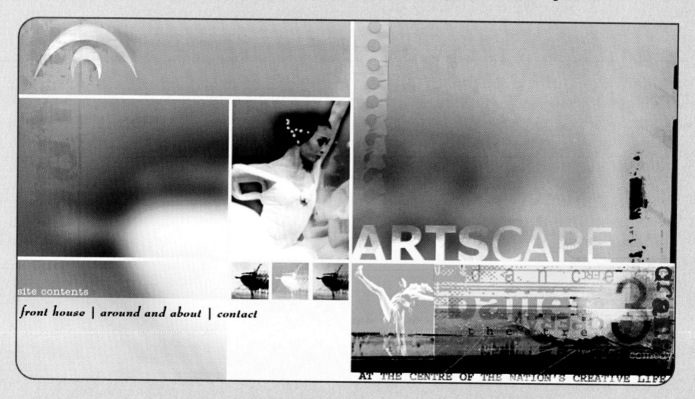

Conclusion: Revisiting the Theme

With the constant reworking of the horizontal and vertical flow, and the break-up of the images, I feel that I've created a fairly strong focal point to the work, centered roughly on the beginning of the "Artscape" text. Also, there's a prevalent diagonal flow to the work (from top left to bottom right), which works from an information point of view: first the logo, then the company name, then the by-line, but picking up visual information the whole way through this journey. This is certainly something I tried to create throughout the design process: a strong sense of visual flow.

On viewing the (now completed) image, I feel that my constant reworking has, to some extent, lost the initial impact of having one dancer in focus, and the rest blurred. This was prevalent in the early versions of the work, but got 'designed over' as things progressed. It's not entirely lost, but if I could change anything, it would be to reintroduce this feature somehow. A positive outcome, on the other hand, is that the reworking has given the design a good surface depth. There are many different levels to the design, some clearly in focus, and some unformed.

If you look at the original scamps, and then at the completed work, you can see that I've gone from the idea of representing the concepts of art and literature fairly literally, to a more 'street hype' kind of style. I think the balance of the work might have tipped a little *too* far towards the funky end, but I feel this travel of concept is a good one. Anyway, old people can be cool too...

The visual message I was hoping to get across was to open up a dialog between my client and their clients:

- There are many distinct facets to the theater, each with their unique attractions

- Theater is for people from all walks of life

- Theater can hold something for you that you wouldn't ordinarily see

- Theater doesn't have to be predictable or boring; it can be fresh and raw, and different

When the final changes were presented, the work was well received by the client. What remains is to create the other skins, but retaining the original look and feel. The project continues, but it should be completed in a month or two.

te contents

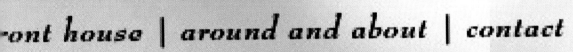

ront house | around and about | contact

ARTSCAPE

dance theatre
.com

chapter 1

chapter 2

chapter 3

chapter 4

chapter 5

chapter 6

chapter 7

chapter 8

chapter 9

chapter 10

chapter 11

chapter 12

chapter 13

chapter 14

chapter 15

chapter 16

outro

"Never underestimate the power of frustration."

Derek Lea
www.dereklea.com

Psychosurgery

Never underestimate the power of frustration. It certainly helped motivate me to begin my career as a digital artist. For years, I had worked at art-related jobs: I was (briefly) an art director, spent many years as a designer, and a few more retouching images at a photography studio – but I felt unsatisfied, like I was going around and around in circles, getting nowhere. It was that sense of frustration that led me to create my first piece of digital art. I wanted a seamless blend of photography, digital art, and traditional illustration; something I had never really attempted before. But I also had a strong urge to create something rich and intelligent, something that had meaning.

The years I spent retouching certainly weren't wasted. I really got to know Photoshop inside out. I began to develop my own techniques for retouching images, using layers and channels often. My technique of stacking duplicate layers with multiple blending modes evolved out of a constant need for flexibility. The same can be said for stacking adjustment layers. The ongoing concern in those days was to manipulate images in a way that didn't deteriorate the photography, and to leave the working layered files flexible enough that any revisions wouldn't mean going back to square one.

Through experimentation I found inspiration. A pleasant surprise in discovering a new technique would start to spark ideas. And while I sat at my computer retouching jewelry, or cars, or whatever, my mind would begin to wander. I started to formulate ideas of what fantastic images I could create by employing these techniques. I figured that I could create masterpieces using Photoshop. I just needed to stop thinking about it and actually start doing something.

I think the most valuable skill I developed while working with photographers was a way to assemble images in a realistic manner – marrying two or more completely different shots so that they looked as if they belonged together in their environment. I began to get more involved in the initial planning of the photo shoots, and pondering the best lighting arrangements, so that I could make the image manipulation more believable. While I was experimenting with my Photoshop techniques, I began to realize that I could execute exactly what I wanted, in the way that I visualized it, if I was doing the photography myself as well. I started asking the photographers technical questions, and tried some shooting. It was time to create something that was entirely my own.

My first image was called *Iterance*. I remember reading through a thesaurus to help me to come up with some ideas, because it was very important to me that the image should mean something. When I found the word 'iterance', and saw that it meant the same thing as 'repetition', it started to spark ideas. I began sketching a main circular shape, and incorporated diverse visual elements that represented repetitive cycles. I was pleased with the result – actually, I was quite surprised that the image had come from me. With hindsight, I see how autobiographical the subject matter was. I felt so stuck in a rut, just going around in circles.

The next image I created was about the concept of reinventing yourself through art. I think it was inspired by the feelings of liberation I got from *Iterance*. I called it *Catharsis*, and the main visual component was all about being reborn or set free. The secondary elements represented things like feeling fragmented, empty, or lacking focus. Again, looking back, it was entirely autobiographical – and coincidentally, it really did set me free. It won several awards, and the phone started ringing. Since then, I've been working steadily and independently. *Iterance* and *Catharsis* hang above computers in my studio, and while I don't know if it's possible to draw true inspiration from one's own work, these images inspire me every day. They remind me of how frustrated I was, and how lucky I am to be making a living doing something that I love.

Psychosurgery

I have always liked artwork that feels mysterious, and I enjoy the idea of creating something that makes people a little uncertain or uneasy. H. R. Giger is the master of this – I could spend countless hours looking at his work. There's always a feeling of being immersed in some terrible world filled with mysterious and ominous creatures. Giger's attention to detail really rewards those who take the time to look closely. I've also found inspiration in many of Salvador Dali's surreal landscapes, and some of M. C. Escher's more three-dimensional works.

Further fantastic examples of conveying something mysterious can be found in the art of Dave McKean – in fact, it was seeing some of his covers for the *Sandman* series of graphic novels that really started me thinking about getting creative in Photoshop. There was such a beautiful blend of things that were real, with digital tools. I think what I like so much about his work is that the mixed media pieces make you really focus on the subject and what he is saying, rather than the digital techniques and tools involved.

In terms of producing art with a computer, one of the first things to inspire me was the *Myst* CD-ROM. It's not so much that it was a game, but that the whole thing was so beautiful – the fantastic richness of the imagery and the attention to detail were unparalleled at the time. I think the virtual world itself was captivating, and combined with the ambient soundtrack, it was a totally immersing experience. The fact that it was wholly digital really appealed to me too – as an artist who works digitally, it makes the medium seem more valid when there are digital artworks that are recognized as such by the rest of the world.

© Myst III: Exile from Ubi Soft Entertainment

Away from physical imagery, I find inspiration in music – usually multi-layered or complex pieces like Fripp & Eno's album *No Pussyfooting*, with its long, sprawling soundscapes. I think that strange and interesting music can help you snap out of the mundane and unleash some good ideas, and I always try to have something on when I'm working. Julian Cope's CD, *Odin*, is a 73-minute vocal mantra – a meditation on Silbury & Waden Hill in Wiltshire, England. He describes it as, "A simultaneously-synthesized parallel-harmonic breathing meditation of 73 minutes and 45 seconds' duration." It's unlike anything else I've ever heard, and it's great music to work to.

One of my most fulfilling projects to date was music-related. I was asked by Lark Popov and George Vona to create the images and packaging for a music CD and accompanying CD-ROM called *The Book of Mirrors*. Popov and Vona are classical pianists who commissioned avant-garde and highly conceptual musical compositions, employing percussion as bizarre as riding crops and breaking glass. The music itself was so inspiring and full of ideas that I must have made around a hundred images for the project. At www.bookofmirrors.com, you can hear samples of the music, and see some more of the rich content that I was moved to create.

www.bookofmirrors.com
(C) 1999 Lark Popov and George Vona

www.bookofmirrors.com
(C) 1999 Lark Popov and George Vona

Psychosurgery

In all my work, I like to incorporate an impression of something tactile – I don't want it to feel cold, or computer-generated. When you're working digitally, there's a danger that you can make things too perfect, but I think that some of the most appealing things around us are the imperfections. I find beauty and inspiration in rusted metals, peeling paint, etc. – and when I see such things, I take photographs, and use bits and pieces of the photos in my images as textures or backgrounds. This can really help in conveying the feeling of imperfection that I think helps to ground an image and bring it back to earth.

I truly enjoy the time I spend scouring antique and junk shops, which can be treasure troves of inspiration – although sometimes, you have to look beyond the obvious to find it. The other day, for example, I purchased a very old, hand-bound Chinese book. It's turning brown, the cover is coming apart in thin layers, and the corners are bent and folded. I'll never read it, but I think it's stunning: I'll scan or photograph it, and maybe use a couple of the creases or the bumpy surface to overlay an image.

On other occasions, I'll get out my watercolors and start painting. Then, I'll scan the paintings, and use them as textures or as small sections of background. Or perhaps I'll tear up the paintings, and just scan bits and pieces of them. There are times when I create an alpha channel from a scan of something as simple as crumpled paper, and generate a surface texture from that.

I've also spent my fair share of time sifting through old, broken computer parts – video cards, motherboards, that kind of thing – to compile a collection of real-world technological elements to use in relevant images. Again, finding something unique can inspire a new direction in an image that would otherwise follow a predictable theme. I recently grabbed the insides of an old television set that someone was going to throw away, and I can't wait for a chance to use it in a technology-related piece.

Not all of my photography is done in the studio. Often, I go out on unplanned shoots, and end up in abandoned warehouses, or deserted, dilapidated, industrial areas. There are so many fabulous textures in these places. Sometimes, something as simple as an old brick wall with crumbling mortar can trigger an idea. Again, it's not always the literal object that is the beautiful part; it may be something as down-to-earth as the ragged edge of a piece of rusted metal, or a single support beam of a railway bridge, or a link in the chain that makes up a fence. I have literally hundreds of images like this on file, and I'm always on the lookout for new ones.

Recently, inspiration has come in an unexpected and rather non-literal way. My wife and I began traveling to Great Britain in 1998, to explore some of the Neolithic monuments. Never before have I experienced such a profound sense of 'place'. Whether they are stone circles, long barrows, or dolmens doesn't seem to matter; they each have a commanding presence that I can't entirely explain. Some of them are off the beaten path, but they're thousands of years old, and still standing – places on the land, marked by ancient peoples eons ago. What could be more fascinating or mysterious?

I don't know exactly what impact these sites have had or will have on my work, but they have enriched my life in a way that I'm sure is bound to come across somehow. I've taken photos of many sites, and hope to create a series of personal images of a megalithic nature. It would be great to make rubbings of some of the rock engravings in the Irish Passage tombs – maybe the Kilmartin Valley cup and ring marks as well – and use them in my pieces. I think it would be an interesting way to combine truly ancient artwork with its most contemporary counterpart. It's just a matter of finding the time to do it. Perhaps the next Photoshop upgrade will incorporate a 'stop time' option of some sort?

Psychosurgery

Photoshop artwork is no more immune to fashion than is traditional illustration or photography. Every year there are styles that seem to be mimicked by many different artists. I try not to get seduced by what's popular at the moment, or to jump on bandwagons. I think it's much more important that I concentrate on refining my own personal style. I think that the truly great artists – the ones that people remember – are the ones who exhibit a style and technique that is all their own. That's my goal, too.

Even so, although I find decaying buildings, rusted metal, old books, and cracked concrete inspiring, these elements aren't always appropriate. Many of the images I'm commissioned to produce are of a more technological nature, where ominous environments and warm colors aren't always appropriate. In those circumstances, I do pay attention to what's going on 'out there'. In fact, I've found the most beneficial aspect of looking at others' artwork is to examine their approach to color, and I'm always on the lookout for an innovative combination that I can use in an image. In different ways, though, I still try to add the same feelings of tactility, and real world imperfections.

A feeling that has always appealed to and motivated me, is that of being lost inside something – something so strong that it can pull you in and make you forget about everything else. It can be a painting, a photograph, some music, a book, a CD-ROM, or even an actual place you can visit. I think the greatest thing any artist can achieve is to create something that totally immerses the viewer.

In my work, I like to tell a story. I want the image to convey something immediately, but also to be rewarding to those who take the time to look closely. Sometimes, I'll add in secondary visual elements, to reveal more of the story. This is the main reason why I enjoy editorial work so much.

The image used in the following tutorial, for example, was originally an editorial commission – a two-page illustration in Elm Street magazine. It opened an article on the resurgence of psychosurgery, and its implications. The art director wanted to focus on the testimony of one of the patients mentioned in the article, who had described the feeling of relief after having a lobotomy as "releasing black butterflies". That was such a strong visual statement that I was struck with the appropriate image immediately.

I wanted to show someone who had been suffering from their affliction. That's why the figure's complexion is blue, and there are dark circles under the eyes (which are closed due to fatigue). But I wanted the release to be intense, which is why the top of the head is bursting open, with beams of light shining out. There's a huge cloud of black butterflies that are scattering as they're released; black resin drips and spatters off them, to show that they are foul and unhealthy things.

After the art director approved the sketch, and we had discussed the overall feeling and color scheme, I got started. To find such a dark-colored butterfly, I felt sure that I would end up having to alter a monarch, or something similar, but that day I was lucky: a phone call to a local junk shop proved fruitful. I photographed the model, some torn paper, and the butterfly, paying special attention to the lighting situations. I scanned the transparencies, and the tactile elements for the textures. The next stage was plenty of time spent in Photoshop; and in the following pages, step by step, I'll show you exactly how it was done.

Psychosurgery

Note: As the author has described, the image in this tutorial was originally used to illustrate a magazine article, and unfortunately we are unable to supply source files for you to experiment on. We hope you'll find, though, that the techniques described can usefully be applied to a range of different projects.

As I explained, this image needed to have an ominous feel to it – psychosurgery is a terrifying and very serious subject. I wanted some moody lighting that would fall off to dark areas around the edges, so as usual when I need something like that, I created the initial background image using Painter. The main reason for this is familiarity; I started using the lighting effects way back in Painter version 3.0, when I found them to be more versatile and intuitive than those available in Photoshop at the time. As a consequence, I've never felt the need to go into Photoshop's lighting effects, although I'm sure they've evolved since then, and with a bit of experimentation you could probably achieve similar results.

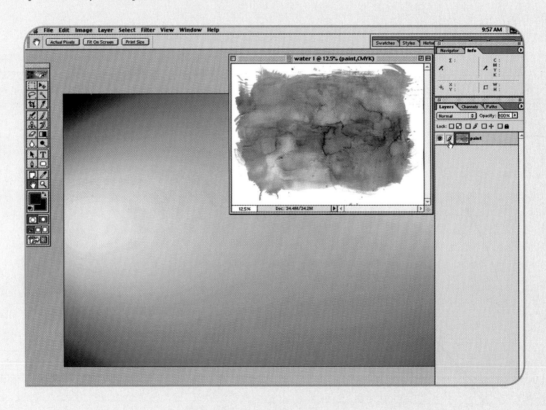

I also painted a watercolor painting, and scanned it. I'm rather impatient, so I find that it's always useful to keep a hairdryer on hand to speed up the drying process. Believe me, you don't want little bits of wet paint stuck to the glass of your scanner! In the painting, I used some warm colors that would go well with the background I'd created; I wanted to overlay the watercolor painting on top of the background in a way that would express the strokes and texture of the watercolor, but still show the lighting and dark edges of the background. To get started I dragged and dropped the watercolor scan into the background image file as a new layer called paint.

Since I wanted the watercolor to look as if it had been painted directly on the background image, I changed the blending mode of the layer to Multiply. This added the color into the layer underneath, simulating a water stain effect, eliminating the highlights, and letting all of the dark areas around the edges show through.

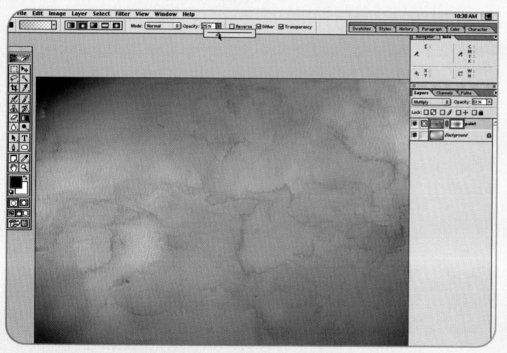

In order to lessen the effect slightly, I reduced the layer's opacity, and added a layer mask. Using the Gradient tool, I began to mask out a bit of the paint in the center of the image. Nothing too drastic – a few radial gradients from black to transparent with an opacity setting of around 25% was all I needed. The idea here was just to lessen the effect in the center of the background, so that when I introduced the main elements of the image, the background didn't compete with them.

Psychosurgery

Wanting to make the watermarks stand out a little and reduce the rather murky mid-tones, I duplicated the paint layer and changed its blending mode to Overlay. This created a bit too much contrast, so I reduced the opacity to 20%. Then, wanting to darken just the edges a bit, I duplicated this layer and changed its blending mode to Multiply. Since I only wanted to darken the edges, I used the Gradient tool in the layer mask again to mask out almost the entire center. This technique of duplicating or stacking layers is a good way to experiment with different combinations of blending modes; it can often reveal some surprises that prove to be useful knowledge later on.

With the background completed, I dragged in a scan of the original rough sketch I'd made as a separate layer called sketch, and changed the layer blending mode to Multiply at 42% opacity. I would use this simply as an aid to placing the other elements in their appropriate positions, switching it on and off as necessary. It was really just a template to ensure that the resulting image was similar to what the art director had approved.

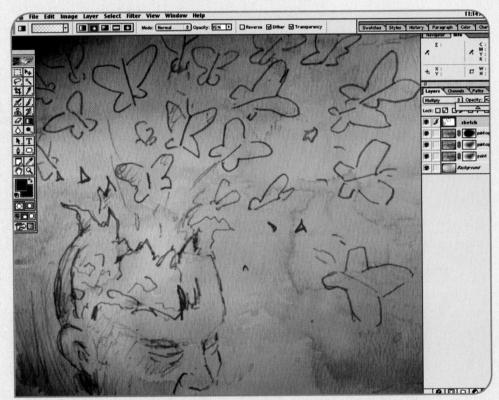

The Head

The next step was to create the sickly blue head from which the butterflies would burst. It started out as a simple photograph of a woman's head, and I drew a path around her face, and the shape of where her head would be under her hair. (There was no need to worry about drawing around the hair, since I wanted the figure's head to be bald.) After converting the path into a selection, I dragged the image inside the active selection into the working file as a new layer that I named head. I then resized the head using Free Transform (Edit > Free Transform), and positioned it according to the sketch layer.

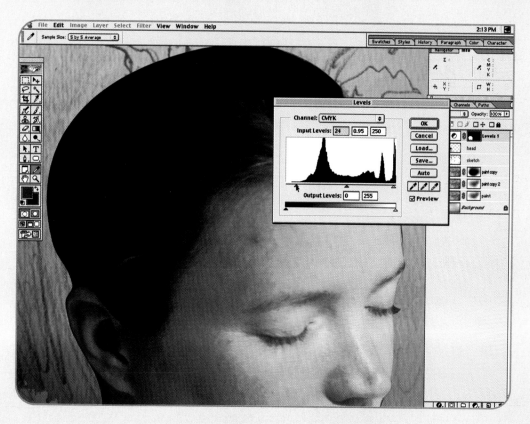

Psychosurgery

Now all I needed to adjust was the color and contrast of the head. I like to use adjustment layers whenever possible, as doing so makes things a lot more flexible, and you can continue performing adjustments or changing things without stripping away information or deteriorating your images. You can also employ the same layer stacking sensibilities with adjustment layers as I did with the background layers. First up was the contrast adjustment, so I Command-clicked on the head layer's icon in the Layers palette to generate a selection from it. With the selection active, I created a Levels adjustment layer, and increased the contrast. You could achieve the same result using a Curves adjustment layer, or even (in this case) a Brightness/Contrast layer, since individual channel adjustments weren't required.

The next thing to consider was the color. Again, using the same active selection, I created another adjustment layer – this time, a Selective Color layer. In this, I performed a series of rather drastic adjustments, adding a considerable amount of cyan to the reds, magentas, and neutrals. It was actually necessary to create a second Selective Color adjustment layer, in order to shift the color sufficiently.

Once the overall color was basically the way I wanted it, I decided to paint some more color into a few other areas. I created a new layer called color above the adjustment layers and changed its blending mode to Color, in order that anything I painted on this layer only affected the color of what was underneath it. Inside a selection generated from the head shape, I began to paint over certain areas using a variety of brush widths and opacities.

The color adjustments really brought out all of the faint spots and speckled areas in the skin, as well as some of the film grain. However, I wanted a smooth face –

almost like porcelain – so on a new layer (called smooth 1), using the same selection from the head shape to constrain the adjustments, I used a combination of tools to smooth out the skin. The first of these was the Clone Stamp; with the Use All Layers function enabled, I began cloning out some of the rough spots. Using opacities between 25% and 50%, I began to clone over areas like the cheeks and forehead, using a number of soft edged brushes, going over some spots several times until they started to look smoother. I used the same tool to remove the hairline as well, and to make the figure look bald.

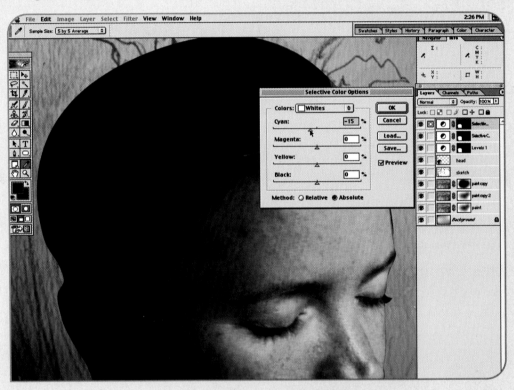

To continue smoothing out the face, I used the Smudge and Blur tools, always with Use All Layers enabled. I used the Smudge tool mainly in the face area – specifically, the eyelids, cheeks, and nose – with smaller brush sizes in order to control what was happening a little better. I used the Blur tool mostly in areas like the forehead, with a large, soft brush. For the majority of this operation, the pressure of the Blur tool was set at 100%.

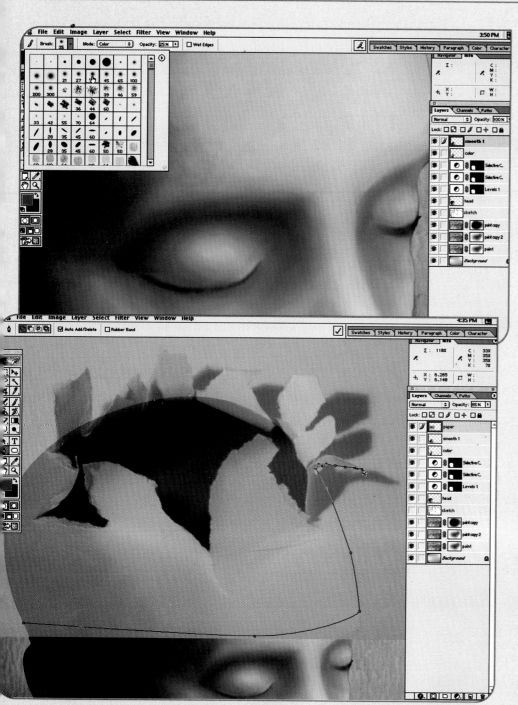

After all of the cloning, smudging, and blurring, I decided to add some dark circles under the eyes. I picked up some of the darker colors with the Eyedropper tool and then began to paint around and under the eyes using smaller, soft brushes with an average opacity of 25%. After I'd painted in the small strokes, I softened the effect by using the Smudge and Blur tools on them, too.

To go on the top of the head, I photographed a torn piece of paper. When you get the chance, lighting all of your shots in a similar manner can make things look more like they belong together, and save you a lot of retouching in the long run when you try to marry two completely alien photos. I dragged and dropped the scanned image into the working file as a new layer (called paper), and drew a path around the areas of the paper that I wanted to use in the image. By briefly reducing the opacity of the layer, I could see the curve of the head underneath, and made the edge of the paper match up. Once I'd finished drawing the path, I made a selection from it and added a layer mask that masked everything outside of the selection.

Psychosurgery

By using a large, soft-edged brush on the layer mask, I was able to make a smooth transition between the bottom of the paper photo and the head underneath. I used Selective Color to adjust the color of the paper so that it started to match the front of the forehead, mainly adding some cyan into the neutrals and whites, and pulling out a little magenta. I also added a hint of yellow and black, but not much.

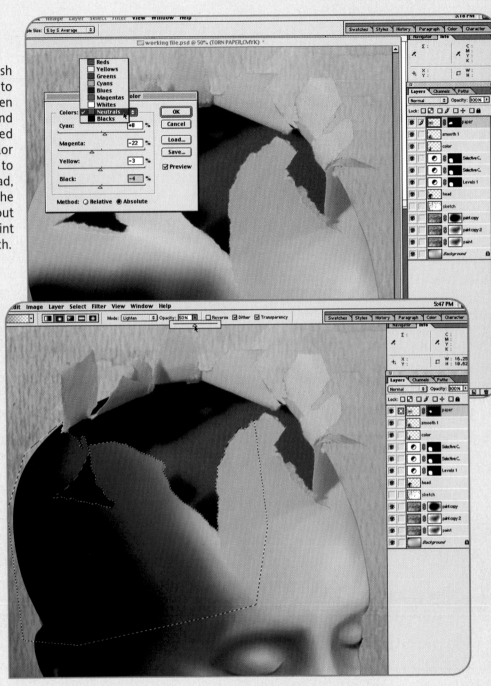

The next problem was that the light-colored paper looked out of place towards the back of the head, so I drew a path around the paper fragments in that area, made a selection from it, and masked out the unwanted areas using the Gradient tool and some soft brushes on the existing layer mask. I double-clicked the path icon in the Paths palette and named it, because I knew it would come in handy again later on, as you'll soon see.

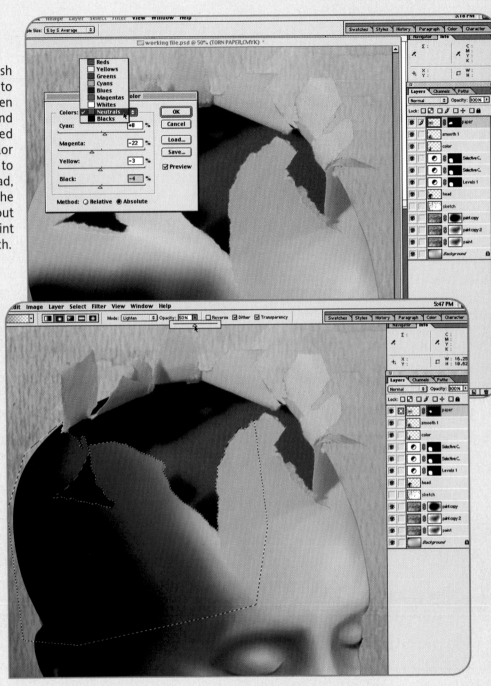

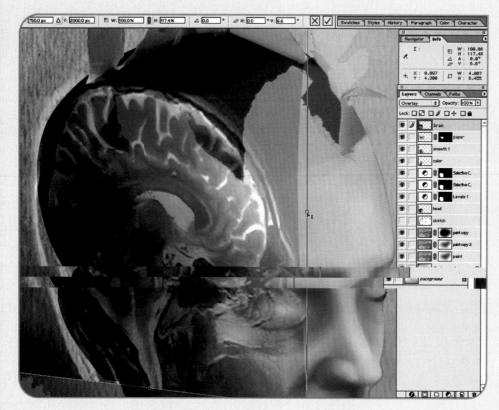

Any illustration on the subject of psychosurgery simply has to have a brain in it, and with this in mind I dragged and dropped in a grayscale image of an MRI scan as a new layer named brain. It was adjusted to fit in with the existing angles using Free Transform, and its blending mode was changed to Overlay.

I added a layer mask to remove all areas of the MRI scan, *except* where it overlapped the side of the head – once again, I used a few different large brushes and the Gradient tool on the mask to edit it. Then, I generated a selection from the path that was created previously, inversed it, and used a soft brush inside the inversed selection to mask out the area where the MRI scan overlapped the inside of the hole on top of the head.

At this point, the image was really beginning to take shape. For a start, the hole in the head was looking believable. And, although the subject matter was far from realistic, things were fitting together in a realistic manner. The things that I wanted to fix were the edges where the head and paper met the background, and the first idea to come to mind was to add a layer mask to the head layer, and then take a small, soft-edged brush and use it to paint out the hard edge. The problem with this, however, is that we would also need to mask all of the adjustment layers affecting the head in the exact same way. Trying to make each one match up would be a nightmare!

Psychosurgery

This is where Layer Sets come in handy. I created a new set (called head set), and dragged all of the layers that make up the head into it, one by one. Even though the layers inside the set all have masks of their own, you can add a further mask to the set itself, so that any adjustments you make to the layer set mask affect all of the layers within the set. I took a small, soft-edged brush, and painted around the head and paper edges on the layer set mask to get rid of the 'hard' look. This technique can really help remedy the cut-and-pasted look.

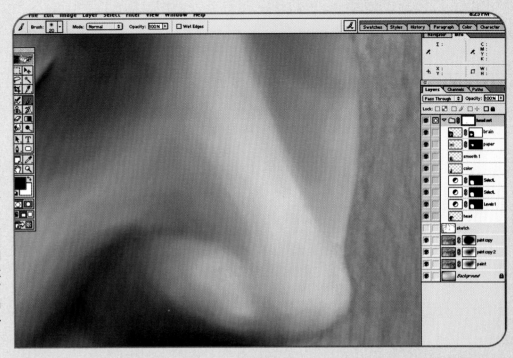

The completion of that last step sort of represents the turning point in the image. For me, every image is a little daunting until the first desired result becomes clear. Because the head is such a major visual element, I breathed a sigh of relief knowing that it was going to work. It never seems to change – even after hundreds of images, I get a feeling of insecurity until each image reaches its turning point. At that stage, it's a lot easier to face the image first thing in the morning!

This method of stacking layer upon layer with mask upon mask can get pretty greedy in terms of memory usage. You may notice that your screen redraws are getting slower, that you're running out of scratch disk space, or that you don't have enough disk space to save. You can remedy some of the file size issues by merging layers, but generally I choose not to do this unless I absolutely have to. I find that having the flexibility of keeping all the individual layers and masks can come in handy if you change your mind later – or worse yet, if the client starts to change things after you're finished.

The Butterflies
Because I wanted a cluster of butterflies going in different directions, I shot the butterfly a number of times, from various angles.

This makes for a more realistic result, because starting off with something shot at the proper angle is always more convincing than relying entirely on Photoshop's transform functions to alter the perspective. Since the scans were looking a little fuzzy, though, I used the Unsharp Mask filter to sharpen the images (Filter > Sharpen > Unsharp Mask).

Psychosurgery

The next step was to increase the contrast and adjust the color of the butterfly. First, I added a Levels adjustment layer, mainly focusing on adding some black and cyan into the dark areas and mid-tones, while removing magenta and yellow overall. You could also use Curves to do this sort of adjustment; it's really just a matter of which tool is more intuitive for you. On top of the Levels layer, I created a Selective Color adjustment layer and continued to add cyan into the mid-tones and dark areas, while stripping all colors away from the highlights.

Still wanting to alter the color more, mainly towards the center of the butterfly, I created a new layer called color with a blending mode of Color, and began to paint over certain areas. There was no need to worry about constraining any of this to a selected area, though, since I was going to cut the butterfly out and drag it into the working file.

Again, just like the figure's face, the butterfly was starting to show a lot of enhanced speckles and film grain. In fact, this often comes as a result of such drastic color and contrast adjustments. It was fixed once again by creating a new layer called smooth, and then smudging and blurring over the problem areas with Use All Layers enabled in the Smudge and Blur tool options.

Since all of the butterfly shots used the same film, lighting conditions, and scanning parameters, I was able to apply the same adjustment layers to each of them. I simply dragged and dropped the adjustment layers (in the same order) into the other butterfly files, then went ahead with the same painting with color and smudging and blurring effects that I'd used in the first one.

When each butterfly was ready, I flattened the image. Then, I drew a path around the butterfly, generated a selection from the path, and dragged the area inside the active selection into the working file as a new layer called butterflies. Some of the edges of the butterfly looked a little too hard, so using the Blur tool I painted over and softened them. (This time, Use All Layers was deactivated, as I didn't want to incorporate the underlying layers into the blur, just the butterfly.) Lastly, the butterfly was scaled and rotated into place using Free Transform.

I started dragging and dropping other butterfly images into the file as new layers, and I also duplicated some butterflies within the same layer. All of the butterflies had some of their hard edges blurred, were resized, positioned, and rotated into place until there was a multi-layered cluster of butterflies rising out of the hole in the head.

The next issue with the butterflies was to not have them overlapping the torn paper in the front of the hole – they were supposed to look as though they were tucked in behind the paper in the foreground, rising out of the hole, not sitting in front of it. To remedy this, I created a new layer set named butterfly set, and added all of the butterfly layers to it. I added a mask to the layer set, and using a small hard edged brush, masked out the bits of the butterflies that were sitting in front of the foreground torn paper.

Psychosurgery

Now, even though the butterflies looked as if they were rising up out of the head, it still seemed as though they were just sitting there in space. I decided to add some dimension to the image by giving them a slight shadow, as well as trying to convey a feeling of movement.

I duplicated some of the butterfly layers, and then moved these duplicates *beneath* the originals in the layer hierarchy. They were slightly offset, and I scaled them down a little, reduced their opacities to around 30%, and changed the blending modes to Multiply. Then I selected the duplicates individually, and applied the Motion Blur filter to each one (Filter > Blur > Motion Blur). Varying the settings slightly from one to the next conveyed the feeling that they were moving up and out of the head, rather than all flying in the same direction. Some of the layers had masks applied to them in which I lessened the blur and shadow effects in certain areas by adding very subtle linear gradients.

Because the overall composition still seemed a little bleak, and to give the impression of *lots* of butterflies without making the overall image too busy, I decided to add some of the butterfly elements to the background texture.

To do this, I duplicated one of the single butterfly layers and moved it right down in the layer hierarchy, below the head layers. Then, on the same layer, I duplicated the butterfly over and over again, rotating each one slightly to convey the feeling that the group of butterflies was emanating from the head. I also scaled the ones closer to the head down slightly. After that, I switched the layer's blending mode to Luminosity (to make it feel more like a part of the background), and reduced the opacity of the layer. Finally, I added a layer mask and used a radial gradient to fade out some of the butterflies surrounding the open area to the right.

Since this illustration was for a two-page spread that started a magazine article, that open area to the right was essential, as (in the page layout) it would contain the head and strap for the article.

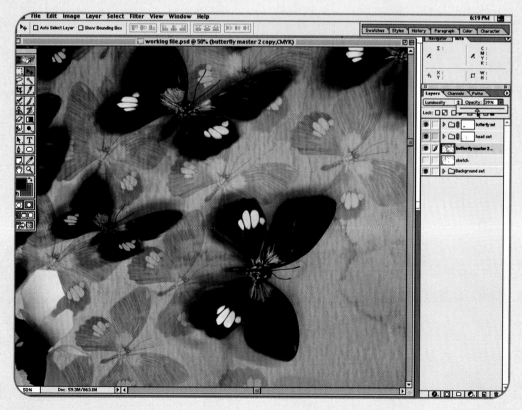

Psychosurgery

Shadows

Something that continued to bother me was that the head still didn't look as if it was part of the environment. There was a dark black shadow at the back of the head, and yet no shadow was cast on the background. To resolve this, I created a new layer called shadows under the head layer set, and changed its blending mode to Multiply.

To begin making the shadow shape, I Command-clicked the head layer's icon in the Layers palette, to make a selection from the contents of the layer. Then, holding down the Shift key, I Command-clicked some of the butterfly layer icons, to add the contents of those layers to the selection. To cast the shadow at an angle, I then switched to Quick Mask mode, in which I could see and edit the selection in the same manner as for any alpha channel. I used the Free Transform function to stretch, shear, and reposition the selection.

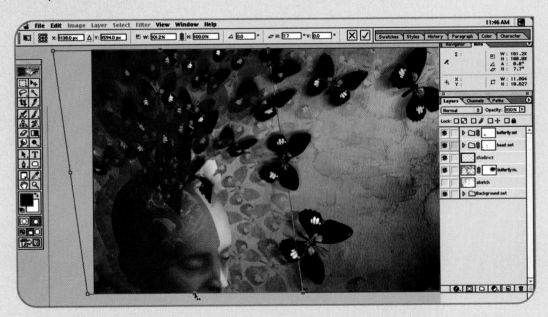

After exiting Quick Mask mode, I drew a linear gradient, from black to transparent, upwards, inside the selection on the new layer. Seeing this result, I decided to make a second shadow on the same layer in front of the head, as if there were a second light source coming from the side. I used the same method as the first shadow, but this time I left the butterflies out of the selection.

Obviously, the edges of both shadows were far too sharp, so I deselected everything and applied a generous amount of Gaussian blur to the entire layer. I then added a layer mask to the shadows layer, and blended the image further using a series of radial gradients with varying opacity within the mask.

The Bursting Effect

To make the bursting effect more dramatic, and to emphasize the feeling of release, I decided to have some rays of light emanating from inside the head. On a new layer named light, I drew the light beam shape with the Polygonal Lasso tool. Inside the selection, I drew a gradient from light yellow to transparent using the Radial Gradient tool, dragging from the bottom of the selection to the top.

After deselecting, I applied a substantial Gaussian blur to this layer, in the way that I'd done with the shadows. However, I wanted more of a glowing effect than just a yellow gradient, so I switched the layer's blending mode to Screen, and slightly reduced the opacity.

I added a layer mask, and using a combination of hard and soft brushes, I masked out the bottom part of the glow so that it looked as if it was emanating from inside the head, not sitting on top of it.

While working in the same layer mask, I generated some selections from certain butterflies by Command-clicking their layer icons in the Layers palette. I used the Gradient tool inside these selections to make it look as if just the tops or upper halves of some of the butterflies were emerging from the glow.

Since I wanted the head to look like it had just popped open, I needed to add in some little pieces of debris. I created a new layer called bits, and used the Lasso tool to draw some ragged shapes that could resemble little bits of torn paper. Inside the selections, I painted in colors that I picked up from the figure's head with the Eyedropper tool. I used a variety of soft brushes with varying opacities to blend the colors together gently.

To keep the pieces looking realistic, I kept the color scheme similar to that of the head. For instance, the pieces at the back of the head were darker cyans and blues, whereas the pieces near the front were much lighter, since theoretically they were showing their undersides.

Psychosurgery

Surface Texture

I wanted to give the image an overall worn and bumpy surface texture, to incorporate a bit more of the tactile, and to help bring all of the elements together. To do this, I started by scanning an old, worn book cover, and pasted it into a new alpha channel within the file, using Free Transform to size and position it properly. Some sections of it were edited or duplicated using the Clone Stamp tool. Then, I used levels to adjust the grayscale image in the channel to greatly increase its contrast – really, I just wanted to make the highlights in the channel stand out, and darken most of the mid-tones so there was less tonal range.

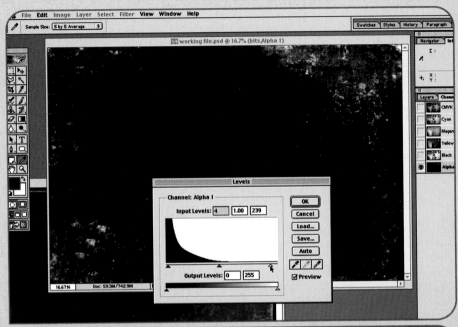

To generate a selection from it, I Command-clicked the channel, and then created a new layer called scratches and filled the selection with a light yellow color. I set the layer's blending mode to Overlay, because I wanted the worn areas to look almost bleached with age. I applied a mask to this layer, and used the radial gradient tool to mask out areas around the head where I didn't want too much texture.

After this initial work, the effect was a little too subtle, so I duplicated the layer, changed its blending mode to Normal and reduced the opacity to 70%. I masked out more areas on this layer, so that I mainly just accentuated the outer edges.

Ink Splats

Last of all, I wanted the butterflies to look dirty, like they were dripping with some foul resin. Remember, they were meant to represent mental illness. The first thing I did was to take some India ink, and spatter it on a sheet of paper in a number of places. Then I scanned the sheet of paper and adjusted the contrast of the image, using Levels to eliminate most of the mid-tones. In the working file, I created a new alpha channel.

Next, I used the rectangular Marquee tool to select sections of ink and drag them into the new alpha channel in the working file. I resized, rotated and positioned the ink splats using Free Transform, placing splats of different sizes and degrees of rotation on a number of different butterflies.

Psychosurgery

After that, I Command-clicked the alpha channel's icon in the Channels palette to make a selection from it, and on a new layer called ink splats, I filled the selection with black. Then, I added a layer mask and used subtle radial gradients on the mask to fade out sections of the layer. Finally, I scanned another sheet of paper containing ink droplets, and used the same procedure to add some droplets of ink into the image surrounding the ink splats.

So there you have it: the image is finished. But if I'd wanted to, I could have kept on going. The technique of stacking layers within sets leaves things rather open-ended. You could go in and move adjustment layers up and down in the layer hierarchy, to experiment with different combinations. You could add new ones within those sets, and the Layer Set masks would still keep things neat and tidy.

Stacking layers with different blending modes can often reveal unexpected and beautiful results. Try duplicating some layers, and playing around with modes and opacity. Try masking more of a layer, so that just a small section of it affects the underlying elements. You could even use selections generated from scanned tactile elements to manipulate areas of masks, or build some new and bizarre adjustment layers.

Experiment with entire sets – you can duplicate layer sets as well. When you create a new layer set, you'll notice that its default blending mode is set to Pass Through, which basically leaves the blending modes of the layers contained in the set alone. But you can change the blending modes of entire sets, to adjust how *all* the layers within will affect the underlying layers.

I always keep an eye out for the next beautiful surface texture that may come along. Never be afraid to throw something unconventional on your scanner. Even if it doesn't look beautiful in color, you may be able to create some stunning effects by using it, or even small sections of it, as channels.

Have Fun!

chapter 1

chapter 2

chapter 3

chapter 4

chapter 5

chapter 6

chapter 7

chapter 8

chapter 9

chapter 10

chapter 11

chapter 12

chapter 13

chapter 14

chapter 15

chapter 16

outro

"I feel like a clown trying not to trip over my big shoes."

Eun-Ha Paek
www.milkyelephant.com

Daydream

I fell in love with animation while studying illustration at the Rhode Island School of Design. It happened gradually during Animation 101. Before each class, the lights would go off, and the instructor would screen experimental animations from around the world. Up to that point, I had only seen Disney movies and Saturday morning cartoons, but works by artists like Len Lye and Sally Cruikshank changed my preconceptions. By taking away the conventional narrative storytelling and characters, these animators opened up so many possibilities. I knew that this was what I wanted to do, too. I wanted people to sit in darkened rooms and enjoy a moment that I had made.

Illustration had been my puppy love. I enjoyed working with different visual styles, and playing with compositions, colors, and contrasts to communicate a concept or a story. When I discovered the possibilities offered by animation, I knew that I'd only been in training. Now, I could add other layers – sequence, sound, and motion – to the visuals, in order to create an immersing experience. The work was more labor intensive, and riskier: I could spend a week working on five seconds of animation, and then have to throw it out if it didn't work. But it was worth it for the times that it did work. I loved that the images were always moving just out of reach, and that no one image could be scrutinized alone. The individual pieces didn't even have to amount to much – the magic could happen in how they all came together. It was exciting to learn how to balance so many different types of media and elements, and to assemble them in space and time.

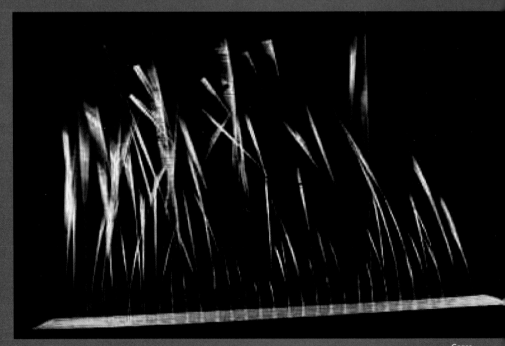

Grass
© Len Lye Foundation

I am most inspired by unexpected combinations, and therefore by artists who successfully perform the balancing act between different elements with a lot of finesse. I look up in awe at these folks; they're doing the high wire act, while I feel like a clown trying not to trip over my big shoes.

Len Lye, a filmmaker and kinetic artist, pioneered camera-less animation by scratching directly onto film, while his kinetic sculptures are similarly elegant and sparse. The materials he used (sheets of steel attached to motors) have the potential to be dangerous, but they result in graceful, refined structures. In his sculpture called *Grass* I love the tension between the material, and what it represents.

From Lye's work, I learned the importance of context – and it's important not to overlook the role that sound can play in this regard. In his scratching-on-film animations, disordered-looking scratches are turned into powerful, abstract, dancing shapes when synched with African drumbeats. We not only hear the rhythm, but we see it as well.

Watching Sally Cruikshank's animations never fails to leave me feeling refreshed. I feel like I've just woken up to find that I'm a kid again: the possibilities are endless, the laws of gravity are suspended, and motion is pure fun.

Characters and scenes bounce around, barely able to contain themselves. There is such exuberance and fluidity to her work that it makes me want to dance. I aspire to get that same feeling across in the pieces I create.

© Sally Cruikshank

Daydream

Examining the varied styles and techniques of animators from around the world got me to ask myself some questions. How can I say more by simplifying? What can the title of a piece imply? What types of sound can I use to change an image? How can pacing get a point across? What inherent qualities in a medium can be used to convey a mood?

For some answers, here are some sample frames from my 16mm animated film, Peek a Boo. It was created using Super-8 film footage, puppet animation, painting under the camera, cutouts, live action, computer printouts, ink and watercolor drawings, and cell animation.

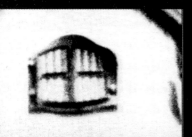  

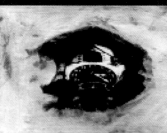

To create a dream sequence, film can be overexposed to create a grainy and blurry world. Hinting at objects, and leaving out detail, allows more room for the imagination to work its magic.

I also tried shooting film footage straight from a computer monitor. The top two images here show the unaltered film footage, while the bottom two came from the screen. I'd used Macromedia Director to composite a cutout puppet animation over some film footage, but I didn't have the means to transfer the digital files to film. This method worked just as well, though, and added an unplanned level of dreaminess to the scene when the monitor cast a blue glow around the whites.

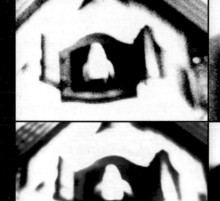 

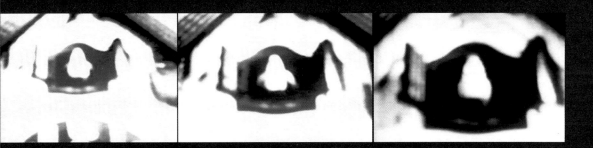

Contrast can also be used to build mood. For the following sequence, I photocopied an image a few times to enhance the contrast, getting rid of detail, and again leaving more to be imagined. Darkness seems more menacing when you don't know what's hidden in it.

I also experiment with texture and color. In the next set of images, abstract washes of red are used around a drawing of an eye to add an air of discomfort. By itself, the drawing is pretty innocuous – but when the red is added, the setting changes. The wash of color resembles smeared blood, and suggests violence.

Daydream

Lastly, in this set I tried combining different techniques in time, to see whether adding detail to an image progressively would make a scene more surreal.

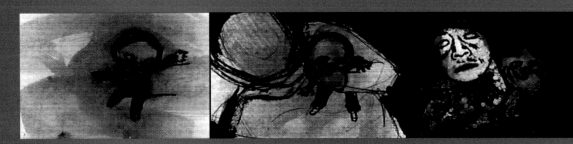

Then I played up the disjointedness of the imagery by interspersing the progression with a few seconds of darkness. The dark pauses enhance the struggle the character is experiencing. Like the character, we struggle to see what's happening – things shift in and out of darkness, reappearing a little differently each time. It's always a surprise what will emerge from the shadows, helping to build anticipation.

To show the changes a character goes through, I use a variety of styles – but by giving the character a distinct pose and coloring, he can undergo many shifts in appearance and remain recognizable.

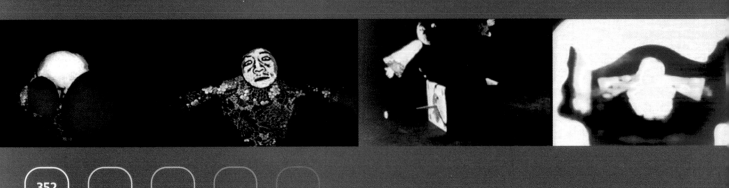

I'm still in love with animation, but I try not to let it be my main focus. If it's to be understood and appreciated fully, it needs to be compared and given context. If I want to get an idea across with abstractions, I need to understand the principles of storytelling. How can composition, lighting, and colors make a scene more dramatic, funny, dreamy, creepy, or sad?

In the single frame at the top, I've tried to depict sadness by placing my elephant character, Ellie, behind the metal bar that dissects the photo. She's separated from the rest of the world, looking out, alone, at the life on the other side. The lighting is dreary where she is, but opposite her, above the lively town, the sky has hints of lightness and color as the fog lifts away.

In the next frame, the subject matter is a little creepy – Ellie is spying on the girl. The uneasiness is enhanced by placing Ellie in a spot that would make it easy to look up the girl's skirt, and by making the girl's legs long and her skirt short. I've added to the discomfort further by cutting the characters in half, and to accentuate the oddness, the characters are placed on different sides of the picture, which in turn is cut in half by the railing. The strange cropping makes *our* view seem voyeuristic as well.

To portray dreaminess in the last picture, the border fades to pink, making the scene soft and airy. By combining elements that don't quite fit together, like the line drawings at the top and the odd layers of color in the photograph, the picture seems a little ethereal.

Milky Elephant

Thing of the Day

MUMBLEBOY

EUN-HA PAEK

KARL ACKERMANN

To master flow and pacing, I need better to understand how to create movement without using motion, and for that I look to the work of graphic novelists. They control the flow of a story from panel to panel, with their choice of composition and style. This is motion that I can scrutinize. By studying their methods of working within the restrictions of the page, I'm able to learn more ways to enhance my storytelling techniques. Taiyo Matsumoto's series of comic books *Black & White* mixes sophisticated and childish drawings to complement his story about a couple of little kids on the tough streets. I love how his style enhances the narrative. For instance, he breaks form by making slight changes in the way he draws his characters: in some scenes, they will be drawn in detail; in others, detail will be left out. The resulting 'blankness' can enhance their posture and words, and the discontinuity of style has the opposite effect of what one might assume. By changing his style, Matsumoto creates even tighter continuity.

Of course, that's not to say that that continuity can or should always be achieved by changing one's style. In *Skibber Bee-Bye*, by Ron Rege Jr., there are pages that are filled with panels that look almost identical. The similarity of the panels makes the odd scenes look familiar, and time passes slowly. By pacing the story this way, it makes the scenes that do change in composition appear even more dramatic by comparison.

Rege is published by www.highwaterbooks.com, and if you check out the 'weekly strips' section of this site (as I often do!), you'll find that the other artists are equally inventive. The only reason I'm not mentioning them by name is because they don't have elephants crying in their work, and I'm a little biased!

Finally, I can't go without mentioning Scott McCloud, and his books *Understanding Comics* and *Reinventing Comics*. He goes into great depth about many different methods that aid visual storytelling.

Daydream

The following example of my work involves a fairly traditional use of flow, and slow pacing. The camera is fixed on the two characters, with focus placed on the character that's currently talking by either zooming in, or blurring out. Thought clouds turn into real clouds as the elephant dreams about some newfound information.

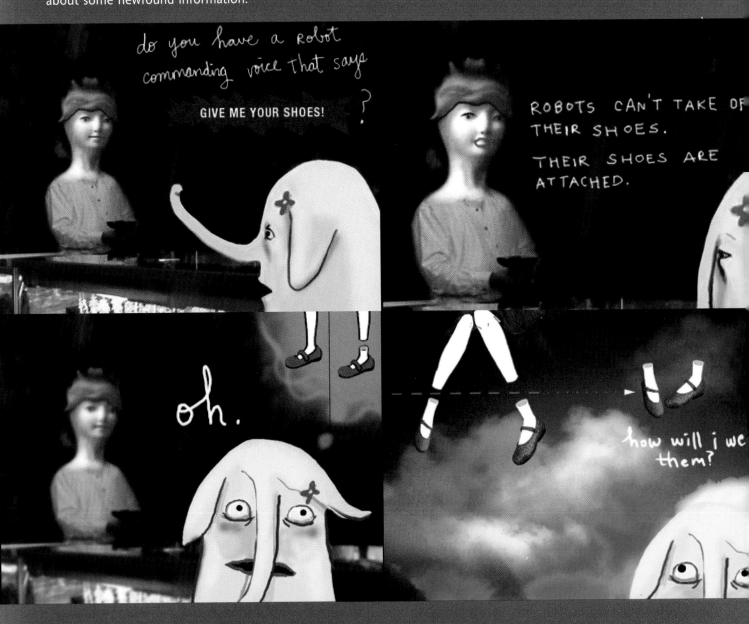

I wondered what would happen if the reader had more control over the pacing, so, in Photoshop, I made the next part of the story into a free-flowing series of imagery. The scene is sectioned loosely into panels that are not obviously delineated.

Eun-Ha Paek

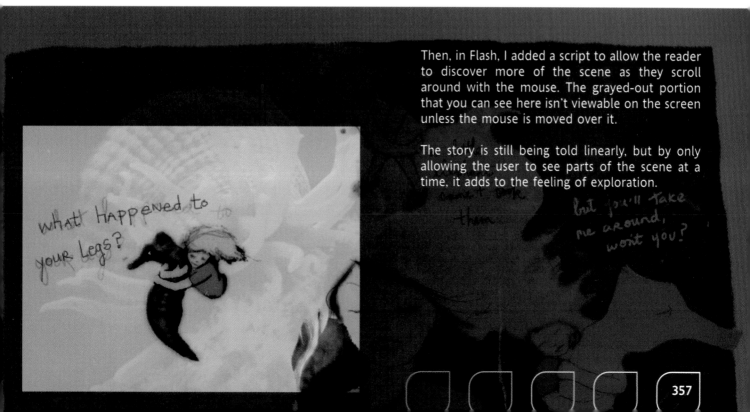

Then, in Flash, I added a script to allow the reader to discover more of the scene as they scroll around with the mouse. The grayed-out portion that you can see here isn't viewable on the screen unless the mouse is moved over it.

The story is still being told linearly, but by only allowing the user to see parts of the scene at a time, it adds to the feeling of exploration.

Daydream

I like to look at other things besides visual art for sources of inspiration. One of my favorite books is called *Lightness*, written by Adriaan Beukers and Ed van Hinte. It's an in-depth look at the history, application, and function of lightweight structures, and how what we learn from nature (even Claudia Schiffer's waist can teach us a thing or two!) can be applied not only to bridges and buildings, but also to anything from draping fabrics to boomerangs. It's a good book about the correlation between objects, both manmade and natural. Knowing how nature and engineers construct lightweight objects gives me ideas that trickle down to how I structure my projects, and even how I use composition and plot.

With this drawing, for example, the triangle that strengthens the bench is echoed by the shape of the girl's legs and arms. In conjunction with the text about the weakest point of a structure, I use the angles to point at her neck and waist as a form of foreshadowing.

In the next scene, the girl is standing next to a plank that's bent in the middle. It's easy to imagine how she could also be snapped in half with relatively little effort. A dotted line is drawn through both the girl and the plank to reinforce the connection.

they say that the weakest point of a structure

is in the middle

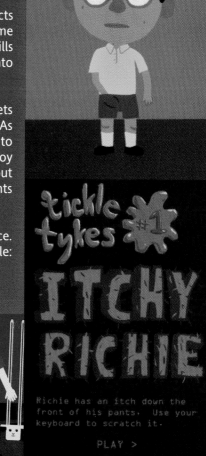

Although I love animation and all its complexity, I continue to learn from projects that don't have the same intricacies. Solving different sets of puzzles helps me gain perspective in solving the ones I'm familiar with. Honing smaller sets of skills has also improved my big-picture abilities, and gives me more insight into different possibilities.

In the workforce, I found it difficult to find the time to experiment. With budgets and timelines to abide by, there wasn't much room for trying new techniques. As an outlet, I decided to try contributing daily (rather than every other month) to the Milky Elephant collective, a group that includes Karl Ackermann, Mumbleboy (Kinya Hanada), and myself. We met in college, and Milky Elephant was born out of our need to continue experimenting, without having to worry about clients and marketing objectives.

Karl and Mumbleboy both inspire me to try to keep doing things in my own voice. Karl's use of humor, for example, is unmistakable:

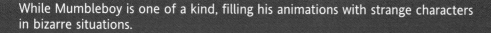

While Mumbleboy is one of a kind, filling his animations with strange characters in bizarre situations.

Since the images of elephants I posted to the Milky Elephant site were replaced daily, I didn't feel any pressure to make them perfect. This allowed me to try many different interpretations, while giving me the discipline of having a framework. Within the idea, the boundaries existed only in my preconceptions. Although the drawings individually did not amount to much, after a few months, their sheer number gave them another context. Just like animation, it's all about how the individual pieces come together. The beauty happens in the connection, and in achieving a satisfying balance between different elements.

Daydream

Whether I'm making animations, drawings, or designs, Photoshop is always part of my process. Other programs have come and gone, but this is the only one that I'm still using as an integral part of my workflow. For my Flash animations, I use Photoshop to create layered bitmap images that provide some contrast with Flash's vector shapes. With my drawings, I can quickly turn a pencil sketch into a finished piece by painting onto it in Photoshop. Unlike 'real' objects, I don't have to worry about messing up, since any step can be deleted in the History palette.

In the following tutorial, I will talk about how I use different techniques in Photoshop, without the finished article looking 'Photoshopped'. While filters can be great, some of them tend to be overused. When I first started using Photoshop, all I did was play with the filters – it was so much fun to make text blurry, to spherize photos of my friends' faces, and to invert images, just because it was possible. Before Photoshop, these things were difficult to achieve. Now anyone can do them, and a lot of people do. I soon realized that just applying filters to my work would result in images that could quickly be identified as having been done with Photoshop filters. Effects like drop shadows and blurry text can work if they're used in the right context, but they can end up looking amateurish if used extraneously.

However, going wild playing with filters and effects in Photoshop has paid off. By trying out all the features to see what they do, all the different possibilities have become a part of my vocabulary. Now, using these effects is second nature, like using words to form a sentence. This allows me to construct complicated techniques that flow from a desire to convey a specific idea, or to achieve a certain look. Once the tool's capabilities are mastered, the process becomes fluid, like speaking. Concentration can be placed on achieving balance in an image with the use of color, composition and subject matter, rather than disrupting a train of thought by having to search for a specific effect.

In this tutorial, we will look at two techniques that go into making the drawings and animations that appear in my print work and on my web site. In the first part, we will alter a scanned-in pencil sketch to give it the look of an aquatint etching; this was later used as part of a calendar design. In the second part, we will see how a similar drawing can be incorporated into a collage with photographs; this was subsequently used for a scene in one of my animations.

My main goal in using the techniques in this tutorial is to steer clear of letting the medium dictate the look of a piece. Photoshop is a great tool to achieve any type of style. For my illustrations, I've been interested in recreating the appearance and texture of traditional printmaking techniques, while taking advantage of working on a computer. I can have multiple 'undo's and version control, instead of acid baths and messy solvents!

Faking It in Photoshop

I love the look of hard ground etchings with aquatint. This type of etching creates prints that are similar in appearance to pen and ink drawings. The process of aquatinting creates tonal range like that of a watercolor wash.

Working in Photoshop, I can turn a pencil sketch into something that resembles such an etching. Although the quality might not quite match the texture and line quality of a real print, it's the closest I can get without having to mess with tubs of acid. My Photoshop file is similar to an etching plate, a master that can be used to make multiple prints.

First, let's start with a pencil sketch. I'm using a very simple drawing as an example, to show how even a loose sketch can be transformed in just a few, simple steps.

Besides creating variations in the stroke and weight of the pencil line, there are other things that you can try in order to add more gradations in line, tone and texture. If you draw something and then erase it, for example, the scanner will pick up the grooves created by the pencil on the paper. I drew the elephants' trunks a couple of times, and then erased them to get hints of some trunk action. To accentuate the elephants' affection, I also drew in some drool and wiped it away.

Since the drawing will be printed once I've finished with it in Photoshop, I scanned it in CMYK color, using at least 300dpi. Even though this is a black and white drawing, scanning it in color gives the tint a warm cast instead of a cold, gray one. This will come in handy later. CMYK color is used so that I won't have to worry about converting the image color mode in Photoshop later for printing. Of course, you can also convert to CMYK right before you print, but my personal preference is to do it from the start so that I won't forget later! More usefully, I know that there won't be any shifts in color when it's converted from RGB to CMYK.

Daydream

The resolution needs to be high in order for the scanner to pick up all the details of the drawing, and the texture of the paper. Picking up the texture of the paper is important because it will lend the drawing a degree of roughness that will make it look more organic and not computer-generated. And since it will be printed, the image needs to be at least 300dpi to be of sufficient quality for that purpose.

Playing with Contrast

Open up the file `original elephant image.tif` in Photoshop. Notice how the texture of the paper gives the scanned image an overall tint. Since this is a pencil sketch, though, there isn't very much contrast between the lines and the paper, resulting in poor overall tonal range. Let's fix that by adjusting the levels. This is where the subtleties added in the pencil sketch will be brought out.

Plan A

To automatically adjust the levels: Let's try the Image > Adjust > Auto Levels feature first. Most of the time, the results are satisfactory – but sometimes, more needs to be done. In this case, there isn't enough contrast in the lines of the elephants.

The image now has good tonal range in the background, and you can see that the elephants are drooling, but some details could still be heightened. Let's revert back to the original image to try Plan B.

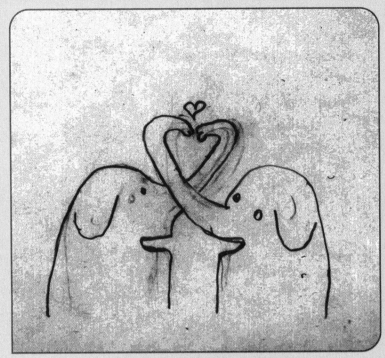

Plan B

To adjust the levels manually: Click on the adjustment layer icon (the black and white circle) at the bottom of the Layers palette, select Levels, and the dialog box pops up (also Layer > New Adjustment layer > Levels). The benefit of using an adjustment layer is that the original image is not altered.

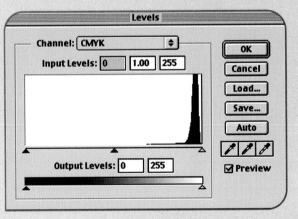

The histogram represents the tonal range of the image. An image with a balanced tonal range will have an even distribution of lines in the graph, which represent the dark tones (left side) and the light tones (right side). Note that the left side is empty and the lines are clustered to the right. This is because the image is very light. Let's adjust the tonal range to achieve a better balance.

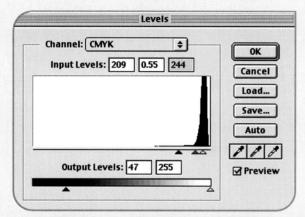

Move the black arrow to where the lines start. This will redefine the dark pixels; it's like telling Photoshop to change a gray into a black, and to adjust all the tones in between. When we adjusted the levels automatically, this is what Photoshop did. Since that wasn't satisfactory, we can manually move the arrows here, to gain more precise control over the placement of the tones in between black and white. Move the white arrow to adjust the light tones, and the gray arrow to adjust the mid-range pixels. Adjust the settings until you find a level of detail in the elephants that you like. These are the Levels settings that I used for my corrected image.

In order to bring out the texture and lines of the elephants, the even tone of the background was sacrificed by heightening the contrast when we adjusted our levels. Now, though, the image fades to white in the left corner. To correct that, let's use an 'auto-adjusted' version of the image, and utilize its background texture to cover up the fade to white.

Daydream

Duplicate the original image (Layer > Duplicate Layer) and name the new layer auto adjusted. Move this layer above the one we adjusted manually, and apply Image > Adjust > Auto Levels. Set the layer blending mode to Multiply, and reduce its opacity to 70% so that the original drawing shows through. Now the background isn't as washed out.

Bleeding Lines

One of my favorite qualities of an etching is the darkness of the lines, accentuated by a slight bleeding of the ink. The lines of the elephants became darker when we layered the same image in the previous step, but to look even more like an etching, we could make them darker still and bleed a bit more.

Duplicate the original image layer, and move this new layer above the auto adjusted layer. Name this layer the bleed, and give it a layer blending mode of Multiply. Select Image > Adjust > Brightness/Contrast and adjust the settings to isolate the lines to bleed from the background, as shown in the picture. Reduce the colors to black and white as far as you can without getting the lines too 'jaggy'.

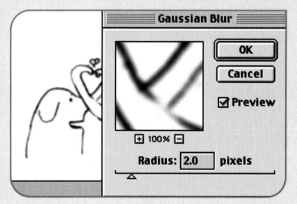

The lines are now isolated, so a blur can be applied to the lines alone, leaving the rest of the image unaffected. The blurred lines will give the illusion of bleeding ink by creating some softness around the edges.

Select Filter > Blur > Gaussian Blur. From the Gaussian Blur dialog box, apply a Radius of 2 pixels to make the lines thick and blurry.

Adding Color

To give the piece some warmth, a wash of color will be added. Since the elephants are in love, let's select a pink with CMYK values of 0, 89, 71, 0. Create a new layer called overall color, change the foreground color, and fill the image using Edit > Fill. Set the layer blending mode to Overlay, and reduce the opacity to 60%.

The Overlay mode is good to use, because it doesn't have much impact on the tonal range, unless you are using very light or very dark colors. (You'll see an example of this when we add highlights later.) This method works well when you just want to superimpose your color over the image – it's kind of like looking at your image through tinted glasses. You could also make a hue/saturation adjustment layer to get a similar effect. But my personal preference lies with overlaying color fills.

Daydream

Now the elephants are blending into the background a little too much, so in order to bring them out a bit more and separate them from the background, we'll add some highlights to their features. We'll give the elephants some dimensionality by hinting at some light hitting their curves. Since a diffuse light will work well for the highlights, let's use the Airbrush tool.

I like to use a Wacom tablet to draw in the highlights, because variations in width and opacity can be achieved through applying different amounts of pressure to the tablet, much like using a real brush to paint. Make a new layer named elephant color, and select white as your color. Click on the Paintbrush tool, and then activate the Brush Dynamics icon at the right of the tool options bar. In the dialog that appears, set both Size and Opacity to Stylus. (This option only works if you're using a stylus.) Set the paintbrush opacity to 25%, and paint the areas that you want to make lighter. Then, set the layer blending mode to Overlay, and reduce the opacity to 60%. This time, you'll notice that the Overlay mode has a different effect from before: since the color we're overlaying is very light, it *does* have an effect on the underlying pixels.

For the final touch, let's emphasize the heart. Add a new layer, and name it heart color. Choose a strong red color, and color in the heart with the Brush tool. Set the layer blending mode to Multiply so that the heart's outline can show through. Here's the altered image (`elephants_in_love.psd`) next to the original for comparison.

Here are some other techniques you might try using when making pencil sketches:

Work on very thin paper (like typing paper) and draw things on the back – they will show through in the scan. This can create some nice ghostlike effects that are good for giving a sense of atmospheric perspective, or indeed for drawing ghosts.

Try using scrap paper, so that the words on the back show through. This can create more texture or can come in handy for sending someone a secret message.

Make a rubbing of a textured surface, like fabric or concrete. Combining a realistic texture pattern with a loose, sketchy drawing can create a nice combination.

Although this technique is a simple one, it provides a good base image for making other things like:

Magnets
The magnets are made by importing the finished images into FreeHand, and then assembling them to print on a sheet of paper. The printouts from my inkjet printer are then attached to an adhesive-backed magnet sheet (available from www.woodcraftsupplies.com, among others). If necessary, cut them to size with a paper cutter. You can also purchase adhesive-backed magnets that are pre-cut to business card size from most office supply stores. They are thicker and better quality, but more costly.

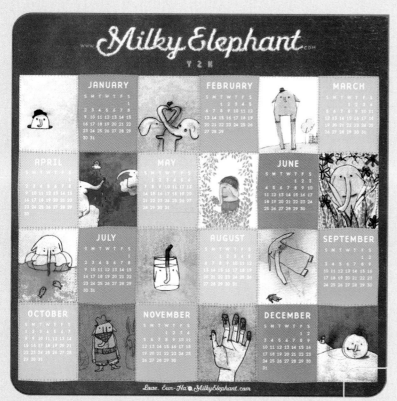

Animations
We'll go further into this in the next part of the tutorial.

Collages with photographs or graphical elements
Here's a calendar composed of drawings I've made with this technique. I use the context of a quilt to balance between the hodgepodge of colors and textures. Like a quilt, these scraps are pieced together to form a unifying whole. Once the drawings are completed in Photoshop, they are imported into FreeHand where I make a stitching pattern to 'sew' the drawings together with the colored date blocks. Real embroidery is used for the heading, to reinforce the concept of the 'quilt'.

Here's the end result.

Blending Drawings and Photos

The next part of this tutorial will investigate combining drawings with photographs in a collage. When drawings and photos are used together in a Photoshop image, you have a lot of freedom to play around with the different layers and blending modes. It can take several minor adjustments to get the final image looking the way you want, as you'll see.

Drawings can be created on the computer and still have the same organic feel as those made on paper. My preferred tool for drawing on the computer is Meta Creations' Painter (www.metacreations.com/products/painter6), which comes with a good assortment of brush effects. While Photoshop's brush tools are great for quick touches here and there, I find that they don't compare with Painter's in creating brushstrokes that imitate the look of natural media.

A variety of textures can be made using Painter's brush tools; the pastel brush, for example, is particularly nice for sketching. It creates roughness around the edges, recreating the look of pastel rubbed over textured paper. The grain of the paper can also be adjusted to simulate different types of paper. Furthermore, all the tools are pressure sensitive, so it works well with my Wacom tablet. In this image, I used the pencil brush to make the finer, cleaner lines. I kept the number of colors in the drawing to a minimum, so that they wouldn't conflict with the colors in the photographs that will be added later in Photoshop.

To make the drawing look like it was taking place underwater, I brought it into Photoshop, so open up `original painter image.tif`. Note that since the final destination of this image will be the Web, the drawing is in RGB mode.

First, I gathered some photographs of underwater scenes taken during a trip to the aquarium. `seascene.tif` is a photograph that has general areas of light and dark that would be nice to replicate. The cloudy quality of the anemones will also work well in bringing some tone to the drawing.

Cut and paste this photograph into the `original painter image.tif` file, and position it on the right of the canvas. Name the resulting layer sea 01, and drag it below the original painter image layer.

In order to create different levels of depth and texture, this photograph should show up only through the dark blue area in the drawing. To do that, let's separate the dark blues from the rest of the drawing. With the original painter image layer selected, go to Select > Color Range. From the dialog box, use the Eyedropper to choose the color you want to select from the original painter image layer (a dark blue from the top right is what you're after). Use the Fuzziness slider to determine the degree of sensitivity.

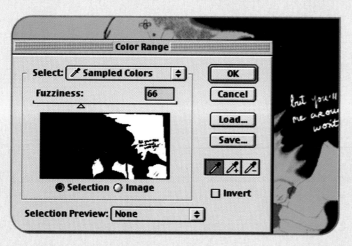

(Fuzziness set at 0 will only pick up the color you choose, resulting in an aliased and jaggy selection. The higher the fuzziness, the higher the range of colors will be; somewhere in the middle usually works best.) Having the Selection radio button checked presents a preview of your selection in the dialog box. If you want to preview your selection in your image, use the Selection Preview drop-down menu to change from None to Grayscale. If you want to see a colored preview, you can use Black Matte or White Matte to view the color that is being selected, with all the other areas covered by either a black or white matte.

Daydream

Here is the dark blue area separated at a fuzziness level of 66.

In order to push the dark blue area further back in space, and also to supply some tonal range, we need more variation in our values. We can heighten the spatial depth by adding some gradations in the blue, which we'll do by utilizing the changes in coloration that occur in the photograph. In order to keep the area 'in the background', the color from the photograph should be muted, and we can use Hard Light mode to get the desired effect. This is similar to Multiply, with the exception that it creates a sort of 'spotlight' effect on the image. It also brightens the light tones, while making dark colors darker still. In this case, since we're using a dark color as our blend color, our dark tones will become inky, like the depths of the sea.

Cut and paste the dark blue selection you just made into a new layer, and name it image darks. Rename the layer without the darks as image lights. To allow the photograph to show through in the desired way, set the layer blending mode of image darks to Hard Light.

Here's the image with the photograph added; the dark area is now pushed back because of the variation and gradation in tone and texture. This helps to create some atmospheric perspective. It also enhances the impression that the scene is taking place deep underwater, since we have some murkiness created by the anemone shapes.

Next, we'll add some texture to the light blue areas. I chose this next photograph (`seascene2.tif`) because the tentacles of the anemone repeat the shape and motion of the tendrils in the girl's hair. The subject matter will also give the image another underwater reference point.

We'll superimpose this photograph over the image. The photograph is kind of dark, and it could make the light blue area darker, but using Screen mode will prevent that from happening. The photograph and light blue area will retain their coloration while blending in together. Photoshop Help has a good analogy: "This effect is similar to projecting multiple photographic slides on top of each other." Imagine that the photograph we are layering is coming from a slide projector, and our original image is already on the wall. The resulting combination will be brighter, because of the light coming from the projector.

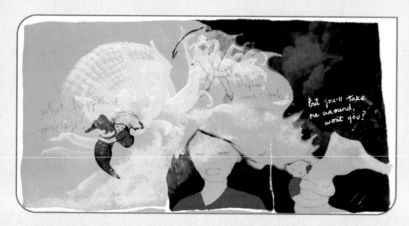

Cut and paste the photograph into a layer above image lights and image darks, and position it on the left of the canvas. Name this layer sea 02, and set the layer blending mode to Screen.

The scene seems dreamier, because the details of the photograph in sea 02 are harder to see, and the colors are faded to blue. A sense of depth is also added to the dark areas where the colors in sea 02 augment the variations in tone of sea 01.

Since the characters' features are now obscured by the photograph, however, it is still a little flat. We'll bring out the characters' features so that it will look like the underwater scene is happening behind them (rather than through them) by creating a mask for the layer sea 02, and painting in the areas of the photograph that we want to make invisible. To maintain the dreaminess of the scene, let's use a soft, fuzzy brush to avoid any hard lines. Checking the Wet Edges option in the Paintbrush options bar will make the brushstrokes a little transparent, which will have a nice effect that matches the underwater theme.

Daydream

Add a mask to the photo layer (Layer > Add Layer Mask > Reveal All). Select the Brush tool, and in the options bar choose the soft, round, 9-pixel brush. Check the Wet Edges box, and then paint the areas where you don't want the photo to show through, like the areas over the characters.

Here's the image with those parts masked out. Note the messiness of the brushstrokes; it adds to the blurry, watery feeling not to have these areas explicitly defined. It also gives the mask a little tonal range; this will keep the mask from looking too 'cut out', and will blend in nicely with the scene.

The outlines of the characters are a little too hard-edged at the moment, but adding a slight glow to the light blue area will help create to a diffuse light that will soften up the picture. The light blues now seem a little too bright and artificial, so let's darken that whole area by creating a duplicate version of image lights, blurring it, and then Multiplying that over the original.

Duplicate the image lights layer, and name the copy glow. Move it above the photograph layer sea 02, and then apply a Gaussian Blur with a radius of 4 pixels.

A lot of detail is obscured now, but we can reduce the glow in order to bring some of the detail back, and make the light blue slightly darker. Set the layer blending mode to Multiply, and since that makes the overall image a little *too* dark, change the opacity of the layer to 50%.

Although the drawing now has more depth, the layering of photographs and blurring of images has sacrificed the legibility of the words in the image. Other details, like the characters' features, are also getting lost. Let's delineate these parts of the drawing by going over and redrawing them with the Brush tool.

Create a new layer, and name it details. Then, select the Brush tool, choose a 1-pixel brush, and zoom into the writing in order to see it better. Select a slightly darker color for the text than was originally used, and rewrite the text, taking care *not* to match it exactly – the slight shifting of the text will echo the rippling water. The difference in color will also reinforce the idea that the scene is taking place underwater, by making the text look like it is in flux, as if it were in between the states reflected in a ripple. Also add in any additional details that need delineating, especially over the characters' features.

Daydream

Let's examine the drawing further to see if there are any other details that could be added to complete the picture.

It seems a little awkward that the girl's hair on the left is cropped high, near her eye. It would benefit from repeating the tendril shapes of the anemone. This will also help further connect the elements in the photograph to the light blue shape.

Create a new layer, and name it tendrils. Using the Eyedropper tool, select the light blue color of the rest of the hair. Then, select the Brush tool, and choose a 9-pixel brush. Check Wet Edges in the Paintbrush options, and draw in the tendrils, looking at the anemone tentacles to get general guidelines for the shape.

My final image is `underwater_scene.psd` on the CD. Here are the initial and final images, for comparison:

Incorporating Drawings into Animations

Once these techniques have been applied, I like to incorporate the drawings into my animations. The final drawing can be imported into Macromedia Flash or Adobe LiveMotion to create animations (SWF files) for the Web. LiveMotion is great at handling Photoshop files – you can just drag and drop your PSD files into the LiveMotion work area, and it will import the layers and preserve the alignment.

In this case, I added some ambient bubble animations to the scene to make it look like it's underwater. In order to create a rippling motion with the image, I create a slightly blurred version in Photoshop by applying a Gaussian Blur of 5 pixels. Then, the normal image and the blurry one are alternated with an animated rippling mask, making for a nice, billowy motion. To see the final result, check out /www.milkyelephant.com/eun-ha/who_is/faux/04.

a little elephant came + took them
but you'll take me around, won't you?
SU

chapter 1

chapter 2

chapter 3

chapter 4

chapter 5

chapter 6

chapter 7

chapter 8

chapter 9

chapter 10

chapter 11

chapter 12

chapter 13

chapter 14

chapter 15

chapter 16

outro

"Don't just repeat what we see every day, or no one will even know you've changed anything."

Michael Young
www.weworkforthem.com
www.designgraphik.com

379

Structure

To find true inspiration for myself, I cannot be looking for it. In art school, I looked for it time and again, only to find myself repeating what past artists and designers had done, leading to endless repetition. This 'process of creativeness' drove me insane, but it got me a job, which was a start. To me, though, it wasn't enough, because being in design isn't just about a paycheck – it's what makes me look forward to getting up in the morning. I love the feeling of knowing that every day, I'm going to learn something new that will advance me as a designer. Where do the ideas come from that I look forward so much to developing? They come from me and my life, nothing more and nothing less.

I laugh when I think of why I got into this industry. In 1996, I had not a clue what I wanted to do with myself, and I was actually about to apply for a business degree at the University of Tennessee, when my mother suggested that I check out Roane State Community College. I knew nothing about it, other than it was a hell of a drive to get to, but my mother had mentioned something about computers and art together in their program. This caught my attention, as I had been into art all my life, and was just getting into computers on my own time at home. I had practically given up hope on traditional art being my talent, because I was nowhere near as good as some other students I knew, but this new computer art thing sounded like something I could succeed at.

At the open day, the school tour staff were showing us this and that, but my objective was to get to the computer art room and see what was going on. When I found it, the lead professor, Anne Powers, sat me down and showed me some of the basic techniques I would learn in her department: using an old version of Strata Blitz, she made a shiny sphere above a checkerboard floor, the floor being reflected in the sphere. These days I'd laugh my pants off if someone showed me that – pure cheese! – but back then it was a stunning effect, and she was doing it so easily. I'd never seen anything like it before, and right then I saw my future as Reflective Sphere Master! Well, not exactly, but I knew I wanted to do something that involved doing this on computers all day.

When I began the art program, I remember that it wasn't as exciting as I had expected, because it was quite slow going. In response, I would wait for the other students to leave, and then take over like a monster. I don't even remember what my inspiration was back then; I think it was more that I wanted to explore this new artistic medium, than I had any particular ideas to express.

After about a year, I started to break off into my own little world. I think this is when my real artistic expression started to take off, and I began to conceive ideas that could be realized digitally. I can remember that I wanted to express emotions through digital imagery, rather than with words or drawings. In my last year in Tennessee, I started paying attention to the design community as a whole, to gain more ideas and knowledge of the field. I looked at signs, posters, movies, television, fashion, billboards, books, web sites, and – best of all – CD cover art. I remember seeing amazing album artwork for the band Tool, the introduction to the movie *Seven*, and David Carson's book *The End Of Print*. To this day, shopping for CDs is a great way to see what's going on in design, and what new things (and old things) people are pulling off.

After Roane State, I received a scholarship at the Minneapolis College of Art and Design. I moved there not knowing anyone, but I soon became close friends with my roommates, and with some other artists from classes and social gatherings. I started to find inspiration now in talking to people, discussing different media and their importance. I was usually in the most uncomfortable position because I was the digital kid in the group; the others were traditional artists – painters, sketch artists, and photographers. I remember debating digital art, and whether I considered what I did to be art, design, or just a commercial product. Today, I still use those debates as my inspiration to push what I do beyond any of these categories – if I'm always moving forward, there's never time for me to sit around and wonder about being right or wrong.

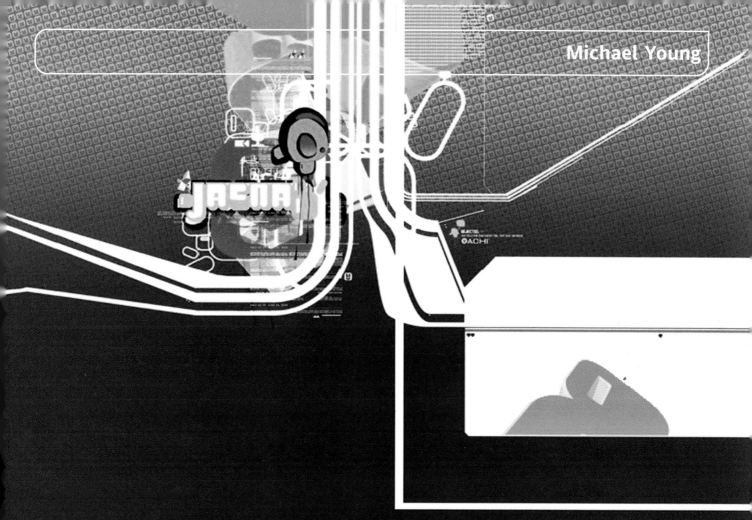

The fun part about making friends in Minneapolis was learning other artists' feelings and thoughts, and their enthusiasm for their own medium. I began to ask whether they were interested in seeing what I could do digitally to their work. They gave me any photograph, drawing, or painting I wanted, and told me to do whatever I liked with them – it was free rein! Sometimes, I even asked them to produce an original for something that I had an idea about, and they were always good enough to help me out. That feeling of open collaboration was the best personal artistic technique I took from that school.

In Minneapolis, I not only learned about collaboration and how much it can help your work, but also took classes in traditional media in order to understand techniques that I could bring back into Photoshop. I discovered a deep passion for painting in my second semester, and hardly ever touched my computer. I wanted to understand color, and the power it could hold in my artwork – and to this day I'm still comfortable using color because I went to an outside source to find inspiration for digital combinations. Painting also helped me to understand how to look at objects in new ways: instead of thinking that you have to make a mirror image of something, you can share with people the way *you* see it. That single idea has changed my work remarkably in the past two years – it has become much more abstract, and I've begun to disobey rules so that I can pursue my own vision of the way things look, based only on my visual concept of them.

Structure

In the summer of 1999, I got an e-mail from someone who'd seen my portfolio online – a company called Vir2l, in Washington DC. They asked me to come in for an interview to check them out for a senior designer position. I took the opportunity, and also took the job after seeing what they did: it was the same kind of Photoshop work I'd been doing for the past two years, but they were doing it commercially. I worked at Vir2l for two years, eventually becoming Art Director at the Washington DC studio. While there, I came across countless new ways to find inspiration, and new ways to create, but most important remained the one I picked up back in art school: learning from others. From Minneapolis, to Vir2l, to the present day, working side by side with other artists has made me who I am.

At Vir2l, we shared all of our ideas. We shared music, books, movies, web sites, and fonts. We talked about good design, mediocre design, and terrible design. We understood what was going on, how one another thought, and who to ask for help or criticism on a particular project. Inspiration at Vir2l came as a result of everything; not a single person, object, application, or piece of equipment. The ideas, collaborations, and watching other people work harder and harder, drove me forward. I learned how to work faster, and think smarter, and spend less time nitpicking. And yet I also learned how to fine-tune my ideas before laying them down.

While with this group, I absorbed more and more things from outside of design. I remember Anders Schroeder (www.dform1shiftfunc.net) talking about monster trucks and chainsaws with me, and in these silly conversations he and I shared ideas about heavy machinery that would later advance our 3D work. I know it sounds far-fetched, but it's quite true. My modeling in 3D now is very robotic, because he inspired me to think that way. I remember how James Widegren (www.threeoh.com) and I would come up with insane ideas, and I'd wonder how we could ever pull them off. But James would just show me a trick in Photoshop, and there it was: the idea on the screen, in no time at all. This was when I realized that you really can do anything you want in Photoshop – you just need the idea to get you started.

Structure

While at Vir2l, I also started two personal projects, to deprive myself of sleep even more. Designgraphik began back in 1999, in my first days at Vir2l, so that I could break off and see what I could do as an individual. I wanted not only to understand the teamwork at Vir2l, but also to maintain my own goals in art. It's still my outlet for studying a new subject that I have an idea for, or for when I want to practice. The odd thing about Designgraphik is that its main goal now was inspired by its own work: in *Serving 3*, I created a piece entitled *Southbound 83*, in which I took a picture of myself in an Atari shirt and modified it – I made the logo extend off the shirt as lines of continuation. A few weeks later, I noticed that I'd stumbled across something interesting, and I began studying the continuation and subtraction of interior and exterior environments with two-dimensional and three-dimensional elements. In *Serving 4*, I launched my new study, using the addition of 3D objects to interior spaces.

My second personal project goes by the name Submethod, and I started it with the aim of collaborating with people working in other media. The group I put together included Nineteen Point Five Collective (NPFC) as the audio artists, Stanley W as the textual artist, and myself as the visual artist. It was something of a learning exercise for me, because I'd never worked with musicians or writers before. NPFC would send me songs, Stanley would send me scripts, and I'd get ideas from combinations of the two. In my opinion, everyone should have a Submethod, simply because you'll be amazed at what ideas others will bring to the team, without anyone having to think about it.

One of the most amazing things to happen at Submethod was our second launch for the Reboot of 2001. I remember talking to Stanley in London at the turn of the year, and we started to conceive some ideas about layering narratives. What we wanted was to make something that was meant *not* to work, and to see if any interesting accidents happened along the way. The new site was to contain three narratives, one each by NPFC, Stanley W, and myself. Each artist was to come up with a story dealing with ten major marking points that highlighted certain events in their day. The goal was for the artists to produce a 'timeline' of their average day.

If you view the movie, you'll see the form and movement with which I try to express emotions, and the pace of my days. I used very detailed objects to express focusing on many things, and the motion is slow, to show my very focused work process. The audio is another layer that explains many things, such as morning urination, a car wash, talking to office workers, and being in a bar. The amazing thing about these works is not only that they're documenting their markers, but also that they're stories being told musically.

In the textual narrative, the words are placed in the titles of documents in a web browser. Many viewers think these words are the movies' titles too, because that's the way they've been trained to think. If you put all ten words together in order, however, you'll see that the author is telling a story as well, but with a single word at a time. In the final piece, *0010*, the top word is "McDonalds", chosen because it described the last event in his day: ending the evening on his way home to his flat near a McDonalds in London, and smelling the stench of the trash.

Structure

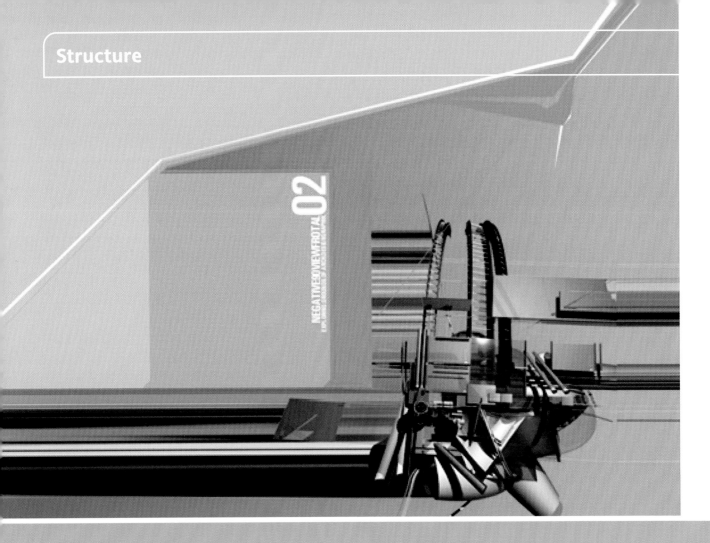

I left Vir2l in the early part of 2001 to pursue personal goals in art and design, but Tennessee, Minneapolis, and Vir2l were growing stages of my artistic life, and they're important to me. I'm only in my early twenties, though, and I still see myself as being at the beginning of my career. The thing I miss most about working with a team is that feeling of knowing there are others sitting next to you who'll help out in a tight fix. To try and patch this problem, I've started to open a dialog with other online artists – people like Michael Cina (www.trueistrue.com) – to absorb and share ideas and techniques with them. My reasons for doing this are the same as your reasons for reading this book: I want to understand others' motives and methods.

When I'm working, I'm usually very focused on what I'm doing, so I don't have time to think about new ideas for myself or my clients. In response, I have begun to drive more in my car, get away and think, go on vacations, and exercise, giving myself plenty of time for ideas just to come to me. When I drive, that's all I do, and I always have a pen, paper, and camera in the car with me. I don't know if this is the safest thing in the world, but it's certainly generated an enormous number of ideas. I've also restarted shopping for CDs in stores, and I've begun to watch more DVDs in order to understand motion and sound relationships.

Lately, my primary visual inspiration has come from architecture. At Vir2l, many of the other artists had started slowly to turn me onto it, but it never really hit me hard. One day, though, I took a look at some books on architecture and was absolutely blown away. Suddenly, I was looking everywhere for buildings and structures, just for the beauty in the outlines, and the forms these structures created. To me, the outline of a structure can sometimes be more powerful than the structure itself. I've now taken these insights to my personal work by creating huge, architecturally influenced 3D objects, and then using only the outlines of the objects in my finished work. In Photoshop, I just make a selection of the object, and fill it with a solid color or gradient. This has been a feature of my recent work, and the inspiration again came from outside of my profession.

I've been in this industry for almost six years now, and the things I've talked about here are what have helped me to progress as an artist, and in my thinking as an artist. The most important thing for me is to understand what others are doing, and to know what they won't do. I have learned these things to help guide me to new ideas, but I'm also trying to *unlearn* them, to start afresh for inspirations still to come. To me, inspiration is not just reading, or listening to music, or watching the latest new movie. It's about the way you think, and open yourself up for change, because with change you will constantly have new ideas and a positive feeling of personal achievement.

05
UPSIDE.DWN.FRONT.VIEW

Structure

In a lot of my recent work, I play with the technique of using three- and two-dimensional elements together with my photography, to give a sense of continuation and addition. A lot of making all of this work together involves using Photoshop to merge all the elements into a smooth flow, in a professional manner. Many applications, including the program that I used to make to the model in this tutorial, can put imagery together, but I've found that Photoshop gives me the best overall control, and makes it easiest to correct mistakes.

As I explained earlier in this chapter, a lot of what goes into making all this happen is patience and concentration – without these your errors, and the corners you've cut, will easily be seen. Never forget the details, because those are what will make your work stand out from the rest. In this tutorial, I'm going to show you how to create the image below, by importing the 3D model and 2D elements into Photoshop. The illusion given is that the 3D object is actually 'on' the sign – but in a strange way, so that it still feels as if it's fake, so not too Hollywood.

Before I get into the tutorial, however, I want to return to the piece that first helped me to discover the style that I'm currently addicted to. *Southbound 83* – that modified photograph of me in an Atari T-shirt – was a complete accident. As I'm beginning to realize, though, my accidents have often been my greatest accomplishments, concept-wise.

The work was a piece that I started with the intention of continuing my little theme of always having a piece to do with video games of some sort in all my Designgraphik servings. I had just recently bought a new T-shirt, and this purchase was right in time to be the last artwork for the new Designgraphik. In a mirror, I took a picture of myself wearing the shirt, with the camera obscuring my face to make sure that all the focus went onto that logo. Until I began to work on the file, though, it had never really hit me what to do with this piece to make it stand out.

I'd recently been motivated to start using Adobe Illustrator by my friend Justin Fines (www.demo-design.com), to help advance the two-dimensional areas of my artworks. I began to play with lines on the image, and then it hit me: I noticed the logo at a new perspective, and started to draw off from the logo, outside the shirt. I then made the canvas much wider, and started to play with continuing the lines still further. I began to take advantage of this discovery, and it has now become my obsession in visual creation, with either photographs or 3D renders.

Warning Sign

To begin the tutorial, I'm going to start with a photograph of a warning sign by a water dam in Tennessee, taken with a digital camera (A_warning.jpg). Now, most digital cameras still show some artifacts of JPG compression when you zoom up close to the image, so I take all my photographs at a very high resolution, and then shrink them down in Photoshop. This leads us to the first step, which is to reduce the original image. Go to Image > Image Size, and you'll see that the size of the image is 1200 pixels wide by 1600 high. You should cut both of those in half, so that the new image is just 600 x 800 pixels.

I'm seldom happy with the way things from real life look in my photographs, so before I do anything else, I invariably change the color balance of my imagery (Image > Adjust > Color Balance). On this occasion, I'm just going to add a slight modification to the Midtones to stylize the photograph a tad. Looking at the three empty fields at the top of the Color Balance window, I changed the first to +14, the second to +15, and the third to -36.

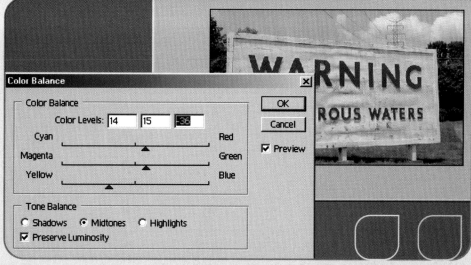

Structure

Another way to control the color levels would be to try some of the other menus under Image > Adjust. It's typical of Photoshop that people tend to get comfortable with their own way of doing this sort of thing, as I'm sure you'll have seen in other chapters. There are many people who, like me, are happy using the Color Balance options, but there are others who say that the channel mixer gives more control. If you take the time to learn to work with all the options, there are almost endless possibilities. Another possibility, for example, is to use the Threshold tool (Image > Adjust > Threshold) to create an outline of the image, and then to overlay that on the original at a low opacity setting.

I'm now going to clean the sign up and give it my own message, which obviously involves removing the 'WARNING dangerous waters" text. The easiest way to do this is by using the Clone Stamp tool to duplicate an area of the image that you select by Alt+clicking, and then painting it over the area where you place the tool cursor. Make sure that you select a nice clean part of the sign that won't be too obvious when duplicated; I chose an area to the left of the W, and repeated the process until the sign was completely cleared of the text.

Achieving the best possible results means getting some variety on the sign, so choose a few different source points from different areas, so that it doesn't look faked. At the end of the process, you can see that I've got rid of the text, and also added some variety to the texture of the sign.

When using the Clone Stamp tool, the longer you spend and the more patient you are, the better the result will be. If you rush through it, your manipulation will be pretty obvious, but if you pay close attention to the selections, the result will look more real and organic.

The 2D Element

We're now going to add some 2D elements on top of the sign to give it its own unique, abstract personality. Open the file `twodee.ai` from Illustrator, and place it over the sign. You'll need to tweak it slightly so that it looks as if it really *belongs* on the sign – when I paste a vector graphic over an image, I usually scale and skew the former so that it looks right. As you can see, when I first pasted the graphic, it looked completely out of place.

The way to get it into the right position is to use Photoshop's Free Transform (Edit > Free Transform) and Skew (Edit > Transform > Skew) tools.

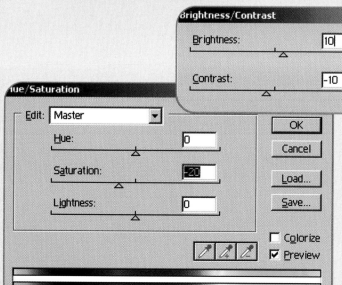

The next step is to tweak the brightness and color of the 2D elements, and also to change the layer blending mode to Multiply, so that they absorb the texture of the sign. When you switch to Multiply, the bright red is affected by the color of the sign, so that it fits in more smoothly.

If you then change the brightness and contrast of the new layer slightly (Image > Adjust > Brightness/Contrast), and make a modification to lower the saturation (Image > Adjust > Hue/Saturation) it should look something like this:

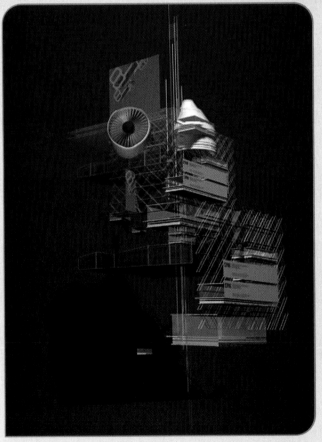

The 3D Element

My next step is to add the 3D element (`three_dimensional.tif`), which will add more depth to the image, and affect its 'realistic' appearance. To do this, I'm going to use an alpha channel, which can make matters easier when you're laying something over an already-set background image. When I open the 3D image, you can see that it has a dark gray background.

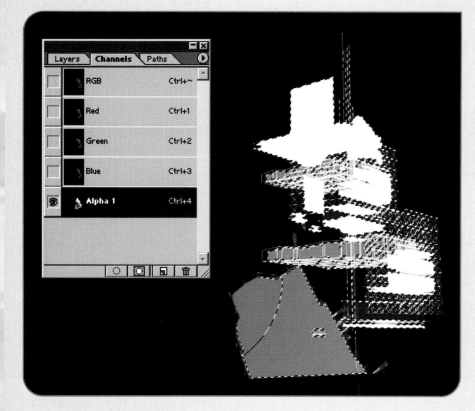

Open the Channels palette and select the appropriate channel for the image by clicking on the Alpha channel and the Load channel as selection icon (empty dotted circle) at the bottom of the palette.

Now return to the Layers palette, select the main layer containing the 3D image, and then copy and paste it into the main image file. You'll notice it fits into the correct spot, but it doesn't look quite right.

To fix this problem, and using exactly the same settings as for the 2D imagery, I changed the brightness and contrast, and the hue and saturation, so that it matched the rest of the image more closely.

Stylizing

Although I've done all that, I still feel as though the image needs another touch to even the whole thing out. The penultimate step is to add a new layer of color with a blending mode of Multiply. This will stylize everything to the one color tone I choose, and also add more emotion and mystery to the picture. I created a new layer and filled it with a fluorescent green (#C6F93C) to alter the image's color presence, and then changed the layer blending mode as described. The result should look something like this:

I will now go and add a few tick marks and dots, and a 5-pixel border (using the Pencil tool) to finalize the image and smooth it all out. I often add a 2D element or some header text over the top of my work, just to break the flow of everything working as part of the photograph. I find that it's good not only to add your own little continuation of real life, but also to add some conflict, so that it doesn't look *too* perfect. That's what you can see in my finished piece, which I showed you at the beginning of this section.

Set yourself apart

Manipulating pictures and adding new elements to them is incredibly simple to do in Photoshop. The key is to set yourself apart from other designers by showing things the way *you* see and feel them. Get creative: don't just repeat what we see every day, or no one will even know you've changed anything. To make this really work as a technique for you, you need to try new things and explore abstract ideas that you would actually like to see in real life, but which do not exist. This is what I do and enjoy.

I would like to finish up with a little soapbox ranting on how you can use Photoshop to your advantage. When they first begin, many users try to imitate what they see going on around them. There is nothing wrong with this – it's a natural way of learning – but the key to success with Photoshop is not to get stuck forever in this hole. If you want to break out and be known, and to set new boundaries, then you need to think unnaturally. Look beyond what everyone else is doing, and think about how to advance your concepts further.

I've received so much e-mail asking what program I use, and what filters, and how I achieve a certain effect. The funny thing is, I only use a filter about twice a year

in Photoshop – to be quite honest, I hate them. As a tool for editing imagery, Photoshop can do anything you want it to, but that's the thing: it's *your* tool, so don't sit there pressing all the pre-rigged buttons. Come up with your own effects. I get my ideas for new effects from real-life events, such as seeing a TV channel go all crazy when the cable goes out. At that moment, I see about eight thousand little details and effects that totally blow my mind as a new way to animate something.

As you saw in the Atari piece, my work doesn't really involve tricks; it revolves around knowing Photoshop as a tool, and how to use it. The key is to learn how all the tools in the basic toolbox work (such as the Clone Stamp tool that I used in my tutorial). Understanding these tools properly will be what pushes your work to a higher level. The other most important tool in my work is the basic Select > All command. It's as easy as that: learn how to use the Select > All command and the Magic Wand tool for techniques such as feathering, which can soften the edges of cuts for slow fading.

Using the Magic Wand tool can also help you to unleash some amazing pattern effects. For example, if you have a pattern on the screen, and you make a selection of that pattern using the Magic Wand, and then go to your image layer and use the Cut command, you'll see it cut that pattern from your image.

Something as straightforward as the Pencil tool can also be very useful, especially if you're working for screen rather than print. Sometimes, I even use the Pencil tool to write my text for (say) a small navigation menu. The Pencil tool can allow you to create crisp details that will turn out very sharp in the final image.

Structure

The very last image that I'm going to refer to here is the wallpaper from my company site that I'm developing in partnership with Michael Cina: *WeWorkForThem* (www.weworkforthem.com).

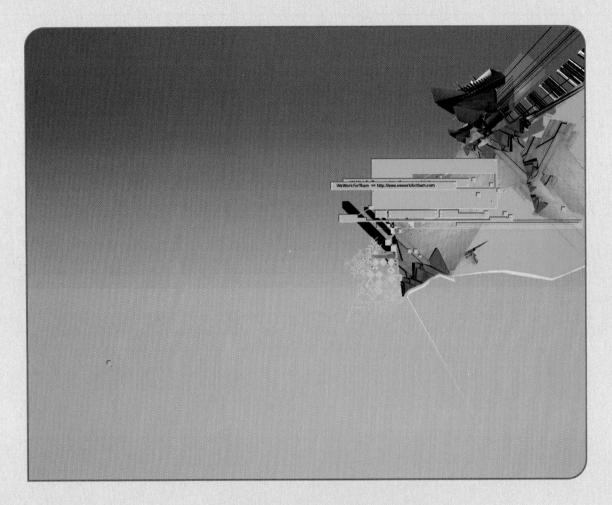

This shows a 3D object with some Illustrator shape details, flat planes, and a bunch of fake, stylized web form fields. I always had some kind of weird liking for form fields on web sites, once I saw that you could personalize their color, font, and size in Internet Explorer. This led me to bring them into my work as elements, but in a way that was more chaotic and out of control. I wanted to make form fields that looked broken, loose, and way over- or under-sized.

In this image, you can see that I have quite a few different shapes, but creating them comes down, once again, to understanding Photoshop's tools. Only two tools were used to make those 'fields': the Pencil tool, and the Paint Bucket tool. First of all, I drew a light colored line for the bottom right part. Then, to finish the box outline, I drew with a dark color at the top left. As you can see, it adds a strange effect to the image – it appears to be 'on top'. Then, if you want to finish it, just get out your Paint Bucket tool, turn off Anti-aliased, and make sure that Contiguous is off as well. That will fill inside the outline you have made, and create the box shape. From there, you can take it wherever you want. In my image you can see that I began to cut out the boxes more, and also to make them in different shapes and angles.

Every tool in Photoshop has a vast array of different settings. Once you've learned how to tweak all the tools to your satisfaction, you're beginning to customize the program to do what *you* want it to do, and not just pressing its presets.

chapter 1

chapter 2

chapter 3

chapter 4

chapter 5

chapter 6

chapter 7

chapter 8

chapter 9

chapter 10

chapter 11

chapter 12

chapter 13

chapter 14

chapter 15

chapter 16

outro

"I was drawing silly, evil little bunnies everywhere I could."

Norma V. Toraya
www.crankbunny.com

Obsession

I was a very picky eater as a child, so when my non-traditional housewife mom found something that I actually liked to eat, she would 'milk' it. If little Normita liked to eat baked chicken with mashed potatoes, little Normita would eat baked chicken with mashed potatoes for dinner three weeks straight, until one day little Normita would wake up as a baked chicken – wings, sauce, and all. Mom didn't have the patience to fuss with making me eat my vegetables, but made priorities out of having me do my homework, go to school, comb my hair, and stop running around the house with scissors. This was the point in my life where I learned how to obsess over particular things. Now, the things that I obsess over have come to influence and inspire me.

With 'obsession', though, also comes the word 'obnoxious': I become obsessed with particular random things that interest me, to the point of being obnoxious. A lot of people ask me what Crankbunny is, to which I reply that for three years now, Crankbunny has been a pool of the most obnoxious, obsessive constants in my life. It was a word that I just blurted out one day, because at the time I was drawing silly, evil little bunnies everywhere I could. On my bedroom walls, on paper napkins, on timesheets at work, on sketchbooks – they were everywhere. For the sake of background, I'd better briefly explain my work.

Norma V. Toraya

A lot of our wonder will become synthetic

Crankbunny (www.crankbunny.com) is an ongoing project comprising videos and interactive Internet movies. Each part of the project tells a story of the future – a futuristic fairytale, if you like. A prophecy of the future human (think cyborgs!), the movies are my prediction of what the human condition may become. It will probably be a place where only a few remember how to feel, and those who do will suffer over sensitivity – pure emotion – because they end up feeling everything that others cannot. The movies don't pinpoint the future, but they do give a general sense of what's going on. I never attempt to map out what cities will look like, or the jet-propelled cars that will zoom us around; rather, I try to use the kind of communication that happens when one listens to a song. This is done through exploring different types of narrative, usually using non-linear and abstract forms of storytelling. The value in this, I feel, is giving the viewer a different sense of information, and a different overall experience.

Obsession

My early fascination in animation came from an interest in 'magic lanterns', and a desire to understand just why people are so drawn by having a story told to them visually. Lantern slides – the precursors of slide projectors, film, television, and video media – started to appear publicly in the 1820s. These 'lanterns' worked like slide projectors, in that they had slides which light passed through, and people could look at several slides in a row. The most exciting type of lanterns, though, were the ones that used mechanical 'slides' featuring slipping plates, pulleys, and levers. With these, different parts of the slide would move, to mimic motion and life.

This is cinema at its most primal. If we were to compare it with the evolutionary timeline of man, that monkey-like creature on the left side of the chart is what lantern slides are to the history of cinema. But from that monkey lantern, we can learn the essence of telling a story in pictures. I like looking at lantern slides because they remind me how easy it is to tell a story. Sometimes, people don't need complicated special effects in order to feel something. When I watch lantern slides, I find it a very grounding experience.

I've always been interested in how we see things, especially when those things are moving. Are there ways to draw people's attention to certain points on the screen? Can I use this to my advantage, so that I can communicate something relatively complex in a simple way? What do our eyes miss when the things they see are in motion?

In 1878, English photographer Eadweard Muybridge settled a bet for Leland Stanford, who was the governor of California and a horse racing enthusiast: Did a trotting horse keep at least one hoof on the ground at all times? Muybridge set up twelve cameras at trackside, with shutters activated by tripwires. The resulting pictures proved that the horse did indeed raise all four hooves off the ground while trotting – something our eye can't detect when the motion is at full speed. I find this example very exciting, because it proves to me that the eyes in our heads have a very limited 'shutter speed' – in other words, there are certain things we don't and won't see. It can be hard for a viewer to understand all that's going on in a non-linear storyline, but when I'm telling a story in pictures, I don't need to worry about everything within a scene. By concentrating on and exemplifying visually what I find important, I can tell my stories in a more effective manner.

Motion of a Galloping Horse
Eadweard Muybridge's photo series showing that all of a horse's legs are off the ground at one time as it gallops.
© CORBIS
Photographed by Eadweard Muybridge ca. 1887

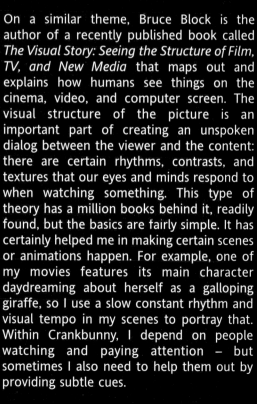

On a similar theme, Bruce Block is the author of a recently published book called *The Visual Story: Seeing the Structure of Film, TV, and New Media* that maps out and explains how humans see things on the cinema, video, and computer screen. The visual structure of the picture is an important part of creating an unspoken dialog between the viewer and the content: there are certain rhythms, contrasts, and textures that our eyes and minds respond to when watching something. This type of theory has a million books behind it, readily found, but the basics are fairly simple. It has certainly helped me in making certain scenes or animations happen. For example, one of my movies features its main character daydreaming about herself as a galloping giraffe, so I use a slow constant rhythm and visual tempo in my scenes to portray that. Within Crankbunny, I depend on people watching and paying attention – but sometimes I also need to help them out by providing subtle cues.

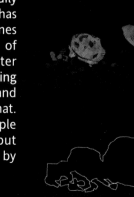

Obsession

The Quay Brothers are known for their stop-motion animation shorts that delve into the world of the miniature, and the odd livelihoods of little objects, and their work gave me a new and entirely different view of animation. Their films display an almost passionate amount of detail and texture. Every single object seems to carry a past that has no significance, but is nonetheless precious. The visual textures created by these objects and their tiny worlds are amplified to something unforgettably dreamlike.

Beyond all these remarkable characteristics, the Quay Brothers' use of metaphor and music that meld like a poem has always inspired me. They believe in a different type of storytelling – a visual aesthetic that never relies upon dialog. Many of their animations are centered on scores of music that have already been created.

The first three minutes of *Rehearsals for Extinct Anatomies* mesmerized me with the beauty of using subtle detail. Sometimes, movement doesn't have to be exuberant or flowing. The idea of communicating a story without words, and expressionism based on music, has recently grounded me into thinking about and creating my Crankbunny work differently. It amazes me how comfortable people are with music, and how ready to accept it. When people watch something abstract, I find that they're more ambivalent towards it than if (say) they were listening to jazz, which can be considered an abstract form of music.

Rehearsal for Extinct Anatomies

In the three years I've been working on the Crankbunny projects, I've had a lot of people tell me that the movies are too vague; that the subtle details I've left in the movies aren't doing their job; that I needed to refine the abstract things I was trying to communicate through better execution and more obvious intent. As a result, I've worked on the contrast between music and visuals to make things clearer for the viewer. In *Future Installment Two: Naissance*, there's a scene in which the screen goes dark for three minutes while a beautiful part of a song by Godspeed You Black Emperor plays. The message is that you're not going to be told the rest of the story with a picture, but with a song.

Away from the Quay Brothers, there's another movie that's strongly influenced the way I use sound in the Crankbunny projects. *Akira*, by Katsuhiro Otomo, is without doubt the most epic Manga ever made, and for me the most powerful scene of all comes right at the end. When the character Tetsuo is engulfed in the vortex created by Akira, there is no sound at all. The silence is so profound that it becomes a soundscape in its own right; because the entire scene is about Tetsuo obtaining internal peace, using silence is a perfect way of communicating the transition he's going though. This abstract use of sound makes for a very strong climax – the end of Akira started to make me think about how, while sound is certainly sound, no sound can sometimes be sound as well.

I have a big obsession with two types of Japanese toys. In the 1970s, Shotaro Ishimori created *Robocon*, a Japanese kids' show that had a resurgence in the late 1990s. It focused on life in a future world where robots go to school in order to learn how best to perform their duties. From what I can tell, many of these robots were built from household objects, or based upon household items. It's all very simple, and the plot and the scenery are absolutely ridiculous, but creatively, Robocon has allowed me to look and think about the future in a less *Blade Runner* way. It made me realize that the future doesn't have to make sense, and that if I wanted my main character to be a half-human-half-noodle delivery scooter, it could be that way.

Doreamon, created by Fujimoto Hiroshi, is probably a little more recognizable, because the blue cat looks a lot like a *Hello Kitty* character. It features a young boy called

Nobita who finds a strange being in his desk drawer: a round, blue, cat-shaped robot. Now, Nobita's great-great-grandson lives in the 22nd century, but thanks to Nobita's mistakes, the entire family is living in poverty. To rectify this, Nobita's descendant has sent Doreamon back to the past, to help prevent Nobita from making those mistakes. Now, this is a difficult task, since Nobita is the weakest and least intelligent child in his class. And initially, Doreamon isn't the smartest of robots, either. He does, however, have a four-dimensional pocket on his front, which contains all manner of cool gadgets from the 22nd century, and it is with these toys that Doreamon will try to save Nobita from a future of poverty and failure.

Maybe now you can start to see where I'm coming from? With their cyborg cats and futuristic robot schools, storylines from both Robocon and Doreamon have influenced many of the stories I like to tell with Crankbunny.

My obsession with old, odd, funny objects explains why I admire the Quay Brothers' work, while my obsessions with the future explain my interest in *Robocon*, *Doreamon*, and *Akira*. So, when I came face to face with a large, abandoned steel mill in Pittsburgh, Pennsylvania, I became enamored with what I always refer to as 'the machine'. It was an overwhelming experience for me, and opened up many doors in my head, and within Crankbunny. You see, I actually studied sculpture in college, and was always attracted to found objects that were usually broken, but had so much character and texture. Back then, I felt that all those trinkets carried a universal meaning.

So, my friend Ryan brought me to the mill, and I confronted this enormous architectural edifice. In essence, the steel mill, which sat on a five-acre piece of land and hadn't been used in about 40 years, was a very large machine. Walking around, I saw how the pipes that ran through the various holding warehouses – used to transport water or steam, I guess – had diameters the size of two-storey buildings. I felt very small. I also felt like I was staring at an ancient animal, with vast, exposed organs. That day, I realized that I'd discovered a very large found object indeed, which I now constantly refer to in Crankbunny movies as 'the machine'.

The machine is a quality that's enveloping all of us ever more, as we become part of the future. The characters in Crankbunny are part technological, but they're also part of a grander technological machine – the world they live in is run by machines, and filled with ruin and loss. This large mill that I met was the epitome of all that, but I realized that it wasn't cold and harsh. Instead, this mill and world of the future was just a very large, unnatural organism that housed so much – so much that it had gained the character of something natural and old.

409

Obsession

I'm a sucker for toys and pop culture; I'm more of a consumer than I am a socially correct artist. I love music videos and commercials. Many people find commercials annoying and without much merit, but when you think about it, they have a very tough job to do. Music videos and commercials both contain strong visual techniques, and sometimes gimmicks, that communicate with the viewer quickly and effectively. In fact, they're probably the strongest examples of work that achieves the goals I set out when I talked about how we see. I actually find some commercials, and especially certain music videos, beautiful.

One company that consistently creates amazing videos is Shynola – four art school friends who got into animation and took up a flat in North London. Their unique perceptions and fresh animations have got them noticed, giving them the opportunity to create animations and slick-looking videos for the likes of U.N.K.L.E., Grooverider, Quannum and – most famously – Radiohead. Much of their work seems playful, vague, and naturally sincere – especially the way they treat their storylines and visual elements. The video for Radiohead's *Pyramid Song* is a great example of this – a stark, brooding song, accompanied by an honest, human interpretation.

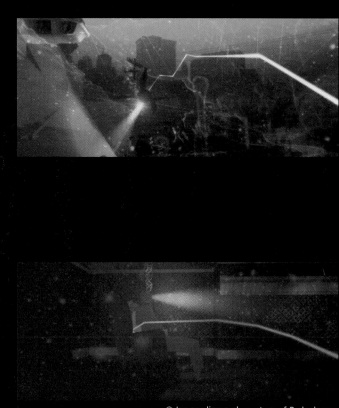

The animated video revolves around a flat, geometrical man moving himself around an underwater city. The everyday things shown – floating papers, a book, a church, and a dining room table – reveal this as a place the man might have known as a home. Out of habit, the man sits in an armchair to watch TV, and as the camera pans out the lyrics explain, "There was nothing to fear and nothing to doubt." The man cuts his life-saving oxygen cord, and the camera follows it as it whips up to the surface, leaving him down there to drown, but finally be home.

It's refreshing to come across a group of people who love to do what they're doing, and get away with doing it. My obsession with Shynola is cemented within this work ethic, and in their belief in themselves.

So, all that is Crankbunny is the product of all these obsessions. And in short, obsession – not the perfume – has been an effective tool for letting my interests drive me. I also find it very safe to obsess randomly over things like toys and TV, because I've never found myself in ruts where I don't know where to look. And the fact that my mother fed me the same thing for three weeks in a row ultimately means I don't have a problem with focusing on one thing and getting bored with it.

When little Normita was 14 years of age, she would make still images in Photoshop – each one a little bit different from the last – and print them out on her father's printer. Then, little Normita would run over to the old Super-8 camera, and take a picture of each piece of paper to make a movie. I've grown up a bit now, using Photoshop to lay out the moving elements into different layers, and then importing them into a video-editing program. I also set up a lot of special effects within Photoshop. In this tutorial, I'll talk about how I built one particular Crankbunny movie called *Level 10* within Photoshop, and then transferred it over to a timeline program for editing together the narrative.

At heart, this tutorial is about the fact that Photoshop has become a means of getting into motion graphics, animation, and digital video in a very reasonable and harmless way. When I started to use Photoshop in this manner, I never had to face the issue of buying and using expensive video equipment, or even a video camera. In the beginning, I found that working with still images and animating them presented less of a challenge in composing/editing than actual video footage.

The movie we'll look at here is about a girl who is daydreaming, and pictures herself as a galloping giraffe. When her daydream ends, she is brought back to reality. This was the narrative and simple verbal storyboard I started with. Although I usually create a physical storyboard for my movies, drawing out each scene with its different changes, I build some of the smaller ones (like this one) as I go along. I have my drawings beforehand, but as I start building the Photoshop file that will eventually become my movie, I make certain decisions about animation, transitions, and other montage techniques that are the basis to telling the story in a certain way. I wanted to present the girl in a private, intimate way that was oddly surreal, but which the viewer still understood. Before looking at the tutorial, I recommend having a look at the finished SWF file, `working.swf`.

Blending the Component Images Together

As stated above, I knew the basic story idea before I started to make my PSD file, so my main concern was working out how to tell it so that people could intimate what this girl was thinking about. I had a drawing of the girl, and a photograph of the room I imagined her in. I decided to show her sitting in this room, but to introduce her very slowly – I wanted the viewer to feel as though they were scanning the surface of her. In the drawing, she is looking away from the 'camera', so the viewer feels very voyeuristic.

I decided to pan the entire final image of her sitting and daydreaming. By moving the whole image, the viewer's attention is drawn to certain aspects of the scene – to the girl, certainly, but also to the sinking feeling as the image moves from top to

bottom at a slight angle. They would scan the girl, but also sink with her into her head. Horizontal movement isn't very 'significant', because people are used to seeing it. Vertical movement is a little more powerful, but anything at a slight diagonal is always a more intense sensation.

In the whole movie, there are three drawings of the girl: one seated (above), one standing, and one as a giraffe. All three began in the same way, with a pencil drawing like this one.

Pencil drawings need to be cleaned up, and that's what we're going to look at first. I scanned in my black and white drawing of the giraffe girl as a grayscale image at 150dpi, and saved it as `giraffe_running_bw.jpg`. Open up this file in Photoshop, and zoom in close with the Zoom tool. Then, select the Curves feature (Image > Adjust > Curves).

Obsession

With Curves, you can set what counts as 'black' and 'white' within your picture. Then, every other tone in the picture is set to fall within the range between your selected 'black' and 'white'. I find this very helpful for cleaning up scanned drawings, where all I really need is the black outline and a crisp, anti-aliased border to the ink of the drawing. Choose the far-right eyedropper in the dialog box (Set White Point), and click on the light gray pencil marks that I didn't manage to get rid of with my gum eraser.

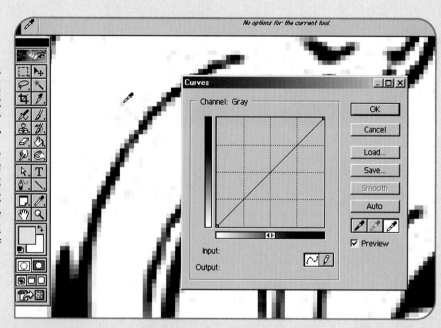

When you click on these marks, you're telling Photoshop that you want to set this light gray as your 'white', and the start of a tonal scale from white to black.

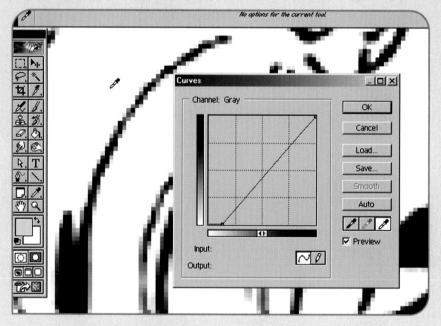

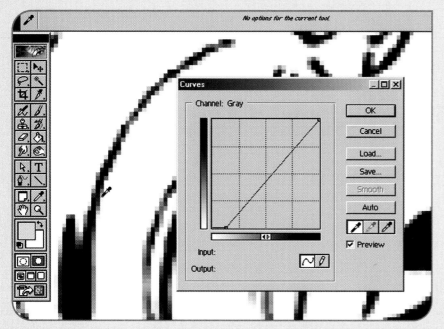

Then, select the far-left eyedropper in the dialog box (Set Black Point), and click on the inked lines of the drawing. Sometimes, the black ink will get scanned in as a darker gray.

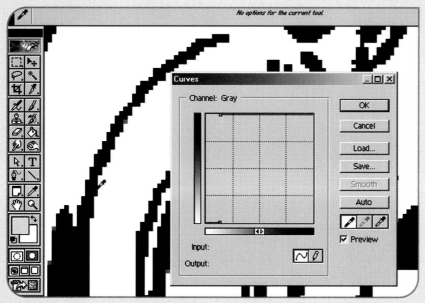

After a lot of fiddling around with those eyedroppers, going back and forth, you'll end up with mostly black and white pixels.

This will prove very useful when I start coloring in the clothing, or the skin tones — I can use the Magic Wand to select the area, and just fill. I won't get any of those icky stray white pixels.

Obsession

Once I'd applied these techniques to all three images, I proceeded to color them in. Without getting into specifics, for tasks like these I tend to use the Magic Wand tool, and select areas together. I usually check the Anti-aliased box, and set the Tolerance to 25. Sometimes I use the Airbrush tool at different opacities and different hues; on other occasions I'll actually fill the areas with cloned pieces of other scanned-in material.

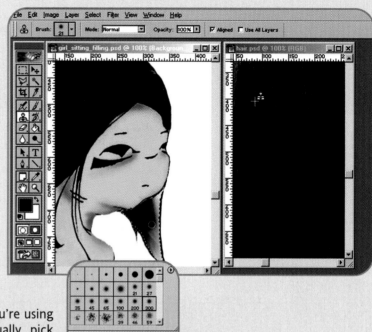

Filling can be quite tricky at first, especially when you're using textures from other scanned photographs. I usually pick textures that will be recognizable at different scales, and can repeat over themselves easily. To help, I use a large, 'fluffy' brush.

You can imagine using fill patterns like these as being a bit like using watercolor paints. By giving slightly different opacities and hues to your airbrush (not to mention using a fluffy brush), you can color in images slowly and carefully, and build up the fill. If you go too far, you can always go back in the History palette. This is what the girl looked like, once I had colored her in.

I also had a photograph of a room that I had scanned in. The room's perspective appears to be similar to that of the drawing, which is ultimately why I chose it, although I also liked the window blinds at the side. I opened the photograph of the room and dragged the colored image of the girl into it, making a new layer within the file. Then, I placed the girl in the photograph so that she looks like she's sitting on the floor.

Color Correction

A lot of successful film/video/composite work in which two or more images are put together depends on color correction. When objects sit together within a space, they affect each other. If someone took a picture of me sitting in a very bright orange room, for example, it's likely that in the photograph, I'd have a slight orange tinge to my skin. This essentially is color theory – the ways colors interact with each other.

The way I had colored the drawing was different from the colors in the room. The girl was warmer in skin and hair tone than the rest of the icy green room, and she stuck out like a sore thumb. To put this right, I selected the layer containing the girl, and went to Image > Adjust > Color Balance. Because the image of the girl had too many warm colors, I added green, and blue, and a bit more cyan.

Perhaps the most difficult part of color correction is determining exactly what must be done to fix the image. This is a combination of realizing what is wrong, and what you would like the image to be – and a little knowledge of color theory is absolutely essential. Photoshop's color wheel for an RGB image is made up of cyan, magenta, yellow, blue, green, and red. Cyan is opposite to red, magenta is opposite to green, and yellow is opposite to blue. When you color-correct something, you actually decrease the amount of one color in an image by increasing the amount of its opposite on the color wheel.

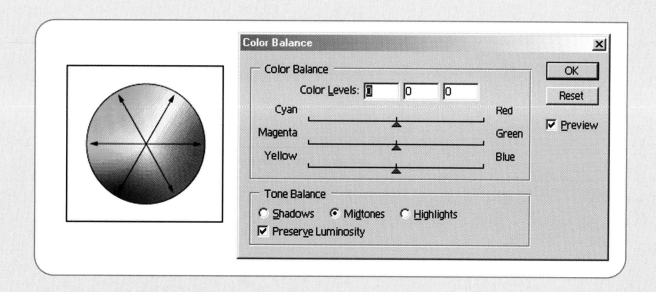

Obsession

So when I looked at my girl sitting down, and decided that there was too much red (warm colors) in the image, I moved the arrow slightly towards the Cyan end of the scale. You can also increase and decrease a color by adjusting the two adjacent colors on the wheel, or even by adjusting the two colors adjacent to its opposite.

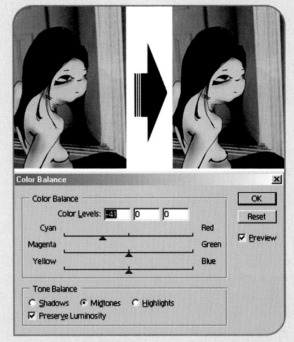

Another problem with the drawing was that it was a bit too saturated – I noticed a lot of subdued grays in the photograph of the room. To fix this, I went to Image > Adjust > Hue/Saturation, and lowered the saturation till I saw in the preview that she fitted in properly with her surroundings.

no color-correction   color-correction   less saturation

By performing this balancing act, I was able to match up the girl to the room, so the new image would look realistic, and not like something out of Monty Python! Even though I love Terry Gilliam's animations, way back when I started Crankbunny, I determined that I wanted the images to be more realistic and serious in tone. Anyhow, I merged the two layers of the girl and the room together into a single image that I saved in its own file, called introlook.psd.

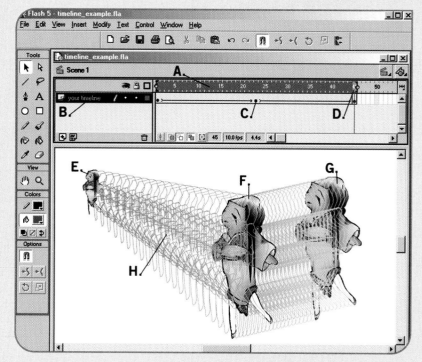

The actual panning of the entire image was done in Macromedia Flash by setting keyframes. (I used Flash to build *Level 10* because I intended it to be one of the many little scenes found in the first installment of the Crankbunny movie.) I imported introlook.psd into Flash, and gave it a layer of its own within the timeline.

If you're not familiar with Flash, here's a quick primer. The way that layers and their contents move within your movie is by means of *keyframes* that are set along a *timeline*. The keyframes are little markers or cues that define where an object must be at a certain time. You can move these marks to different frames in the timeline, and have as many of them as you want. Flash works out the differences between the keyframes, and does the work of getting the object from one place to another, once you've told it what kind of action you want it to make.

A. This is your timeline, and the frames that make it up.

B. This is a layer within a timeline.

C. This is what a keyframe looks like. It's usually a dot (or some sort of mark) to`` distinguish it from other frames.

D. This is the playhead of your timeline, which you can use to navigate around your movie. It lets you examine a movie one frame at a time.

E. This smaller image of the girl is the first keyframe on the timeline.

F. In the second keyframe, the girl from the first keyframe has been repositioned and resized.

G. The final keyframe shows the girl in another position.

H. The blue outlines you see represent the animation and change made by Flash in each frame to get from one keyframe to the other, and then to the final keyframe.

Obsession

To create the pan of the girl in the room, I placed the image near the bottom of the viewable area where I wanted the pan to start, and set a keyframe at the very beginning of the timeline. Then, five seconds along the timeline, I made another keyframe and then selected the image and moved its position up to where I wanted the diagonal pan to end. By creating a 'motion tween' between these keyframes, I generated the panning effect.

Because the image was so big in relation to the size of my preview movie area, it was very close-up, and a lot of the image was cut off. That worked to my advantage, though, because the resulting pan doesn't seem as cheesy and obvious.

Getting the Masks Ready

For the background sound, I chose a loop from a song called *Rollerball* by Mogwai. It's just a piano piece, but there's a certain repetition and sense of daydreaming that made me want to use it. Because the pan was so large and slow, and might not match the rhythm of the music, I decided that the left side of the movie would have to have something 'dancing' in time to the music – a contrast of sorts, as the viewer could get bored looking at the static image of the girl in the room. This contrast was enhanced further by having the material of the dancing elements appear very close-up and textured. I really didn't want the introduction of this character to be boring, so I thought these strips of texture would be interesting, and add to the intimacy of the moment.

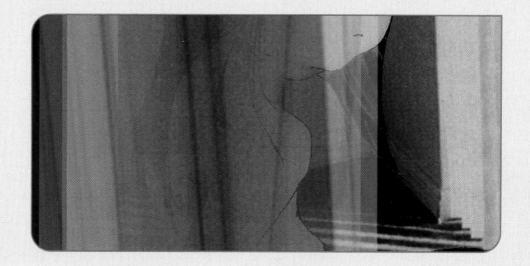

The way the strips of texture dance back and forth, revealing the background pan through gaps, is a product of various masks over images that also move over each other. It's worth mentioning, though, that 'masks' are treated a little differently in Photoshop and Flash. If you create a mask over a Photoshop layer, it becomes a part of that layer – a characteristic of it, if you like. In Flash, the 'masks' you use are separate layers in their own right.

In the case of the *Level 10* movie, I wanted the mask to change and move over the image. I needed my mask not to be a 'characteristic', but an image that I could animate separately and set keyframes to. I needed to create my Photoshop masks as layers in their own right, but they were quite easy to do: simple rectangular areas – skinny boxes and thicker boxes.

I took an overall screenshot of what I had already done with my movie in Flash, making sure that the preview window was scaled at 100% when I did so. Then I created a new document in Photoshop, pasted the screenshot into the new file, and saved it as `overall_screen_of_pan.jpg`.

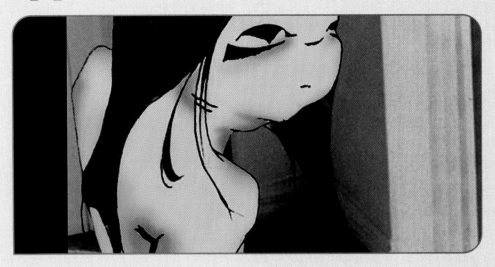

Open `introlook.psd` in Photoshop, and using the Rectangular Marquee tool, select various areas from it.

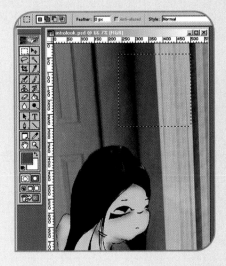  

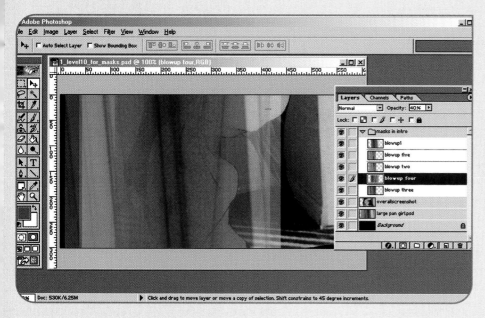

With each area that you select, copy and paste it into the Photoshop document that began with `overall_screen_of_pan.jpg`. New layers will be created automatically as you do so. In the end, I made five selections, and named their layers blowup one to blowup five. I then enlarged each of these layers, as I wanted them for the close-ups of the textures.

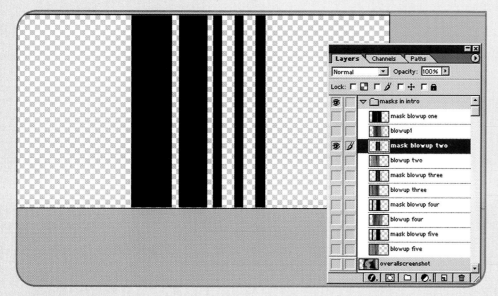

I arranged all these layers to the left side of the screen, and positioned them where I wanted them to appear at the start of the movie. I also varied the opacity of each layer between 40% and 60%. Above each new texture layer, I added a new blank layer, in which I made various big black rectangular shapes that would be the mask.

When I was done, I had five different textures in their own layers, each with their own mask layer right above them.

I then saved the file as `Level10.psd`. Eventually, this would become the final Photoshop file with all the layers that I'd import into Flash.

I had to export the layers individually into JPG files, but what to do about the mask layers that just had just big black masses on them? Well, I exported those as individual JPG files too, and imported them into Flash. I then had to break apart the images, outline the masked blob area, and make a separate vector shape from the outline. I finally got my layers and mask layers moving by setting keyframes to affect their scale, position, rotation, brightness, and other characteristics.

Transition between Scenes

Now that we've introduced the main character of *Level 10*, and visually explained her daydream and its layout, there needs to be a transition into the next scene. This will feature the girl imagining herself as a giraffe, tall and colorful, and galloping around. This transition also has to give the impression that the viewer is going inside the girl's head.

I chose to make this transition like a progression from real to make-believe. I saw these two worlds as polar opposites, so I decided to use swiping planes of black and white coming in slowly at first, and then repeating over and over at a faster speed each time. This would create an ever-quickening rhythm, causing the viewer to *expect* something to happen. I also hoped that the rhythm would amplify the looping of the Mogwai piano sound. You can use visual rhythm or repetition like this as a metaphor, setting a tempo that other visuals, transitions, and movements can match. Unconsciously, the viewer of your film will respond to this tempo, and experience your movie in a more intense way.

In my `Level10.psd` file, I created two new layers above the mask layers. Using the Paint Bucket tool, I filled one with black and labeled it black, and filled the other with white and labeled it white. Because this transition would primarily be based on me setting a lot of keyframes in Flash to make the black and white swoosh across the screen, that was basically all the Photoshop work I had to do! Yay, for easy black and white layers!

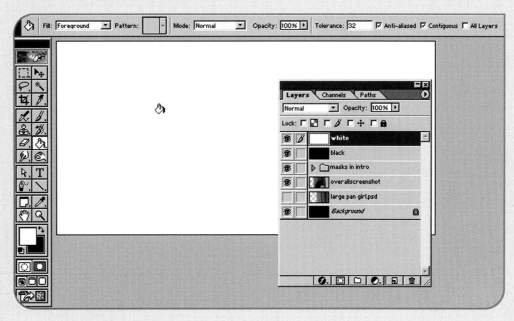

The Giraffe

The next scene in the movie would be the giraffe girl running in and around the subconscious brain. I always remember this little dog that I used to play with in my grandma's neighborhood. I used to sit on the grass in the backyard, and the dog would run around and around. One trick it especially liked to pull was going off about 50 yards, and making a sharp turn back towards me at a very high doggy speed. It would head straight for me, but when it got to about a foot away, it would turn slightly – barely missing me. The whole time, the little white dog would have this big, happy expression on its face, like: "Ha, gonna run you over! – Ha, *just missed you*!" This is the kind of feeling I wanted to have for the giraffe: galloping in from the darkness, and bulldozing the viewer's perspective.

Obsession

Using perspective in your images and videos is a very valuable thing, and there are several different ways to do it. First, as you know, you can change the size of your object: large objects seem to be closer and become part of the foreground, while small objects seem farther away and become part of the background.

A second technique, though, is textural diffusion, where objects that are closer are given more detail. As objects fall into the background, they lose detail – imagine looking at the crowd in a sports stadium at different magnifications, and you'll know what I mean. Detail (or lack of it) can also be substituted with focus. Furthermore, I think the movement of an object is very important in giving a sense of space.

Let's take the giraffe file that we were looking at earlier (now colored in), and drop it into `Level10.psd` on a new layer above the black and white layers. It's time to get down to the nitty-gritty of animating a character in Photoshop, which consists of looking at the giraffe and deciding which parts make this thing run.

We will then give each of those parts its own layer in Photoshop. In the case of the giraffe, I saw that each part of the legs – the top calf, lower calf, and hoof – would have to be in a separate layer. The torso and the tail would also be in separate layers. The neck of the giraffe, I divided into two parts (on two layers). Finally, the head would have its own layer, too.

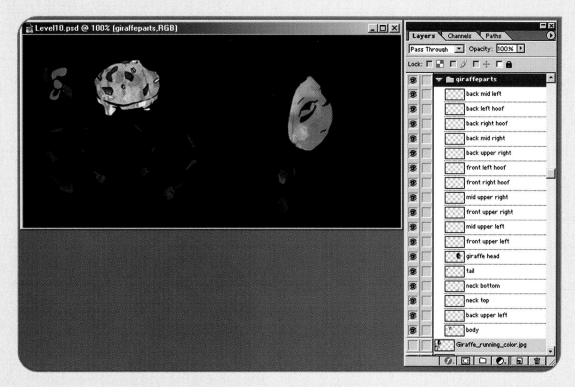

Divide these parts by zooming into the giraffe picture, and carefully selecting the part you need to section off with the Lasso tool. Then copy the selection, delete it, and paste it back into the file (making a new layer). Don't forget to name each layer, as you'll end up with a lot of them, and it could become very confusing. In the case of my giraffe drawing, where I'd cut out a leg and part of the leg was now missing because another leg had been over it, I'd make up the rest of that part in situ by drawing and painting it in.

After sectioning off all the parts of the character into their own layers, I placed them together in such a way that I could tell which parts went together. This is just so that when I imported the Level10.psd into Flash, I wouldn't have a lot of giraffe limbs flying around that I wouldn't be able to make sense of.

Obsession

In Flash, I proceeded to make the animal run in place with a series of keyframes, each keyframe capturing one instant of the giraffe running.

Using Flash's 'movie clips', it's possible to make a small movie that contains an instance of movement – like a loop of someone walking – and then to use that instance in its own layer that you can set further keyframes to. It's like having a movie within a movie.

Once I had the giraffe running in place, I used this instance as a layer in my main movie, and added keyframes to make it move from the top left to the bottom right of the scene. Between these keyframes, I changed the position, the scale, and the opacity of the giraffe – so it seemed as if the giraffe was galloping out from the darkness into your face.

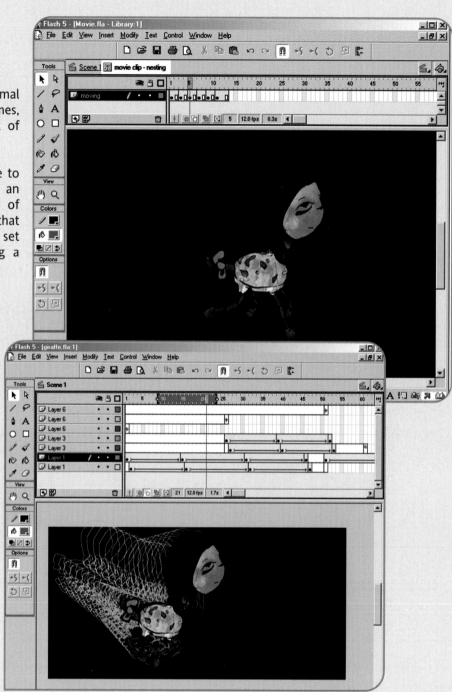

Lighting Effects

The final thing I'm going to explain is one of the elements in the final scene, where we're back to the girl standing up. This is a split screen, with the right side containing the girl, and the left side containing the black 'head space' that the giraffe runs across. When they meet each other's glance, the giraffe falls and is reduced to an outline.

There are very subtle additions that you can make to any video in order to hint at a different experience. In animation like this, or when you're editing live video footage, you can easily add or change the lighting in your scenes. In the closing scene of *Level 10*, the girl is standing in front of a window. Rays of sunlight lightly filter through and onto her. (The same thing happens earlier on, when the girl is sitting and the light washes through the blinds.) When I find myself with a static image that has to sit on the screen for some time, I often add lighting effects that move or dance just a little – it stops the image from seeming too still and stagnant.

Once again, I had a scanned drawing of the girl standing up. I cleaned and colored the drawing as before, eventually flattening and saving it as `girl_standing_color.jpg`.

Open this file, and bring it into the `Level10.psd` file on its own layer. Place this layer at the top of the Layers palette, and turn off all the other layers for the moment.

Obsession

Airbrush the left side of the scene with black, to blend in the room with the black space a bit more.

Next, I took a good look at the window, and its position in relation to the standing girl. There are several ways to make rays of light, but the first thing was to make a new blank layer.

Choose the Polygonal Lasso tool and then make selections of the area where you think the light would shoot from and across to. Usually, they tend to look like a very skewed rectangle – they start out narrow at the closest point to the light source, and progressively get larger towards the other side.

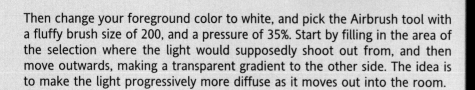

Then change your foreground color to white, and pick the Airbrush tool with a fluffy brush size of 200, and a pressure of 35%. Start by filling in the area of the selection where the light would supposedly shoot out from, and then move outwards, making a transparent gradient to the other side. The idea is to make the light progressively more diffuse as it moves out into the room.

If your new light layer seems too much like a shaft, I find it also helps to play with its opacity. In this case, deselect the area, and set the opacity of your new light layer to 70%.

Don't be afraid also to grab the Eraser tool (set to a similar brush size, and a pressure of 10%) to take away any white that may be making the light effect seem fake. Finally, use the Gaussian blur filter (Filter > Blur > Gaussian Blur) with a radius of 5.6 pixels (or whatever it takes to make the image look good).

If you wish, you can make more layers in this way, and I actually ended up lowering the new light layers' opacities even more. It's a lot of playing around, but essentially what we're creating here are simplified special effects.

If you want to include shadows, they're just as easy to add, and similar to produce. Instead of filling your selected areas with faint gradients of white, you do it with black, and lower the opacity just a little more.

The Final Product

I had a finished Photoshop file laid out just I how wanted, and at that stage I was ready to import it into Flash. To do this, I had to convert each layer into its own individual JPG. (Remember how I explained that Flash doesn't understand the layers and transparencies that make up Photoshop PSD files?) This can get tricky if you have layers that are very transparent or work with other background layers, so I had to make a decision and pick an overall opaque background color with which to merge transparent layers, or merge layers with other layers that were already opaque. I ended up with a lot of JPGs that had to be broken up and cut out separately after importing into Flash.

After all that, I started setting keyframes to move the layers of my `Level10.psd` around – and in the end, I had a small movie that communicated what I had wanted from the beginning.

Conclusion

Using Photoshop to help with the creation of video is actually very flexible and not at all intimidating, once you start fiddling around with it. Starting off in Photoshop is actually a very easy way of delving into the world of motion. If you're not experienced in thinking in terms of a 'timeline', you can at least feel comfortable at the beginning, while you're setting something up. I usually think of the bottom of my Layers palette as the beginning of my movie, and as my movie progresses, more and more layers are added. As we get to the very top of the layer list, that's the end of the movie.

There are many other things to know about Photoshop and video. Maybe, after trying out the above and getting comfortable doing your own movies, you can start thinking differently. It's possible, for example, to bring video footage into Photoshop (kind of the reverse of what I've explained in this tutorial), and this is a technique that I've used in a lot of my Crankbunny pieces. Basically, you take the captured video footage file, and open up each frame in Photoshop for manipulation – either in separate files, or as one huge PSD.

I hope this tutorial has shown how Photoshop can be used as a way to start exploring the world of motion. On the Internet now, a lot of web designers have started using motion, interactivity, and video-like qualities in their work, because they have picked up Flash. They have moved on from a 'flat' idea of web design to a multidimensional one, making web sites that look good, entertain the viewer, and communicate a message – even if it's just "have a laugh!"

Maybe you don't want to make a web site? Maybe you want to learn about video? Like designers starting to use Flash to get visuals moving on the Internet, Photoshop can be used to learn about video and animation. Once you're in your video program and comfortable with the basics, you really can find all the answers you need from the Help section – that's really how I've learned to fiddle with keyframes and export the video finally onto a tape or a file for the Internet. In any case, it's very exciting to know that this might make people who are not familiar with timelines and keyframes at least a little less shy of the whole idea of doing animation and making motion. Just always remember: you're tremendous.

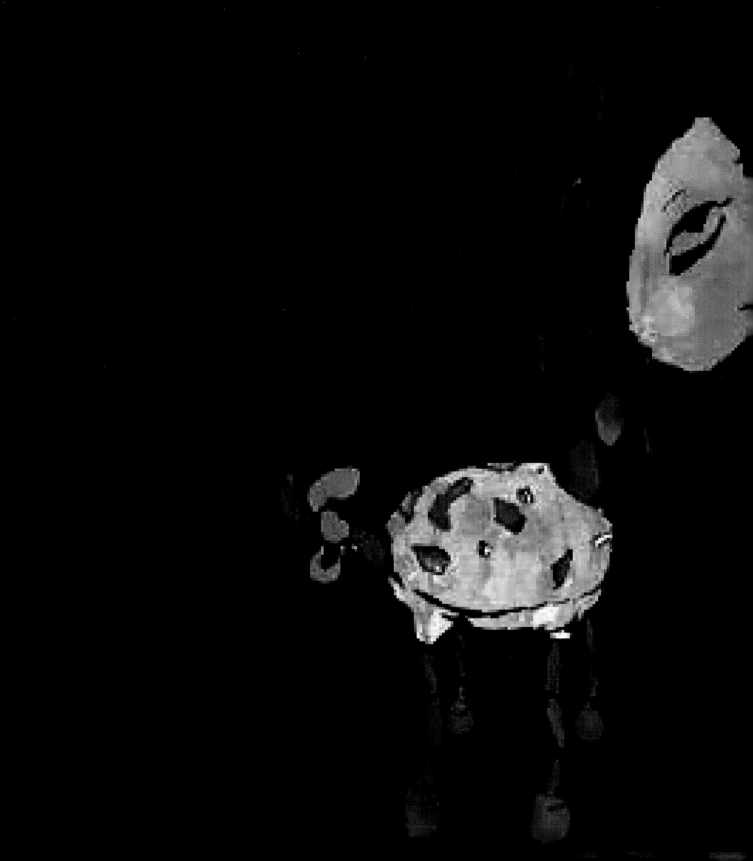

chapter 1

chapter 2

chapter 3

chapter 4

chapter 5

chapter 6

chapter 7

chapter 8

chapter 9

chapter 10

chapter 11

chapter 12

chapter 13

chapter 14

chapter 15

chapter 16

outro

"We make an image to find out what the rules are."

Andrew Park & Wojtek Madej
www.pandamediaallstars.com

Effective Spaces

Whenever Photoshop starts up, and I see all the names on the splash screen – Mark Hamburg, Sau Tam, Karen Gauthier, and the rest of the programmers – I think to myself that these are the geniuses. I'm just a monkey playing with their invention. As Ian Dury put it so eloquently in his song, "There ain't half been some clever bastards!"

Photoshop's interface does a good job of masking its quantum values, which are essentially just zeros and ones. When we think about Photoshop, we do so in the way that we think about pencils and brushes: when we use a pencil,

we seldom consider the atomic structure of graphite. Adobe has understood the creative needs of artists and designers; it has gauged what people require, and accommodated them in its application, making it intuitive to use.

In terms of being 'New Masters of Photoshop', Wojtek and myself are both honored, but we blush at being placed under this banner. It seems to be rather grandiose when speaking about us, who in essence are a couple of gibbons that enjoy pressing buttons and moving sliders about.

Wojtek and I make our work in a very collaborative way. At the moment, for example, we're working on a series of prints called *Days of Code*, about two medieval knights and their brotherhood, which are fighting an ongoing battle with demons. We arrived at this project because we wanted to work together and experiment with Photoshop, and because it combines some of our mutual visual interests. Primarily, it is a narrative, and we've been treating it as though we were children playing with toys. These characters are role-play for us: we guide them through a world, and sometimes accidents guide us, and lead the narrative in different directions.

The first image we made together, *Undercover Levels*, started with the knight here, which I made while I was staying with Wojtek in Poland. He was out for the day, and I was just doodling using a digital camera, paper, pens, paints, a scanner, and Photoshop. When he came back, I had the basics down: a rather normal-looking image, almost Pre-Raphaelite in feel.

Wojtek suggested that I 'break' it, by which he meant that I should disrupt its static qualities. Often, the first iteration of an image can seem to be a bit undercooked, but we need to be careful at this stage that we don't just finesse what is only our first idea – it's important to be experimental. Any image has a number of stress points, but it's crucial that we test all of them, and don't back off if it starts to look a little ugly. It's only when we take it past those stress points that we can truly see the potential of the initial idea.

I experimented with the image, using layers, and filters, and additional drawing, and got it to the position you can see here. This is where a visual conversation started, because Wojtek, inspired by the stuff I had made, started his figure on the left, using the same kinds of techniques that I had used. Initially we planned only to make one image in collaboration, but the conversation began to take on a life of its own, inspiring further images through a process of action and reaction.

Effective Spaces

Because we our work tends to be born out of conversation, we thought it best to articulate ourselves here in the same way.

AP: I know that you're a skilled printmaker and woodcarver. What do you think are the main differences between traditional techniques and new media like Photoshop?

WM: In terms of woodcarving and printmaking, both disciplines force you to make early decisions about the final result. Because they are very time-consuming, you become aware that your work is being channeled in a way that accommodates the medium. Your choices are limited; there is no turning back. You can't replace what you have chiseled or burned away, and I think that you could say the same thing in terms of being a painter.

It's different with Photoshop, because it enables you to put back the things you might have taken away. It also provides you with the ability to layer your work, in a way that just doesn't exist in printmaking. In Photoshop, your mind is free from concern for the lengthy preplanning you might need in order to make a print in a conventional manner. It's like playing chess without having to think sixteen moves ahead; you can concentrate on the next move, and if you get yourself in check, you can always go back.

AP: I should say that you can put things back in painting, but it takes a long time, and you often end up making a mess. For me, painting has always been a long process. I usually try to assemble lots of different elements together, and then to integrate them seamlessly with each other – it sounds a bit like collage, but it isn't. I assemble elements from a wide variety of sources and paint them onto the canvas. I wasn't aware of Photoshop when I first started painting, and I spent a lot of time trying to achieve results from different source materials manually, giving myself headaches in the process. I spent lots of time in the college bar trying to visualize a Gaussian blur before I knew what it was. In painting, there is no Ctrl+Z.

Despite its rapid rate of development, though, I still think that computer art is in its infancy. Current applications are in the transitional stage between being tools that technically minded people can use, and tools that artists can use. Artists are just getting to grips with using them, but I think that there's a push to create broader spaces within this environment – to permit greater expression. It's a desire to employ traditional thinking, but with new tools.

WM: Yes. I think that Photoshop is like having a studio. It's a repository for our ideas and thoughts, a playground for us to experiment in.

AP: Graphic designer Paul Rand once said, "The fundamental skill of a designer is talent, and talent is a rare commodity. It's all intuition. And you can't teach intuition." I think this is very important. Photoshop won't do the work for you. I find it almost impossible to start working on a computer without using my sketchbook first. I like to use sketchbooks in my everyday life to find images and capture ideas, my train of thought.

It's the same creative process that I'd go through if I were to make paintings. Ideas don't come bundled with software – I wish they did! They usually arise out of conversations with friends who all seem as perplexed as I am about the ludicrousness of life. Little things can be a springboard for great ideas.

James Baylay is a friend of mine, and a talented painter; he is also someone who I consider to have a unique point of view. He's currently creating a world built around a word he said in his sleep: he shouted "Bollivans!" and it's a place he's just finding out about. Essentially, he's trying to make sense of his subconscious.

WM: I think we treat Photoshop as our sound stage or theatre. Once we've given a working title the green light, we know that we're going to have to prepare the script, find our performers, build sets, and make a 'film'. The best part of this process, though, is the collaboration. It's so much better to work together. Ideas hide when you're on your own.

AP: Films make for a good comparison. Photoshop is a two-dimensional environment, of course, but I see it differently. Two-dimensional pictures can offer interesting stories to people who are willing to engage at a slightly deeper level. When I made paintings, they were essentially like films. I tried to make images that encapsulated their own worlds within the confines of a canvas. I wanted to tell stories that had some kind of range and depth.

The most obvious and celebrated purveyor of this technique that I can think of is Cindy Sherman, whose photographs are like small, frozen pieces from larger narratives. Her early work in particular is reminiscent of stills taken from film noir, or something Jean-Luc Godard might have made. They use their style, composition, and character to suggest this, and by doing so they seem to hold the tension of a much bigger story.

Effective Spaces

WM: I've always loved self-contained worlds. The language of gesture, so perfectly used in medieval illustrations, is a universal code that can easily express the notion of a third dimension: that of time. The sequence of events and how they are read, along with their composition, helps an image to achieve a feeling of reality.

AP: Time is certainly an important component. We're interested in being able to guide the spectator's eye along a path, which hopefully indicates several passages of time and emotion. Of course, we can't be sure that everyone will be interested enough to find the paths we've set in our images – we just enjoy 'encoding' semiotic clues into our narratives. Our intention is to construct an image that has many points of attraction for the spectator, all of which are hooks that hopefully drive a narrative from that reference point.

If we look at *The Messengers of the Temple*, we see our two knights returning home after they've traveled a long road. They're coming out of the forest, which is a metaphor in itself. In the tree we see a bird, which takes flight. The bird belongs to another brother of the temple, and represents that our knights are nearly home. Also, if we look at the composition, there is a definite shift from the condensed forest on the left, to the wide-open space on the right. This is to show that the way ahead is clear: they are, quite literally, out of the woods. We wanted to show the transition of time and place from *Undercover Levels*, which took place in a hot desert country. A lot of what's in our image was influenced by Pieter Breugel's painting, *Hunters in the Snow*.

WM: Yes, that's a good example. Breugel's is a beautiful painting. The foreground and the background work together to create a reality in which the lives of many people intersect. You can imagine life outside the confines of the frame, which is always magical. We can only hope that we've managed to use some of that quality in our image.

The Messengers of the Temple

Hunters in the Snow (January)
Pieter Brueghel the Elder, 1565
© Francis G. Mayer/CORBIS

M.72.67.2
The Raising of Lazarus, circa 1630
Rembrandt van Rijn
Los Angeles County Museum of Art, Gift of H. F. Ahmanson and Company,
in memory of Howard F. Ahmanson
Photograph ©2001 Museum Associates/LACMA

I've always liked Rembrandt too, particularly because of the way that he uses light in his work. By illuminating the areas that drive the narrative, he indicates where you should look – but if you examine his images more closely, there's always something hidden in the shadows. In The Raising of Lazarus, the narrative is easily recognized, due to the fact that Rembrandt has shown us the way with light. He lights his paintings like stage plays: you always know instinctively where your attention ought to be focused.

AP: I believe that using computers has helped me to understand visual language a little better. Just tinkering around in, say, sound-editing software makes you aware of creative 'building blocks'. I was fascinated to discover, for example, that sound has certain shapes. When you're primarily visually aware, this is a revelation, because you can start constructing sound in a very visual way. The digital age has heightened my awareness of 'chunks' of data, analogous to brushstrokes and notes, instead of single bits.

WM: It's healthy to have different reference points for visual imagery, from other fields like poetry and sound. They inform the image in a different way. For instance, I find that another influence on my thinking is spirituality.

AP: How so?

WM: Spirituality and tradition sound like subjects you wouldn't really deal with in Photoshop, but it's in these two realms that I verify my work. Spirituality and tradition act as a filter for my experience.

My earliest memories of something you could call 'art' come from my childhood in the Polish village of Paszyn, where I grew up. It was here that a strong sense of Catholic tradition mixed with folk imagination, giving rise to a very special event.

Effective Spaces

AP: Paszyn is the village with the amazing carvings?

WM: Yes. It has a good story, which you know, but I want to tell it. In the early '70s the village priest, Edward Nitka, got fed up with his sinful congregation. As a penance, he gave carving tools to his flock, and asked them to create sculptures and carvings, instead of being idle. The inventive nature of the villagers and what they produced is living proof that spirituality has a great influence over the quality of creation. It wasn't enough just to hand out tools; they needed that spiritual impetus and thrust to make the work.

AP: It's a good point to make. You have to have a reason to make stuff, whatever that is. Tools remain just tools without that driver.

WM: Because of the close relationship my family had with Nitka, sculptures of angels, saints, and demons were always present in our house, and I would often play with them as toys. This, I think, has great bearing on my fascination with medieval art, a world in which stories were told with few symbols, and often hid deeper meaning. I'm a great believer that every product of creation holds secrets. It's a bit like navigating a Flash web site, trying to find the hotspots that take you to another experience. In a two-dimensional image, it's possible to create 'hotspots' that open new experiences in the viewer's mind.

AP: Building images happens over time, and often you find yourself influenced by a number of different things while an image is created, and which become reflected in it. I think this is particularly true in the field of painting, because the timescales involved are so long. With Photoshop, the feedback loops are shortened, and image creation is more immediate. It's an amazing feeling to be able to produce work so fast, and to push forward with ideas and iterations so quickly. I know that working in traditional media, it took time to get the results that I wanted, and that often led me to getting sidetracked or bored. I think that Photoshop allows that magical moment in art when experimentation and expectation meet. This sounds like one of those "Lose weight in two days!" ads, doesn't it? "Photoshop gave me the results I needed in just hours, instead of months with traditional media! Thank you, Adobe!"

WM: Of course, being able to produce fast iterations allows for far greater diversity with an image or within a set of images, because you're not constrained by the time factor, and you're able to produce many variations on a theme. In printmaking, this process would take a lot more time, energy, and motivation to get the same results.

AP: I think it's key to point out, though, that while Photoshop saves a lot of time, the creative process cannot be tackled with shortcuts. There's just one way to get there, and that's by reaching a moment of insight that can only be gained by producing work and iterating it.

Effective Spaces

We want to talk a little bit about our title, *Effective Spaces*. We came up with it by thinking about what we do in Photoshop, and coming to the conclusion that we're trying to make the space as effective as possible in shaping an image. Negative space, emotional space, real space, headspace, they all figure in our compositions. It's in them that our separate ideas come together to form a conversation.

What do we mean by *Effective Spaces*? It's really a loose description, a statement of intent, to remind us that the marks we make must be in the spirit of forging a space that is as exploratory as possible. Harold Pinter will often start his plays with an exchange of dialog between unknown characters in an unknown setting and unknown circumstances. It is his job to 'find out' what exactly is happening.

It is paramount that we look carefully at what is unfolding, without being too prescriptive. John Berger says that, "When a painting is lifeless, it is the result of the painter not having the nerve to get close enough for a collaboration to start. He stays at a *copying* distance. Or, as in mannerist periods like today, he stays at an art-historical distance, playing stylistic tricks that the model knows nothing about."

"To go in close means forgetting convention, reputation, reasoning, hierarchies and self. It also means risking incoherence." We're not saying that we are being brave and heroic, but we do like to throw caution to the wind, and lose and then find ourselves in our images. We make an image to find out what the rules are.

To say we had numerous goals for this image might be a little excessive. We wanted to collaborate. Collaboration for us is like running a relay race: we hand off successive iterations like a baton for the other person to run with. We wanted to produce an image that described an event that we shared. The goal was to make something that we were both happy with, and that meant something to us. We wanted to enjoy the freedom of not working to a brief.

Subject matter is important. You can choose to make art about anything you want – it's wide open. We like to use elements from our own personal experiences, and while we don't spend a lot of time working in the same place (because we live in different countries), when we do get together, we always have fond memories and experiences to call upon. We decided that it might be good to make an image of us driving in a car, so we took a ride from Wojtek's family home in Nowy Sacz back to his own home in Sulkowice. Not an overly eventful journey – we listened to some Delta Blues, ate ice cream, and took some photos. Earlier that day, we'd bought three folk sculptures representing two angels and a demon from the village of Paszyn that Wojtek mentioned earlier. Later in the journey, driving along a dark country road, a hare leapt into the road and froze in front of our car's headlights; we hit it with an almighty thud. Poor thing.

In the making of this picture, we're hoping to present a visual diary of those events. We're making it for ourselves, because it crystallizes that moment in our lives, which we shared. It also has a new meaning now, because we're making the picture for this book, and it crystallizes the time we spent together doing so. Obviously, we can have a lot of fun representing the elements we both remember, and have a visual conversation with each other about that time and this.

Because our images are made up of hundreds of different experimental improvisations, it would be a very long process to try and make a tutorial from the beginning. We tend to deal with an image like printmaking or painting, but I suppose that a better analogy for it would be modeling with clay. You sculpt by building up clay, and then you take bits off, build up, and take off again, until a recognizable form takes shape. What we have done is to make the image as free flowing as possible, and got it to a certain point. Our tutorial, therefore, will focus on a small slice of activity. We hope that showing a little bit of our technique and creative process will provide, at a recursive level, an illustration of how we achieved the overall effect in the final image.

The Bluesman

If you look at the image below, you can see that we really did start off with a blank canvas – just two figures sitting in the middle of all that space. As we progressed, we experimented with the image, using lots of layered elements, filters, hue/saturation, drawing directly on screen, etc. Sometimes, an image requires you to turn away from it for a couple of hours – coming back with a fresh pair of eyes can be an enormous help, because it's then when you manage to spot all the things that don't sit right. We consider an image to be finished when all the narrative and visual elements are in place, with their levels turned up to the right volume and pitch, and in balance with each other. (This is not to say symmetrical, because everything has the right amount of tension to hold the image together.) You can tell when an image is ready – if it isn't, it either lacks something, or it has too much. Refining an image doesn't get easier, but you do learn what to look for in your own work.

So because we were listening to Delta Blues in the car, we wanted to represent that by having a bluesman overlooking the journey. Our tutorial will concentrate on the integration of the bluesman into our image, and see how he informs the decisions we make after that point.

The composition of something like this is always intuitive. You have to think about the narrative elements you need: How detailed do you want them to be? In our example, the blues playing in the car was only a minor element of the journey, but when you choose to represent this visually and make the choice to bring in an image of a bluesman, that will have an effect on the composition as a whole. A lot of the time, an image will speak to you and tell you what it needs. It's all part of the fun.

For you, the starting point for the tutorial is the Photoshop file, `car.psd`. We've chosen to start in true Blue Peter fashion, with an image that we prepared earlier, so there's already some shape for us to build from. In it, we're already in the car – I'm riding shotgun, and Wojtek is driving.

When we start an image, we always try to look for the non-obvious, and to make our images a balance between the information necessary to tell the story, and elements that please the eye. Looking at the image in this state, we consider it about 30% complete. We are waiting for the arrival of our bluesman, so he can tell us which direction we need to go next.

Open up `Bluesman.png`, and move the image onto a new layer in `car.psd`. When you first open the file, the bluesman's movement will be locked, so click on the Lock Position icon (the crossed arrows) that you'll find just under Opacity in the Layers palette. Then just drag and drop the image across as usual, and name the new layer Bluesman.

As soon as he's in, the bluesman instantly starts singing, "I'm so outta place, I need to change... whoa yeah!" Don't worry: you can move him about and see where he fits in best. If we were to place him on the right of the image, though, he'd be blocking some of the space we intend to use later. This negative space leads to the dead hare, an area of narrative we want eventually to lead the eye to.

The bluesman is quite an imposing figure, who demands attention, but we don't want him to be the main focus; he needs to fit in with the rest of the image. He has his role to play, though, so it's our job to find a balance where each of the elements tells its own story. We enlarged him a bit using Edit > Free Transform (don't forget to press the Shift key and move the corners to constrain his proportions), and positioned him at the far left of the screen.

We did this for a reason: the car has energy and movement, but the image also has a lot of space that could draw the eye's attention. We need to give the eye a starting point. At the moment, the bluesman is large and in charge – all the attention seems to be focused on him. We need to calm him down a little bit, so we're going to break him up in order that he becomes a more integral part of the image. This is where the fun starts, and it's very much a time to experiment. The only goal we have in our minds at the moment is making the bluesman harmonious with the other areas of the image; there are no rules for how this is to be done.

Thinking about our image, we don't really want to get rid of the photographic look of our bluesman, but we do need to integrate him with the rest of the elements. The pixelated shape that represents the car hood (the blue area, to the left) sort of mirrors the bluesman's checkered jacket, and we thought it would be good to make this more explicit by changing the color of the latter to match (Image > Adjust > Color Balance). There are other ways of getting the right color, but I've always mixed them by eye – being a painter, this seems to come more naturally to me.

For the next step, we need to move the Bluesman layer below the car hood layer. In our picture, we also placed his feet below the pink bar at the bottom, but

because you have a ready-made file, this layer has been flattened. We suggest you leave the feet for now, because you may want to move the image later. Now create another layer called white lines, and using the paintbrush with a medium width, draw a few white lines over the blue, pixelated area.

Now we're going to use the mosaic filter (Filter > Pixelate > Mosaic) at quite a low, subtle setting. This really lightens the whole area, linking it more to the white space below the car.

Looking at the figure, he's still a little too strong for us. We want him to *represent* music – he's just a metaphor – so we need to take him back further. Use the Rectangular Marquee tool to select his jacket, and adjust the Hue/Saturation: drop the Saturation, and increase Lightness. Again, this was just done by eye. We like the fact that his face is still quite clear, and how the jacket melts into the pixelation.

Effective Spaces

Now add another layer called polygon, and use the Polygonal Lasso tool to draw a shape over the bluesman's shoulder. Fill it with white, and adjust the layer transparency to 64%. This shape is needed to dampen the bluesman down even more, to hold the pixelation at the bottom of the screen, and also to indicate the hood of the car.

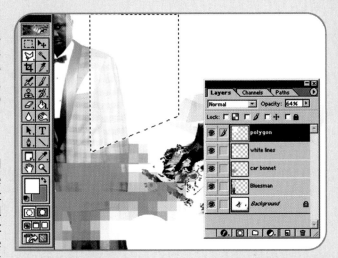

Rain And Movement

The image is taking shape, but there's a long way to go, and so many experimental decisions to be made. I wanted to use something to represent rain, so I took up my Wacom tablet and drew into a new layer with a hard, round, 5-pixel paintbrush, using a bright red color. We chose red because it can also represent the blood of the hare. At first, I liked the idea of the rain coming in from behind the car, so that's where I put it.

Select Image > Liquify, and another interface pops up showing your current layer – in our case, the red rain. Use the Warp tool (top left) to push the rain around into more spattery shapes. (We had the brush size set to 79, and the pressure set to 58.) Once you're happy with the effect, press OK.

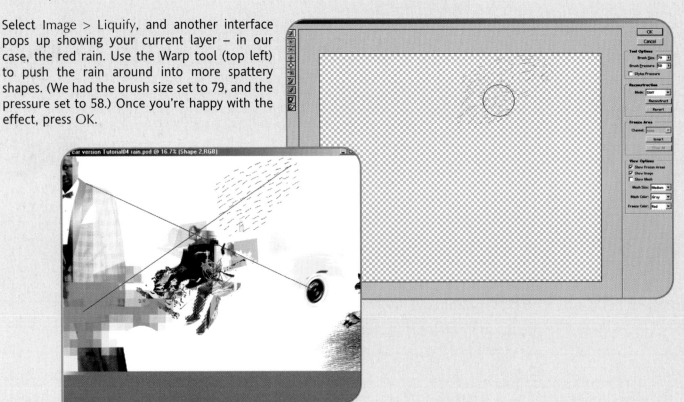

We decided, however, that the rain at the top of the car created an "X" shape on the canvas. In most art, and especially in master paintings, there are often compositional devices that lead the viewer's eye to a given point. We felt that we had unintentionally made that cross with the elements we had placed in our image. This is something we wanted to avoid.

The invisible cross is noticeable from the bluesman's shoulder to the rear wheel of the car, and from the car hood to the rain in the top right, as indicated in the screenshot on the last page. Sometimes, even though it's hard to see the patterns that develop within an image, those patterns can be stifling. We really wanted the flow to be from bottom left to bottom right, so I moved the red rain down below the bluesman, breaking up the heavy gray square of his trousers.

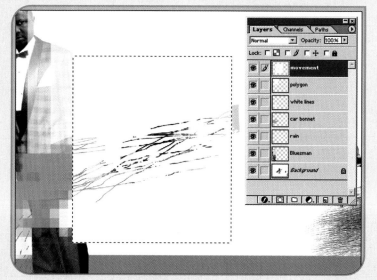

Looking at the car now, we want to get some feeling of movement, and also to make it less overly explicit that it *is* a car. We don't like images that are too obvious, and it's part of the fun to try and play visual games with the different elements. One thing informs another: the negative space of one element becomes the positive space of another element, and so on.

Create a new layer called movement, making sure that it's at the top of the Layers palette. On it, draw a square with the Rectangular Marquee tool, and fill it with white. Using the Eraser tool in Paintbrush mode (hard, round, 5 pixels), draw some lines into the white square that run diagonally down to the left, across the figures in the car. These can be quite rough.

Then, take the layer's opacity down to 35%. These lines, we think, unify the bluesman and the car, and create a sense of speed. We like the way that some of the richer colors come through from the car underneath.

The Lyrics

We wanted to break up the elements on the left of the image a little more, and we thought it might be good to include some text. And since we were playing the blues, we decided to use some blues lyrics. We thought it might be fun to feature the words of Robert Johnson's *Crossroads*, because they fit in with our story well.

After obtaining the lyrics, I copied them into Photoshop by selecting the Type tool, holding down the left mouse button and drawing a bounding box of approximate size. (At this point, we simply wanted to get the text on the page; we find that an element's visual dynamic will usually inform you where you should ultimately place it in the larger image.) I selected quite a lyrical font (Edwardian Script ITC), and colored it black.

The next thing was to resize all the text to use a 12pt font. It looked too big before; this is not a text-based image and we're using the text as a *visual* element. Some of the words will be relevant, but we want it to be something that can be discovered in the image, rather than being relied upon to do all the 'talking'. Still using the Type tool, I selected the words that I felt told the story of the dead hare ("I fell" and "lord have mercy"), and then enlarged them by switching to a 72pt font. You may have to move the bounding box around in order to accommodate the newly enlarged text.

I selected the phrase "I'm sinking down" at the end of the song, cut-and-pasted it into a new layer, and changed its size to 72pt and its color to white. I then moved it over the pink bar at the bottom of the image. After that, I applied a Gaussian Blur filter, so that it was softened a little, but not too much – I wanted it still to be legible.

I enlarged the "Oooo, oooeeee" section of the text to 72pt, just as I had with some of the other lyrics; I felt there should be something holding it at the bottom, otherwise it seemed rather to trail off. Then I went back to the black text layer and applied the Liquify tool to it, using the Warp tool to distort the text just a little. Next, selecting the same phrase with the Rectangular Marquee tool, I changed the Hue/Saturation, clicking the Colorize box and adjusting the sliders to obtain a reddish orange color.

The text now appears to have three distinct lines, but this needs to be broken up, as it disturbs the eye a bit. Making sure that the appropriate layer was active, I selected "lord have mercy" with the Rectangular Marquee tool and enlarged it (Edit > Transform > Scale). We then cut and pasted the selection to a new layer, giving us more freedom to play around with the positioning, but less with the actual content. Remember: once you've copied and pasted the selection to a new layer, it no longer remains editable text: it becomes a rendered graphic.

We wanted to change the color, because the black seemed too heavy for the area it was in. Using a simple invert (Image > Adjust > Invert), we selected this layer, changed the text to white and positioned it down near the red text. Now, the text seems to be creating interesting shapes; I really like how the Liquify tool has distorted it.

Effective Spaces

Finally, we took "fell" from the main body of the text, using the Rectangular Marquee tool, cut and pasted to a new layer (as before), and then positioned it near the other text in order to crowd it a bit. Basically, we've just chopped the text up to play around with the composition and color.

Balancing Spaces

What we have now appears to be a hole represented by the gray square of the bluesman's legs. With all this sound coming from it, could it be a hole down to hell? We also have the impression of the front wheel, created in negative space between the blue pixelation above (which has the wheel arch) and curve of the red text below, making the form of the car more visible.

In basic drawing classes, students learn that there are three basic elements of a composition: the frame, the positive space, and the negative space. The positive space is the easiest to understand: generally, it's the space occupied by your subject. Negative space is the space that is not your subject. The negative space is defined by the edges of the positive space, and the frame or border – the third element.

We wanted to add more text to the right hand corner, to split the strong pink edge at the bottom of the image, which now has three distinct areas. There's the bluesman and the hole to hell on the left, the car and its passengers in the middle, and the dead hare scene to the right. All three areas are joined by a curve that runs along the center of the image, starting in the middle of the blue pixelation, and ending along the gray shape above the back wheel. We're happy with this because it really represents the whole side of the car without us needing to be too explicit about it.

At this stage, we decided to do something about the amount of white space – starting, counter-intuitively, by enlarging the canvas by 10cm in both directions

(Image > Canvas Size). Now, I very rarely crop my images when they exist outside the frame (I like to keep my options open), so in making the canvas bigger, our bluesman shows a bit more of himself. This is not exactly how much we want to show, so on this occasion we did crop the image, with the Crop tool.

Having done that, you'll notice that the pink bar doesn't stretch across the image anymore, so you'll need to make a new selection with the Rectangular Marquee tool to form your new bar. Then use the Eyedropper tool to select the pink color, and fill the selection.

As you can see, in order to keep all the action inside a frame, we also made black bars at the top and bottom of the image. In a new layer named Black Bars, we drew rectangles in the appropriate places, made sure that Add to Selection was in operation, and filled them with black. Finally, we drew a rectangular marquee with a feather of 30 pixels on the left side of our bluesman, and adjusted the Hue/Saturation to darken that area. (Saturation +54, Lightness -16.)

Serious Reggae

As we continue with it, we're finding out that this piece of work is just as much about itself and our time spent making it, as it is about the original journey. While we were making it, we went to my local Chinese takeaway, where there's a really interesting character who sells bootleg reggae CDs and always seems to be herbally happy. While we were waiting for our food, someone came in to look at the sun-faded, photocopied covers, prompting our man behind the counter to say, "Yeah man, this is serious reggae."

This struck a chord with Wojtek, who asked me to write it down in my sketchbook for later reference. Wojtek wanted to use this phrase in our print, so he made some type that resembled old car lettering, and placed it on the right of the image. You do get inspiration from the most bizarre places! We thought it would be good to use this text element to break up the pink line at the bottom of the image. At the moment it is very strong, and needs to be subdued.

To make the text for Serious Reggae, we created a new file and set the image size at 20cm wide by 8cm high, at 200 dpi with a white background. Then, choosing a 50s'-style font (we used ScriptMTBold, not a standard Photoshop font), we typed the word "Reggae".

We enlarged the second "g" in the word by selecting it with the Type tool and changing the value in the Character palette, which is a handy thing to have around if you do a lot of work with type. Happy so far, we rasterized it to make it into a graphic that we could chop up (Layer > Rasterize > Type).

It's good to have fun with fonts. I like to treat them as graphical elements, cutting bits up and moving things around. I suspect that real font junkies would go mad to see what I do to their descenders and spines! On this occasion, we cut away a few sections from the word, and then closed up the resulting gaps between letters, using our old friend the Rectangular Marquee tool.

The last of the above images shows the result of selecting the Type tool once more, and clicking on the image to create a new layer. The word "serious" appears in the Photoshop Large font, set to 72pt and a regular style. After typing it, I moved it in close to "Reggae", so that the "s" lined up with the "R". Being a bit finicky, and using the Rectangle Marquee tool again, I chopped another bit of the R's leg off in order to create a bit more room for the letters to sit together.

Effective Spaces

This is fine for now, but we need to move it to our main image to see how it works there. In your Layers palette, link the layers by clicking the boxes between the eye icons and the layer names, and choose Merge Linked from the palette's drop-down menu. Then, with both files open, drag the text into your main image, and move the layer to the top of your Layers palette.

When we moved the text over the bar, so that it broke the surface of the straight line, we thought the black color of the text was too strong – so we inverted it to white. After that, things started to look a little better, and it seemed to fit into the image a bit more. To make the top of the "R" visible against the white background, we drew a rectangle, stopping just on the pink bar. Then we adjusted the Hue/Saturation by moving the sliders. (Hue +128, Saturation +64, Lightness -25).

To end this phase, one more cut was made from the large "g" in "Reggae", using the Marquee tool once again. As you've probably gathered, we like the rectangular tool a lot, because it allows you to be quite choppy with an image. It's not a precise implement (unless you *want* rectangles and squares), but sometimes, if you go in using it broadly, it takes things away by accident. And the way we use the program, accident is a friend to us.

We wanted a little bit of movement in the text, so we created yet another new layer, called Blips. With the color white selected, we used a paintbrush (hard, 9 pixels) to draw some quick squiggles and blips down at the bottom left of the text. To complete the effect, we added a Motion Blur filter, and took the layer's opacity down to 44%. Once again, we used the marquee tool to chop off the bottom of the blips.

The finishing touches were added when the Blips and Reggae layers were linked and merged, and a few last parts of the element were teased away with the Eraser tool set to Paintbrush (soft, round, 13 pixels). We think that this text is a nice counter to the Robert Johnson lyrics on the left of the image. There's something anchoring about it; it draws the eye towards the right of the scene, where the "serious reggae" of the hare's death is happening.

Demon Element

We then needed to represent the angels and demon in the back seat, so we quickly drew some pictograms representing them, and scanned them in. They just happened to be in red pen, because it was the first thing I picked up when I thought of the idea. When you're working with Photoshop, it doesn't really matter – you can always change the colors.

Originally, we were going to go with the actual demon that I bought from Paszyn, and you can see that the two ways I tried to represent it are very different in concept. The common feature, however, is that both try to simplify the imagery somewhat, in order to counter the quite hectic quality of the rest of the composition. Open the `Angel & Demon.jpg` file; this is a screenshot, so you'll need to crop it first. Double click the layer in the Layers palette, and then click OK; this will turn it into an editable layer. Then, use the Crop tool to select the drawing alone, and drag it into the main image.

We wanted to make the glyphs something that could be discovered in the image – that is, we didn't want them to be too obvious – so to start with, we reduced their scale. Then, we selected the demon glyph on the left, and changed the Hue/Saturation to color it blue (Hue -136, Saturation -45, Lightness -6).

Finally, we only wanted there to be the notion of the presence of the angels and demon in the car, so we dropped the opacity down to 10%.

At this point, Wojtek decided that he didn't like the look of the rear wheel – he thought it was too bold for the image. Use the Magnetic Lasso tool to select the tire, and then copy and paste it onto a new layer. Once you have that, you can draw a rectangular marquee over the bottom half of it, and invert the selection.

Finally, we created a new layer called blue square, and drew a square from the top left of the demon, to overlap some of the hare. We filled it with a really pale blue, and adjusted the opacity so that most of the images underneath could be seen. This square represents the field of influence the angels and demon have over the hare: they are fighting for its soul.

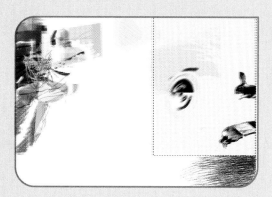 

Finishing The Image

At this point, the step-by-step description of the project ends – it would take far too long to show every single step and decision we made. In the middle of a piece, nothing really gets concluded, but we hope to have given some insight into our creative and decision-making processes. It's all a balancing act: one thing will outweigh another, until you take countermeasures. It's a struggle, and you have to wrestle with an image until you have both exhausted each other. We thought we might be near a conclusion here, but a night away from the computer showed us there was still a long way to go. Too many things were inconclusive, and too much space was still unruly. We sat down to fight some more.

We were aware of the huge holes in the image, and we needed to anchor the elements to each other, so they weren't just floating separately in space. Lots of energy was escaping up into the white void above the car. After lots of effort, tea drinking, and tag-team action, we wrestled the image to a resting-place. We're pleased with it, but like everything you produce, you remain critical. We see this creation as being one that has to be read small areas at a time, until the larger image can be understood.

In our final version, we decided to make use of the top part of the canvas, using the dark blue representation of the sky to force the car to exist in the middle. We've also tried to give some sense of time of day and landscape, as well as enhancing the suggestion of the car with further negative and positive space. *Effective Space*, you might say.

I went to the crossr

I went to the crossroad, fell *down* on my knees

Standin' at the crossroad, I tried to flag a
Didn't nobody seem to know me, everybody p

fell

on my knees

dark *Lord*

me here

Mmmmm, stan goin' down, boo

Lord

Hazel

have poor Bob, if you please"

at the crossroad, I tried to flag a ride

You can run, tell my friend-boy, Willie Brown?
Lord, that I'm standin' at the crossroad, babe, I believe

seriousReggae

chapter   1

chapter   2

chapter   3

chapter   4

chapter   5

chapter   6

chapter   7

chapter   8

chapter   9

chapter 10

chapter 11

chapter 12

chapter 13

chapter 14

chapter 15

chapter 16

outro

"If I can move one person to change their way
of thinking, I have succeeded."

Adrian Luna
www.purusdesign.com

Reflective

It feels as though your eyes are going to burst because the light has become so bright. As the air somehow finds its way to the second story window, it's redirected to your face by the turning blades of the ceiling fan. The climate is cold and brisk; it is yet another day. You roll to your side and bring the covers up to your neck – they're warm from many hours of concentrated body exposure. Your eyes feel as though they were open for nearly forty-eight hours the day before. As you look at the clock, you promise to get up in another fifteen minutes. As your rise and stretch your legs, back, and arms thirty minutes later, you feel your muscles as if they were being stretched for the first time.

You look out into the passing traffic, and think what a relief it is not to be in one of those strange metal boxes that squeak down the road. Somehow, you find yourself in the bathroom, and cannot bring yourself to recall the last five minutes of your morning. The shower is like that morning blanket – a comfortable place indeed. Cleansed, you clothe yourself and make your way downstairs to the place you love most. You tap the keys, and a few seconds later, the monitor clicks and snaps and flickers until the tubes become warm with energy. And once again, you're there. You're in that state of mind: alone, yet free of the daily burdens and realities that define life. You let go and search for your true self, the self that is an artist.

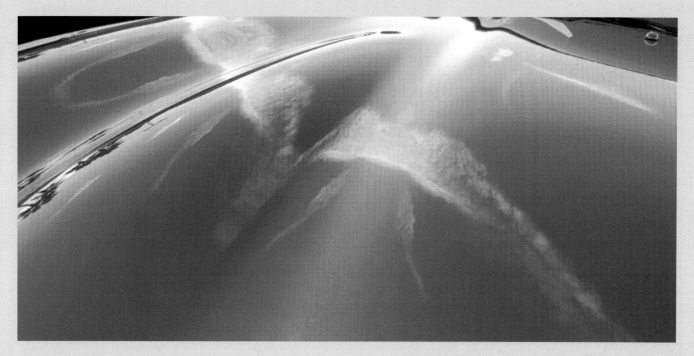

I was born and raised in Southern California. Everyone seems to be in a hurry around here. But things were different for me. In high school, I remember my classmates asking one another where they were planning to attend college after graduation. Some would say UCLA; others would mention USC. But when the question was posed to me, I had no answer. After high school, I took a year off. This was the time for me to step back and find my direction. I would spend most of my days at the beach: I would surf when the waves were good, and sit upon the tabletops while the wind was onshore. I picked up sketching and drawing, and a friend recommended that I look into the Art Institute in Laguna Canyon. On a trip to the coast, I decided to stop by to view the campus, where I was given a short tour during some of the classes. Nude models posed for a crowd of mature onlookers. In the outer yard, sculptors shaped rock into beautiful form. The studios were full of charisma and youth. It was exhilarating being there for that one day. My life was different from that day forth.

I studied for four years at the Art Institute of Southern California in Laguna Beach, and graduated with a Bachelors degree in Fine Arts and Graphic Design. During that time, I was disciplined in many media, methods, and practices. I was exposed to a talented group of individuals, and together we made our way through the fog and haze to find clarity and precision. As a group, we were exposed to many famous works, by artists alive and gone. Fine Art was beauty expressed. It was form captured. It was light reflected. I never thought I would spend two full years of my life concentrating on a few bowls of fruit. It was mind-boggling. It was enough to make you go mad – and some did. I suppose that added to the flavor of art school. You could tell which ones were going to make it the full four years.

Reflective

    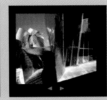

When, during my pursuit of education, I ventured into the professional world, I was inspired by modern feats of architecture. Driving through Los Angeles will make an artist faint. It's a treasure! The buildings on Wilshire will make you feel tiny by comparison. The Getty along the hills of Sunset will make you blush. But the major structures are not what touched my heart; it was the smaller constructions that caught my eye. There are a few along Sawtelle Boulevard that made me wonder. They sat just two blocks shy of a ghetto, alone and cold, but illuminated with warmth from the life churning within. The light seemed not so much reflected as repelled by the surface – it was as if the material chosen for the outer extremities of this building was polished so fine that you could see your own thoughts in it.

In Laguna Beach, I was inspired by a small structure once again, standing between a pottery store and a nightclub. Its purpose was simple and pure: it was a place of worship. The glass was tinted with green to cleanse the light as it made its way through. The stone along the outside, on the other hand, had a matte gray finish that absorbed any light that touched it. There was a stain wash finish to the varnished cement floor along the inside. Halogen lights dangled from the ceiling, and bolts were thrust into the walls to harness untouchable abstract artwork. This structure was brilliant yet subdued, and I still dream of having it as my studio. Maybe one day it will be so.

Reflective

While in San Diego on a field trip, I was moved to the beat of contemporary art. Startling installations made my skin tingle. Photographs of a murderer's diary and tools of destruction. Down the hall, Francis Bacon's art kissed the wall. I'm not as big a fan of his work as I am of his personality. A video played in the same corridor. He drank wine like never before. It was a pleasure to see him prance and stumble around the room during his interview.

As I walked to the next set of installations, my ears picked up a menacing, high-pitched sound. In the wall were three small televisions stripped of all their external coverings. In unison, the screens flickered a sequence of cold, stale imagery in which the color was desaturated by about eighty percent. This was the first time that I had ever experienced new media – it wasn't interactive or on the Internet, but it was a version of what we might ordinarily conceive as being new.

To the left of this exhibit was an elongated table that tapered at the end, gave the illusion of closeness. If you were to sit at the welcome end of the table, you'd see a small television opposite you – it seemed to be the size of one of those sets that you'd see in the kitchen of an upper

class home. But if you stood from the seat and walked to the right of the table, you'd discover that it was actually twenty feet long, and that the seemingly small television at the end suddenly grew to about twenty-six inches.

There was even an installation that involved the use of the ocean breeze. The artist cut a six by six-foot square from the Plexiglas window; the art was the phenomenon produced by the unusual paradox of being enclosed in a room, yet having the cool ocean breeze soothe your skin. There was actually a line indicating the spot on the floor that the artist intended you to stand on.

These contemporary artists used their minds to create this art. They took everyday objects and occurrences, and put them to work. It's like turning a water turbine sideways: one moment it's producing energy, and the next it's producing mist that cools the bodies of young children in the summertime. The first position offered function, and the second position offered a choice. The choice is an option offered to you without a price. If the option is taken, it's up to you to make something of it. The result could be nothing, but more likely the world will change in more ways than one.

Four Views by Robert Rauschenberg
© Geoffrey Clements/CORBIS

Persimmon by Robert Rauschenberg
© Burstein Collection/CORBIS

In the later years of my education, I was exposed to the glorious works of Robert Rauschenberg – In Transparency was showing at the Orange County Museum of Art. His work was groundbreaking, and he was the first to use Plexiglas as a medium for communication. Using silk screening as his technique for transferring art to the surface, Rauschenberg used it to create oversized books, posters, and installations. The effect was amazing; it was the first time that imagery had been placed in multiple layers while natural sunlight was projected through; it was as though Rauschenberg had invented the concept of Photoshop. His work was so powerful that I rethought my entire design philosophy. What seemed to be a glimpse into his prestigious career has moved me into the beginning of my own. Thank you for the inspiration, Robert.

Motion graphics offer a wealth of media for exploitation. You can develop audio, color effects, filters, transitions, multiple movie clips and more to communicate a message. To me, the most productive and moving motion graphics are the ones that begin with no theme. As they are created, they become vehicles for message. They are beautified and brought to life without the contamination of function; the art is pure.

This has been the methodology of Matt Owens, of http://volumeone.com. During a conference in Sweden, he presented examples of his process. Many were curious as to how he was able to bridge the gap between experimental and functional work. As a collective, he and his fellow artisans would create 'enigmas' that would act as skeletons for future projects – but the puzzles were blank, without function or meaning. Alike in method, the WDDG (http://wddg.com/anamorph) have created a beautified visual representation of the merging of humans and technology. The style of that piece is so beautiful, and I would love to see how it evolved.

As noted by Catharin Eure of http://breathedesign.com, there is a difference between design and art. In design, the client takes precedence over the work. In art, the work takes precedence over the client. But what if you were to take this philosophy and redefine it, to extract the best of both worlds? My proposal is to give an artist the freedom of creation, to view the creation, and then to modify it to become a vehicle for meaning – just as the people and group mentioned here have done so well. This will give you the aesthetic beauty of a finished piece of art, and the functionality of a vehicle for meaning.

http://anamorph.wddg.com Anamorph © 2001 WDDG

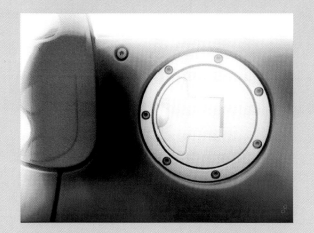 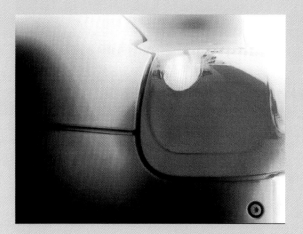

Audio is the most powerful element in a new media artist's repertoire. In combination with images and motion, it can convey unstoppable emotion. As a student, I only combined all three elements successfully once, in a piece so powerful that when he viewed it for the first time, my instructor began to cry. I had photographed my mother with traditional black and white film, grainy and weathered. The room around her was cold and stark. The piece started with a simple black and white image, and faded into a duotone that brought the warmth of her skin to life. In the background, audio that I had extracted from her personal classical collection merged into the imagery. The mood was dark and painful, and deep with sorrow – but for me, it was cleansing. Together, my mother and I dealt with family issues – issues that many of us have – and moved forth with our lives.

Imagery can capture the meaning of life. If you take a picture of a group of halogen lights in the ceiling, you can almost feel the life being sucked from you as you view that image once again. If you photograph a beautiful orchid on the beachfront, you capture the youth and vibrancy of its color. In turn, this youth and vibrancy will illuminate your work. Take notice of the environment in which you live. I understand that you know what's around you at the moment, but I need you to look again. Look deeper into the edges of the walls. Look down to where they meet the floor. Think about what's in the wall: visualize the cables, and the energy that runs through them to light the room. Imagine if you could capture that energy, and make it work for you. This again would come through in your work. By strategically organizing the elements in your photography, you can validate your work. So choose well.

Another mentor during my schooling was Gary Birch of statmedia.com. A unique challenge during my studies with Gary involved this statement: "Interactive digital media: the new literacy." He asked that we visualize it, and doing so required redefinition of the words. What is interactive digital media? And why is it the new literacy? And if this is new, what is old? I could have spent hours asking myself where to begin, but instead I took the simple path. Rather than proposing that people were going to have to become literate in this new language, I argued that it wasn't new at all, and that people already knew it. I took three scenarios and visualized them in an interactive piece. These were the rollover states: "Have you ever used your cell phone in the garden?" "Have you ever used your laptop in the park?" "Have you ever glanced at your watch while strolling across the grass?" People know new media, but just need a little help to notice it.

There can be emotion in your work: lust and greed can devour your canvas. Have you ever stayed up late in bed, thinking about your dreams? It's strange how the mind never sleeps. Sadness feels good at times – it can bring out the best of me. The sensation of another's touch can give you warmth and security. Untouched beauty awaits your redefinition. As I was hiking in the wilderness the other day, I came across a type of plant that I had never seen before. In the corner of my eye it looked like a flower, but its form was that of a hanging bulb. It dangled from its branch as if it was sad, but its beauty shone through.

Happiness in others can make my day – have you ever given a gift just to see the look on someone's face? Doesn't that feel great? Together with Photoshop and the flower experienced the day before, I can give this gift to the world. If, in my daily life, I encounter an object of such beauty, I return to capture it. After I've done so, I can begin to work on it in Photoshop. Once I have the image on my machine, I feel free – as though I've already succeeded, even though I've only just begun. At that point, I'm creating art: the piece is touched and soothed in my personal fashion; I erase the edges to blend into the background, and feather the petals to wisp into a synthetic breeze.

Freedom defines who I am. I do not work in a cubicle, nor will I ever. But I'm not an anarchist, and I won't frown upon the desire of others to do so – it just isn't for me. I split on a full time job a few years back because the summer swell was so good. It was the best vacation of my life. Solitude is important: I wouldn't suggest that you exclude others from your life, but I would encourage a small vacation from reality every now and then. The mind needs a rest. And as it rests, the best thinking can be done. Just don't tell my wife I said that.

I wish to create visual phenomena, utilizing the final image as a vehicle to communicate emotion. Using photographic images of readily available objects and everyday occurrences, I hope to inspire others to do the same. In translating from the mind's visions to the final piece, you find yourself – it's as though you've broken the law of mind, because what is thought is not meant to be visualized. What a special feeling it is. If I can move one person to change their way of thinking, I have succeeded. If I can help someone to better his or her situation, I have succeeded. If I can spread positive emotions to one person, I have succeeded. I wish to create new media that will change people's lives. With this, we could make the world a better place, a place of visual stimulation and thought. Imagine that.

Reflective

There can be nothing more rewarding than listening to and observing someone else. At times, I just sit in the park and watch people as they pass by. Some are calm and without words, some are chatting quietly, and some are in tight and tense arguments. To me, this park setting is a stage for discovery. Without prying into these people's lives, you're able to see what may happen in their situation, without having to endure the consequences.

With a couple that was arguing, I noticed a few things. The husband was not speaking. It seemed as if the wife needed some time to speak. It was her time to be heard. At that moment, I looked down in discomfort; I knew what it was like to experience brutal truth said in anger. But as my head lifted and I looked around, they were nowhere to be seen. It was strange, but then I noticed them sitting at the edge of the path under a large oak tree. The man had lifted his arm and wrapped it around her shoulders. In that one simple gesture, he'd said a thousand words.

This was enlightening to me, because I've often been confronted with situations that offered multiple solutions. Instead of retaliating and setting up a wall of defense, the man gave in and opened his arms to the woman. Thanks to that occasion, I learned something about relationships, but I wondered if I could also translate the experience to other things in life. And I could. Some may argue that signs and events are only metaphorical and cannot be universal, but I beg to differ. If you are creative, and you're willing to mix and match the elements, you will become stronger than the person who is still arguing the obvious.

In the same way, I'm willing to share what I have learned, in the hope of making your work better. As a designer, I've been exposed to many projects with tight delivery dates that have posed a threat to the aesthetic outcome of the final product. Though under pressure, I always promise myself that I'll deliver an enticing solution, no matter what the restrictions may be. What I hope to do here is to elevate the quality of *your* product delivery.

In design, there are just a few major elements: type, image, hue, and shape. In new media, audio, motion, and audience interaction can be added to that list. By elevating your attention to detail and aesthetic quality in just one element, your work will become better. If you can elevate your attention to detail and aesthetic quality in all of the elements, your work will become beautiful. I'm still working on image, and when I feel comfortable, I'll move on to the next one. I alone may not be a force, but the combined group of creative Photoshop artists within this book will give you a repertoire of methods like you would never believe. Instead of sitting alone, absorb what is around you, and apply it as you see fit.

From job to job, the subject matter will change. For this tutorial, I've selected something that I hope will be interesting to you, although of course the methods I've used can be applied to almost any imagery. The pictures for this tutorial were shot at an elevation of 5,687 feet, on Modjeska peak in California. Together, a few close friends and I decided to take on this challenge, and at the top Bob Messersmith and Karla Winrow were to be married. I chose my mountain bike as the way to get to the top; others chose their dusty and battered running shoes. On a test run three days prior to this ride, I made it eight miles before my camel pack dried up. To complete the ride, I would have had to climb for one and a half miles more without water — a risk I wasn't willing to take. Instead, I proceeded to descend for 47 minutes. It was a blast!

The morning of the climb arrived. It was still dark out as I threw my trusty homegrown Schwinn into the trunk of my car. The air was icy as it entered my mouth and nose. As I pulled up to the dirt parking lot in my lowered streetcar, people turned and wondered why this city slicker was pulling in so early. It was so funny. There I met my friends, and together we began the journey.

3 hours and 26 minutes later, we reached the top. Our legs were cramping and our clothes were wet with perspiration — and because of the elevation and the dry air, I had sprung a bloody nose. I wasn't in the best of shape, but I had done it! I had climbed over 5,000 feet and more than 9 miles to the top of this mountain! It was one of the most inspiring moments of my life. And as a surprise to Karla, at the end of the wedding ceremony Bob had a helicopter come to the top of the peak to fly them off to their reception. It was an awesome day. And as a bonus, I got to shoot that cool chopper! The imagery may seem arbitrary and universal to many, but it is inspirational to me. If you want to see more of the trip up the mountain, visit http://purusdesign.com/gift/

Recycling Imagery

It can be relatively easy to create one spectacular image, but what if you have to create four more that are in the same ballpark of beauty? This might not be a difficult subject to undertake if you have a splendid database of good imagery, but unfortunately this is not usually the case. Composition is key to success here, and in order to achieve it I suggest placing your elements in unexpected places, stirring interest in the viewers' minds. Also, play with the rotation and the size of the canvas after you've 'completed' the piece. There may be a more interesting and appealing solution just degrees away.

Image `1_1.jpg` is of a helicopter rotor blade, but it's a bit overexposed, so I'd tend to place it towards the bottom of the layer stack in order to get a lighter effect from it. If you want a deep tone for your final image, place a darker image in the background.

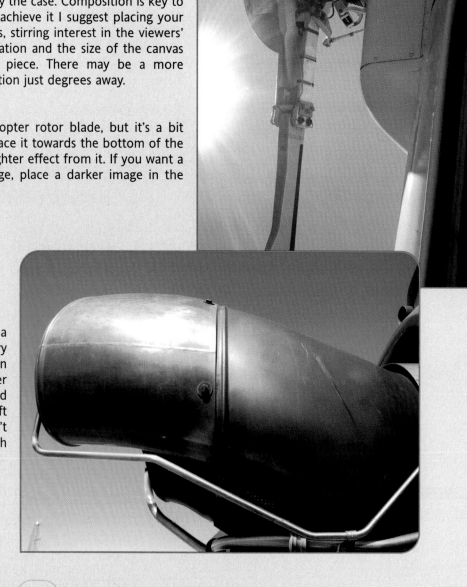

Image `1_2.jpg` is of a helicopter turbine. This is a very strong image that I'll use again as the background for another piece, but in this case I've used it as an overlay, to give a soft appearance. Overall, it doesn't overwhelm the canvas with form; rather, it adds accent.

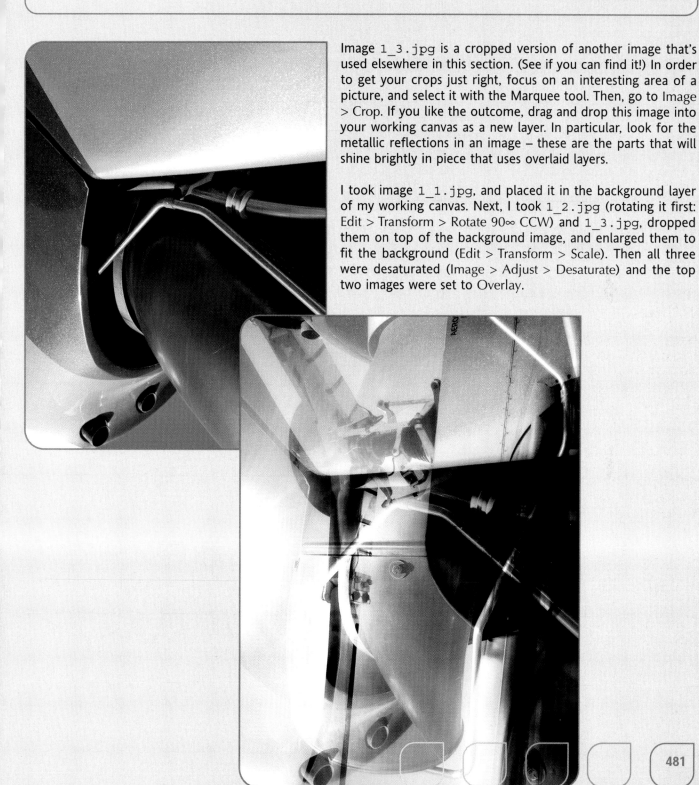

Image `1_3.jpg` is a cropped version of another image that's used elsewhere in this section. (See if you can find it!) In order to get your crops just right, focus on an interesting area of a picture, and select it with the Marquee tool. Then, go to Image > Crop. If you like the outcome, drag and drop this image into your working canvas as a new layer. In particular, look for the metallic reflections in an image – these are the parts that will shine brightly in piece that uses overlaid layers.

I took image `1_1.jpg`, and placed it in the background layer of my working canvas. Next, I took `1_2.jpg` (rotating it first: Edit > Transform > Rotate 90∞ CCW) and `1_3.jpg`, dropped them on top of the background image, and enlarged them to fit the background (Edit > Transform > Scale). Then all three were desaturated (Image > Adjust > Desaturate) and the top two images were set to Overlay.

Reflective

Next, I selected the Airbrush tool, and softened the highlights of the image. I set the radius to approximately 100, and the pressure to about 5%, and then proceeded (on a new layer) to brush over the areas that I wanted to highlight. (In the screenshot opposite, these areas have been set on a gray background, to help them stand out.) This is a technique commonly used by photographers for retouching portraits. Instead of using it on teeth, I thought I could use it to bring out the whites in the forms and structures I had captured. Because this layer will be purely white, be sure to keep it *under* the layer that we'll talk about in the next section.

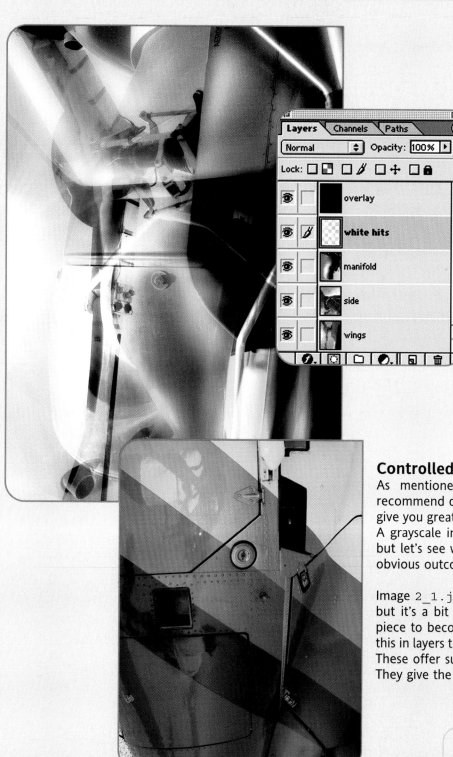

Lastly, having desaturated all the layers, I decided to add a dark blue (R: 11, G: 56, B: 67) layer in Overlay mode, and as a final adjustment I dropped the opacity of the 1_3.jpg layer to 65%.

Controlled Surprise

As mentioned in other parts of this tutorial, I recommend desaturation of the layers of imagery, to give you greater control over the final hue of a piece. A grayscale image creates a simple and clean form, but let's see what we can do to break free from the obvious outcome.

Image 2_1.jpg is of the side panel of a helicopter, but it's a bit flat. Because I wouldn't want my final piece to become flat, I suggest utilizing imagery like this in layers that employ the Overlay blending mode. These offer subtle changes, and a touch of contrast. They give the image a boost, so to speak.

Reflective

For the second image in this tutorial, we'll again use `1_2.jpg`: the helicopter turbine. You can almost feel the intensity and power that have been experienced by the metals of this piece of machinery. There's a bit of plasma coloration happening along the foremost panel of the metal, from extreme heat exposure. You can find this effect in oil, or if you were to combine chemicals with water.

Using the image of the turbine as a background layer gives us a solid foundation for a piece. Because I wanted to see something unusual, though, I left the side panel colored, while desaturating the turbine. I dragged the former to sit upon the latter, and set the blending mode to Overlay. To add some essence, I again highlighted the white areas that I thought would improve the final piece – highlights are a gift of the heavens!

Because I already had some cool colors in the mix, thanks to those blues in the side panel image, I wanted to add a warmer hue. I started by adding a white layer, set to Soft Light mode, beneath the highlights. Then I created another new layer at the top of the stack, filled it with a dusky red (R: 170, G: 54, B: 98), and set it to Color Burn at 60% opacity.

Color burn is one of my favorite effects in Photoshop. After you've taken the images and set them to Overlay, you have the choice of desaturating the imagery, or leaving it as-is. If you decide on the latter, though, adding a Color Burn layer can posterize or make the colors muddy. I would suggest either desaturating all of the imagery, and placing a color burn layer at the top of the stack; or else leaving just one color while all the others are desaturated, as I have here.

Composition Complexity

After you've become comfortable with the methods we've looked at so far, you may feel the need for a challenge. In order to control this medium, you have to overcome your fears of breaking the canvas. Remember that we're dealing with a synthetic medium, so the consequences of failure are minor.

Image `3_2.jpg` of the helicopter's exhaust is strong, clean, and sharp. Lens flares and bright spots in images can add exciting elements to your work: if the image with the lens flare is in the background, setting the layer above that to Overlay mode will add form to that area, while benefiting from the gradation of the lens flare. Two unique occurrences will be captured at one time.

Image `3_1.jpg` of the helicopter's rotors is dynamic, and rich in perspective. Once I'd dragged it into my composition and performed my usual desaturation and highlighting, though, I felt that the picture needed extra form – so I duplicated it (Layer > Duplicate Layer), and flipped it horizontally (Edit > Transform > Flip Horizontal). To finish off, I created two new layers on top of the others: one filled with white, set to Soft Light at 20% opacity; the other filled with a blue-gray color (R: 77, G: 114, B: 154) and set to Color Burn at 70% opacity.

The result is a dynamic, strong, and bold image.

Morphing Imagery

Because it's so difficult to find two images from two different photographs that can be united together in one composition, I have developed a method that can offer some assistance. During a photo shoot, use your tripod to capture one strong image. Then, rotate your camera slightly, using the features of the tripod. This will give you a great variety of images that are able to be overlayed and 'morphed'.

Because of the success of this particular shoot, I was able to mix and match the shots as I pleased, without the additional problems of having to modify lightness and darkness. If I were to attempt this with images of two separate objects in two separate environments, I could run into trouble – but because I have control of the surroundings, lighting, and subject matter, such things will come easily.

Image `4_1.jpg` is of the central part of the helicopter's main rotors. It is a complex image, offering high contrast and cool mechanical forms. Cables, blades, and hard edges can be fun!

Image `4_2.jpg` is of the rear helicopter rotor. This image offers the same aspects that `4_1.jpg` does. Together, they should fit just fine.

What I'm looking for is a focal point in the images. To find it, I prepared both by desaturating them, and then setting one as the background and the other as the overlay. Because they're so similar, I could have used either one as the background, but I finally decided on `4_1.jpg`. Once you've got them together, the focal point is obvious: it's where the rotor meets the body of the helicopter.

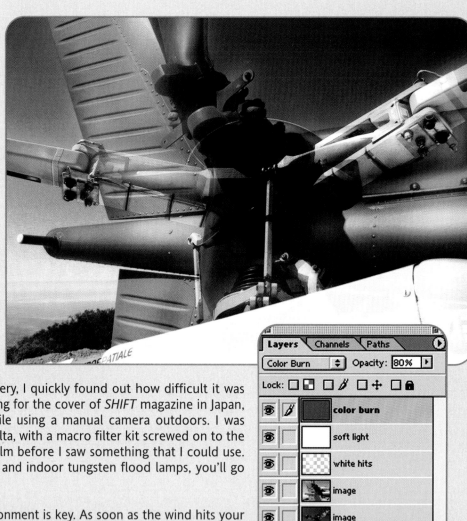

Next, I softened the highlights with the airbrush, added a white Soft Light layer at 50% opacity, and placed a new orange-colored layer on top of that (R: 204, G: 107, B: 52, Color Burn at 80% opacity). Because the images are of similar subjects, the illusion created is rather like morphing from one to the other. The images are not one, but they contain the same elements and brightness values.

Gaussian Halo Technique

During my first ventures into imagery, I quickly found out how difficult it was to get a perfect shot. While shooting for the cover of *SHIFT* magazine in Japan, I came across many problems while using a manual camera outdoors. I was using a 35-millimeter manual Minolta, with a macro filter kit screwed on to the lens. I must have shot 10 rolls of film before I saw something that I could use. Without proper macro equipment and indoor tungsten flood lamps, you'll go nowhere.

Furthermore, controlling the environment is key. As soon as the wind hits your subject, it's going to shift. It might only be a centimeter of movement, but if it's in the middle of the shutter opening, your shot is lost. On that shoot, it was most likely the macro kit that gave me problems, but I have since created methods for ironing out *any* nicks and scratches you may find in your imagery.

For example, you may have discovered a sweet shot in one of your photo shoots, but the image may still have problems. It could have an inconsistent grain pattern, or waffle effects from a fouled-up scan. In print, it's vital to have a clean image without dust, grain, or scratches. I have developed a very simple technique that can soften edges and overall textures in imagery, giving them that Purus feel.

In image `5_1.jpg`, I have a decent shot of a helicopter exhaust pipe. The image has a good amount of detail, and lots of gradated surfaces.

First, I duplicate the `5_1.jpg` layer, and add Filter > Blur > Gaussian Blur set at 10 pixels. Next, I take this layer and lower its opacity to about 30%. This is where the excitement begins; you see the difference immediately. With this one maneuver, you are able to achieve the awesome effects of the Gaussian blur, while retaining the clarity of the original imagery in the background.

Then, I duplicate the blurred layer again, but set its blending mode to Overlay, with opacity of around 50%. Something interesting happens when you set a Gaussian layer to overlay. It's very cool. If you were to take the sharp background image, duplicate it, and set *it* to Overlay, you would see a drastic change in edge sharpness and the overall contrast of the piece. (Of course, if you want an edgy feel to your image, this is exactly the right thing to do.) But if the layer being set to overlay is blurred, it just feels right. It's so sweet. I hope you can use this in your work – people will be looking over your shoulder asking, "Where did you buy that image from?" The coolest thing about this technique is that you can make a snapshot look like a staged event.

Edge Control

Creating an interesting composition with photography can be challenging. It's not because of your body placement while shooting, but because of the uncontrollable data that may appear in the background. Perspective is a challenging subject, but if you can bring it to your work, the depth alone can make your viewers wonder why they are so enchanted. Though perspective is a challenge to create, though, it can actually be quite simple to capture. By this, I mean putting your face to the wall and searching for an interesting composition. Or maybe crouching down to get that worm's-eye perspective. Or on the flip side, climbing a fire escape to grab that bird's-eye view. It's all there for us; we just have to find it.

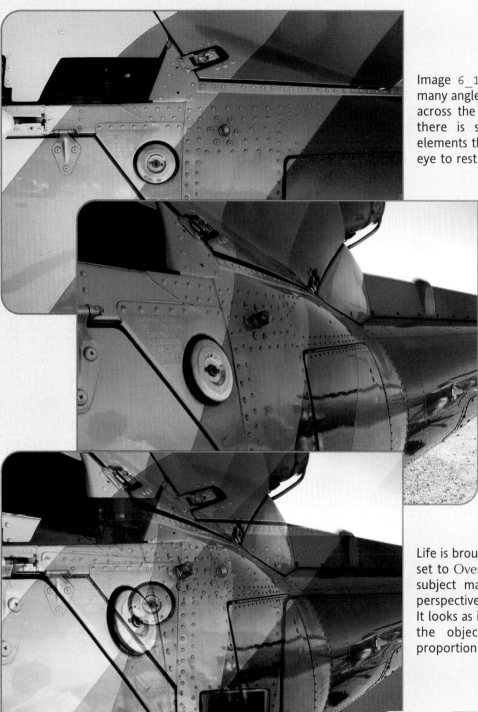

Image `6_1.jpg` is a strong one: there are many angles and paths that will guide the eye across the canvas during presentation. Plus, there is some eye candy: smaller visual elements that act as stopping points for your eye to rest at when viewing an entire canvas.

Image `6_2.jpg` offers an interesting composition, and a taste of perspective. But in order to capture it, I had to bring in a piece of the ground, too. I thought it was a small price to pay, but because I don't want to ground the viewer, I'd like to replace that section with a duplicate of the sky.

I selected the undesirable piece of ground with the Polygonal Lasso tool, feathered the selection (Select > Feather, set at 2 pixels) and deleted it.

Life is brought to the piece when `6_1.jpg` is set to Overlay above `6_2.jpg`. Because the subject matter is alike, but in a different perspective, interesting things are happening. It looks as if the second image is skewed, but the objects in the foreground are in proportion to one another.

Reflective

I would like to simulate the gradation of the sky that's happening in the top right hand corner of the image. This will give a cool-looking halo effect to the tail of the helicopter, and it's really quite easy to create. First, select a deep blue piece of sky using the Eyedropper tool, and fill the deleted-ground selection with your blue on a new layer.

Then, place a new layer over the blue layer, select the Gradient tool (under the Paint Bucket tool), and create a gradient path at a 45-degree angle, moving from left to right (left-click and drag, holding down the Shift key). While doing this, I used white as my foreground color and the tool was set to work in Foreground to Transparent mode.

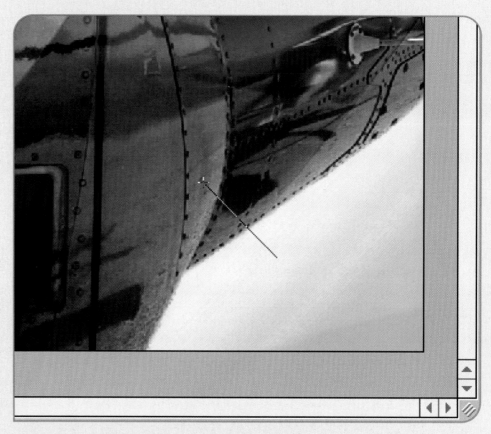

Finally, to create an interesting composition, I rotated the canvas 90 degrees counterclockwise (Image > Rotate Canvas > 90° CCW). During my studies, I was challenged to rotate my canvas while painting a still life – and curious as ever, I did so. Immediately I saw flaws and distortions that I would not have seen before the rotation.

This technique opened my eyes. Before my first rotation, I felt as if I was bound to a path without the option of distortion. Try this with your work, perhaps even rotating it through 180 degrees, or flipping it horizontally. In some cultures, people read from right to left, or from top to bottom, rather than the left to right that I'm familiar with. When I flip my canvas, maybe I get a glimpse of how they see it? I've noticed that a large amount of the traffic to my site comes from Japan. This makes me wonder whether I'm catering to their reading style more than my own.

You can become a smarter designer by knowing your audience. Who is going to be reading your article? Who is going to be reviewing your work? You can save yourself from countless revisions if you understand what you are creating for. By doing so, I have been able to excel in my work and in life together.

chapter 1

chapter 2

chapter 3

chapter 4

chapter 5

chapter 6

chapter 7

chapter 8

chapter 9

chapter 10

chapter 11

chapter 12

chapter 13

chapter 14

chapter 15

chapter 16

outro

"Forcing yourself to design is like exercising:
the more you do, the stronger you become."

Michael Cina
www.weworkforthem.com
www.trueistrue.com

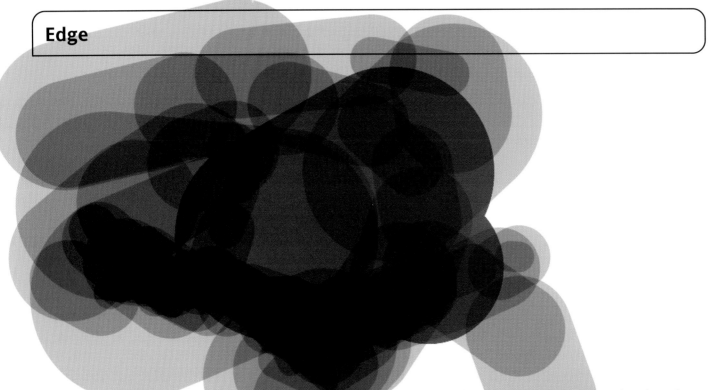

Edge

Like many of the other artists and designers who've contributed to this book, Photoshop has always been my application of choice. Actually, now that I think about it, I *didn't* choose Photoshop; rather, it chose me. When I started out in this field, Photoshop was the only image editing application around, and while it was difficult for me to grasp at times, I used it again and again, on one project after another, until eventually it became second nature. In this chapter, I'm going to talk a little about how I work, tell you about some of the people I look to for inspiration, and take you through some of the techniques that I use when I'm putting an image together.

During my time as a designer, my work has covered a wide range of styles, with a correspondingly broad set of influences. My work is constantly evolving, and the images we'll look at later are ones in which I used Photoshop in a different way than I have in the past. A lot of people pull their inspiration from current trends in design, but there are so many awesome things to learn about from outside your chosen field. The more you can look around, and read, and discover, the stronger a designer you will be. I'm influenced by art, and information and product design, sure, but I also find fascination in architecture, music, theatre, friends, God, nature, film, accidents, junk, science, photography, illustration, literature... the list is almost endless.

If you were to ask me what things characterize my work – the things that I really focus on – many of them can be found in the methodology of one of my biggest influences, the Bauhaus school. People such as El Lissitzky, Herbert Bayer, Le Corbusier, Moholy-Nagy, Walter Gropius, Max Bill, Johannes Itten, Josef Albers, Wassily Kandinsky – architects and painters – had great things to say. Their quest for simplicity in form, and their research into color, shape, and grids, is as relevant today as it was in the 1920s. This magazine cover, for example, can be linked to recent work like the Designers Republic's sleeve for Sun Electric's 1993 EP, *O'locco*. Produced in 1926, it's so well organized. I love the bold use of type; they were hand-lettering the fonts, and drawing the images.

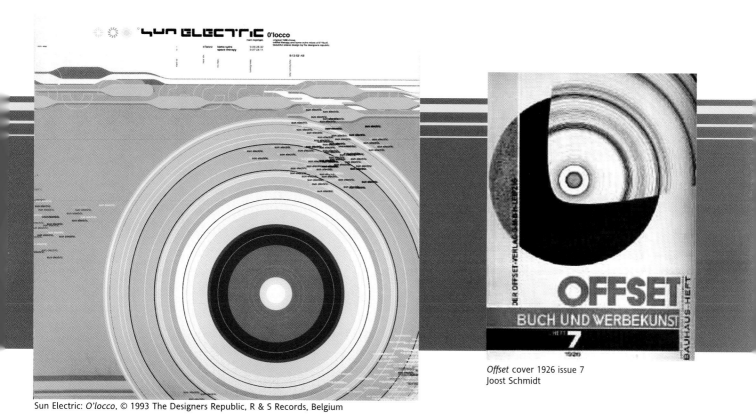

Offset cover 1926 issue 7
Joost Schmidt

Sun Electric: *O'locco*, © 1993 The Designers Republic, R & S Records, Belgium

Edge

When I design an image, I think about hierarchy of form: What is the most important part of the image? What do I want to stand out? Then, while working, I create a dialog in my mind about what I'm going to do with the image – what it is, and how it should perform. After that, I'll approach it with a lot of different ideas, throwing layer after layer of work into the PSD file. Most of these will quickly be deleted, or at least made invisible, but this technique allows me to experiment quickly, and the layers that do remain at the end are the strong ones.

Take, for example, the project that I worked on for a London-based stock art company. They asked me to create thirty images for a series called *Abstract*; apart from that, there were no restrictions at all. When I approached the project, I gave myself little themes for each image by picking words like "commerce", "technology", etc. The particular image we'll look at here started its life as a creation in Strata 3D, and because the series was going to be print-based, I generated it at 300dpi.

Once prepared, I imported the image into Photoshop, and adjusted the color using the Curves dialog box (Image > Adjust > Curves), until it had the color and contrast that I wanted. Having control over your color is a very important thing; seeing pictures that are off-color can be painful if you know how they should have looked.

For this image, I knew that I was looking for some sort of 'lightning' effect to divide the page, so I generated about half a dozen shapes that I thought might work, and tried them all until I eventually found something that I liked. In addition, a theme of the whole series was to include subtle background detail that would look good when printed, like the small crosses that I incorporated next. These are actually just '+' symbols, at a very small font size. Details are what make an image for me, but it's important not to overdo them. I like to keep them at the bare essentials.

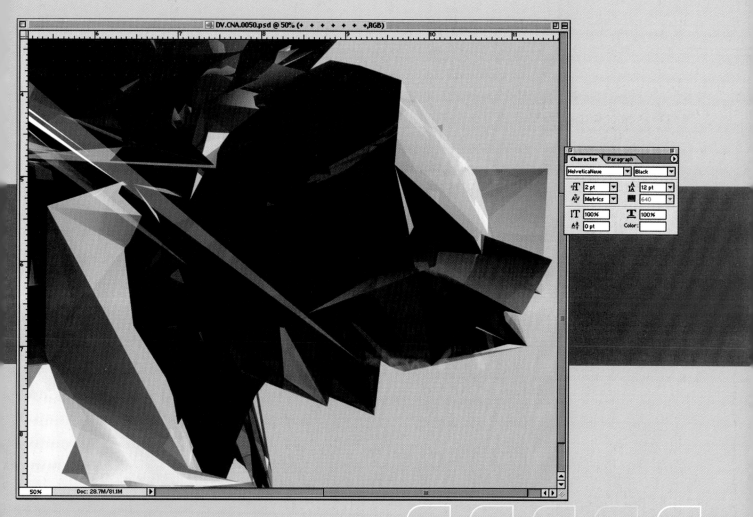

Edge

At this point, to my surprise, all these 3D shapes started to inspire me to work on some typography. I began to make typographic elements in Adobe Illustrator, and then imported them into Photoshop where I played with their properties to make them work with the image, generally by lowering their opacity. Sometimes, if I felt that something was still drawing too much attention to itself, I blurred it a little too.

Another trait of mine is to slip little factual elements into my work, like the number 0049 at the top – this was the 49th image I tried for the series. If you look very closely, you might also see the letters "cin" and "yng", standing for Cina and Young, and the "lfe" over the red bar. There, I was thinking of the word "life", because the more I looked at this image, the more I saw a big planet forming, or something like that. Keeping myself entertained in this way is always important!

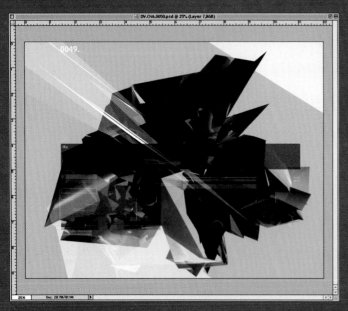

The final image is very center-focused. I placed the red bar in the middle, and lined up the rest of the text elements with it. One of the reasons for this result is that I almost always work within some type of grid, to the extent that turning on Photoshop's grid, or making guides, is usually the first thing I do when opening a new file. The grid is second nature to me, and I rarely think about it when I design.

As a result of all my experimentation, at this stage of creating an image I usually have about twenty layers that are turned off, and I'll go through all of them to see if anything works better, and move elements around to see if anything stands out. Usually, this takes about an hour before I realize that I'm going nowhere, and I will save the image and quit.

The Bauhaus school was playing with layout and letterform, and doing it well, but the Swiss picked up where the Bauhaus left off, taking design to another level. Among others, Emil Ruder, Josef Müller-Brockmann, Richard Paul Lohse, Wim Crouwel, Wolfgang Weingart, and Armin Hofmann are individuals whom I admire greatly. They helped bring about a new 'good form': a mindset that presented information logically, with the aid of graphical elements. These are the people I look to now, in order to learn more about design.

In fact, Wim Crouwel had impressed me before I even knew who he was – his "New Alphabet" appeared on the cover of Joy Division's *Substance* album. I remember being amazed when this CD came out in 1988 – I'd never seen such abstract lettering. The cover itself was designed by Peter Saville, and although he used the typeface incorrectly (when the glyph is underlined, the letter 'n' should be interpreted as an 'm'), it still looks stunning.

As I've already hinted, typography is an important part of my work too, and I believe it should be in the top three skills on every designer's list. Type is how most people communicate their message, and how you use the typeface is key. When I first started to design, I worked for the University of North Texas. We had no budget and 20 typefaces, so I had to make the most of what I was given, and I quickly learned the importance of type and color. College taught me a bit about how to use type, but it wasn't until I started making typefaces of my own that I really began to learn how it functions. Think of it as being like taking a computer apart: you get to see exactly how it's constructed.

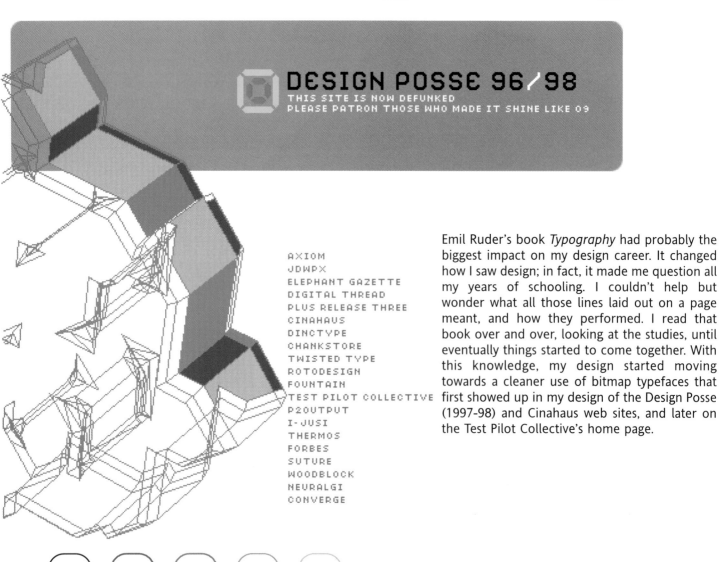

DESIGN POSSE 96/98
THIS SITE IS NOW DEFUNKED
PLEASE PATRON THOSE WHO MADE IT SHINE LIKE 09

AXIOM
JDWPX
ELEPHANT GAZETTE
DIGITAL THREAD
PLUS RELEASE THREE
CINAHAUS
DINCTYPE
CHANKSTORE
TWISTED TYPE
ROTODESIGN
FOUNTAIN
TEST PILOT COLLECTIVE
P2OUTPUT
I-JUSI
THERMOS
FORBES
SUTURE
WOODBLOCK
NEURALGI
CONVERGE

Emil Ruder's book *Typography* had probably the biggest impact on my design career. It changed how I saw design; in fact, it made me question all my years of schooling. I couldn't help but wonder what all those lines laid out on a page meant, and how they performed. I read that book over and over, looking at the studies, until eventually things started to come together. With this knowledge, my design started moving towards a cleaner use of bitmap typefaces that first showed up in my design of the Design Posse (1997-98) and Cinahaus web sites, and later on the Test Pilot Collective's home page.

The next project I want to show you also features some typography, and it started out just as an idea in my head. What I wanted was to have an image that was dark at the top, with a transition into a lighter area – like the clouds falling down, or something. I also knew that I wanted the image to be green.

I find that I do a lot of work in my head, before I ever actually open Photoshop. When I try to 'sketch' in a program, with no idea of what I want to do, a lot of time gets wasted and the outcome is usually not as good. I've been doing this for so long that I can usually envision a whole image, layout and all, but even if that doesn't work for you I'd still advise you to sketch out images on paper before you start working at the computer.

All the 3D elements I used in this image were created using a program from 1995 called Infini-D. I guess it's a bit dated now, but I've used it for six years, and know it fairly well. And anyway, don't all 3D programs do pretty much the same thing? I'm certainly no expert at generating 3D images, but I think that's what gives my work a raw feel. Like musicians that use keyboards they don't know anything about, I get great results from using them a way that probably wasn't intended.

This image uses five layers of 3D generated artwork, and two layers of wireframes – but once again, these were chosen from a selection of around four times as many. My work is sometimes criticized for being 'simple' or 'plain', but I put in tons of work to get it there. I always over-create, and then delete until I end up with the essence of the image. It's a more educated and reductive process than putting up every idea or layer that I have.

The 'bottom' layer of the finished PSD file looks like this, although in truth you can hardly see it at all in the final composition. This is because I took the opacity right down to 6% in the Layers palette.

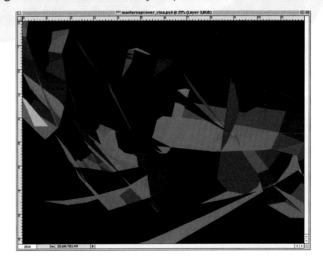

Edge

I actually started the project off with the next image, and took things from there. Layers like this are important for the final outcome – I wanted a sort of 'whirlwind' feel to it, like something was being stirred up.

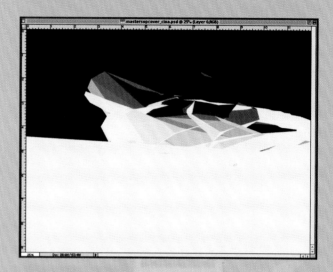

The first layer I showed you was then added, and helped to bring more texture to the piece. I feel this is most important part of the entire image – it really pulls everything together, as you'll see when I add the 'main' parts of the final image. All these layers help to support one another. Without any one of them, the image doesn't work.

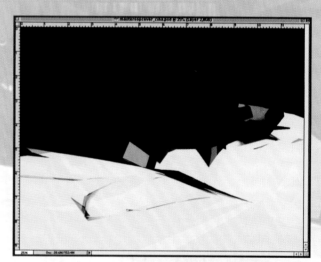

I probably spent about half an hour getting these layers to work properly with each other, adding, removing, and cloning until the final look was achieved. When you're overlaying images, it's important not to have open parts that will 'shine' through – you really need to finesse your layers to get them to work right. Still, you will almost *never* know exactly how your final work will look when printed, or viewed online by others – the top part of this one, for example, has some nice textures going on that you can't see on the screen. That's one of the joys of printing!

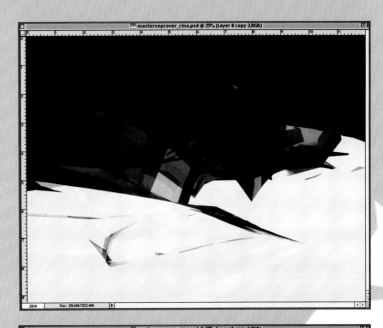

My two favorite parts of this image are the piece that comes down from the top left and points to the bottom right part, and the part to the left that looks like a scorpion tail. I made sure that they would be seen when I finished the image. To accent the extrusion that points to the bottom right, I made a shape in Illustrator and pulled it in to my document. Its blending mode was set to Screen, and I dropped its opacity to 25%.

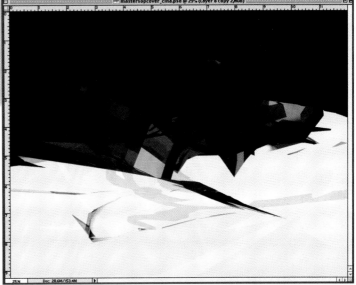

My new element was getting lost in the dark area, so I placed another image that brought a sense of movement to the piece. After trying a lot of different combinations, this one was given Multiply mode, and set to 27% opacity. When designing these images, I tried to design from the inside of the page out, instead of outside in, which is the way I usually think about things.

Edge

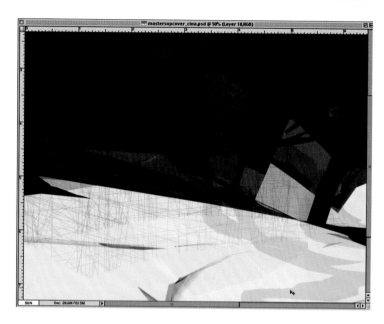

The piece still needed more, so I generated some wireframes from some existing 3D objects that I had lying around. From the half dozen or so that I made, I ended up putting just one of them over the piece, giving it a dark blue color and screening it down to 19% opacity. This gave it a light texture that worked with the piece and didn't stick out too much. Then I duplicated the wireframe again, and gave it 63% opacity. I also added some little dots on the top of the image, to give it more texture and detail. This all helps to build a solid piece, without being too heavy with imagery.

At this stage, I started to add some more small elements to the piece, like lines and dots. Again, these were at low opacity, because I didn't want to draw any attention to them – all I wanted was some texture. I also started to create icons to place in the image. I often do this kind of thing when I get to a 'stopping point', or when I find myself doing pointless things with the layers. You know: over-thinking, and over-designing.

To get from here to the final image that you can see at the end of the chapter, I put some type over the image, using a font that I created specifically for this piece – I needed something long and geometric. After I'd rasterized the type and brought it into Photoshop, I continued to make alterations by deleting pixels from it, and adding little details that made it more interesting. Most likely, I will now make those alterations to the font when I make the full typeface family. Isn't the designing process lovely? This is why I always have too much work to do.

On a project like this, it's important that you make the type interact with the rest of the piece, so I started to import some little design elements that worked with the type. On this occasion, the type is being used more as a design element itself, but it would work with functional type too. I think about color a lot at this stage, making all the elements work together, and pulling out an accent color to make the image pop. Aspects like these are things that I learned from my art classes.

Finally, I moved some of the elements around, and made them line up on tangents. I love it when things are lined up with one another, and it's something that I've been doing forever – even my teacher used to call me "Tangent Man". Don't you ever call me that, though: I may chase you down in my riding lawnmower.

As you've probably gathered, music is definitely in the list of my top ten inspiration sources, and has been since long before I started designing. I remember being seven years old and listening to music, sometimes shutting my eyes to see what pictures would come to mind. I don't know how it does it, but music can move the soul.

Growing up, I was surrounded by a music-loving family. My father would play music non-stop when he was at home. One of my favorite memories is of going shopping for records with him – I loved looking at the album covers, and hearing what new music was coming out. Sometimes he would find a rare gem, and tell me a story about the band or their music. The thing that always interested me most, though, was the cover art. I could get lost looking at the imagery, and reading the liner notes. As I got older, I picked up where my father left off – so much so that in high school, my parents had a talk with me about buying too many albums, a problem I still have. It's an addiction of sorts.

This addiction led me to start DJing in 1989. I was going to nightclubs quite often, and thought that I could do a better job myself. What could be better than getting paid to spin records? I bought turntables and a mixer, and began to learn how to match beats per minute. My DJ career took off in 1993, and I began to mix at various parties and clubs in Dallas, Texas. Some nights I would get lost in the music, like I was in another world – I could see the music moving in my head. Drums, and the other instruments, would all appear and behave in a particular way. The whole thing usually ended up looking like an abstract equalizer or chart.

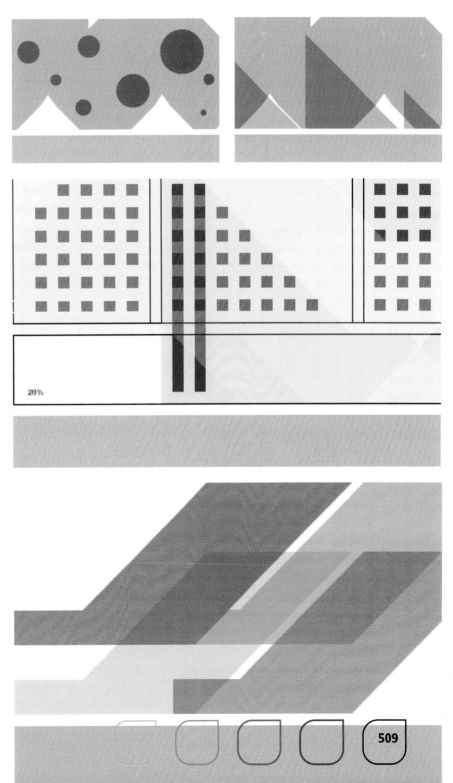

Going clubbing could also be very inspiring – hearing great DJ's from around the world was always a real treat. Songs like Urban Soul's *Alright* and Style Council's remake of the Joe Smooth classic *Promised Land* always touch me deeply when I hear them. Now, when I design, I almost always listen to music, because it can set a mood in a way that nothing else can. If I need to work late, I will put on some driving music (drum 'n' bass, hard house, breakbeat), or a good mix tape. groovetech.com and betalounge.com are two great sites to find good mix sets. I basically program my music when I start, and use it like another tool.

One of the pastimes I enjoy the most is to take a song and design a graphic to it. When I was learning design, this was my favorite thing to do, because trying to think what a song looks like is a great exercise. Colors, fonts, images, style, theme… they can all be established fairly easily, based on the music. Not only did this help develop my visual language, but also it sharpened my skills. Forcing yourself to design is like exercising: the more you do, the stronger you become.

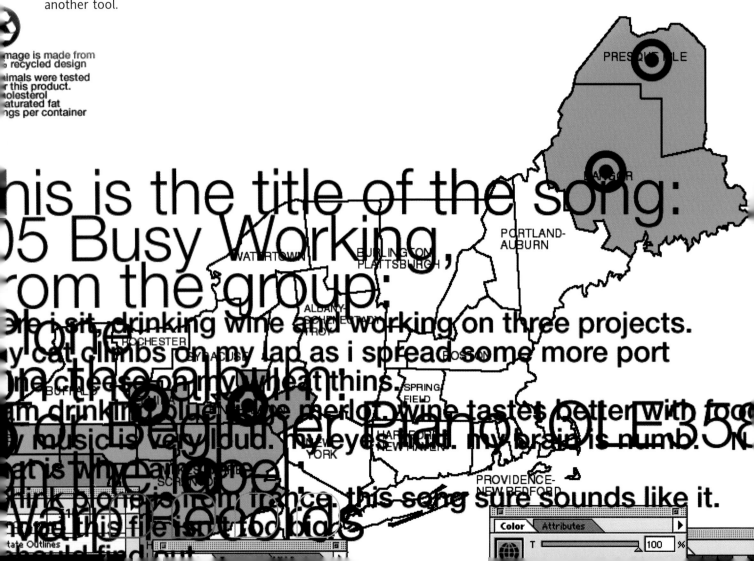

I surround myself with little projects, so that I can always be inspired in some way, depending on my mood. If the Internet isn't calling my name, I have scrapbooks to work in. Or else there's painting, or screen-printing... the list goes on and on. I keep a sketchbook with me all the time – something that ought to be mandatory for every creative person. I don't know a better way to record ideas, or sketches, or a cool sticker, or anything else that you happen to find. My house is usually packed with trash, just waiting to get pasted into a scrapbook. Ha.

One of my Internet projects, the Test Pilot Collective, was a web site that I worked on with Joseph Kral and Matt Desmond. It was to be a type studio where we could sell the typefaces that we created. Joseph and I would bounce ideas back and forth about process and design, and he started to develop a typeface called Xerxes that was based on a 72dpi grid. I was beginning to use a lot of flat color in my work, turning off anti-aliasing on the Line and Pencil tools in Photoshop to create a very simplistic and clean look.

I believe that this was a merging of print design (limited use of color and typefaces), and the exploration of technology (only using bitmaps to create the image, resulting in a small file size). I experimented with these ideas day and night, trying to use my knowledge of the grid system. It got to the point where I would never use a JPG in any of my work – it was all hand-drawn (pixel by pixel) GIF files. I remember getting frustrated if my image was bigger than 20 kilobytes. To this day, people still think that I used Illustrator to create those Test Pilot Collective images.

Edge

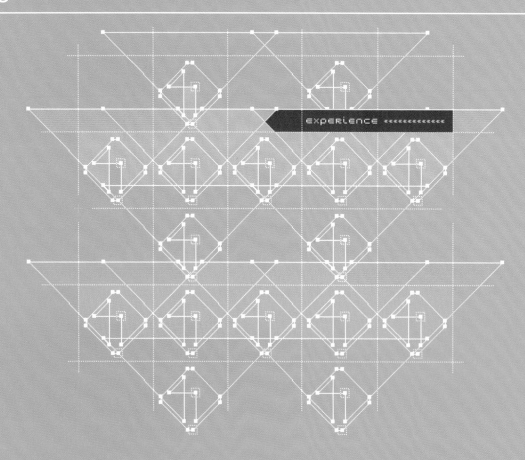

EXPERIENCE «««««««««

the countdoyn begins

Because I was making a lot of fonts at this time, the process of doing so inspired all my other work as well. I was forever drawing geometric typefaces in Fontographer, so I was dealing with clean vector lines every day. When I got into Photoshop, I was really doing much the same: drawing lines to make images.

This image was actually created in Fontographer – it's just a screenshot of an icon I was making that I pulled into Photoshop. Then I altered the color (another important aspect of design), and exported it as a GIF. You can see the influence of Wim Crouwel again in the text at the bottom of the image – and once again, that was drawn by hand, pixel-by-pixel.

I buy books obsessively, and over the years my collection has grown to a huge size. Recently, I've learned to cut down a little – not having a lot of money helps! – but I still find them difficult to resist. I'm a firm believer in continuing to learn after attending college, and books are a wonderful means of self-education. There's a wealth of knowledge out there, and for anyone to believe that they know it all is laughable. I read a lot about design history, which has taught me where different people fit into the scheme of things. Learning how other people work is a great place to grow from, and the following is a list of just some of the titles I keep on my shelves.

Design

Josef Müller-Brockmann: Pioneer of Swiss Graphic Design (Müller, Rand)
Dutch Graphic Design: A Century (Broos, Hefting, Broos)
Maeda @ Media (John Maeda)
Experience (Perkins, Ardill, Caddy)
Design: Vignelli (Paul Goldberger)
Herbert Bayer: The Complete Work (Arthur Allen Cohen)

History

A History of Graphic Design (Philip Meggs)
Graphic Design in America: A Visual Language History (Walker Art Center)
Graphic Design, a Concise History (Richard Hollis)
The Thames and Hudson Dictionary of Graphic Design and Designers (Alan and Isabella Livingston)

Grids

Grid Systems in Graphic Design (Josef Müller-Brockmann)
Typography (Emil Ruder)

Typography

Typography (Wolfgang Weingart)
Typography (Friedl, Ott, Stein)
Twentieth-Century Type (Remix) (Lewis Blackwell)
Typographic Communications Today (Edward Gottschall)
Typographic Design: Form and Communication (Carter, Day, Meggs)
Basic Typography: Design with Letters (Ruedi Ruegg)
Typography: Macro + Micro Aesthetics (Willi Kunz)
The Elements of Typographic Style (Robert Bringhurst)

Logos

Marks of Excellence (Per Mollerup)

Color

Theory and Use of Color (Luigina de Grandis)
Basic Law of Color Theory (Harald Kueppers)
Interaction of Color (Josef Albers)

Theory

Ways of Seeing (John Berger)
Design Without Boundaries (Rick Poynor)
Looking Closer (Michael Bierut)

Information design

Information Design (Richard Saul Wurman)
Anything by Edward Tufte

Web sites

www.kiiroi.nu
www.k10k.com
www.h73.com
www.linkdup.com
www.surfstation.lu
www.designiskinky.net
www.shift.jp.org
www.australianinfront.com.au
www.threeoh.com

As you've made your way through this chapter, I hope that I've managed to give you a glimpse into how I work, and what inspires me. Most of all, though, I find that inspiration comes as a result of opening myself to new ideas, and to new ways of looking at things. Next time you're out, do something that you wouldn't normally do – get out of your bubble. Drive home a different way, look at an architecture magazine, a sports magazine, a fashion magazine; you'll be shocked at how they can set you thinking. Just make sure that you have your sketchbook or wallet handy.

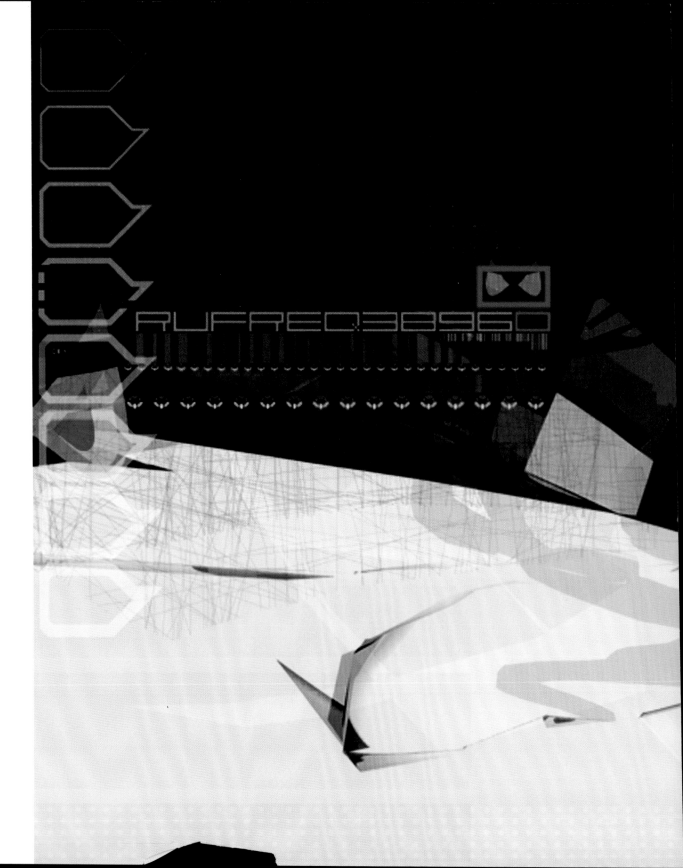

Index

The index is arranged hierarchically, in alphabetical order, with symbols preceding the letter A. Many second-level entries also occur as first-level entries. This is to ensure that users will find the information they require however they choose to search for it.

100% Photoshop (tutorial)
adding color to chrome ring 197
adding depth to body 204
adding grooves to lens joins 191
adding layer style to grip pimples 194
adding noise 191
Airbrush tool 204
aluminum effect 206
applying custom gradient 190
applying layer styles 194
Bevel and Emboss 194
beveled lens sections 191
camera body 198
Chisel Hard setting 194
chrome effect 197
chrome ring 196
color stops 189
creating new channel 202, 205
customized gradients 189
drop shadows 208
feathering transitions 207
Free Transform tool 191, 193, 196
Gaussian Blur filter 202, 205, 207
Gradient tool 189, 196
grip layer 194
lens barrel 188, 190
levels of reflectivity 188
line layer 192
Line tool 191
linking body part layers 201
Marquee tool 190, 193
matt surface effect 189
Overlay layer blending mode 192
pattern background layer 196
Pattern fill 193
Pinch filter 196
Polygonal Lasso tool 199, 201
positioning and resizing grip 196
producing lens sections 191
rough shapes of body parts 199
rounded corners 203
rubber grip 192
Spherize filter 195
texture map 205
wraparound effect 194
3D image (tutorial)

3D artwork layers 505
adding small elements 508
adding type 508
bottom layer 505
composition 507
Multiply layer blending mode 507
overlaying images 506
Screen layer blending mode 507
wireframe layers 505, 508
3D programs 505
3D rendering 137
3D Studio Max 43, 63
4-Up button 265

A

ABC Warriors (comic strip) 143
abstract (tutorial)
adjusting image color 501
background detail 501
factual elements in work 502
lightning effect 501
positioning red bar 502
text elements 502
working within grids 502
Ackermann, Karl 359
adjustment layers 14, 17, 66, 312, 324
Adobe 63, 438
Airbrush tool 19, 133, 204, 366, 482
Akira (film) 407
Albers, Josef (painter) 499
All Japan: The Catalogue of
Everything Japanese (book) 98
alpha channels 4, 202, 316, 392
Alright (song) 510
Anderson, Charles S. (designer) 28, 32
Animal-Vegetal (book) 217
anti-aliasing 264
The Aphex Twin (band) 5
Auto Levels feature 362

B

background color 224
Bacon, Francis (painter) 472
Barker, Clive (novelist) 146
base twice (tutorial)

adding grille 45
adding hexagons 45
adding list of figures 48
adjusting color of skeleton lines 42
adjusting color of target layer 46
back 3D element layer 38, 49
background color 37
basetwice2.psd 36
composition 36
creating shadows 48, 50
crop circles layer 44
cylinders layer 44
Eraser tool 39, 43, 45, 47
Eyedropper tool 40, 42, 48
flattening image 51
Free Transform tool 48
front 3D element layer 41, 43
graphic text layer 41
half-finished 3D object effect 43
Hard Light layer blending mode 45, 47
Lighten layer blending mode 42
lines layer 39
logo layer 44
Luminosity layer blending mode 38
Magic Wand tool 42
matosill.ai 37, 42
Multiply layer blending mode 48
non-flattened image 51
Overlay layer blending mode 44, 47
Paint Bucket tool 39
Paintbrush tool 48, 50
Pencil tool 39
pixelated writing layer 44
preparation of graphic elements in
Illustrator 36
radiation layer 47
rectangles layer 37, 38, 49
Rectangular Marquee tool 37
ruler 180 layer 40
'ruler' elements 40
ruler layer 40
screen fill pattern 39
Screen layer blending mode 40
shadows layer 48, 50
skeleton 3D element layer 42
sketch 36

Index

Soft Light layer blending mode 45
target layer 46
target.ai 46
wireframe effect 41
bathroom (tutorial) 93
adjusting color of Bathroom layer 109
Bathroom layer 109
BathroomPic_3_Orig.jpg 106
cleaning up collage 106
Collage layer 107, 108, 109
CollageOrigScan600dpi.psd 106
color field layer 110
composition 111
cropping photo 106
Eraser tool 106
Eyedropper tool 110
inserting color omissions 111
Lasso tool 113
Magic Wand tool 108
Multiply layer blending mode 110
placing collage on Bathroom layer 108
Rectangular Marquee tool 106, 107, 111
removing collage background 108
restroom photos 105
scanning in collage 106
Sharpen filter 106
shrinking image to work on 107
source material 104
Zoom tool 113
Batman – Arkham Asylum (graphic novel) 146
Bayer, Herbert 499
Baylay, James (painter) 441
Belvedere (picture) 123
Berger, John (art critic) 446
Beukers, Adriaan 358
Bill, Max (designer) 28, 499
Birch, Gary (web designer) 475
Bird, Tim. See also skateboard (tutorial)
abstract backgrounds 9, 12
club flyers 3
design background 3
experimentation with Photoshop 4
favorite artists 8

favorite photographers 7
introduction to Photoshop 3
London 3
Man in Gas Mask picture 6
photo retouching 5
rave scene 3
scanning everyday objects 12
surreal imagery 2
Trellick TV picture 5
Bisley, Simon (artist) 143
bitmap graphics 74
Black & White (manga) 354
BlahBlahBlah (magazine) 147
Block, Bruce (writer) 405
Blue Peter (British TV show) 449
Blur tool 69, 326
Boccioni, Umberto (sculptor) 144
Bond of Union (picture) 123
The Book of Mirrors (album) 315
Braque, George 220
Breugel, Pieter (painter) 442
Brody, Neville (designer) 28, 148
Brooks, Jason (digital artist) 7
Brothers In Arms (song) 62
Brush tool 366
Burn tool 72
bursting effect 338
butterflies (tutorial)
adding butterfly elements to background texture 335
adding circles under eyes 327
adding ink droplets 342
adjustment layers 324, 332
background 321
bits layer 339
blending paper and head 328
Blur tool 326, 332
book cover scan 340
brain layer 329
building cluster of butterflies 333
bursting effect 338
butterflies layer 333
butterfly color and contrast 332
butterfly images 332
butterfly set layer 333
Clone Stamp tool 326, 340

Color layer blending mode 325, 332
color layer 325, 332
creating blue head 323
Eyedropper tool 327, 339
Free Transform tool 329, 333, 336, 340
Gaussian Blur filter 337
glowing effect 338
Gradient tool 321, 322, 328, 339
head color and contrast 324
head debris 339
head layer 323
head set 330
head shadow 336
ink splats layer 341, 342
Lasso tool 339
layer hierarchy 342
layer masks 321, 327, 329, 333
Layer Sets 330, 342
Levels adjustment layer 324, 332
light layer 338
lighting effects 320
Luminosity layer blending mode 335
Marquee tool 341
Motion Blur filter 334
Multiply layer blending mode 321, 334, 336
Overlay layer blending mode 322, 329, 340
paint layer 321
paper layer 327
Polygonal Lasso tool 338
Quick Mask mode 336
radial gradients 335, 337, 340, 342
reducing blur and shadow effects 334
scanning painting 321
scratches layer 340
Screen layer blending mode 338
Selective Color adjustment layer 332
Selective Color layer 325
shadow effects 334
shadows layer 336, 337
sketch layer 322
smooth 1layer 326
smooth layer 332
smoothing butterflies 332
smoothing out head 326

Smudge tool 326, 332
stacking layers 322, 324
surface texture 340
torn paper photograph 327
Unsharp Mask filter 331
water stain effect 321

C

C404 (digital design company) 101
Caldwell, John 250
camera lens gradient 190
Candyman (film) 146
Canon Rebel 2000 camera 188
CAP&Design (magazine) 62
Caravaggio (painter) 145
'Careless talk costs lives' poster 183
Carson, David (designer) 28, 147, 380
Cassian, Nina (poet) 218
channels feature 200
chapter3.net 124
Chase, Margo (designer) 28
Cherry Moon (club) 182
Chisel Hard setting 197
Cina, Michael 386, 396. See also
abstract (tutorial) . See also 3D
image (tutorial)
    Abstract project 500
    Bauhaus 499, 503
    Cinahaus web site 504
    Design Posse web site 504
    designing graphics for songs 510
    DJing 509
    grids 502
    hierarchy of form 500
    introduction to Photoshop 498
    music 509, 510
    sketching 505, 511
    sources of inspiration 498
    suggested reading list 513
    Swiss design 503
    'Tangent Man' 508
    Test Pilot Collective project 511
    typography 503, 508
    working methods 500, 502
Clipping Group symbol 134
Clone Stamp tool 123, 154, 226, 326,

390
cmart.design.ru 124
CMYK color 29, 34, 152, 224, 361
collage (tutorial)
    adjusting portrait 230, 232
    Airbrush tool 229
    altering layer opacity 221
    background layer 224
    base image 222
    Brightness/Contrast Adjustment layer
    241
    broken mirror image 237
    Clone Stamp tool 226, 228
    Color Balance 229
    composition 238, 242
    Difference layer blending mode 225
    digital cameras 223
    file preparation 223
    file resolution 223
    flattening image 225, 243
    frame color 229
    frame layers 228
    frame shadows 238
    Hard Light layer blending mode 236,
    240
    Hue/Saturation palette 239
    image size 224
    layer masks 222, 230, 234, 236
    Luminosity layer blending mode 222,
    227, 236
    man image 236
    Multiply layer blending mode 232, 235,
    239
    Normal layer blending mode 231, 236
    Overlay layer blending mode 222, 241
    pinboard images 233
    portrait layer 226, 230, 236
    reflections layer 227, 231, 239, 242
    RGB mode 224
    Screen layer blending mode 240
    shadow effects 234
    side frames images 233
    Smudge tool 235
    Soft Light layer blending mode 230
    tonal contrast 238
    triptych format 223

    triptych frames 227, 228
Color Balance 229
Color Burn layer blending mode 77,
160, 484
color correction 417
Color Dodge layer blending mode 12,
72, 160
color psychology 242
Color Range 17
color stops
    adding color stops 189
    duplicating color stops 190
    removing color stops 190
color theory 417
Come To Daddy (video) 5
Computer Arts (magazine) 62
Constable, John (painter) 185
Cooper, Kyle (designer) 9, 29
Cope, Julian (musician) 315
CorelDraw 199
The Cornfield (painting) 185
Cromhout, Gavin. See also dancers
(tutorial)
    abstract creation 278
    artistic influences 275
    Artscape project 280
    Gestalt theory 276
    grandfather's influence 272
    History of Art study 272
    individual transformation of the visible
    277
    interactivity of Web 272
    intuitive principle 277
    photography 272
    principles of web site design 274, 276
    Russian Avant-Garde artists 275
    texture, structure and style 279
Crop tool 457
Crossroads (song) 454
Crouwel, Wim 503, 512
Cruikshank, Sally (animator) 348, 349
Crustation (band) 62
Cubadust 27
Cudworth, Nick (artist) 8
Curves feature 413

Index

D

Dali, Salvador 8, 314
Dallal, Melissa 101
dancers (tutorial)
  1. dancers.psd 283
  3. final dancer.psd 287
  4. fragmented dancer.psd 289
  5. Adding information.psd 291
  6. Filling out and texturising.psd 295
  8. final.psd 305
  adding Artscape logo 294
  adding border 288
  adding gray strip 298
  adding handwritten text 289
  adding texture 291, 305
  adjustment layer 298
  applying layer mask to principal dancer 284
  background layer 286
  breaking up boundary lines 301
  breaking up image plane 287
  breakup layer 290
  breakup.psd 292
  changing color of adjustment layer 299
  color block layers 301
  color layer 288
  color selection 282
  composition 281, 298, 306
  customizable skins of web site 296, 307
  dancer 1 layer 283
  dancer 2 layer 283
  dancer 3 layer 286
  dancers picture 282
  design brief 280, 307
  design elements 281
  eggshell border layer 288, 293
  erasing background around dancer's head 286
  Exclusion layer blending mode 296
  film3.psd 293
  flat and complex color combination 289
  Gaussian Blur filter 283
  Hard Light layer blending mode 293
  Hue/Saturation adjustment layer 285, 287
  icondancer layers 296
  increasing surface depth 287
  initial scamps 280
  listofwords.psd 289
  Luminosity layer blending mode 293, 296
  Marquee tool 283
  morebreakup.psd 291
  Multiply layer blending mode 290, 292, 293, 305
  navigational elements 296, 298
  Overlay layer blending mode 293, 302
  photobreakup layer 291, 292
  photocopy layer 292
  Rectangular Marquee tool 284
  ringunbound.psd 300
  scanned_in.psd 290
  Screen layer blending mode 286, 288, 293
  segmenting image 283
  selective blurring effect 283
  smalldancers.psd 287
  Soft Light layer blending mode 304
  target audience 280
  visual flow 306
  yellowover layer 292
day-dream.com 101
de Kooning, Willem (painter) 248
De La Soul (band) 62
Dead Ringer (album) 143
Designers' Republic (design collective) d499
Desmond, Matt (web designer) 511
Despeckle filter 75
Difference layer blending mode 225
digital cameras 223, 389
Dire Straits (band) 62
Director 350
Discreet 63
Do It Yourself (painting) 248
Dodge tool 72
Dogme films 61
Donwood, Stanley (artist) 9
The Doors (band) 62
Doreamon 408
drawing (tutorial)
  adding color 365
  adding highlights 366
  adjustment layer 362
  Airbrush tool 366
  auto adjusted layer 364
  Auto Levels feature 362
  background texture 363
  bleed layer 364
  Brush tool 366
  elephant color layer 366
  elephants_in_love.psd 366
  Gaussian Blur filter 365
  heart color layer 366
  image resolution 362
  Levels settings 363
  Multiply layer blending mode 364
  original elephant image.tif 362
  overall color layer 365
  Overlay layer blending mode 365, 366
  Paintbrush tool 366
  scanning in pencil sketch 361
  tonal range histogram 362
  Wacom tablet 366
Duffy Design 28
Duffy, Joe (designer) 28
Dungeons & Dragons (game) 96
Dury, Ian (singer) 438

E

e13.com 101
Edwardian Script ITC font 454
Effective Spaces (tutorial)
  adding black bars 457
  adding text 454
  adjusting color of jacket 450
  adjusting saturation of jacket 451
  adjusting size of text 454
  Angel & Demon.jpg 462
  angel and demon pictograms 462
  Black Bars layer 457
  Blips layer 461
  blue square layer 463
  Bluesman layer 449
  Bluesman.png 449

car hood layer 450
car.psd 449
composition 453, 456, 463
creating Serious Reggae text 458
Crop tool 457, 462
Edwardian Script ITC font 454
enlarging bluesman image 450
enlarging canvas 456
Eraser tool 453, 461
Eyedropper tool 457
Free Transform tool 450
Gaussian Blur filter 455
integrating bluesman into composition 450
Liquify tool 455
liquifying effect 452
Magnetic Lasso tool 462
merging layers 460
Mosaic filter 451
Motion Blur filter 461
movement layer 453
moving red rain 453
narrative elements 448
negative space 449, 456, 463
polygon layer 452
Polygonal Lasso tool 452
rasterizing text 459
Rectangular Marquee tool 451, 453, 455, 457, 459
red rain layer 452
Reggae layer 458, 461
ScriptMTBold font 458
text layers 455
Type tool 454, 459
Wacom tablet 452
Warp tool 452, 455
white lines layer 451
EFX Art & Design (magazine) 62
Eikes Grafischer Hort (design collective) 105, 112
Element K Journals 62
Elliptical Marquee tool 75
Elm Street (magazine) 319
The End (song) 62
The End Of Print (book) 380
Eno, Brian (musician) 315

Erased de Kooning Drawing 248
Eraser tool 39, 106, 431, 453
Escher, M.C. (artist) 29, 98, 118, 123, 125, 314
Eure, Catherin (web designer) 474
Exclusion layer blending mode 296
Eyedropper tool 40, 110, 327, 457, 492

F

Fallon, Josh. See also rind (tutorial)
art training 118
artistic influences
Bond of Union 2001 125
favorite web sites 124
images of hands 119, 121
Inspiration project 123, 137
introduction to Photoshop 119
sketching process
Spiral Hand 125
file size 34, 72, 257, 261, 330
fill patterns 416
filter effects 4, 35, 394
Finders, Keepers (book) 215
Fines, Justin 388
Flagg, James Montgomery 183
Flash 419
combining with Photoshop 254, 257, 265
importing from Photoshop 34, 375, 432
keyframes and timelines primer 419
movie clips 428
use on Internet 433
vector-based program 260
fluorescent lamps (tutorial)
2d layer 79
2d_grid_sample.psd 79, 81
adding 2D graphics 79
adding fluorescent light to ceiling 87
adding glow and fog 78
adding light rays and sparks 83
adjusting Hue/Saturation of background layer 77
adjusting Hue/Saturation of fluorescent light 85
adjusting light levels in photo 76

Airbrush tool 77
background layer 76, 77
blur 11 filter 85
Blur tool 88
Color Burn layer blending mode 77
creating fluorescent light 83
dark edges layer 77
dark glow layer 79
deleting light behind pillar 87
distorting grid 81
fluorescent 2 layer 87
fluorescent layer 87
focal depth effect 88
Gaussian Blur filter 78, 82, 85, 86
glow layer 78
green 26 layer 85
grid glow layer 82
grid layer 81, 82
linking light layers 86
Move tool 86
Overlay layer blending mode 78, 79, 82
Polar Coordinates filter 83, 84
Polygonal Lasso tool 82
rectangles.psd 83
rotating grid 80
rotating picture 76
scaling and tiling lights 86
Screen layer blending mode 78, 79
Stockholm_airport.jpg 76
using grid when adding perspective, 79
Wave filter 84
Wind filter 83
yellow layer 77, 78
focal depth effect 69, 88
Fontographer 512
fonts 459
Free Transform tool 18, 65, 191, 391, 450
FreeHand 34, 199, 367
Fripp, Robert (musician) 314
Fujimoto, Hiroshi 408
Fukuda, Shigao (artist) 98
Fuzziness slider 369

G

Gaussian Blur filter 69, 202, 283, 337,

Index

489
Gaussian Halo technique 488
Gauthier, Karen 438
Giger, H. R. (artist) 29, 314
Gilliam, Terry (animator) 419
glow effect 73
Godard, Jean-Luc (film director) 441
Godspeed You Black Emperor (band) 407
Gould, Steven Jay (writer) 215
Gradient tool 16, 189, 196, 321, 492
gradients 188
Grass (sculpture) 349
Gray's Anatomy (book) 215
The Great and Secret Show (novel) 146
Grooverider (band) 410
groovetech.com 510
Gropius, Walter (architect) 499

H

half-finished 3D object effect 43, 45
The Hallucinogenic Toreador (painting) 8
halo effect 492
Hamburg, Mark 438
Hames, Paul (photographer) 6
Hanada, Kinya (Mumbleboy) 359
Hard Light layer blending mode 15, 159, 236, 293, 370
Head of a Centaur (drawing) 145
helicopter (tutorial)
    1_1.jpg 480
    1_2.jpg 480, 484
    1_3.jpg 481
    2_1.jpg 483
    3_1.jpg 485
    3_2.jpg 485
    4_1.jpg 487
    4_2.jpg 487
    5_1.jpg 489
    6_1.jpg 491
    6_2.jpg 491
    Airbrush tool 482
    background layer 481
    blue-gray layer 485

Color Burn layer blending mode 484, 485, 488
    composition 480, 490, 491, 492
    dark blue layer 483
    desaturating images 481, 483, 484, 487
    edge control 490
    Eyedropper tool 492
    Gaussian Blur filter 489
    Gradient tool 492
    grayscale images 483
    halo effect 492
    Marquee tool 481
    morphing rear and central rotors 487
    orange-colored layer 488
    Overlay layer blending mode 481, 483, 485, 490, 491
    Paint Bucket tool 492
    personal background to project 479
    Polygonal Lasso tool 491
    red layer 484
    replacing ground with sky 491
    rotating canvas 492
    scaling and rotating images 481
    simulating sky gradation 492
    Soft Light layer blending mode 484, 485, 488
    softening highlights 482
    white layer 484, 485, 488
Hello Kitty 408
Hellraiser (film) 146
Hofmann, Armin 503
Horn, Rolfe (photographer) 7
Hue layer blending mode 66
Hue/Saturation box 197
Hunters in the Snow (painting) 442

I

Illuminations (book) 215
Illustrator 7, 111, 199, 388, 502
    KPT Vector Effects plug-in 38, 46
image resolution 257, 259, 262
image size 224
In Transparency (art exhibition) 473
Infini-D 505
inkjet printers 257, 262
Internet Explorer 396

Ishimori, Shotaro 408
Itten, Johannes 499

J

Jensen, Dr Jerry (designer) 183
Johns, Jasper (painter) 248
Johnson, Robert (blues guitarist) 454
Joy Division (band) 503

K

Kandinsky, Wassily (painter) 499
Karlsson, Jens Magnus. See also www.threeoh.com. See also fluorescent lamps (tutorial). See also light waves (tutorial)
    astronomy 60
    Chapter Three web site 59
    Desktop Imperium web site 62
    Emotional Abstracts project 59
    experimentation with photographic techniques 57
    favorite artists 61
    favorite designers 57
    favorite music 62
    Highly Graphic Technology 58
    introduction to Internet 57
    introduction to Photoshop 57
    light effects 63
    online design community 57, 62
    photography 56, 58, 60
    Sweden 57
    wallpaper 62
Kent, Stacey (musician) 62
The Kiss (painting) 145
Klimt, Gustav (painter) 145
konstruktiv.net 124
KPT Vector Effects plug-in 38, 46
Kral, Joseph (web designer) 511

L

Lasso tool 113, 128, 427
layer blending modes 135, 192
    multiple blending modes 312
    stacking layers with different blending

modes 343
layer masks 17, 155, 285
Layer Sets 330
layers 4, 10, 440
applying layers 221
Photoshop 3 221
Le Corbusier (architect) 499
Lea, Derek. See also www.bookofmirrors.com, See also butterflies (tutorial).
autobiographical elements in work 313
The Book of Mirrors (album) 315
Catharsis 313
digital art 312
editorial work 319
fashions in Photoshop 318
favorite artists 314
favorite music 315
Iterance project 313
junk shops 316
Neolithic monuments 317
old computer parts 317
photography 316, 317
Photoshop techniques 312
starts to create original images 313
tactile inspirations 316
viewer immersion 319
watercolor painting 316, 321
Lehndorff, Vera 215
lens flare effect 35
lens flares 485
Leonardo da Vinci 121, 122
Level 10 (tutorial)
Airbrush tool 416, 430
animating texture and mask layers 424
background photograph 416
background sound 421, 424
black layer 425
blowup one to blowup five layers 423
cleaning up scanned drawings 414, 429
color correction 417
color saturation 418
coloring in drawings 416, 429
Curves feature 413
dancing elements 421
diagonal camera movement 413

Eraser tool 431
fill patterns 416
Gaussian Blur filter 431
giraffe motion 425, 428
giraffe movement layers 426
giraffe_running_bw.jpg 413
girl_standing_color.jpg 429
introlook.psd 419, 422
Lasso tool 427
Level10.psd 424, 426, 429
lighting effects 429
Magic Wand tool 415
making rays of light 430
mask layers 423
merging girl and room layers 419
motion tween 420
overall_screen_of_pan.jpg 422, 423
panning image 419
perspective 426
Polygonal Lasso tool 430
preliminary sketches 413
Rectangular Marquee tool 422
scene transition 424
texture layers 423
transition effect 424
white layer 425
working.swf 412
Zoom tool 413
Levine, Gemma (writer) 97
Lichtenstein, Roy (painter) 248
light waves (tutorial)
adding atmospheric light 74
adding glow to light wave 72
adding perspective to spiral 67
adjusting Hue/Saturation of Colorize layers 71
adjusting Hue/Saturation of spiral 69
adjustment layers 66
ambient light layer 74
base.psd 64, 65
BLUE layer 66, 74
blur 1.3 layer 66
Blur 10.0 layer 70
Blur 45 layer 70
Blur tool 69
blurring spiral 69

Color Dodge layer blending mode 72
Colorize layers 70
colorizing light sparks layer 75
colorizing light wave 70
complete.psd 64
creating light rays 66
dark background 64
Dodge layer 72
duplicating and tiling spiral 65
Elliptical Marquee tool 75
focal depth effect 69
Free Transform tool 65
Gaussian Blur filter 69, 73, 76
glow effect 73
high-resolution file for spiral 64
Hue layer blending mode 66
Layer1 65, 66
light sparks layer 74
light_in_motion.jpg 74
linking light wave layers 73
Median filter 75
motion blur effect 72
Move tool 65
opening glow layer 73
Overlay layer blending mode 72, 73
pink and blue RGB values 66
Rectangular Marquee tool 65
RED layer 65, 75
scaling down spiral 65
Screen layer blending mode 74, 75
spiral.psd 64
Trace layer 72, 74
volumetric fog layer 75
Lighten layer blending mode 42
lighting effects 429
Lightness (book) 358
lightweight structures 358
Line tool 191
Liquify tool 455
liquifying effect 452
Lissitzky, El (artist) 499
LiveMotion
importing from Photoshop 375
Lohse, Richard Paul 503
Luminosity layer blending mode 38, 222, 236, 293, 335

Index

**Luna, Adrian. See also
purusdesign.com. See also helicopter
(tutorial)**
architecture 470
art installations 472
art school 469
artistic influences 473
audio 475
California 469
cycling 479
design 478
everyday inspirations 476
Gaussian Halo technique 488
imagery 475
interactive digital media 475
Japan 492
Laguna Beach 469, 471
Los Angeles 470
motion graphics 474
photography 488, 490
relationships 478
San Diego 472
surfing 469
Lye, Len (artist) 348

M

**Madej, Wojtek. See also Park,
Andrew. See also Effective Spaces
(tutorial)**
Catholicism 443
collaborative work 441, 446
Effective Spaces project 446
medieval art 444
narrative in painting 443
Nowy Sacz 447
Paszyn (village in Poland) 443, 447
Photoshop as theatre 441
printmaking 440
self-contained worlds 442
spirituality 443
Sulkowice 447
tradition 443
woodcarving 440, 444
Magic Torch (design company) 7
**Magic Wand tool 42, 108, 131, 395,
415**

Magnetic Lasso tool 462
Mandalay (band) 62
manga 407
Maroc (book) 217
Marquee tool 190, 193, 283, 481
The Matrix (film) 184
Matsumoto, Taiyo (manga artist) 354
McCloud, Scott (comics artist) 355
**McGregor-Mento, Matthew 101. See
also www.c404.com**
**McIntyre,Catherine. See also collage
(tutorial)**
anatomy 215
artistic influences 215
collage 214
computer graphic design 214
illustrated books 218
important themes in work 218
life drawing 214
photography 214, 216
poetry 218
use of nudes in work 218
visual symbolism 219, 222
**McKean, Dave (comics artist) 142,
146, 217, 314**
Meatloaf (singer) 143
Median filter 75
Medicine (painting) 145
Meta Creations 368
**The Metamorphosis Of Narcissus
(painting) 8**
Michelangelo 121, 142, 145
Milky Elephant collective 359
Mogwai (band) 421
Moholy-Nagy, Laszlo (artist) 499
**Mohr, Jason. See also Sodeoka, Yoshi.
See also www.c404.com
See also www.sissyfight.com. See also
www.pixeltime.com. See also bath-
room (tutorial).** artistic influences 97
Be Prepared project 95
C404 (digital design company) 101,
112
Californian youth culture 99
collage 104
creative process 102

early sources of inspiration 97
father's influence 94
Fifteen project 100
film posters 96, 100
Furniture web site interface 94
interface design 102
Japanese culture 98
kindergarten 94
LEGO 94
organic objects 97
parents 96
pixel-perfect style 103
San Fernando Valley 99
sketching 102
surfer culture 99
video games 99
Mona Lisa (painting) 121
Moore, Henry (sculptor) 97
morphing imagery 486
Mosaic filter 119, 451
motion blur effect 72
Motion Blur filter 334, 461
Move tool 11, 65, 130
Muggleton, Kevin (photographer) 5, 7
Müller-Brockmann, Josef 503
**Multiply layer blending mode 48, 110,
290, 364, 507**
correcting overexposure 15
Mumbleboy 359
**Muybridge, Eadweard (photographer)
404**
Myst (computer game) 314

N

Neofrog 180
Neolithic monuments 317
New Alphabet (font) 503
**Nineteen Point Five Collective (NPFC)
384**
No Pussyfooting (album) 315
Normal mode 231, 236
Nova (tutorial)
4-Up button 265
adding line drawings 263
adding screenshot 264
avoiding anti-aliasing 264

enlarging image 261
file size 261, 265
image resolution 258, 262
importing image into Flash 260
optimizing image in sections 265
preparing image for web site 265
Publish command 265
redrawing scrollbar in Flash 265
Resample Image 264

O

O'locco (EP) 499
Odin (album) 315
OK Computer (album) 9
Oliver, Vaughan (designer) 148
Oppenheim, David 101
Otomo, Katsuhiro 407
Overlay layer blending mode 44, 160,
192, 293, 481
Owens, Matt (web designer) 474

P

Paek, Eun-Ha. See also www.milkyele-
phant.com. See also drawing (tutorial). See also seascape (tutorial).
animation 348, 352, 353, 359
aquatint 361
calendar 367
contrast, texture and color 351
Ellie (elephant character) 353
etchings 361
experimental film techniques 350
favorite comics artists 354
Flash 360
illustration 348
image composition 358
interactive storytelling 357
magnets 367
Milky Elephant collective 359
Peek a Boo film 350
Photoshop 360
sketching techniques 367
storytelling 353
Paint Bucket tool 39, 397, 492
Paintbrush tool 48, 366

Painter
brush tools 368
lighting effects 320
Paiva, Troy (photographer) 7
Park, Andrew. See also Madej, Wojtek.
See also Effective Spaces (tutorial)
'breaking' images 439
collaborative work 439, 446
computer art 440
Days of Code project 439
Delta Blues 448
Effective Spaces project 446
films 441
fonts 459
The Messengers of the Temple (picture) 442
painting 440
'serious reggae' 458
sketchbooks 441
Undercover Levels project 439, 442
Pasciolini, Mirco (web designer) 57
Pass Through layer blending blending
mode 343
pattern effects 395
pattern manipulation 188
patterns feature 192
Pen tool 128
Pencil tool 39, 394, 397
The Persistence Of Memory (painting)
8
Personal Space (tutorial)
adding 'personal' type 168
adding 'space' type 161
adding dictionary text 169
airbrushing areas of image 155
aligning portrait and Mad_Pic layers
164
blank canvas specifications 152
blending edges of steps 158
blending railing sections 157
Bridge layer 153
brush size 155, 158
Burn tool 169
Car Park_1 layer 154
Car Park_2 layer 156
changing portrait coloring 163

Clone Stamp tool 154
Color Burn layer blending mode 162,
163
Color Dodge layer blending mode 160,
163
distort facility 170
dropping opacity of portrait layer 166
duplicating Mad_Pic layers 171
filling shape with color 167
Gaussian blur filter 161
Hard Light layer blending mode 159,
162, 166, 169
increasing scale of layer 153
Lasso tool 166
Line tool 172
Lines layer 172
lining up railing sections 156
linking portrait and Mad_Pic layers 165
Mad_Pic copy layer 170
Mad_Pic copy2 layer 171
Mad_Pic layer 164, 170
Marquee tool 165
merging all visible layers 159
merging portrait layers 163
Orange Quadrangle layer 166
Portrait layer 162
rasterizing type 161
removing top and bottom of portrait
layers 165
removing type layers 172
removing unwanted figure 154
RGB color profile 152
selection of base images 150
Steps_1layer 158
Structures layer 159, 160
text copy layer 160, 166
text layer 160
transparent background 152
Type tool 161, 168, 172
perspective 426
textural diffusion 426
photographic transparencies 13
Photoshop
absence of constraints 142
adjustment layers 15, 17
alpha channels 4

Index

animation 412, 433
bitmap images 360
channels feature 200
collage 221
color wheel 417
combining with Flash 254, 257, 266
correcting mistakes 388
creative potential 34, 266
design elements formed from 'mistakes' 273
exporting to Flash 375
fashions in Photoshop 318
filter effects 4, 35, 360, 394
Help section 433
history feature 147
image manipulation 220, 252, 312, 394
immediacy of image creation 445
importing into Flash 34, 432
importing video footage 433
interface 438
interface design 102
intuitive working 34
layer blending modes 131
layer masks 17
layer modes 9
layers 4, 10, 57, 214, 440
Layers palette 433
learning through experimentation 273
manipulating vector images 199
masking 126, 421
McKean, Dave, influence of 217
pattern effects 395
patterns feature 192
Photoshop 3 221
retouching 312
Select All command 395
special effects 412
tonal control 197
tools 395
use by professional photographers 4
use for layout alternatives
vector functions 30
Photoshop World Convention 187
Picasso, Pablo 30, 220
Pinch filter 196
Pinter, Harold (playwright) 446

Plain Mosaic filter 11
Plath, Sylvia (poet) 218
Polar Coordinates filter 83, 84
Pollock, Jackson (painter) 266
Polygonal Lasso tool 82, 199, 338, 430, 491
Popov, Lark (musician) 315
Promised Land (song) 510
Publish command 265
Puni, Ivan (artist) 276
Purcell, Rosamund Wolff 215
purusdesign.com 479
Pyramid Song (video) 410

Q

Quannum (band) 410
Quark XPress 3
Quay Brothers, (filmmakers) 406
Qvicker, Anders 180

R

Radiohead (band) 9, 410
The Raising of Lazarus (painting) 443
Rand, Paul (graphic designer) 441
Rauschenberg, Robert (painter) 248, 473
Ray, Man (artist) 61
Raygun (magazine) 147
Reboot of 2001 385
Rectangular Marquee tool 20, 65, 106, 284, 422
reflection effects 188, 240
Rege, Ron Jr. (comics artist) 355
Rehearsals for Extinct Anatomies (film) 406
Reinventing Comics (book) 355
Rembrandt 443
Rempel, Byron 180
Renaissance art 121
resolution 34, 362
retouching 312
RGB color 152, 202, 224, 361, 417
rind (tutorial)
adding mask to orange layer 128
adding shading 134

adjustment layer 135
aim of project 127
aligning rind sketch layer with orange layer 130
back rind layer 131, 132
back rind shading layer 134, 135
background layer 127
brush sizes 133
clipping mask 134
color balance adjustment 135
Color Overlay 132
creating back of rind 131
creating edges of rind 132
drawing edges in by hand 133
image size 127
levels adjustment of scanned image 130
masking front of rind 131
Multiply layer blending mode 131
orange layer 127, 131, 132
perspective 133
radial gradient overlay 136
rind edge layer 133
rind sketch layer 130, 132
scanning in rind sketch 129
Screen layer blending mode 135
sketching rind outline 128
Ritts, Herb (photographer) 29
Robocon (Japanese TV show) 408
Rollerball (song) 421
Rosevear, Eric 101
Rozanova, Olga (artist) 277
Ruder, Emil 503, 504

S

Sabin, Tracy (designer) 32
Saksi, Miika (web designer) 57
Sandman (graphic novels) 314
Saville, Peter (designer) 503
scanners 6, 12
Schroeder, Anders 383
Screen layer blending mode 11, 74, 135, 286, 338
ScriptMTBold font 458
seascape (tutorial)
adding blue gradations 370

adding bubble animations 375
adding texture 371
atmospheric perspective 370
Brush tool 372, 373, 374
details layer 373
emphasizing characters' features 371, 373
Eyedropper tool 369, 374
Fuzziness slider 369
Gaussian Blur filter 373, 375
glow layer 373
Hard Light layer blending mode 370
image darks layer 370
image lights layer 370
layer mask 371
Multiply layer blending mode 370, 372, 373
painter image layer 369
painter image.tif 368
RGB mode 368
Screen layer blending mode 371
sea 01layer 369
sea 02 layer 371, 373
seascene.tif 369
seascene2.tif 371
separating dark blues 369
tendrils layer 374
underwater_scene.psd 374
Select All command 395
selective blurring effect 283
Seven (film) 9, 29, 381
shadow effects 134, 234, 334, 431
Sharpen filter 106
Sherman, Cindy (artist) 61, 441
Shevchenko, Alexander (artist) 276, 279
SHIFT (magazine) 488
Shift Rojo 27
Shynola (video production company) 410
Sigismondi, Floria (photographer) 61
sign (tutorial)
  2D elements 391
  3D element 392
  adjusting brightness and color of 2D elements 391

adjusting color balance of 3D image 393
adjusting color balance of photograph 389
Alpha channel 392
A_warning.jpg 389
Clone Stamp tool 390
Color Balance options 390
fluorescent green layer 394
Free Transform tool 391
image resolution 389
Multiply layer blending mode 391, 394
Pencil tool 394
removing sign text 390
Skew tool 391
three_dimensional.tif 392
Threshold tool 390
twodee.ai 391
warning sign photograph 389
Sinclair, Paul. See also Personal Space (tutorial)
  anatomy 144
  artistic influences 144
  Daemons project 143
  Death's Doorway project 146
  digital art 149, 173
  discovers Photoshop 142, 146
  early artistic ambitions 142
  fantasy art 143
  industrial and urban imagery 148
  Personal Space project 149, 172
  photography 148
  Renaissance art 145
Sistine Chapel 121
skateboard (tutorial)
  adding barcode 18
  adding black border 20
  adding crane picture 19
  adding helicopters picture 20
  adding noise 21
  adding text 18
  Airbrush tool 19
  applying global color 15
  applying sepia tone to eyes 15
  background 13
  BARCODE 1layer 18

barcode.tif 18
BORDER layer 20
Color Dodge layer blending mode 12
Color Range 17
combining EYE layers 14
combining skaters layers 11
copters.tif 20
darkening edges of picture 16
DEEP layer 18
deep.tif 17
duplicating EYE layer 13
element sources 10
EYE DUO layer 15
EYE layer 13
eye.tif 13
Free Transform tool 18
fuzz.tif 12
Gradient tool 16, 21
Hard Light layer blending mode 15, 19
Move tool 11, 13, 18
Multiply layer blending mode 17, 18, 20
Overlay layer blending mode 18
Plain Mosaic filter 11
Rectangular Marquee tool 20
removing layer mask 15
rough scan of eye image 13
Screen layer blending mode 11
site.tif 19
skate1.jpg 11
skate2.jpg 11
SKATERS 1 layer 11, 21
SKATERS 2 layer 11, 21
TV FUZZ layer 12, 15
sketching techniques 366
Skew tool 391
Skibber Bee-Bye (comic strip) 355
Slaine – Horned God (graphic novel) 143
Smith, Colin. See also www.photo-shopcafe.com. See also 100% Photoshop (tutorial).
  100% Photoshop project 187
  Alien Station project 187
  Cherry Moon flyer 182
  early days of Internet 179

Index

effect of Internet on design work 180
evocative power of imagery 183
favorite movies 184
graphic design 180
importance of functionality in design 183
learns HTML 179
less is more principle 186
love of realism in art 185
model-making 185
photorealism 188
sorces of inspiration 181
Voice (magazine) 183
Waitahanui River 181
wins Guru Award 187
Smudge tool 235, 326
Sodeoka,Yoshi 98, 101, 105. See also www.c404.com. See also bathroom (tutorial)
Soft Light layer blending mode 45, 304, 484
Spherize filter 195
St Catherine 219
St Jerome 219
stacking layers 322, 343
Stanick, Peter. See also www.stanick.com. See also Nova (tutorial)
    4:3 ratio 257
    All Mod Cons (painting) 250
    Art About Art exhibition 248, 250
    art critics 249
    Beat Surrender (painting) 249
    Contact Music 255
    creative possibilities of Internet 267
    Dance Craze (painting) 255
    digital images 254, 256
    Fight Gridlock (painting) 249
    first use of Internet 252
    first use of Photoshop 252
    Flash 254
    He's Not a Bum (painting) 251
    Hibiya Line Grey (painting) 250
    It's Just a Flag (painting) 251
    Japanese graphics 258
    large images on screen 257

Marlboro (painting) 255
minimalism in digital art 267
natural progression from painting to Photoshop 266
New York 249
pop art 248, 251
Relax (painting) 255
selection of images 255
size of paintings 258
Stockholm 251
Tube (painting) 255
uses text in paintings 251
Yahoo (painting) 255
Stanley W 384
Star Wars (film) 96, 184
storyboards 412
Strata 3D 500
Strata Blitz 380
Struzan, Drew (artist) 96
Style Council (band) 510
Substance (album) 503
Sun Electric (band) 499
Supper at Emmaus (painting) 145
Swanky (web site) 57

T
Tadanori, Yokoo (designer) 100
Tam, Sau 438
Target (painting) 248
Tempest (arcade game) 99
The Temprees (band) 62
Terretatz, Johann. See also base twice (tutorial)
    collaborative projects 27
    design 27
    favorite artists 29
    favorite designers 28
    Geneva 26
    introduction to Photoshop 30
    love of books 31
    mistrust of ready-made effects 35
    sources of inspiration 26
    style of work 33
    surfboard and snowboard design 31
    traditional design background 30
    typography 28

    varied clientele 35
    working habits 31
Test Pilot Collective (design collective) 504, 511
textural diffusion 426
Threshold tool 390
Toadies filters 11
tonal control 197
Tool (band) 380
Toraya, Norma V. See also www.crankbunny.com See also Level 10 (tutorial).
    abandoned steel mill 409
    animation 405
    commercials 410
    Crankbunny project 403, 405, 407, 433
    early Photoshop work 412
    favorite films 406
    Future Installment Two: Naissance (film) 407
    little white dog 425
    'the machine' 409
    magic lanterns 404
    manga and anime influences 408
    music videos 410
    obsession 411
    picky eater as child 402
    pop culture 410
tracy.sabin.com 32
Transfigurations (book) 215
Tron (arcade game) 99
Trülzsch,Holger 215
Type tool 454
Typography (book) 504
Typography Now: The Next Wave (book) 148

U

U.N.K.L.E. (band) 410
Uncle Sam poster 183
Understanding Comics (book) 355
Unique Forms of Continuity in Space (sculpture) 144
Unsharp Mask filter 331
Up and Down (picture) 123
Urban Soul (band) 510

V

Vallejo, Boris (artist) 143
Vallhonrat, Javier (photographer) 217
van Hinte, Ed 358
vector images 199
The Visual Story: Seeing the Structure of Film, TV, and New Media (book) 405
Voice (magazine) 183
volumeone.com 474
Von Trier, Lars (film director) 61
Vona, George (musician) 315

W

Wacom tablet 129, 366, 368, 452
wallpaper 62
Warhol, Andy 29, 248, 266
Warp tool 452
water stain effect 321
Waterfall (picture) 123
Watson, Albert (photographer) 217
Wave filter 84
WDDG (design collective) 474
webagent007.com 124
Weingart, Wolfgang 503
Wesselman, Tom (painter) 248
Why Not Associates 148
Widegren, James (web designer) 57, 383
Wind filter 83
wireframe effect 41
With Henry Moore (book) 97
wraparound effect 195
Wrightson, Bernie (comics artist) 143
www.2Advanced.com 124
www.attik.com 124
www.australianinfront.com.au 513
www.betalounge.com 510
www.bookofmirrors.com 315
www.breathedesign.com 474
www.c404.com 101, 102
www.cemgul.com 124
www.chapter3.net 58, 124
www.cmart.design.ru 124
www.crankbunny.com 403

www.cudworthartworks.co.uk 8
www.demo-design.com 388
www.designgraphik.com 384
    Serving 3 project 384
    Serving 4 project 384
    Southbound 83 project 384, 388
www.designiskinky.net 513
www.designshed.com 7
www.desktopimp.com 62
www.dform1shiftfunc.net 383
www.duffy.com 28
www.elementkjournals.com 62
www.f45.com 7
www.floriasigismondi.com 61
www.folioart.co.uk 7
www.h73.com 513
www.highlygraphic.com 58
www.highwaterbooks.com 355
www.k10k.com 513
www.kiiroi.nu 513
www.konstruktiv.net 124
www.linkdup.com 513
www.magictorch.com 7
www.metacreations.com 368
www.milkyelephant.com 375
www.onyro.com 124
www.photoshopcafe.com 179
www.pixeltime.com 103
www.seven.it 57
www.shift.jp.org 513
www.sissyfight.com 103
www.stanick.com 254
www.statmedia.com 475
www.submethod.com 384
    0010 project 385
    artistic collaboration 384
    Reboot of 2001 385
www.surfstation.lu 513
www.threeoh.com 57, 62, 383, 513
www.trueistrue.com 386
www.wddg.com 474
www.webagent007.com 124
www.weworkforthem.com 396
    wallpaper 396
www.woodcraftsupplies.com 367
www.word.com 95, 100, 101

X

Xerxes (font) 511

Y

Young, Mike. See also www.weworkforthem.com. See also sign (tutorial)
    abstract painting 381
    architecture 387
    art training 381
    artistic collaboration 381, 384
    CD cover art 380, 386
    design community 380
    Designgraphik 384
    form fields 396
    heavy machinery 383
    inspiration 380
    introduction to computer art 380
    Minneapolis 381
    Submethod 384
    Tennessee 380, 386
    Vir2l design firm 382, 386

Z

Zoom tool 113, 413

FreshFroot
www.freshfroot.com

get it daily